Internet Children's Television Series,
1997–2015

Internet Children's Television Series, 1997–2015

VINCENT TERRACE

McFarland & Company, Inc., Publishers
Jefferson, North Carolina

LIBRARY OF CONGRESS CATALOGUING-IN-PUBLICATION DATA

Names: Terrace, Vincent, 1948– author.
Title: Internet children's television series, 1997–2015 / Vincent Terrace.
Description: Jefferson, N.C. : McFarland & Company, Inc.,
Publishers, 2016. | Includes index.
Identifiers: LCCN 2016027887 | ISBN 9781476664620
(softcover : acid free paper) ∞
Subjects: LCSH: Internet television—Encyclopedias. | Television
programs—Plots, themes, etc.—Encyclopedias. | Childrens television
programs—Encyclopedias.
Classification: LCC PN1992.2 .T53 2016 | DDC 384.550285/4678—dc23
LC record available at https://lccn.loc.gov/2016027887

BRITISH LIBRARY CATALOGUING DATA ARE AVAILABLE

ISBN (print) 978-1-4766-6462-0
ISBN (ebook) 978-1-4766-2669-7

On the cover Julia Bushman as Gretel and Josh Elliott Pickel as Hansel,
image from "Sweet Truth" episode of *Or So the Story Goes*,
© 2016 Outtake Productions, LLC

Printed in the United States of America

*McFarland & Company, Inc., Publishers
Box 611, Jefferson, North Carolina 28640
www.mcfarlandpub.com*

TABLE OF CONTENTS

PREFACE

Internet Children's Television Series, 1997–2015, is the fifth volume in a one-of-a-kind series of books that examines various genres of Internet television programming. Like the prior titles (*Internet Horror, Science Fiction and Fantasy Television Series, 1996–2013; Internet Drama and Mystery Television Series, 1996–2014; Internet Lesbian and Gay Television Series, 1996–2014 and Internet Comedy Television Series, 1997–2015*), this volume is also the only book to date that presents a history of children's television programs produced exclusively for the worldwide web.

Internet television programs are produced like a broadcast or cable television series but *without* the big budget and, in most instances, *minus* name performers. The 573 programs contained here are listed alphabetically with cast and credits (where given), story lines, dates and websites. An index of names and titles completes the book.

Series produced for children follow the basic format of similar series created for broadcast and cable television. Production values in most cases, however, do not compare to what is seen elsewhere, and one should not expect to see a high caliber of programming here. While it is difficult at times to figure out what age group some producers are seeking (as, for example, cartoons that are appealing to an adult audience), the programs covered here fall in the category of pre-school children to freshman high school students (about 3 years to 14 years of age).

Internet titles and web site information can be *very* deceiving and what looks and sounds like a children's series is just the opposite and parental guidance is often not suggested. All the programs listed here are for children in the age range indicated with parental guidance issues listed as appropriate (especially in ghost and horror themed series that, although made for children, could venture into the teenage or adult category for their themes. Teenage and adult themed series appear in their appropriate genres in the four prior volumes). Series that produced more than 25 episodes have their episodes listed vertically to make comprehension easy.

The Internet has and is presenting a whole new world of television-like entertainment that, while still in its infancy, is continually growing and maturing. With this series of books about genres of Internet television series, you will have the only printed record presently available of its pioneering, intriguing history.

The author would like to thank James Robert Parish for his assistance on this project.

Note Regarding Web Addresses: At the time of compiling the series listed herein, all were active and could be viewed. Over time, some programs were taken offline and all the information simply disappeared from the Internet. A number of the series in this book have been taken offline and thus a web address will not appear with that entry, as there is simply no way to watch the show or call up its information. A very few still have their titles listed, but searching them will lead to an "Error 404" or "This Domain for Sale" site. It is possible that such series will return but as of April 2016, those listed without web addresses are still offline.

Since all the Doll and Mermaid series listed in this book appear only on YouTube it is suggested you use the following system to find these shows. To find Doll series, type in the series name in the search engine followed by "Doll Series" (for example, "Barbie: Life in the Dream House Doll Series"). For any Mermaid series, type in the series name followed by either "Mermaid Series" or "Ep 1" or Season 1 Ep 1" (for example, "A Splashy Tale, Ep 1"). This insures that the proper title appears as there are sometimes numerous items with the same title. All Doll and Mermaid series have been listed in the index, under those key words, to make finding them easy.

THE SERIES

1 *Adventures in Yumlandia.* youtube.com. 2013 (Children).

A potpourri of entertainment geared to children including puppets, music, the obligatory mad scientist (Professor Macaroni), a robot, quizzes and music. **Cast:** Paul Pittenger (Prof. Macaroni/Think Quick/McSmarty Pants), Mike Patok (Cheese), Cliff Pooh (Bing, Hamlet), Jason Tuck (Ding), Katie Clark (Cookie), Angela Lee Rapp (Candy). **Credits:** *Writer-Director*: Cliffy Pooh. **Comment:** Although they look to be homemade, the puppets are quite enjoyable. Although kids will not get it, the program has commercial breaks that encompass old black and white TV commercials from the 1950s and 1960s (interesting to see). The Professor is not all that "mad" as he does instruct children on how to make things (like a sandwich). Overall, the concept should appeal to the small fry. **Episode List:** *1*. Pilot.

2 *The Adventures of Cute Godzilla.* you tube.com. 2008 (Cartoon).

Godzilla, the legendary King of the Monsters, wrecked havoc in a number of feature films beginning with the 1954 film *Godzilla*. Bad as Godzilla may have been, he did have a "childhood" and did live in Japan but in a world where he could speak and function like a human child. And just like any kid, Godzilla does have a best friend named Kirby (there is even a kid Rodan) and the program follows the roughly drawn, but still cute Godzilla as he deals with all the problems and pressures of being a kid monster. **Voices (as credited):** Metroidfannumber1 (Godzilla/Goku/Argurius), Marshmallowpeepz (Kirby). Keckoaquanmermaid (Rodan). **Credits:** *Art and Animation*: Marshmallowpeepz. **Comment:** The program was abandoned after two episodes with an explanation given that the girl who created the series (identified only as Marshmallowpeepz) lost interest. The animation is crude but the program did show potential for being interesting; it in no way compares in story or production to the animated *Godzilla* series produced for television in the 1980s.

Episode List: 2 untitled episodes, labeled "Episode 1" and "Episode 2" have been produced.

3 *The Adventures of Knickerbock Teetertop.* youtube.com. 2015 (Cartoon).

Knickerbock is a young child who is also the smallest kid on the enchanted Wonderpine Mountain. He looks up to his Grandpa and wishes he were taller and could become a big adventurer like his hero. Determined not to let his size deter him, Knickerbock begins a quest to become a great adventurer but encounters all the pitfalls that are a part of becoming that future somebody. **Voice Cast:** Adam Taylor (Knickerbock), Jim Meskimen (Grandpa), Bailey Gambertoglio, Brittany Dalton (Otto), David Kaye (Maurice). **Credits:** *Producer-Writer*: Melanie Wilson LaBracio, Adam Wilson. **Comment:** Produced in association with Amazon Prime and only available through a purchase of the video. A brief highlight is available on YouTube and judging by it, it is well animated and produced and looks to appeal to children up to six years of age. **Episode List:** *1*. Pilot.

4 *The Adventures of Puss in Boots.* youtube. com. 2015 (Cartoon).

An adaptation of the "Puss in Boots" story that is set in the city of San Lorenzo, a mythical land that is invisible to the outside world due to a magical spell that protects it, its citizens and its mystic treasures. By pure accident a cat (Puss in Boots) breaks the spell and exposes San Lorenzo to the rest of the world. Now, with his city at risk, Puss in Boots must become a hero and protect it from the invaders and marauders who seek to conquer it. *Other Characters*: Dulcinea, the sweet and naïve feline who is also a love interest for Puss in Boots; Artephius, the elderly alchemist; Toby, a pig who holds Puss in Boots in high esteem; Pajuna, a Highland cow and owner of the local cantina; Senora Zapata, the suspicious (of Puss in Boots) manager of the town orphanage; Cleevil, a teenage goblin; Via, the featured orphan; Esme, a five-year-old girl; and Kid Pickles, the child who likes pickles.

Origins: As a poor miller lay dying, two of his three sons took everything for themselves, leaving behind a cat. Sad that he had only the cat to give to his remaining son, that son accepted it but with very little food he had planned on eating it. Magically, the cat spoke and asked the son to give him a bag of carrots and grain, his coat and boots. The son obliged and the cat (called Puss in Boots) set out to save the life of the son in return for the good deed he had done. Through a clever scheme (to make the King believe the miller's son is the Marquis of Carabas), the miller's son is accepted into the King's household and eventually marries his daughter. Puss in Boots, in the meantime, leaves the miller's son and begins a quest to find adventure.

Voice Cast: Eric Bauza (Puss in Boots), Jayma Mays (Dulcinea), Paul Rugg (Artephius), Joshua Rush (Toby), Carla Jimenez (Senora Zapata), Carlos Alazraqui (Mayor Temoroso), Laraine Newman (Pajuna), Gret Griffin (Vina), Candi Milo (Kid Pickles/Cleevil), Ariebella Makana (Esme). **Credits:** *Director*: Luther McLaurin, Lane Lueras, David Mucci Fassett, Douglas Lovelace, Roy Burdine. *Writer*: Doug Langdale, Greg White, Jesse Porter, Ben Acker, Ben Blacker, Tad Stones, Julia Yorks. **Comment:** Although produced for the pay service Netflix, episodes can be viewed for free on YouTube. The computer animation is excellent and there is a good mix of comedy, action and adventure.

Episode List: *1.* Hidden. *2.* Sphinx. *3.* Brothers. *4.* Duchess. *5.* Adventure. *6.* Fountains. *7.* Bravery. *8.* Golem. *9.* Boots. *10.* Sword. *11.* Mouse. *12.* Goblin. *13.* Star. *14.* Pigs. *15.* Luck.

5 All Hail King Julien. *youtube.com.* 2014 (Cartoon).

A prequel series to the feature film *Madagascar* that relates events in Madagascar as seen through the experiences of King Julien XIII, a strict but cowardly ring-tailed lemur.

Voice Cast: Danny Jacobs (King Julien XIII), Andy Richter (Mort), Kevin Michael Richardson (Maurice), Henry Winkler (Uncle King Julien XII), Debra Wilson (Masikura), David Krumholtz (Timo). **Credits:** *Producer*: Mitch Watson, Bret Haaland. **Comment:** Although not on the same caliber as the animation of the feature film, it is well done and captures the flavor of the film. While the series was produced for the pay service Netflix, it can be viewed for free on YouTube.

Season 1 Episode List: *1.* King Me. *2.* Poll Position. *3.* Enter the Fanaloka. *4.* Empty Is the Head. *5.* Return of the Uncle King. *6.* Eat, Prey, Shove. *7.* He Blinded Me with Science. *8.* Viva Mort. *9.* The Really, Really Big Lie. *10.* One More Cup.

Season 2 Episode List: *1.* My Fair Foosa. *2.* Diapers Are the New Black. *3.* Crimson and Clover. *4.*

Pineapple of My Eye. *5.* Gimme, Gimme, Gimme: The Game. *6.* Body Double. *7.* Election. *8.* Daddy Julien. *9.* That's Soo Rob. *10.* The Man in the Iron Booty. *11.* Monkey Planet. *12.* True Bromance. *13.* The King Who Would Be King. *14.* Are You There Frank? It's Me, King Julien. *15.* The Phantom of Club Moist. *16.* King Juli-End?

6 The Amber Project. *youtube.com.* 2014 (Dolls).

Amber Thomas is a 14-year-old girl who has lived with her mother since her parents divorced some years ago. She has a best friend (Phoebe) and one great love: music. A profile of Amber's life at school is presented as she deals with all the drama that surrounds her, especially from Erika and Jamie, the mean girls who taunt her and other students.

Cast (as credited): Josephine Montoya (Amber Thomas), Saige Copeland (Phoebe Williams), Ruth Maxwell (Erika Brown), Corinne Eunas (Jamie Nickles). **Comment:** Very good doll manipulation is coupled with excellent voices and photography.

Episode List: 5 untitled episodes, labeled "Episode 1" through "Episode 5" have been produced.

7 American Girl Mermaid. *youtube.com.* 2012 (Dolls).

American Girl dolls are incorporated to tell the story of Charlotte, an ordinary pre-teen girl who encounters a star pool while swimming and is magically transformed into a Mermaid. How she adjusts to what she has become and learns to use her powers are the focal point of stories.

Cast (as credited): Holly (Voices and Doll Movement). **Comment:** The picture is a bit grainy but the overall production is well done.

Episode List: *1.* Pilot. *2.* New Powers. *3.* New Friend. *4.* The Secret.

8 Anastasia's Fantasy. *youtube.com.* 2015 (Dolls).

It is 1945 and Anastasia, her mother and sisters, Madelyn and Bernadette, have just relocated from England to France. Anastasia is a young girl who loves to tell stories that seem to be fanciful but presented as a mystery (just stories or incidents from Anastasia's past lives?). The LPS (Littlest Pet Shop) dolls are used to relay stories as told by Anastasia.

Voices (as credited): OakStar LPS (all characters except Bernadette, who is voiced by Kelsey). **Comment:** Good voice characterizations are coupled with equally good photography and doll manipulation.

Episode List: *1.* Mum's Stories. *2.* Letters from Lexi. *3.* Disappearance. *4.* Reappearance.

9 Annedroids. *annedroids.com.* 2013–2015 (Comedy).

Anne is a very pretty and brilliant 11-year-old girl who experimented with robotics and eventually created three intelligent androids (Pal, Hand and Eyes). The androids, who can think for themselves, are curious about the human world in which they now live. Although they are programmed not to leave the safety of Anne's lab (which Anne established in her father's junkyard) Pal, Hand and Eyes are eager to absorb more data. As the androids explore their surroundings, Anne and her friends, Nick and Shania, incorporate scientific principals to help them (and children) understand and solve the real-life situations they encounter.

Cast: Addison Holley (Anne), Jadiel Dowlin (Nick), Adrianna DiLiello (Shania), Millie Davis (Pal), Raven Dauda (Nick's mother), James Gangl (Anne's father), Jayne Eastwood (Shania's Grandmother), Joey Nijem (Garth). **Credits:** *Producer*: J.J. Johnson, Matthew J.R. Bishop, Blair Powers, Christin Simms. *Director*: J.J. Johnson, John May, Jeremy Lutter, Craig David Wallace. *Writer*: J.J. Johnson, Christin Simms, Amanda Spagnolo, John May, Suzanne Bolch. Doug Hadders, Adam Rotstein. **Comment:** Enjoyable, very well acted and produced science-themed program geared to 'tween children. The special effects, which are computer generated, are very well done.

Season 1 Episode List: *1.* Pilot. *2.* New Pals. *3.* Pal n' Go Seek. *4.* Reduce, Reuse, Robocycle. *5.* Helping Hand. *6.* Garbage Band. *7.* Eyes Up. *8.* Junkyard Sleepover. *9.* Pal in the Middle. *10.* Android's Best Friend. *11.* The Power of Love. *12.* Electromagnetic Pal. *13.* Out of Hand. *14.* Eyes on the Skies.

Season 2 Episode List: *1.* Message in a Rocket. *2.* Undercover Pigeon. *3.* Experiments in Babysitting. *4.* Parent Swap. *5.* An Android Space Odyssey. *6.* Zack Bot. *7.* Junkyard CSI. *8.* Jurassic Junkyard. *9.* Costume Pal. *10.* Broken Hand. *11.* Lights, Camera, Volcano. *12.* Annebots. *13.* Family Matter.

10 Aqua Girls. 2012 (Fantasy).

Taylor and Alex are friends who have discussed the possibility of Mermaids existing but have come to the conclusion that they are just a myth. Their thinking changes shortly after when the water (in a pool in which they are swimming) activates a recessed gene that transforms them into Mermaids. Taylor and Alex quickly adjust to what has happened but must now keep a secret as they pretend to be ordinary girls.

Cast (as credited): Landri B. (Taylor), Avori V. (Alex). **Comment:** Interesting story and acceptable acting but the program has since been taken offline. **Episode List:** *1.* Something New. *2.* Moonlight Mystery. *3.* S.O.S.

11 Aqua Stars. *youtube.com.* 2014 (Fantasy).

While near a pond, two girls (Ivy and Zoey) find a star-shaped stone that Ivy believes will make a good stone for skipping across the water. As Ivy throws the stone across the pond, the water takes on a shimmering look that mystifies the girls but does not harm them. Later, at Ivy's home, Zoey accidentally spills water on herself and transforms into a Mermaid. Ivy, splashed with the water, transforms into a Mermaid seconds later. The program was to chart the girls "as they decide to have fun and face the thrills of being Mermaids."

Cast: Only Nelly as Ivy is credited. Other characters are Zoey, Kelly, Aquata Silverfish, Tridentia Silverfish and Marina. **Comment:** The girls are pretty and the acting acceptable but poor sound hampers the production. It appears that only one episode has been produced and, although it is listed on YouTube, it is not available for viewing.

Episode List: *1.* Pilot.

12 Aqua Vitae Mermaid. *youtube.com.* 2012 (Fantasy).

Two girls (Karis and Kiley) are at the beach and swimming when a large wave magically transports them to a secret cave. As the sea water begins to fill the cave, the girls begin to panic as there appears to be no way out. Suddenly a light shines from above and the girls see that there is an opening at the top of the cave that allows them to escape and return home to safety. The following day, when Karis and Kiley come in contact with water they transform into Mermaids. The girls are not sure what caused the metamorphosis (the sea water, the light or the cave) but know they must now keep secret what happened and pretend to be ordinary girls as they adjust to becoming Mermaids.

Cast (as credited): Karis and Kiley as Themselves. **Comment:** The girls are pretty, the photography is nice and the acting is good. The only complaint would be the camera lens catching people in the background of a public pool that was used as the cave to which the girls were transported.

Episode List: *1.* Aqua-respire. *2.* Seeing Change.

13 Aqua Waters. 2012 (Fantasy).

While swimming in the ocean, two girls (Hayley and Sierra) encounter what appears to be a sea opening that leads to a cave. While exploring the cave Hayley and Sierra become lost. Although frightened, the girls keep their cool, retrace their steps and soon find themselves safely back in the ocean. Later, when each of the girls comes into contact with water, she is transformed into a Mermaid. Hayley and Sierra now share a secret and their efforts to control their developing powers as well as pretend to be ordinary girls are chronicled.

Cast (as credited): Savannah (Sierra), Jessie (Hayley). **Comment:** While the girls are pretty, the program has poor sound and acceptable photography. It has since been taken offline.

Episode List: *1.* First Wave. *2.* Monster-logy. *3 and*

4. Unknown. 5. Troubled Waters. 6. Siren's Cave. 7. The Ogham Charm. 8. Finale.

14 Are Fishy Little Secret. 2013 (Fantasy).

In an effort to keep the water in a public pool clean, park officials treat it with a supposedly harmless chemical. When the pool is used the following day by two young girls (cousins Brooke and Ember) they are unaware, at first, that the chemical has activated a recessed Mermaid gene each carries. When the girls return home and first come in contact with tap water, they are transformed into Mermaids. While amazed at what has happened, Brooke and Ember quickly adjust to their situation and stories relate their efforts to conceal their secret identities while pretending to be ordinary school girls.

Cast (as credited): Bridgette (Brooke), Rachel (Ember). **Comment:** The young girls handle their roles quite well but the sound and photography are poor. The program has since been taken offline. **Episode List:** 1. Pilot. 2. Whisked Back in Time.

15 Ariana Mermaids. *youtube.com.* 2014 (Fantasy).

Kimi is a young girl with an unnatural fear of water and the full moon. She appears to be an ordinary girl but contact with water or exposure to the light of a full moon transforms her into a Mermaid. As Kimi settles into a new home, she meets and befriends two girls (Aubree and Mariana) who are unaware of Kimi's secret until their association with her places them in an enhanced spell that also transforms them into Mermaids. The mishaps (and adventures) the girls share as they struggle to protect their secret while leading lives as typical school girls are depicted.

Cast (as credited): Jillian (Aubree Henshaw), Isa (Marina Anderson), Jae (Kimi O'Connor). **Comment:** Only one episode has thus far been produced. The sound and photography are poor but the project does show potential for some intrigue as the girls cope with what has happened to them. **Episode List:** 1. Pilot: A New Tail.

16 Aspen Heights. *youtube.com.* 2013 (Dolls).

Aspen Heights is a school that has a sinister past. It was founded a century ago at a time when two groups of people, the Aspens and the Highettes ruled. The Aspens were endowed with magical powers while the Highettes were not. Two sisters, one with Aspen abilities and one devoid of magic (Highettes) founded the school. The sisters despised each other and their lives changed forever when the Highettes sister gained magical powers by joining with evil (the Abandon) to destroy and absorb the power of the Aspens. Each decade a special girl was born, called "The Chosen One," who possessed an Aspen gene that would protect all Aspens from the Abandon. It is the present day when a young girl named Elita, a student at the Aspen Heights School, has come to realize her true calling as "The Chosen One." The program follows Elita as she begins a dangerous quest to defeat the Abandon and save the Aspens.

Cast (as credited): Zoe Flemming, Samantha Parks, Caden Coleman, Felicity Merriman, Aly Grey, Jenna Akina, Julie Albright. Voices by Alexis. **Comment:** American Girl Dolls are used but the story is just hard to understand (or even figure out). While there is a recap episode (which should be watched first) there is no real introduction when the series begins as to what Elita is or what her calling is (something is hinted but not made clear). The doll manipulation and voices are very good. **Episode List:** *Season 1*: 11 untitled episodes; *Season 2*: 9 untitled episodes; *Season 3*: 10 untitled episodes. *Season 4*: 11 untitled episodes.

17 Atlantis Mermaids. 2013 (Fantasy).

While out for a walk, two young girls (Chris and Renee) find two necklaces that, when placed around their necks, secretly activate a recessed gene each of the girl's carries. Nothing happens at first but when each comes in contact with water, they are transformed into Mermaids. Now with a secret each must keep, the program charts their efforts to deal with their power over water yet live their lives as ordinary girls.

Cast (as credited): Chris and Renee as Themselves. **Comment:** Very slow-moving program which appears to have been abandoned. It is produced in Puerto Rico and the acting and photography are only just acceptable. The program has since been taken offline. **Episode List:** 2 untitled episodes, labeled "Episode 1" and "Episode 2" have been produced.

18 The Ballad of Mary and Ernie. *maryandernie.com.* 2010 (Fantasy).

Marshall Ernie, the Marshal of a typical town of the Old West (here in the 1890s) is a big man—not only in the fact that he is the only source of law and order, but that he stands fifty feet tall. Ernie is accepted by the townspeople and believes he was born in the town but others believe he was conceived in outer space and came to the town as a baby. As Ernie grew he considered the town his home and the townspeople his people—people he has sworn to protect. (In a flashback sequence Ernie is seen as large baby and being placed in a cabin with a childless couple. A considerably smaller in size flying saucer is then seen departing. Ernie had always maintained that his height is due to the fact that his mother said "I was big for my age.") Ernie's efforts to just be himself as he protects his beloved town are chronicled.

Mary Venezuela is a mysterious girl who has recently arrived in town to run the saloon. She is as tall as Marshall, but has no recollection as to where she came from or an explanation for her height.

Blad Bart is the town villain, a once prosperous wine salesman with 12 children. It was during the famine of 1888 that his life changed when he found making an honest living impossible and people ate whatever they could to survive. Blad's family mysterious disappeared (hinting that he survived on them) and he came to realize that being an outlaw was his only choice.

The Kid (his first name is The) is Ernie's best friend, an orphan. His parents were killed in a "train robbery/earthquake/typhoon/cheese cake factory explosion" and he has since attached himself to Ernie. The Kid is in love with Mary and excels at "cross-dressing, running faster than cattle and tennis—which won't be invented for another 30 years."

Nan Iceberg is the normal-sized woman who is engaged to Ernie (while Mary is Ernie's size, she is not too fond of him and hates the town).

Cast: James Lane (Marshall Ernie), Vanessa Celzo (Mary Venezuela). *Voice Cast:* Darcy Halsey (Nan/Vinnie), Catherine Reitman (The Kid), Jesse Corti (Blad Bart). **Credits:** *Producer-Writer-Director:* Robert Stadd. **Comment:** Clever take on the *Gulliver's Travels* segment set in Lilliput. Ernie represents Gulliver while the townspeople the Lilliputians. Ernie and Mary are the only live-action characters while others are toy dolls (coupled with miniature sets) to give the illusion that Ernie and Mary are 50 feet tall. Simple as it seems, it works. Ernie does have a horse (that he carries with him rather than riding) and, even though The Kid and Nan are toys, their voices and movement give them an impression as being real. Overall the idea is good; the acting and production values also good and there are definitely numerous possibilities to explore with such a premise should the producers decide to continue the series.

Episode List: *1.* I Got a Kidney Bigger Than Yours. *2.* A Fun Day Was Just Outside of Town. *3.* Back in Town. *4.* And Just Outside of Town. *5.* Jealous. *6.* The Flashback Show.

19 *The Barbie Family Show.* *youtube.com.* 2012–2013 (Dolls).

The Mattel line of Barbie dolls is used to relate incidents in the lives of a family that seem to encounter nothing but mishaps. The program is also known as *The Barbie Happy Family Show* and is based on the Internet series *The Happy Family Show* (see entry).

Voices: Lenore Castillo. **Comment:** Lenore's hands can be seen as she manipulates the dolls. Although she does a good job with the voices, the camera movement is a bit unsteady at times.

Episode List: 14 untitled episodes, labeled "Episode 1" through "Episode 14" have been produced.

20 *Barbie: Life in the Dream House.* *you tube.com.* 2012–2014 (Dolls).

The Barbie fashion dolls produced by Mattel come to life via computer animation to relate events in the life of a beautiful teenage girl (Barbie) and her younger siblings (Skipper, Stacie and Chelsea), who live in a large pink mansion in a fanaticized version of Malibu, California.

Barbie, the iconic doll created in 1959, has remained a bright, charming role model for young girls. She is personable, well-mannered and, although she is considered a Malibu celebrity, she tries to be just a regular girl. Although Barbie has been associated with many occupations via the dolls (from actress to nurse) she is seen as the owner of Barbie's Fashion Boutique on the program.

Ken is Barbie's boyfriend and portrayed here as an inventor whose "gadgets" often malfunction.

Skipper, Stacie and Chelsea are Barbie's sisters. Skipper is a teenager who loves high tech gadgets; Stacie is ten years old and very organized for one so young; Chelsea is six years old and devoted to her pets.

Teresa is Barbie's friend, a girl who is quite chatty and a bit of an airhead. Nikki is Barbie and Teresa's friend, a sassy girl who manages a fashion blog.

Raquelle is a girl who lives in luxury and is seeking to steal Ken from Barbie. She is also very vain and will resort to trickery to get what she wants.

Ryan is Raquelle's twin brother and has been friends with Barbie since they lived in Willows, Wisconsin, as children. While he knows Barbie likes Ken he hopes that one day Barbie will leave Ken and become his girlfriend.

Midge is Barbie's oldest friend (they grew up in Willows, Wisconsin) and has recently moved to Malibu. She is a girl who loves to wear retro clothes (especially from the 1960s) and enjoys arts and crafts.

Summer is Barbie's friend, a girl who enjoys sports and games; Grace is the newest addition to Barbie's circle of friends as she has just moved to Malibu.

Voice Cast: Kate Higgins (Barbie), Sean Hankinson (Ken), Paula Rhodes (Skipper/Stacie), Laura Gerow (Chelsea), Katie Crown (Teresa), Nakia Burrise (Nikki), Haviland Stillwell (Raquelle), Ashlyn Selich (Midge), Charlie Bodin (Ryan), Tara Sands (Summer). **Comment:** The computer animation is very good and it captures the images of the dolls with Barbie's physical attributes (39-18-33) altered somewhat (smaller breasts and a larger waist) to make her more realistic. The voice match-ups are also good and the stories flow smoothly from beginning to end. A real treat to girls who are, were, or still are Barbie fans.

Season 1 Episode List:
1. Closet Princess.
2. Happy Birthday, Chelsea.
3. Pet Peeve.
4. Rhapsody in Butter Cream.
5. Ken-tastic Hair-tastic.
6. Party Foul.
7. Day at the Beach.
8. Sticker It Up.

9. Oh How Campy.
10. Bad Hair Day.
11. License to Drive.
12. I Want My BTV.
13. Gifts Goofs Galore.
14. The Barbie Boutique.
Season 2 Episode List:
1. The Reunion Show.
2. Closet Princess 2.0.
3. Sisters Ahoy.
4. The Shrinkerator.
5. Plethora of Puppies.
6. Closet Clothes Out.
7. Accidentally on Porpoise.
8–9. Gone Glitter Gone.
Season 3 Episode List:
1. Playing Heart to Get.
2. Catty on the Catwalk.
3. Help Wanted.
4. A Spooky Sleepover.
5. A Smidge of Midge.
6. Occupational Hazards.
7. Ooh How Campy, Too.
8. Let's Make a Doll.
Season 4 Episode List:
1. Endless Summer.
2. Sour Loser.
3. Another Day at the Beach.
4. Happy Birthday to You.
5. Cringing in the Rain.
6. The Ken Den.
7. Primp My Ride.
8. Mall Mayhem.
9. The Closet Upgrade.
Season 5 Episode List:
1. Doctor Barbie.
2. Stuck with You.
3. The Only Way to Fly.
4. Perf Pool Party.
5. Trapped in the Dream House.
Season 6 Episode List:
1–2. Style Super Squad.
3. Little Bad Dress.

21 _Barbie Mermaid Chronicles._ _youtube.com._ 2014 (Dolls).

Katie is a teenage girl celebrating her birthday with her friends when things get a bit out of hand and Katie somehow manages to get shoved into her bathtub (it is really difficult to figure out what is happening in this sequence as it is poorly presented). The bathtub, for unexplained reasons, is filled with water and Katie is seen transforming into a Mermaid. Her friends, Chloe, Olivia and Tiffany, coming to her assistance, are touched by the water and also transform into Mermaids. The program offers no explanation as to how four girls acquired their Mermaid abilities (recessed genes?) and sort of just ends with the viewer wondering what will happen next (the pro-gram appears to have been abandoned and will have no doubt followed other Mermaid shows with the girls helping each other keep their secret while pretending to be ordinary girls).

Voices (as credited): LPSKayGirl. **Comment:** The Mattel line of Barbie dolls are incorporated in a program that has good doll manipulation and voices but is poorly constructed per a story line.

Episode List: *1.* Season 1, Episode 1.

22 _Barbie: Sirens of the Sea._ _youtube.com._ 2015 (Dolls).

Sophia is a 17-year-old girl newly arrived in America from Germany. She has been enrolled in high school and is making new friends but she is also hiding a secret: she is a Mermaid. One day, while walking to class with her friend Betsy, Sophia accidentally steps in a puddle of water and transforms into a Mermaid. Although shocked, Betsy promises to keep secret what happened and help Sophia adjust to her Mermaid life, a situation made more complicated when Sirens (evil creatures of the sea) become a threat to Sophia.

Cast (as credited): Sophia Van Der Beck, Betsy McLaughlin. **Comment:** The Mattel Barbie dolls are encompassed with good voices, doll manipulation and photography.

Episode List: *1.* First Day of School. *2.* Hide Your Tail. *3.* A New Discovery. *4.* Who Is She? *5.* Sirens Spell. *6.* Best Friends Forever. *7.* Secrets. *8.* For Real. *9.* Twin Sister. *10.* Chosen. *11.* Problems. *12.* Magic. *13.* Trapped. *14.* Human. *15.* Amnesia. *16.* Remember. *17.* Principal Problem. *18.* Liar. *19.* Caught.

23 _Barbie Vlog._ _youtube.com._ 2015 (Cartoon).

An exclusive YouTube program that incorporates the image of a Barbie doll in computer animated form. It is geared strictly to girls and presents Barbie revealing aspects of her own life as well as items (like fashion and hairstyles) to her audience.

Comment: Unfortunately, other than being identified as Barbie Roberts, there is no cast information. The animation is excellent (comparable to the numerous "Barbie" movies made for DVD) with just wholesome entertainment for children.

Episode List: *1.* 10 Things about Me. *2.* Favorite Fashion and Hairstyles. *3.* *People* magazine catches up with Barbie. *4.* Finger Tutting [making symbols with your hands] and "Raise Our Voice" Challenge.

24 _Barbie: Water Tails._ _youtube.com._ 2012 (Dolls).

Lizzie is a student at Miami Day School who lacks self-confidence and is not well liked by other girls (through unflattering rumors spread by a jealous girl named Chrissy). One day, while hiking through the woods, Lizzie stumbles upon a glowing object and is transported to an enchanted, glass-like cave. As Lizzie explores her surroundings, she is drawn to and swims in its waters. At that exact moment, rays from the moon enter the cave and illuminate the water. Magically she is transported back home and appears to be unaffected—at first. She soon learns that her experience was extraordinary, perhaps supernatural as her first contact with water (taking a bath) transforms her into a beautiful Mermaid—something that boosts Lizzie's self confidence and makes her more respectful of who she is—but a self-confidence that only appears when she is a Mermaid. The program follows Lizzie as she struggles to adjust to a new (and secret) life while also trying to live her normal life—at school and at home with a "Barbie psycho freak" mother and her younger sister Kassidy.

Voice Cast: Lizzie Summers (Lizzie/ Narrator/ Kassidy), Chrissy Carson (Chrissy), Louis Summers, Jason Shaw.

Comment: The program encompasses the Mattel series of Barbie Dolls to tell its story. Lizzie Summers' voice is captivating and she does make the series work. She also handles the dolls and her pain as Lizzie can be felt by the viewer. With the actual dolls as "the stars," it does present something different and it does come with a parental warning as it is not a comedy series but a dramatic look at real problems faced by young girls (although told through dolls) from eating disorders (possessed by Lizzie) to bullying and romance (it also warns against the hazards of swimming with marine life without supervision).

Season 1 Episode List: *1.* Mysterious Waters. *2.* Safety First. *3.* The Secret Is Revealed. *4.* Study Date. *5.* Plastic Surgery. *6.* A New Tail. *7.* The Talent Show.

Season 2 Episode List: *1.* The Chosen Ones. *2.* Sink or Swim. *3.* Thank You. *4.* Work Out Tails Off. *5.* Practice Makes Perfect. *6.* Blown Away. *7.* The End of the Tail.

Season 3 Episode List: *1.* Gotcha. *2.* Violets Are Purple.

25 Batgirl: Spoiled. *youtube.com.* 2012 (Fantasy).

An Adaptation of the *Batgirl* legend based on the Stephanie Brown rendition of the comic book. Although Batgirl's history, as the daughter of the Police Commissioner of Gotham City, is the best known version (wherein Batgirl, alias Barbara Gordon, fought alongside Batman and Robin), here Batgirl (now alias Stephanie Brown), battles evil alone (as a vigilante) after a close call lead to her and Batman breaking ties. It was her encounter with Barbara Gordon, alias Oracle that changed her life when Barbara convinced her to join her in her crusade against evil.

Stephanie is a student at Gotham City University and in order to work as a team and constantly keep in contact with each other, Barbara secures a position as an assistant professor at the school. Stephanie patrols the streets at night, seeking to keep the city safe from diabolical villains but also suffers from inner demons as she re-examines her place in the world. Stephanie's dual life and the problems she encounters trying to keep both worlds separate are depicted.

Cast: Marisha Ray (Stephanie Brown/Batgirl), Jessica Kent (Oracle), Tara Strand (Harley Quinn), Robin Sol (Catwoman), Tim Powers (Penguin), Jennifer Newman (Black Canary), Eric Cash (Tentacles), Bryan Morton (Batman), Matthew Mercer (Batman's voice). **Credits:** *Producer:* Sax Carr, Marisha Ray. *Director:* Damian Beurer. *Writer:* Sax Carr, Marisha Ray, Sam Weller, April Wahlim, Zack S. West. **Comment:** Unfortunately only two episodes were produced as the program showed great potential as being something to look forward to seeing. Marisha Ray is perfect as Batgirl and her befriending and battling other characters familiar to the Batman/Batgirl legend would have only enhanced the program. The acting and production values, writing and directing are very good (comparable to any broadcast or cable TV series). The one major drawback is that there is no character background information given; Batgirl is just there; even a short narration explaining the premise would have helped as not everyone is familiar with Stephanie's history.

Episode List: *1.* Blindside. *2.* Little Lost (Bat) Girl.

26 Batgirl: Year One Motion Comic. *you tube.com.* 2009 (Cartoon).

Barbara Gordon, a recent college graduate, has returned to Gotham City with a sincere desire to battle crime—but not like her detective (later police commissioner) father James Gordon. Although Gotham City is protected by Batman and Robin, Barbara feels there is a need for another mysterious figure for justice and dons her Batgirl costume for the first time (to stop the evil Killer Moth). Barbara, with the help of Batman and Robin (and Black Canary) succeeds and is accepted as a symbol for justice. Stories follow Barbara as Batgirl, as she battles crime, but also seeks to adjust to a dual life.

Voice Cast: Kate Higgins (Barbara Gordon/Batgirl), Erin Fitzgerald (Vicky Vale/Black Canary), Lex Lang, Keith Silverstein, Neil Ross.

Credits: *Producer:* Richard Scott Russo. *Director:* Stephen Fedasz IV. **Comment:** Fast-moving story that is animated in a panel-by-panel style wherein the characters are basically stationary with moving graphics and sound effects. It does take a minute or so to adapt to, but enjoyable once you do.

Episode List: *1.* Masquerade. *2.* Future Tense. *3.* After Glow. *4.* Cave Dweller. *5.* Moth to a Flame. *6.* Bird of Prey. *7.* Hearts of Fire. *8.* Seasoned Crime Fighter. *9.* Gotham Police Station Ablaze.

27 Batman Adventures: Mad Love Motion Comics. *youtube.com.* 2008 (Cartoon).

An unusual program based on a single issue only

comic book of the same title (by Paul Dini and Bruce Timm) that delves into the life of Gotham City criminal Harley Quinn. Before turning evil Harley was a respected psychologist (Dr. Harleen Qunizel) but her encounter with the manipulative Joker at the Arkham Asylum for the criminally insane changed Harley's life (when she fell for the Joker's lies about his troubled childhood then became infatuated with him). To be with her new love, Harley turned to a life of crime as the Joker's accomplice. The Joker, however, has a fixation about killing Batman in a spectacular manner and declines Harley's advances, knowing Batman is more important. To win back the Joker, Harley devises a plan to kill Batman herself—something that infuriates the Joker. The episodes follow both Harley and the Joker as they each seek to kill Batman but for different reasons. **Voice Cast:** Cindy Airey (Harley Quinn), Billy Davis (Batman/Joker), Paul St. Peter (Alfred/Commissioner Gordon). **Credits:** *Producer:* Dan Smith. *Director:* Stephen Fedasz IV. **Comment:** Short animated project that uses comic book-like panels with moving backgrounds and sound effects. The program is enjoyable with a fast-moving story. **Episode List:** *1.* Dental Hi-Jinx/Crazy in Love. *2.* Psycho Therapy/In Like Quinn/The Grand Decep. *3.* A Fish Tale/Breaking Up Is Hard to Do.

28 Batman: Black and White Motion Comic. *youtube.com.* 2008–2009 (Cartoon).

Original stories coupled with adaptations that showcase adventures encountered by the Caped Crusader, Batman, throughout the years. **Voice Cast:** Michael Dobson (Batman), Janyse Jaud (Angelica), John Fitzgerald (Commissioner Gordon), Adam Fulton, Joseph May, Keifer Dobson. **Credits:** *Producer:* Ian Kirby, Ralph Sanchez. *Director:* Ian Kirby, Adam Fulton. *Writer:* Bob Kane, Doug Alexander, John Arcudi, Ed Brubaker, Kelly Puckett. **Comment:** Each animated episode is presented like a snippet as opposed to a full story. The animation is presented like a comic book—with basically still characters set against moving backgrounds and sound effects. **Episode List:** *1.* I'll Be Watching. *2.* Here Be Monsters. *3.* Broken Nose. *4.* Two of a Kind. *5–6.* Black and White Bandit. *7.* Punchline. *8.* Good Evening Midnight. *9.* Hide and Seek. *10.* Night After Night. *11–12.* Catwoman. *13.* Legend. *14.* Heroes. *15.* In Dreams. *16.* Sunrise. *17.* Hands. *18.* A Game of Bat and Rat. *19.* Monster in the Closet. *20.* The Call.

29 Bean's Monkey Business. *youtube.com.* 2011 (Variety).

A purple monkey puppet (Bean) hosts a program wherein children are taught basic reading, counting and drawing skills. Bean is assisted by two very pretty girls (Abyni and Paris) and the program also incorporates songs (mostly lullabies) and stories. **Cast:** Abyni, Paris and Jay as Themselves; a voice for Bean is not credited. **Comment:** The program has excellent photography and acting but it is a bit hard to understand what Bean says at times due to his high-pitched voice. **Episode List:** *1.* Different. *2.* Lullaby Time.

30 Bear in Underwear. *youtube.com.* 2015 (Cartoon).

Shady Glade Woods is home to a group of bears who have become accustomed to wearing "pants" (actually tighty whiteys) that were found years ago by a legendary bear in an abandoned campsite. Eddie is the young cub of that famous bear and has set his goal to become a legend like his father. The program relates Eddie's adventures as he pursues that goal but learns along the way that becoming a legend has its challenges. **Voice Cast:** Griffin Burns (Eddie), Jath Soucie (Rossman), Catherine Taber (Quinn), Ben Diskin (Virgil), Jess Harnell (Ron/Bigfoot), Ali Hillis (Eloise), Brad Grusnick (Lou). **Credits:** *Producer:* Evan Adler, Todd Harris Goldman, David Schiff. *Writer:* Todd Harris Goldman. David Schiff. **Comment:** Based on the book by Todd H. Doodler and produced in association with the pay service Amazon Prime (select episodes can be viewed for free on YouTube). While the animation is acceptable the program itself will appeal only to its target audience, young children. **Episode List:** *1.* Summer Is Over. *2.* S'mores. *3.* Testing the Hat.

31 A Beautiful Secret. 2013 (Fantasy).

Chloe Pruitt is a teenage girl who believes nothing ever exciting happens to her. It's the same old thing day in and day out. One day, while placing water in her backyard bird bath, Chloe finds a necklace and becomes fascinated with it. She takes it into the house, washes it off and places it around her neck. Later that day, when she goes swimming, the water transforms her into a beautiful Mermaid. The program ends here but it is assumed Chloe will struggle to keep secret what happened as she pretends to be an ordinary girl. **Cast:** Cheyenne Watson (Chloe Pruitt). **Comment:** The acting, photography and story are good but it appears that the program has been abandoned after one episode. No explanation is given and the program has since been taken offline. **Episode List:** *1.* Oops.

32 Bee and Puppycat. *youtube.com.* 2014 (Cartoon).

Bee is a young girl with a most unusual pet: Puppycat (looks like a cat but smells like a dog). While the how of the story line is not established, Bee and Puppycat are super heroes and through their leader,

TempBot travel between the reality of their world "and the void of Fishbowl Space." Their adventures in strange worlds are explored as they attempt to help where they are needed.

Voice Cast: Allyn Rachel (Bee), Roz Ryan, Hannah Hart (TempBot). Puppycat is non-speaking. **Credits:** *Producer*: Fred Seibert, Eric Homan, Kevin Kolde. *Director*: Larry Leichliter, Meredith Layne. *Writer*: Natasha Allegri, Madeline Floresi, Frank Gibson. **Comment:** The animation is quite good and stories are aimed at children six years and older.

Episode List: *1.* Bee and Puppycat. *2.* Food. *3.* Farmer. *4.* Beach. *5.* Cats.

33 *Ben and Holly's Little Kingdom. you tube.com.* 2009 (Cartoon).

Little Kingdom is, as its title implies, a land of tiny people called Elves (who live in the Great Elf Tree and earn a living by making toys and wands; they also run a farm and a windmill). King and Queen Thistle, who live in the Little Castle, rule the land. Also residing in this magical kingdom are Fairy Princesses (who reside in homes made of toad stools), witches and gnomes. Principal focus is on Ben Elf and Princess Holly and the adventures they encounter. Ben lives with his parents (Mr. and Mrs. Elf); Holly is the daughter of the King and Queen and has two siblings, Daisy and Poppy. Nanny Plum is Holly, Daisy and Poppy's nanny (and general castle housekeeper); Lucy is Ben and Holly's friend, a normal size human girl.

Voice Cast: Preston Nyman (Ben Elf), Sian Taylor (Holly Thistle), Ian Puleston-Davies (King Thistle), Sara Crowe (Queen Thistle), Zoe Baker (Daisy and Poppy), Sarah Ann Kennedy (Nanny Plum), David Graham (Wise Old Elf), John Sparkes (Mr. Elf), Judy Flynn (Mrs. Elf), Taig McNab (Gaston Ladybird), Lucy Moss (Violet Fairy), Zara Siddiqi (Strawberry Ferry), Alice May (Fleur Fairy), Oriana Pooles, Chaniya Mahon (Rosie Fairy), Oriana Pooles (Tangerine Fairy), Lucy Moss (Dorothy Fairy), Stanley Nickless (Barnaby Elf), Jonny Butler (Jake Elf). **Comment:** British produced series that is aimed at pre-school children with good animation and voice characterizations.

Episode List:
1. The Royal Fairy Picnic.
2. Gaston the Ladybird.
3. Holly's Magic Wand.
4. The Elf Farm.
5. Daisy and Poppy.
6. Queen Thistle's Teapot.
7. The Frog Prince.
8. The King's Busy Day.
9. Fun and Games.
10. King Thistle Is Not Well.
11. The Lost Egg.
12. The Elf Games.
13. Nanny Plum's Lesson.
14. The Elf Factory.
15. Mrs. Witch.
16. Elf Joke Day.
17. King Thistle's New Clothes.
18. The Elf School.
19. The Royal Golf Course.
20. Morning, Noon and Night.
21. Gaston's Visit.
22. A Trip to the Seaside.
23. Ben's Birthday Card.
24. Books.
25. Betty Caterpillar.
26. Queen Holly.
27. The Tooth Fairy.
28. The Elf Windmill.
29. The Elf Band.
30. The Ant Hill.
31. Red Beard the Elf Pirate.
32. Tadpoles.
33. Cows.
34. Queen Thistle's Day Off.
35. Nature Class.
36. Toy Robot.
37. Big Bad Barry.
38. King Thistle's Birthday.
39. The Wand Factory.
40. Camping Out.
41. Dinner Party.
42. The Woodpecker.
43. Daisy and Poppy's Pet.
44. The Elf Rocket.
45. Picnic on the Moon.
46. Lucy's Picnic.
47. Acorn Day.
48. The Elf Submarine.
49. Visiting the Marigolds.
50. The Party.
51. Snow.
52. The North Pole.
53. Strawberry Soufflé.
54. King for a Day.
55. Giants in the Meadow.
56. Mrs. Fig's Magic School.
57. Daisy and Poppy's Playground.
58. No Magic Day.
59. Spies.
60. Hard Times.
61. Gaston Goes to School.
62. Elf Rescue.
63. Lucy's School.
64. Baby Dragon.
65. Dolly Plum.
66. The Lost City.
67. The Shooting Star.
68. Nanny's Magic Test.
69. Gaston to the Rescue.
70. Miss Cookie's Nature Trail.
71. The New Wand.
72. Super Heroes.
73. Mrs. Witch's Spring Clean.

34 *Beneath the Waves.* 2014 (Fantasy).

It is a Friday the 13th and to some people it means a day of bad luck. Thera is a young girl who disbelieves that and decides to go swimming. But unforeseen powers see things differently and as Thera swims she is engulfed by the water's magical powers and transformed into a Mermaid. Although she quickly adjusts to what has happened, she must now encompass her developing powers while at the same time pretending to be an ordinary young girl.

Cast (as credited): Kayla (Thera), Jayla (Octavia), Amber (Isabel), Our Friend (Anabeth), Susie, Kolby. **Comment:** Typical Mermaid series with pretty girls and acceptable acting and photography; it has since been taken offline.

Episode List: *1.* Friday the 13th. *2.* Born or Turned? *3.* Through New Eyes. *4.* Christmas Gift. *5.* Sisters Stick Together. *6.* Darker Side. *7.* Teach Me How to Be Human. *8.* Moon Sickness Not? *9.* Happy New Powers. *10.* The Beginning of the End.

35 *Best Fins Forever. youtube.com.* 2012 (Fantasy).

Serena and Kendra are swimming in the ocean when they spot a cave, enter it and find a bottle with a note inside that warns them to be careful of a full moon and magic. The water then begins to bubble but Serena and Kendra appear to be fine. Later, when the girls return home and first come in contact with water, they transform into Mermaids. Now, as Mermaids, they must learn to keep secret what has hap-

pened, learn to control their powers and lead lives as ordinary girls.

Cast (as credited): Hannah (Serena), Lexi (Kendra). **Comment:** Although the acting is good, the production suffers from bad camera work (very shaky picture).

Episode List: *1.* The Mermaid's Curse.

36 *BFF Mermaids. youtube.com.* 2013 (Fantasy).

Reeva and Ashley are best friends who have a fascination with Mermaids. One day, while Ashley is with Reeva in her bedroom, they discover a clear plastic box that appears to contain gumballs. Believing they have something to do with Mermaids, Reeva and Ashley each take one. As the box mysteriously disappears, the girls are transformed into Mermaids but are now fearful of water and a full moon (which can also cause a transformation). As Ashley and Reeva slowly adjust to what has happened to them, their lives take a turn for the worse when they begin exploring an old abandoned house and disturb the peace of a Siren, whose awakening has angered her and made them a target of her revenge. The program charts the mishaps that befall Ashley and Reeva as they try to maintain their secret, live lives as ordinary school girls and somehow find a way to defeat the Siren before she destroys them.

Cast (as credited): Alyssa (Ashley), Phoebe (Reeva). **Comment:** The introduction of a Siren adds some intrigue in the Mermaid saga but the sound and editing are very poor and the photography only just acceptable.

Episode List: *1.* Tail Scale Change. *2.* The Bag. *3.* Episode 3. *4.* Not Understood. *5.* New Moon. *6.* The Siren.

37 *Bike Tales.* 2010 (Children).

A friendship developed when two young girls (Sofia and Ren) bonded over a bicycle. It was Ren who taught Sofia how to ride a two wheeler and, based on what has been released it would follow the comic mishaps Ren and Sofia encounter.

Cast: Emily Delahuaty (Ren), Erika Forest (Sofia), Adrien Cote (Ren's father), Alison Ward (Ren's mother), Al Miro (Sofia's father). **Credits:** *Producer:* Ramiya Pushparajah, Zakim Muraney. *Director:* Jaselle Martino. *Writer:* Piers Rae. **Comment:** Gentle tale of two young girls that is well acted and produced. It has since been taken offline.

Episode List: Pilot (although listed as a trailer that runs 13 min. and 24 sec.).

38 *Blue Moon Crystal Tails. youtube.com.* 2013 (Fantasy).

After awakening from a nap, a young girl (Eclipse) finds a crystal on her bed. As she holds it up to the light, the glimmer from the crystal appears to memorize her for a few seconds then causes her to collapse. Eclipse regains consciousness a few minutes later and, without the effects of water, finds that she has been transformed into a Mermaid. Seconds later her tail vanishes and her legs return to normal; but any contact with the crystal from this moment on will cause her to become a Mermaid. Although only a pilot episode has been produced, it appears that the program would have related Eclipse's efforts to conceal her true identity while attempting to discover the mystery of the crystal and who placed it on her bed.

Cast: Heather Leveille (Eclipse). **Comment:** Heather is a very pretty girl and the program, while well acted and photographed, appears to have been abandoned without resolving issues.

Episode List: *1.* Pilot.

39 *Blue Sand.* *youtube.com.* 2013 (Fantasy).

After searching the Internet for information about Mermaids, a teenage girl (Florence) later stumbles upon a book of fairy tales. As she looks through the book, she finds a piece of paper with a strange recipe (due to very low sound and over-powering music, it is very difficult to hear and comprehend what is happening. It appears that Florence will make the recipe and after sampling it will transform into a Mermaid). The episode just ends here and nothing else has appeared.

Cast: Neru Akita (Florence). **Comment:** In addition to the low sound problem at a crucial time, the acting and photography are only just acceptable. It does appear that the program has been abandoned.

Episode List: *1.* Episode 1, Season 1.

40 *Booba.* *youtube.com.* 2015 (Cartoon).

Booba is a cave-man like creature that only grunts and is extremely mishap prone. The program simply places Booba in a situation (like a kitchen) and explores what happens as he tries to do the simplest of things but encounters the most difficult and disastrous outcomes.

Voice Cast: Roman Karev (Booba). **Credits:** *Producer:* Daniyar Khatim, Konstantin Kobzev. *Director:* Sergey Gorobetc. *Writer:* Eveniy Krot. **Comment:** Extremely well done computer animated program that will not only delight children but adults as well. It would make the perfect TV series for The Cartoon Network or Nickelodeon.

Episode List: 3 untitled episodes, labeled "Episode 1," "Episode 2" and "Episode 3" have been produced.

41 *Bravest Warriors.* *youtube.com.* 2012–2013 (Cartoon).

It is the year 3085 and four teenagers (Chris, Beth, Danny and Wallow) use their powers to protect defenseless beings of all worlds.

Chris is the leader of the Bravest Warriors and uses a weapon animal called Little Bee (which can form a sword with a honey-combed hilt and a swarm of bees). Beth is Chris's girlfriend and has a cat, which can transform into a cat-o-nine tails as her animal weapon. Wallow is the smartest member of the team whose glove contains a computer named Pixel. His animal weapon is a falcon that transforms into an axe. Danny formed the Bravest Warriors and his animal weapon is a dog that can transform into a sword or gatling gun. Plum is Beth's friend, a Merewif (a girl who can morph her legs into a mermaid's tail when in the water). She is the unofficial fifth member of the team. Emotion Lord is the old man with warping abilities who is linked to Chris's emotions. Catbug is the child-like creature that is part cat and part ladybug.

Pilot Voice Cast: Charlie Schlatter (Chris Kirkman) Tara Strong (Beth Tezuka), Dan Finnerty (Wallow), Rob Paulsen (Danny Vasquez).

Series Voice Cast: Alex Walsh (Chris Kirkman), Liliana Mumy (Beth Tezuka), Ian Jones-Quartey, Maria Bamford (Pixel), John Omohundo (Danny Vasquez), Tara Strong (Plum), Breehn Burns (Emotion Lord), Michael Leon Wooley (Impossibear), Sam Lavagnino (Catbug). **Credits:** *Producer:* Breehn Burns, Will McRobb, Chris Viscardi, Fred Seibert. *Director:* Randy Myers, Pendleton Ward, Breehn Burns. *Writer:* Pendleton Ward, Breehn Burns. **Comment:** Comical animated science fiction fantasy that would play even better on the Cartoon Network. The animation is good and the stories as silly as animated spoofs are meant to be.

Episode List: *1.* Time Slime. *2.* Emotion Lord. *3.* Butter Lettuce. *4.* Memory Donk. *5.* The Bunless. *6.* Lavarinth. *7.* Gas Powered Stick. *8.* Dan before Time. *9.* Cereal Monster. *10.* Ultra Wankershim. *11.* Catbug. *12.* Sugarbellies. *13.* Moo-Phobia. *14.* Drama Bug. *15.* Browser Fail. *16.* Impossibomb. *17.* Terrabeth Bytes. *18.* Aeon Worm. *19.* RoboChris. *20.* The Lost (Original Pilot) Episode.

42 *Bring Me Alice's Head.* *youtube.com.* 2013 (Fantasy).

An update of the Lewis Carroll story *Alice in Wonderland.* After her experiences in Wonderland, Alice had returned to the real world but always dreamed of one day finding the White Rabbit that enticed her when she was a child. Alice is now grown and has isolated herself from the world, hoping to one day find happiness in Wonderland. Her only pleasure appears to be spending time with her pet white rabbits. Her wishing becomes reality when the White Rabbit appears to her and she asks him to take her back to Wonderland. Before she can get a response, the White Rabbit disappears; however, a stranger overheard Alice and the White Rabbit talking about the magical world of Wonderland. In Wonderland, the White Rabbit relates what happened (a stranger now knows about Wonderland) to the Queen of Hearts who becomes infuriated with Alice for revealing that such a place exists. In retaliation, she orders that Alice be silenced forever (had additional episodes been produced, they would have followed Alice's new adventures as she attempts to escape the Wonderland assassins hired to kill her).

Cast: Raffaella Anzalone (Alice), Andrea Beretta (White Rabbit), Vincenzo De Falco (Queen of Hearts), Simone Baldassari (Cheshire Cat), Martina Rusolo (Lori). **Credits:** *Producer-Writer-Director*: Marco Latour. **Comment:** The program is produced in Italy and captioned in English, but one must activate the closed captioning icon for the subtitles. The acting is acceptable but the production is very dark and difficult to make out what is happening. Having to use the subtitles is also a bit distracting (especially for children) as it draws your attention away from the visual aspects of a scene. The program ends with no conclusion but leads the doorway open for additional episodes.

Episode List: *1.* Bring Me Alice's Head (Pilot).

43 The California Tails. *youtube.com.* 2009 (Fantasy).

A young girl (Abigail) is in the backyard of her home when she finds a necklace and places it around her neck. Later, when she comes in contact with water she transforms into a Mermaid. The episode ends with Abigail's friend, Lisa, arriving at her house. The crucial (to what happens next) episode 2 has been taken offline (no explanation given). As episode three begins it has been established that Lisa is a land Mermaid (like Abigail) and that they have been granted their abilities by Malissa, Queen of the Ocean. Based on what can be determined, it appears that Lisa has been sent to help Abigail develop her powers and together they must use them to protect Mermaids and help good defeat evil.

Cast (as credited): Samantha5999 (Lisa), Loulou5999 (Abigail). **Comment:** While the program is one of the earliest of the Mermaid series it is somewhat confusing as to what happens. The overall production is acceptable and if the missing episode is restored, it will make the program much easier to comprehend.

Episode List: *1.* Findings. *2.* Unknown. *3.* Malissa. *4.* Switching. *5.* Meetings.

44 Camp Pinelake. *youtube.com.* 2011 (Dolls).

Gracie is a fifth grade girl who finds her life changing when her mother enrolls her at a summer retreat called Camp Pinelake. Gracie is not too enthused until she begins making friends and the program follows Gracie and her life at Camp Pinelake.

Voices (as credited): Fey and Allie. **Comment:** American Girl dolls are used as the characters in a pleasant outing that young girls will enjoy. The doll movement and voices are very good.

Episode List: 6 untitled episodes, labeled "Episode 1" through "Episode 6" have been produced.

45 CandyLand. *candylandseries.com.* 2012– 2013 (Comedy).

Pacific Palisades Preschool is not just an ordinary educational institution in Southern California. With its motto, "Where the Top One Percent Get Their Smarts," it is a grammar school for the privileged children of wealthy parents. Children who do not meet its standards are simply not welcomed. Ema is such a young girl, newly enrolled at the school, and through her experiences, a view of school life as few children ever experience is depicted.

Kale, the vegetarian (called a Vegan) is Ema's friend; Pear is the school heartthrob; Bethany #1 and Bethany #2 (sometimes called "The Bethany's") are the super rich, spoiled young girls who are also the school's "back-stabbing bitches"; Lucy, the ultra snob (the school's Queen Bee), leads the Bethany's (all members of the school clique, The Toddlers Tiaras Crew); and Beckham is the spoiled rich kid.

Cast: Tatum Hentemann (Lucy), Katherine Manchester (Ema), Mikey Effe (Pear), Mma-Syrai Alek (Bethany #1), Gracie Hall (Bethany #2), Wes Watson (Beckham), Shayna Brooke Chapman (Kale), Olivia Choate (Ema's mother). **Credits:** *Producer*: Win Bates, Damian Horan, Ali Scher. *Director*: Win Bates, Samian Horan, Ali Scher. *Writer*: Win Bates, Jeremy Cohen, Damian Horan, Jonathan Langager, Ali Scher, Courtney Thomas. **Comment:** A pre-teen version of most notably *Beverly Hills, 90210*, although aspects of *Saved by the Bell* and *The O.C.* can also be seen. The production is top rate and the child performers all handle their roles quite well. It is also a bit of a shock at first glance to see such young children dress and act beyond their years—as it is something that is rarely seen on television in the manner presented here. While Ema is sweet and innocent, the Bethany's are real "adult" bitches and Lucy the ultimate, nasty snob—a unique depiction not even seen on the shows it copies.

Episode List: *1.* The New Girl. *2.* Beckham's Bash. *3.* Keep Your Friends Close. *4.* Confessions of a Bethany. *5.* Mad, Bad and Dangerous to Know. *6.* The Real Lucy. *7.* Oops, I Did It Again.

46 Captain Blasto. *captainblasto.com.* 2008 (Fantasy).

Colin Carter is a high school student who feels life is a drag. He is bored, tired of the same old routine and feels the future is not all that bright. To bring some excitement into his life, Colin decides to become a super hero. Basing his character on his favorite comic book, *Captain Blasto*, Colin begins by designing a costume then, to become that hero, hires a group of people to play the villains in staged criminal acts that Colin will resolve as the mysterious Captain Blasto. The program itself limits itself to what happens when the crimes Colin devises become all too real and he must literally put an end to what has become a crime wave.

Cast: Christopher Preksta (Colin Carter), Daryl Karameikos (Aaron Kleiber), Evan Archer (Curt Wootton), Mark Tierno (Michael Lee), Sam Nicotero (Sam Seigel), Chris Hammel (Tom Moore), Melissa Urbaniak (Abbey Green), Michael Dirocco (Eddie Bendis). **Credits:** *Producer:* Aaron Kleiber, Christopher Preksta, Ashley Urbaniak. *Director:* Christopher Preksta. *Writer:* Aaron Kleiber, Christopher Preksta, Ben Shull. **Comment:** Clever mix of black and white and color images. While not an original idea, it is well presented (although it drags in places) with good acting and comedy spread throughout the production.

Episode List: 11 untitled episodes, labeled "Episode 1" through "Episode 11" have been produced.

47 Captain Canuck. *youtube.com.* 2013 (Cartoon).

Equilibrium is a Canadian-based organization of superheroes that was organized by Michael Evans, the older brother of Tom Evans, alias Captain Canuck. Michael, a scientist, possesses degrees in physics and biology and Tom is not an ordinary superhero. Michael enhanced Tom's body with nanotechnology that not only gave him the abilities of wisdom and strength, but speed and an Eidetic Memory (he can learn simply by watching). He has a strong sense of right and wrong and believes that ignorance and prejudice are the greatest enemies of mankind. Now, as Captain Canuck, Tom battles injustice in a slightly altered world where Canada is a technological superpower.

Redcoat is a top Equilibrium agent and Captain Canuck's constant assistant. She grew up in Brixton in the South of London and is only known by her code name of Redcoat. She learned the lessons of life growing up on the mean streets and at the age of 18 she chose to join a British Army initiative for social undesirables (as she was classified) rather than spending time in jail. The experience changed her life and she distinguished herself in hand-to-hand combat as well as exhibiting extraordinary abilities as a pilot. She was selected to join the SAS Mobility Troop where she became one of their top pilots (one of Lord West's "Redcoats," the shadow arm of the SAS that perform deep-cover espionage missions). When Equilibrium was formed and Lord West became its head, Redcoat also became a member of the organization.

Mister Gold is a billionaire industrialist bent on conquering the world. He was educated at the finest schools and is a master manipulator and funds a weapons manufacturing empire. While he outwardly appears as a gentleman (thanks to his public relations department) he is really brutal and ferocious and takes great pleasure in eliminating anyone who stands in his way. He is secretly financing war and instability around the world and is Tom's number one nemesis.

The Blue Fox is an elusive and deadly killer on which very little is known. She is skilled in the martial arts and is a master assassin. She is also a master of disguise and never lets her targets see she is coming or ever let anyone know she was there. Her services go to the highest bidder but she is always her own master, shifting alliances as she pleases.

Voice Cast: Kris Holden Reid (Captain Canuck), Tatiana Maslany (Redcoat), Laura Vandervoort (Blue Fox), Paul Amos (Mister Gold). **Credits:** *Producer:* Fadi Hakim, Jonas Diamond. *Director:* Sam Chou. *Writer:* Paul Gardner, Dean Heniy. **Comment:** Spectacular animation coupled with a fast-moving story that, unfortunately, ends in an unresolved cliffhanger.

Episode List: *1.* Happy Canada Day. *2.* Outfoxed. *3.* Turned Tables.

48 Carlos Caterpillar. *youtube.com.* 2008–2009 (Cartoon).

The program encompasses 3D animation with a strong multicultural Hispanic flavor (hip Latin music and a Spanish and English bilingual language track) to tell the story of Carlos Caterpillar and his friend, Sluggy (a slug), citizens of Mogan, a bug town in Spain, as they learn valuable lessons about life through the situations they encounter. It is geared to children 4-to-10 years of age and is produced by the Christian media company Vision Video.

Comment: A very well done program that can compare to any animated network or cable cartoon series. For reasons that are not explained, cast and credits are not listed (not on the website, in reviews or even the episodes themselves).

Episode List: *1.* Colossal Tales. *2.* Topsy Turvy. *3.* No Prize Surprise. *4.* Litterbug. *5.* Buggy Bigbucks. *6.* Ultrabug. *7.* Bug-A-Boo. *8.* Batter Chatter. *9.* Buggy Breakup. *10.* Cheater Critters. *11.* Royal Trouble. *12.* Hocus Bogus.

49 Circuit Playground. *youtube.com.* 2015 (Educational).

Like the program *Sylvia's Super Awesome Mini Maker Show* (see entry) the basics regarding electronics are explored; here through a curious robot (Adabot) and a female MIT engineer nicknamed "Ladyada."

Cast: Limor Fried (Ladyada). **Credits:** *Video:* Collin Cunningham, Andrew Baker, Limor Fried, Phillip Torrone, Noe Ruiz, Pedro Ruiz. **Comment:** The episode listing represents what had been produced at the time of publication. In 2005 Limor Fried created a company called Adafruit as an online site for learning electronics and making the best designed products for makers of all ages and skill levels. The series is a brief introduction to the various aspects of the electronics world with very good acting and production values.

Episode List: *1.* A Is for Ampere. *2.* B Is for Battery. *3.* C Is for Capacitor. *4.* D Is for Diode. *5.* F Is for Frequency. *6.* G Is for Ground.

50 Club Kate. *youtube.com.* 2015 (Variety).

An extension program based on *Fun with Kate and Chloe* (see entry) that presents comical videos wherein sisters Kate and Chloe present topics of interest to children.

Host (as credited): Kate and Chloe. **Comment:** Simply a fun program for children with excellent acting and photography.

Episode List: *1.* "Annie" (2014) Movie Review. *2.* Candy Eating Contest Ends in a Mess. *3.* Coolest Item Challenge. *4.* Candy Testing with Kate and Chloe. *5.* Blind Makeup Challenge. *6.* Bean Boozled Gross Candy Challenge. *7.* Cake Decorating Contest. *8.* Atomic Fire Candy Challenge.

51 Cooking with Stacie. *youtube.com.* 2015 (Dolls).

Cooking with a twist: a chef doll (Stacie) who presents young girls with step-by-step recipes to prepare meals (mostly desserts).

Chef: Stacey Oakley. Voices by Elmak Suna (as credited). **Comment:** Meant strictly for entertainment purposes as "Do Not Try This at Home" appears with each episode. It is a different approach to a cooking program and entertaining. The doll movement is also well done.

Episode List: *1.* Cookies. *2.* Strawberry Pie. *3.* Taco Fantastic Sundae. *4.* Lovely Dove Fudge-Filled Brownies. *5.* Christmas Cookies. *6.* Strawberry Cheese Cake. *7.* BBQ.

52 Counting with Paula. *countingwithpaula. com.* 2015 (Cartoon).

Paula is a very bright and articulate young girl who, with her friends Billy and Tim, experience colorful and exciting adventures in exotic places. Each adventure presents them with a problem and through Paula's evaluation of that problem, messages are relayed that help pre-school children count, learn shapes and recognize numbers.

Voice Cast: Vanessa Phang Wan Qing (Paula), Chio Su-Ping (Tim/Billy), Chung Yin Ping (Mr. Banana Tree). **Credits:** *Producer:* Tang Chi Sim, Chung Yin Ping. *Director:* Sacha Doedegebure. *Writer:* Sanjay Revee, Sacha Goedegebure, Chung Yin Ping. **Comment:** The program, produced in Singapore uses computer animation and combines Singapore Math with the United States' Common Core. It is very well done and the characters are most appealing for its target audience.

Episode List: 48 episodes were produced but only the following remain on line: *1.* A Friend Is Missing. *2.* Easter Egg Hunt. *3.* Horsing Around. *4.* Search for New Fruits. *5.* Where's the Wheel? *6.* Mr. Astronaut's Mission. *7.* Toys for Blue Baron. *8.* A Sweet Shape.

53 The Crazy Mermaid Life. 2012–2015 (Fantasy).

While at the beach a young girl (Bella) cuts her foot on an unusual rock. It is the night of a full moon and Bella becomes a bit uneasy over what has happened. As she composes herself, she returns home but the following morning, when she first comes in contact with water, she transforms into a Mermaid. Her cousin, Nikki and their best friend, Payton, have also had a similar experience and have also been transformed into Mermaids. The program follows three girls as they learn to control their Mermaid abilities while at the same time keeping secret what has happened to them.

Cast (as credited): Grayson (Bella Chadwick), Brittany (Payton White), Jessica (Nikki Chadwick), Violet (Blaire Convoy), Sarah (Emily). **Comment:** While the program has since been taken offline, it is an acceptable production with pretty girls, mostly steady video images and decent sound.

Season 1 Episode List:
  1. A Stone Magic.
  2. Mer Freak.
  3. Gooding Around.
  4. Power Play.
  5. Payton's Secret.
  6. Season 1 Finale.
Season 2 Episode List:
  1. New Year, New Cousin.
  2. An Unfortunate Dream.
  3. Cabin Fever.
  4. Sea Sick.
  5. New Member.
  6. Fish Out of Water.
  7. Splash of Knowledge.
  8. New Girl.
  9. A Twist at Grandma's.
  10. Season 2 Finale.
Season 3 Episode List:
  1. Nikki's Back.
  2. Night Fright.
  3. Camp Emily.
  4. Changed Mermaid.
  5. First Sighting.
  6–7. Toil and Trouble.
  8. Change.
  9. The Capture.
  10. Season 3 Finale.
Season 4 Episode List:
  1–2. This Isn't Good.

54 Creative Galaxy. *youtube.com.* 2013–2014 (Cartoon).

The *Creative Spark* is a rocket ship piloted by an adorable alien (Arty) who possesses great artistic skills and hails from the Creative Galaxy. Arty has made Earth his home and has set his goal to help people overcome problems through painting. The program, aimed at pre-school children, attempts to teach them about art by enlisting their help in solving a problem (much like the 1950s TV series *Winky Dink* wherein children were asked to help resolve a problem through their drawings on "The Winky Dink Magic Screen").

Voice Cast: Christian Distefano (Arty), Kira Gelineau (Epiphany), Amariah Faulkner (Annie), Brad Adamson (Pablo), Samantha Bee (Mom), Scott McCord (Captain Paper), Kallan Holley (JuJu), Tricia Brioux (Fabiana), Devan Cohen (Jackson), Cory Doran (Builder Ben), Jennifer Walls (Builder Betty), Cloris Leachman (Gallaia). **Credits:** *Producer:* Amanda Smith-Kolic. *Director:* Larry Jacobs, Michele L. Band, Dee Shipley. *Writer:* Angela Santomero. **Comment:** An original Netflix.com series that can be viewed for free on YouTube. The animation is well done and the premise intriguing for children as they can also learn, through Arty's trips to other planets to find inspiration, that asking for help to give help is also a part of life. Each episode consists of two stories.

Episode List: *1.* Pilot. *2.* Arty's Masterpiece/A Home for Bunny. *3.* Mom's Present/A Home for Baby Georgia. *4.* Jackson's Action Painting/Arty Plays Safari. *5.* Annie's Bracelet/Arty's Team Shirts. *6.* Annie's Flowers/Arty's Indoor Campout. *7.* Jackson's Dog/Arty's Play. *8.* Arty's Art-y Party/Arty's Birthday Treasures. *9.* Bath Time with Arty/Dinner Time. *10.* Family Fun Night/Game Night. *11.* Arty Paints Annie/Arty's Colors. *12.* Arty's Artistic Lunch/Art after Lunch. *13.* Arty's Book/Arty's Grumpy Day. *14.* Baby Georgia's First Christmas/Christmas Memories.

55 Creature of the Deep. *youtube.com.* 2012 (Fantasy).

Erin is a young girl who finds a recipe ("Glass of fresh water in a magic Mermaid shell") and follows its instructions. Within 30 minutes after drinking the mixture, she is magically transformed into a Mermaid and her adventures as she struggles to live two different lives are the focal point of stories.

Cast (as credited): Wiebits (Erin), Jabba (Ruby), Peck (Tessa), Sweetheart (Kirsten). **Comment:** The girls perform their roles well but the sound and photography are poor.

Season 1 Episode List:
1. Ocean Potion.
2. The Voice of Ruby.
3. Ruby Befriends Erin.
4. A Twist in the Tail.
5. Power Hour.
6. Hide-and-Go-Seek-a-Tail.
7. Swimming with Fins.
8. Tail Fever.
9. Lake Swim.
10. Season Finale.
Season 2 Episode List:
11. Moonstruck.
12. A Weird Discovery.
13. An Unexpected Dive.
14. Potion Commotion.
15. A Storm Is Rising.
16. A Tail of Trouble.
17. And Then There Were Four.
18. A Secret Revealed.
19. Christmas Creature.
20. Moonlight Swim.
Season 3 Episode List:
21. Accidents Happen.
22. Mermaids Cove.
23. The Mysterious Realm.
24. The Capture.
25. Evil Unleashed.
26. Split Personalities.
27. Twins!
28. Mini Episode.
29. Fairly Magical.
30. Party Pooper.

56 Crest of the Wave. *youtube.com.* 2014 (Fantasy).

One night a young girl (Rosie) has a weird dream about mysterious images that she cannot explain or understand. The following day, while at the beach and walking along the shore she is stopped in her tracks when magical orbs encircle her. Seconds later she is transformed into a Mermaid and several seconds later she returns to normal. Realizing that the images she saw in her dream were those of the orbs, Rosie accepts what has happened and must now conceal her secret while attempting to live the life of an ordinary school girl.

Cast: Emma Troake (Rosie Crest), Marina Troake (Rosie's mother), Nico Troake (Nico). **Comment:** Typical Mermaid program with acceptable acting and production values.

Episode List: *1.* Ow! Scales Hurt! *2.* Runaway Canine.

57 Crystal Blue. 2013 (Fantasy).

Four friends (Ashley, Jenna, Mia and Savannah) stumble across a container containing a liquid that fascinates them and sort of beckons them to drink it. The liquid causes a metamorphosis and each of the girls transforms into a Mermaid. As the girls now regret doing what they did, they find they have no other choice but to keep secret what has happened and help each other adjust to their developing powers. What has happened has come to the attention of a group of "Mer-Haters" and the program follows the girls as they attempt to escape their pursuers and remain free. **Cast (as credited):** Hannah (Savannah), Haley (Jenna), Ella (Mia), Giovanna (Ashley), Reece (Adam). **Comment:** Although the program has been taken offline and an evaluation based on viewing is not possible, it does sound a bit more intriguing than other Mermaid programs. Here, adding the aspect of discovery and pursuit could have made for an interesting twist. **Season 1 Episode List:** *1.* New Challenge. *2.* Challenges. *3.* Answers Not Found. *4.* New Hardships. *5.* Stunning Truth. **Season 2 Episode List:** *1.* Caught. *2.* The Escape. *3.* Missing Mermaids. *4.* The Fugitives. *5.* A Twist in the Tail. *6.* On the Road Again. *7.* Trapped. *8.* Friend or Foe? *9.* Frenemy? *10.* Days of Sadness? *11.* Finale.

58 *Daughter of the Elements.* 2015 (Fantasy).

One day, after returning home from school, a teenage girl (Elsa) finds a note on her kitchen table that tells her that her parents are away for a week but there is plenty of food in the house. After reading the note Elsa hears a strange female voice followed by a glowing light. The voice tells her that she is The Guardian and to touch water. Elsa obeys the voice and is suddenly transformed into a Mermaid. The voice then instructs her to open a book on the Five Elements (Earth, Sky, Water, Wind and Fire) and study them as she has become their guardian. While it is not clear why or how Elsa has been chosen to become a guardian, the program follows her progress as she learns to master each element so that she may protect them and use their power to help good defeat evil. **Cast:** Nikki Crawford (Elsa McLean, Raven, Melissa, Voice of The Guardian). **Credits:** *Producer:* Starlight Productions. *Writer-Director:* Nikki Crawford. **Comment:** A British production that is well acted and photographed. The program, before being withdrawn, had Elsa attempting to conquer the Fire element. **Episode List:** *1.* The New Elemental Master. *2.* Element Lesson Water. *3.* The Fire Within.

59 *Daughters of the Sea.* youtube.com. 2014 (Fantasy).

It is the night of a blue moon and two friends (Blakelyn and Meredith) decide to go to the nearby lake to witness it. As they wait, a storm appears to be brewing and the girls take refuge under a pier. Suddenly Meredith hears an echoing voice extolling "Come to Me" and feels it is the spirit of her late mother. Believing the voice is beckoning her to swim in the lake, Meredith, followed by Blakelyn, enter the water. Almost immediately, a blue mist (from the moon) appears ahead of them and engulfs them, first leading them to a mysterious cave then magically transporting them back home. The girls appear to be fine after their ordeal but when they come in contact with water, each is transformed into a Mermaid. Blakelyn and Meredith are not sure exactly what happened but know they must keep secret what happened and pretend to be ordinary girls. **Cast:** Savannah Thompson (Meredith Prescott), Kennedy Rodgers (Blakelyn Johnson), Kaitlin Davis, Jessica Moore. **Comment:** Acceptable photography and acting is coupled with a good story line. **Season 1 Episode List:** *1.* Destiny. *2.* Destiny Fulfilled. *3.* The Dryad. *4.* New Things. *5.* MerWolf. *6.* Elements. *7.* Elements Found. *8.* The Last Battle. **Season 2 Episode List:** *1.* Can't Remember. *2.* The Enchantress. *3.* The Blue Stone. *4.* Another Is Coming. *5.* Kidnapped. *6.* Pizza?

60 *A Day in a Life.* 2012 (Variety).

Lexi and Katie are best friends who enjoy doing everything together. One day they decide to do an Internet show based on their daily activities. Although only one episode was produced, it does establish the story line as they share their activities with viewers. **Cast (as credited):** Lexi and Katie as Themselves. **Comment:** An amusing, well-done program with charming hosts and an interesting premise. It has since been taken offline. **Episode List:** *1.* Pilot.

61 *A Day in the Life of a Mermaid.* you tube.com. 2015 (Variety).

Traci Hines is a young woman who plays both a Mermaid (Traci) but also appears as a Princess at various gala functions. The program is simply a fantasy look for children at the world as seen through the eyes of a beautiful Princess. **Cast:** Traci Hines (Princess). **Comment:** An excellent, television quality series that encompasses two fantasies of young girls (Mermaids and Princesses) and presents them in a manner where children can appreciate and better understand them. See also *Traci Hines, Mermaid* and *Hipster Mermaid*. **Episode List:** *1.* Princesses in Hollywood. *2.* Come with Me to Disney's D23 Expo. *3.* Disney's D23 Expo: Meet and Greet + Disney Princess Cosplay. *4.* A Jolly Holiday at Disney's D23 Expo. *5.* Down the Rabbit Hole: Alice Makeup Transformation with Alana Rose. *6.* A Day in the Life of an Urban Mermaid ("Adorkable" Adventures"). *7.* A Day in the Life of a Princess (Magic Carpet Ride).

62 *A Day in the Life of a Mermaid.* 2015 (Fantasy).

After what seemed like an eternity cleaning her bedroom, a young girl (Brooklyn) decides to relax at a nearby pond. There she spies a sea shell in the water and picks it up. She places the shell up to her ear (hoping to hear the ocean) when she suddenly blacks out. Although she had been wearing a bikini, she awakens on her front lawn clothed in a shirt and shorts. Unable to figure out what happened, Brooklyn goes into her house and with her first contact with water transforms into a Mermaid. The program ends here and it is assumed that, if additional episodes are produced, it will follow Brooklyn as she attempts to adjust to her Mermaid abilities while trying to live the life of an ordinary girl.

Cast (as credited): Brooklyn (Herself). **Comment:** Brooklyn is a delight to watch and the program encompasses excellent photography. Over-powering background music, however, makes dialogue a bit difficult to hear at times and the program now appears to have been taken offline.

Episode List: *1.* The Ocean's Gift.

63 *Days of a Mermaid.* youtube.com. 2013 (Dolls).

After seeing an ad on television for a rainbow bikini, a teenage girl (Selena) is inspired to go swimming. At the beach, which appears to be deserted, Selena sees what she believes is the tail of a Mermaid in the ocean. Hoping to discover what she saw, Selena begins a sea search but soon exhausts herself and blacks out. Miraculously, that Mermaid (Starlina) comes to her rescue and returns her to the beach shore. As Selena awakens and discovers what happened, she learns that Starlina is a real Mermaid but has always dreamed of experiencing life as a human. In an effort to repay Starlina for saving her life, Selena invites Starlina to stay with her at her house. Starlina is able to develop human legs when her tail dries and the program follows Starlina as she attempts to live the life of a human teenage girl and Selena's efforts to not only keep her secret, but her own when she, due to contact with Starlina in the ocean, is transformed into a Mermaid.

Cast: Starla Wilson (All character voices). **Credits:** *Producer-Writer-Director:* Starla Wilson. **Comment:** A very well done doll series with good doll movement, voices and photography (with the exception of episode 4, which has a somewhat grainy picture).

Episode List: 5 untitled episodes, labeled "Episode 1" through "Episode 5" have been produced.

64 *Deep Blue Mermaids.* youtube.com. 2012 (Fantasy).

Lea and Nicole, like many young girls, believe in Mermaids and often wish they could become one. One night each girl has a dream that they are descended from Mermaids but shrug it off as just a weird dream. Shortly after, when Lea and Nicole come in contact with water, they are instantly transformed into Mermaids and realize that dreams do

come true. Lea and Nicole are followed as they struggle to protect their secret identities while attempting to live normal lives. (It is later revealed that the girls' great grandmothers were also Mermaids and they inherited a recessed gene.)

Cast (as credited): Te'a/Lynor04 (Lea), Alisia (Nicole), Kailey (Catalina/Winda), Emily (Liv Walters). **Comment:** Poor sound but acceptable photography with capable acting by the young female leads.

Episode List: *1.* The Beginning. *2.* A Fishy Family. *3.* New Life, New Moon. *4–10:* Untitled Episodes.

65 *Deep Down Under Secrets.* youtube.com. 2013 (Fantasy).

Three friends (Serena, Bella and Alex) are sitting beside a swimming pool when a mysterious salesgirl from Magic Solutions approaches them and offers them a product to protect their hair from the chlorine in the water. The girls purchase the product, use it on their hair and transform into Mermaids when they enter the water. Serena, Bella and Alex must now keep secret what happened and adjust to their developing powers while pretending to be ordinary girls.

Cast (as credited): Emily (Serena), Kat (Bella), Sia (Bella). **Comment:** Although the program appears to have been abandoned, it is well-produced with good acting and photography.

Episode List: *1.* Magic Solutions.

66 *Deep Sea Tails.* youtube.com. 2012 (Fantasy).

It is a warm summer day and a young girl (Synde) finds relief from the heat by swimming in the local public pool. While in the water she spies a turquoise gemstone at the bottom of the pool and retrieves it, electing to keep it for herself. Curious about what she has found, and believing it may be related to Mermaids, Synde conducts an Internet search and learns that all Mermaids have a gem in the ocean and whoever finds one will become a Mermaid (how the gem found its way into a public pool is not stated). Synde soon discovers that she is a Mermaid (with a turquoise tail) when water spills on her and she transforms. By drying her tail she regains her human legs and stories follow her adventures—as she attempts to encompass her new abilities and keep her secret from others (her friend, Ruby, discovers her secret in the second episode and vows to not only help her but protect her).

Cast (as credited): Meredith G. (Sydne), Caroline M. (Ruby), Kayla G. (Hailey), Giny A. (Cassidy), Sophie V. (Sofia), Mariah K. (McKayla), Sam Y. (Teddy). **Comment:** Camera microphones do not provide the best sound and the production suffers because of it. The girls perform well and the photography is acceptable.

Season 1 Episode List: *1.* Fish Out of Water. *2.* House Maid. *3.* Halloween Special. *4.* Hypnotized Half Tail. *5.* Water Wastage. *6.* Stranger than the Average Strange. *7.* Fishy Letters. *8.* Truth Be Told. *9.* Dive Deep. *10.* Season 1 Finale.

Season 2 Episode List: *11.* Full Moon Despair. *12.* One Letter Too Far. *13.* New Girl in Town. *14.* Déjà vu. *15.* Fish over Fed.

67 *Deep Waters.* 2015 (Fantasy).

Argon, Chloe and Hailey are enjoying themselves in a hot tube when strange beams, emanating from the star Sirius, affects the water and transforms them into Mermaids. The girls must now keep a secret while pretending to be just ordinary girls.

Cast (as credited): Argon, Chloe and Hailey (Themselves). **Comment:** The girls are cute but the program suffers from poor audio at times. It has since been taken offline.

Episode List: *1.* Storm in a Bottle. *2.* The Splash Effect.

68 *Destiny's Hope. youtube.com.* 2014–2015 (Dolls).

Monster High Dolls are combined with Liv Dolls to present a story about Destiny and Hope, teenage girls who appear as normal school girls by day but transform into (not so scary) monsters at night and their efforts to conceal their dual identities.

Cast (as credited): Gwen and Howleen (Destiny), Lann and Twyla (Hope), Alex (Max), Ava (Jasmine). The show's creator, Ms. Flanclan provides the voices. **Comment:** Excellent doll manipulation coupled with very good voices and photography.

Episode List: 4 untitled episodes, labeled "Episode 1" through "Episode 4" have been produced.

69 *The Diary of Tortov Roddle. youtube. com.* 2009 (Cartoon).

The travels of a man (Tortov Roddle) and his companion (a large pig, presumably descended from the Dali elephants) and their encounters with strange animals and fantasy-like cities. Each story is told through grainy water color drawings and contains no dialogue (although there are cutaway dialogue inserts like those found in an old silent movie).

Credits: *Director-Animator-Creator:* Kunio Katou. **Comment:** There are no real plots to speak of, as each episode merely presents Tortov in a situation with no explanation as to how he got there. The program does not encompass a narrator as stories are told strictly through visual art and the dialogue inserts, translated from the original Japanese cartoon, are not well done (poor English). Once accustomed to the still-like presentation and accepting the fact that Tortov magically appears in places, the program becomes an interesting alternative to the standard animated productions that are typical of movies and television programs.

Episode List: *1.* The City of Light. *2.* Midnight Café. *3.* The Little Town's Movie Gathering. *4.* Moon-

light Travelers. *5.* Melancholy Rain. *6.* The Flower and the Lady.

70 *Dinosaur Office. youtube.com.* 2011–2012 (Comedy).

A look at the everyday lives of a group of dinosaurs, living in the modern-day world and how they cope with life at work.

Voice Cast: Kevin Corrigan (Craig), Caldwell Tanner (Todd), Emily Axford (Sheila), Sam Reich (Terry), Brian Murphy (Richard), Elaine Carroll (Susie Stone). **Credits:** *Producer:* Eric Towner, John Harvatine IV, Spencer Griffin, Janet Dimon, Jeremy Reitz. *Director:* Ethan Marak, David H. Brooks, Harry Chaskin, Ben Joseph, Tennessee Reid Norton, Trisha Gum, Alex Kamer, John Summer. *Writer:* Kevin Corrigan, Caldwell Tanner, Brian Murphy. **Comment:** Very short videos (under one minute) that are amusing, with good voices but no attempt is made to conceal the hands of the people manipulating the toy dinosaurs (which does not distract from the story).

Season 1 Episode List: *1.* Pilot. *2.* Computer Problems. *3.* Downsizing. *4.* Asteroid. *5.* Traffic. *6.* Office 7. Volcano Drill.

Season 2 Episode List: *1.* Viral Videos. *2.* Office Party. *3.* Guys' Night Out. *4.* Bring Your Child to Work Day. *5.* Elevator. *6.* Team Building. *7.* Sick Day. *8.* Coffee Run. *9.* Gym. *10.* Buyout. *11.* New Boss. *12.* The Presentation. *13.* Halloween Spooktacu-rawr. *14.* Thanksgiving.

71 *Dinotrux. youtube.com.* 2015 (Cartoon).

Dinotrux are hybrid creatures that are part dinosaur and part construction vehicles. They live in a modernized prehistoric world called the Mechazoic Era and work to build their city while at the same time battling their enemies, the evil D–Strucks, a T-Rex who threatens to destroy everything they build.

Characters: Ty Rux (part Tyrannosaurus Rex and part excavator); Revvit (part chameleon and part electric drill); Ton-Ton (part Ankylosaurus and part dump truck); Skya, a Craneosaur (part Brachiosaurus and part construction crane); Dozer, a Dozeratops (part Triceratops and part bulldozer); Garby (part Stegosaurus and part garbage truck); D–Strucks (part Tyrannosaurus Rex and part excavator); Click Clack (part lizard and part rotary drill); Ace (part lizard and part wrench); Waldo (part lizard and part monkey wrench); and George, a Dozeratops (part Triceratops and part bulldozer).

Voice Cast: Andrew Francis (Ty Rux), Richard Ian Cox (Revvit), Matt Hill (Ton Ton), Ashleigh Ball (Skya), Brian Drummond (Dozer/George), Trevor Devall (Garby/Skrap-It), Paul Dobson (D–Strucks), Fred Ewanuick (Click Clack), Cree Summer (Ace), Doron Bell (Waldo). **Credits:** *Producer:* Ron Burch, Jeff DeGrandis, David Kidd. *Director:* Michael Millen, Donna Brockopp. **Comment:** Computer generated animation that is well done and being dinosaur related will attract its target audience (children). The program, originally produced for the pay service Netflix, can be viewed for free on YouTube.

Episode List: *1.* Ty and Revvit. *2.* Scrapadactyls. *3.* Garage. *4.* Scraptors. *5.* Pit. *6.* Garby. *7.* Tortools. *8.* Desert. *9.* Sandstorm. *10.* Fake Ravine.

72 *The Discovery: Mountain Mermaid.* *youtube.com.* 2013 (Fantasy).

While hiking along a mountain trail, two young girls (Kylie and Liz) take a wrong turn and suddenly find themselves in an unfamiliar area. As they begin to explore their new surroundings Kylie falls through a grass-covered hole and into a sandy-like area near a cave. As Liz leaves to seek help, Kylie enters the cave and finds herself in waist-high water that is being enhanced by beams of light from the moon. It is not shown how, but Kylie is magically transported back to her home—at the same time Liz had arrived to summon help. Kylie appears to be unaffected by her weird adventure until she comes in contact with water and is transformed into a Mermaid. With Liz witnessing the change, Kylie must now learn to adjust to her Mermaid abilities (with Liz's help) and live the life of a normal girl.

Cast (as credited): Dani (Kylie), Kate (Liz). **Comment:** Good underwater filming and acting by the girls but the program has poor sound and sometimes unsteady indoor scenes.

Episode List: Four untitled episodes, labeled "Episode 1" through "Episode 4" have been produced.

73 *Do You Believe in Magic?* 2013 (Fantasy).

It is the first day of the New Year (2013) when a young girl (Jessica) finds a necklace in the snow. She takes it home and examines it but when she goes to the sink to wash her hands, she is transformed into a Mermaid. Jessica, however, does not keep her secret and reveals what happened to her friend Crystal who shocks Jessica with a secret of her own—she too is a Mermaid (through a found necklace also). Two girls and a shared secret and how they attempt to help each other cope with what has happened to them.

Cast (as credited): MermaidScale 99 (Jessica), Kristen (Crystal). Katie (Nikki). **Comment:** While the idea is good, the program has poor lighting and a jumpy picture at times. It has since been taken offline.

Episode List: *1.* Happy New Tail. *2.* Friendly Secrets. *3.* Untitled. *4.* Dream Needs. *5.* Sneak Peek. *6–7.* Untitled.

74 *Dolls: Hawaii Gone Wrong.* *youtube. com.* 2010 (Dolls).

Bratz Dolls are encompassed to present a spoof of the TV series *Big Brother* (and other such reality series) wherein a group of teenagers (Claire, Amy, Savannah, Lilana, Aubrina and Rina), promised a luxurious trip to Hawaii are instead placed in a home which they cannot leave and must fend for themselves while living together.

Host (as credited): Breese Damon. **Comment:** Good voices, photography and doll manipulation.

Episode List: 5 untitled episodes, labeled "Episode 1" through "Episode 5" have been produced.

75 *Doppelganger.* 2015 (Dolls).

Emily Lee is a young girl who appears to be enjoying a normal life until she crosses the path of her Doppelganger, her evil twin who is seeking to destroy her and take over her life (according to legend everyone has a Doppelganger but few, if any, ever see it. Seeing one's Doppelganger, however, is also omen of doom). The program charts what happens as Emily seeks to destroy her evil twin before it destroys her. American Girl dolls are used and the program ends unresolved.

Cast (as credited): Elline Grace (Emily Lee), Rita Abbott (Coroline Lee), Marzia Pine (Olivia Lee), Carter Jenkins (Kenny), Jasmine Grace (Marie Flower). **Comment:** Although the program deals with an evil topic, it is geared to girls and well produced. The voices and doll movement are very good and the background music is especially appealing. The program has since been taken offline.

Episode List: 2 untitled episodes, labeled "Season 1, Episode 1" and "Episode 2, Season 1" have been produced.

76 *Doraleous and Associates.* *youtube.com.* 2010 (Animated Fantasy).

Nudonia is a magical territory in a land of many kingdoms. To protect the various territories, especially the vulnerable Nudonia, a band of warriors called Doraleous and Associates has been established. Stories follow the band of noble warriors (Doraleous, Drak, Broof, Neebs, Mirdon and Sir Walken) as they battle evil, especially Titanus and his Nanadoo Army.

Voice Cast: Jon Etheridge (Mirdon), Bryan Mahoney (Drak), Nate Panning (Doraleous), Tony Schnur (Sir Walken), Brent Triplett (Neebs). **Credits:** *Director:* Brent Triplett. *Writer:* Jon Etheridge, Bryan Mahoney, Nate Panning, Tony Schnur, Brent Triplett. **Comment:** An amusing, sometimes funny spoof of the medieval age saga of warriors defending their kingdom. The animation is good, the jokes not overly crude (worse is seen on Fox's *The Family Guy*) as the creators considered children might be watching. Episodes are short enough so as not to become a burden to watch in multiple groups.

Episode List:
1. Open for Business.
2. The War Room.

3. The Toll Bridge.
4. The Wetalds.
5. Worst vs. Worst.
6. Mightopolis.
7. The Dungeon.
8. Unexpected Gift.
9. No Horse for Walken.
10. Party Cancelled.
11. Digger Town.
12. Hero Punctuation.
13. The Pyramites.
14. Dongo Tavern.
15. Girl in Mightopolis.
16. The Gladiator.
17. Arzon Prison.
18. Goodbye Drak.
19. The Canyons and Ramparts.
20. Old World Gate.
21. Brothers of the Old World.
22. Battle in Dongo.
23. The Theater.
24. Untitled.
25. Geigh Kingdom.
26. Needbs vs. Titanus.
27. Queer Village.
28. Last Straw.
29. Battle of Hyleria.
30. Testiclees.
31. Wizard Duel.
32. Giopi Invasion.
33. The Black.
34. Ampherny.
35. Broom Salesman.

77 *Drama Queen.* *youtube.com.* 2011 (Dolls).

Incidents in the lives of a group of grammar school girls with a particular focus on Madi, a drama queen who always wants to get her way, especially when it comes to her dream of becoming a dancer. Conflict enters her life when a fellow student (Tess) appears to be better than her and sets Madi on a course to prove who is best. **Cast (as credited):** Ginger Akanor (Madi Linscourt), Kanani Akinai (Tess Falk), Cici Moore (Emma Bank), Ivy Ling (Grace Demi), Ally Freeman (Selena Marsh), Kit Kittredge (Lizzy Dunlap). **Comment:** Well done stop motion photography opens each episode with very good doll manipulation (although certain camera angels expose the girls' hands or arms), voices and photography. **Episode List:** 2 untitled episodes, labeled "Episode 1" and "Episode 2" have been produced.

78 *The Ecliptic Curse.* *youtube.com.* 2015 (Dolls).

In 17th century Salem, Mass., at the time of the Witch Trials, a coven of young witches invoke the Ecliptic Curse to protect themselves and their future generations from the Hunters (also called Hunts-

men), who are seeking to destroy all witches. It is the present day and seven descendants from that original coven have become friends (see cast) and have only just come to realize they are witches. They also realize they have to fear the descendants of the Hunters, who are seeking to find and destroy them. The current coven needs to break the curse for protection but doing so is very difficult as they must find 12 descendants of the original coven that were all born on the first day of their Zodiac cycle. Once the task has been accomplished they must recite a spell that will strip themselves of their powers and thus end the reign of terror begun by the Witch Hunters. The program charts their efforts to keep secret what they really are and find the descendants needed to break the curse. **Cast (as credited):** Marley Copeland (Serena), Emma Akina (Melina), Nathan Coleman (Cole), Weston Stark (Max), Belle Winters (Molly), Beth Cole (Lia). Voices by Alexis. **Comment:** Although produced for children, the program is a bit difficult to comprehend for all that happens. It is well voiced and photographed and the doll manipulation is excellent. **Episode List:** 6 untitled episodes, labeled "Episode 1" through "Episode 6" have been produced.

79 *Emilia.* 2014–2015 (Dolls).

It is August 11, 1834, and a 13-year-old girl (Emilia) is seen in bed in a nightgown. It is the year 2014 when Emilia awakens. Her mother (Jennifer) recognizes her as her daughter but is puzzled why Emilia is wearing a nightgown when she went to bed in pajamas. Emilia knows something bizarre happened as she is in a strange room and puzzled as to why her mother is dressed in such unusual clothes. From this point on, it is very confusing to figure out the story. Emilia adjusts much too quickly to what has happened and assumes the role of a 21st century girl without any knowledge of the era. She attends school like nothing has happened and it is hinted at first that a time traveling experiment switched the 19th century Emilia with the modern-day Emilia. Emilia's efforts to become a part of the present form the basis of the story (it is later revealed that Emilia is part of a scientific experiment that malfunctioned and transported a girl from the past to the present. Jennifer, her mother, was explained as being a robot and programmed to accept Emilia as her daughter). **Cast (as credited):** Izzy Palmer, Skye Abbott, Niomi Rose, Ashlyn Brooks, Demi McIntire, Addison Smith, Lilia Rose, Chrissa Morganstern. **Comment:** While the doll movement and voices are very good, segments of poor sound make it difficult to understand what is happening. It has since been taken offline. **Episode List:** 21 untitled episodes, labeled "Episode 1" through "Episode 21" have been produced.

80 Enchanted (2012). 2012 (Fantasy).

Three girls (Ash, Coy and Aqua) are walking through the woods when they find what appears to be an old box. As they open it they find a number of items (like sea shells and pearls) including an odd-looking key. As they try to figure out what the key opens, Ash spots what appears to be a lock embedded in a rock and places the key in it. As she turns the key, a doorway opens and transports them to an alternate world called Ezonklo, a world where magic and evil exists. The program follows Ash, Coy and Aqua as they seek a way to return to their own world while battling the evil forces that prevent them from doing so.

Cast (as credited): Kady (Ash), Cali (Coy), Samantha (Aqua). **Comment:** For a kid-produced show, it is quite intriguing. The concept is good and the acting and photography also very good. Some outdoor scenes do present a problem with wind blowing into the microphone making is difficult to understand what is being said. It has since been taken offline.

Episode List: *1.* The Beginning. *2.* In the Real World. *3.* Ezonklo. *4.* Ezonklo Headquarters. *5.* Zombie Graveyard.

81 Enchanted (2013). 2013 (Fantasy).

A school called The Princess Academy has been established in America for young girls destined to become princesses. Alice, Elizabeth, Isis and Pandora, descendants from ancient Greek goddesses, have enrolled in the school to further their training. There are also girls from America who yearn to become royalty. The program relates what happens at the school as true royalty mixes with "wanabee" royalty and how the true royalty girls attempt to adjust to life in America (where they are not pampered as they were in Greece).

Cast (as credited): Maddy (Alice), Elena (Elizabeth), Eloise (Pandora), Zea (Isis), Em (Laura). **Comment:** A well acted and produced program that transforms the ancient Greek gods into young girls to expose them to a world outside of their comfort zones. The program has since been taken offline.

Episode List: *1.* Princess Alice and Princess Elizabeth. *2.* Princesses Isis and Pandora. *3.* Welcome to America. *4.* Settling in America. *5.* Good vs. Bad.

82 Enchanted Mermaid. *youtube.com.* 2011 (Fantasy).

While playing outside their home, two sisters (Christie and Nicki) find a pair of necklaces with a note attached: "The person reading this prepare for a fishy surprise." Christina and Nicki do get the surprise of their lives: they are transformed into Mermaids as the episode concludes. It appears the program has been abandoned and would have most likely followed their efforts to keep secret what happened to them.

Cast (as credited): Mermaid Animation (Christie), 1199 Briannai (Nicki). **Comment:** The stars are African-American but the production is below par with bad photography and sound.

Episode List: *1.* Enchanted Necklace.

83 Endless Oceans. *youtube.com.* 2013 (Fantasy).

Two young girls (Marina and Serena) are swimming in a pool when they spy a mysterious staircase. Intrigued, they climb the stairs and suddenly find themselves in a secret tunnel that leads to the ocean. Fearful of what they might find, the girls leave. When they return to the pool they realize that their little excursion has changed them as they are growing scales. Marina and Serena soon discover who they really are when, on their eleventh birthday, they transform into Mermaids at their first contact with water. Marina and Serena must now keep secret what happened and pretend to be just ordinary girls as they adjust to their developing powers.

Cast (as credited): Sofie (Marina), Stephanie (Serena). **Comment:** The girls are pretty and the overall production pleasing to watch.

Episode List: *1.* Passage to a Secret. *2.* Marina's Discovery.

84 eScape. *facebook.com.* 2012 (Fantasy).

Camp Quest is a seemingly typical summer retreat for children operated by James Fantaro, owner of a video game company called Fantaro Games. As a group of campers begin adjusting to their new surroundings, they suddenly find they are alone when the adult counselors mysteriously disappear. The children soon realize they are trapped in one of the video games created by Fantaro and must use their gaming skills to escape. Stories follow their efforts, given powers by the programmer, as they battle monsters and attempt to overcome various video game quests to win their freedom.

Cast: Noah Berliner (Jack), Patrick Reilly (Steven), Emma Guilfoyle (Myrna), Jake Prescott (Joshy), Sarah Sharifpour (Lexa), Livi Prescott (Olivia), Belle Babcock (Belle), Jessica Babcock (Caitlyn), Alex Wesley (Chris), Spencer Worley (Spencer). **Credits:** *Producer-Writer-Director:* Mike Feurstein. **Comment:** While not an original idea (the Australian TV series *Pirate Islands* used the same trapped-in-a-video game format), it is an interesting variation and well done.

Season 1 Episode List: *1.* Jooker. *2.* Aggro. *3.* Zling. *4.* Romo. *5.* Kite. *6.* Rollerback.

Season 2 Episode List: *7.* The Man in White. *8.* Guild. *9.* Bot. *10.* Drop. *11.* Mirror. *12.* Retcon. *13.* Rez. *14.* Torrent.

85 Ever After High. *everafterhigh.com.* 2013 (Cartoon).

Ever After High is a fairy tale world school where

the children of famous (but fictitious) characters are not only educated but where they must learn to make their own decisions. But when choices have to be made, there is also conflict and thus two factions have grown: The Royals and The Rebels. The Royals believe all fairytale characters must remain true to what they are or else their stories will disappear forever while The Rebels oppose their "happily ever-after" world and must become their own individuals. Stories relate the conflicts that such characters face as they contemplate the lives they now have and what awaits them if they should deviate from what they have become.

Characters:

Apple White, the daughter of Snow White, is a Royal (and leader of the Royal Faction). An incident from her childhood (falling down a well) has made her afraid of a different future and will do what it takes to keep the world she loves (Happily Ever After) from disappearing forever.

Raven Queen, Apple White's roommate, is the daughter of the Evil Queen and the Good King. Although she is a Rebel and leader of that faction, she has a good heart but is not interested in assuming the role destiny has planned for her.

Briar Beauty, the daughter of Sleeping Beauty, is Apple White's best friend and a Royal (she fears the prospect of sleeping for 100 years and suffers from sleeping spells at inopportune moments). It appears Briar's goal is to acquire as much knowledge as possible before falling under that sleeping spell.

Madeline Hatter, called Maddie, is the daughter of the Mad Hatter and Raven's best friend. Although Maddie is a Royal and is looking forward to her destiny in *Alice and Wonderland* she sides with the Rebels and believes everyone should have the right of free choice. She and her father live in the village of Book End and run a tea shop together.

C.C. Cupid, the adopted daughter of the gods Eros and Psyche, believes the conflict between the Royals and Rebels is foolish but sides with the Rebels as she believes destiny should not get in the way of love. She has the power to unite people through love and has become the school's advisor on romantic problems.

Ashlynn Ella, the daughter of Cinderella, is a Royal who owns the Glass Slipper shoe store. Like her mother, she is a nature lover and, because a slipper brought her mother and Prince Charming together, she is only interested in fashion if there are sensational shoes to go along with it. She is sweet and kind and fears she will lose her heritage if the Rebels get their way.

Hunter Huntsman, the son of The Huntsman (a character in *Snow White* and *Little Red Riding Hood*) is a Rebel and the boyfriend of Ashlynn Ella, something he must hide as he is not a part of her story and characters are not permitted to become a part of a story for which they were not written.

Blondie Locks, the daughter of Goldilocks, is a Royal and Cupid's roommate (she is also best friends with Apple White and Briar Beauty). At school she runs a Mirror-Cast Show (a newscast), loves to gossip and has the uncanny ability to open any lock.

Cedar Wood is a Rebel and the daughter of Pinocchio. She is a life-size puppet made of Cedar and cursed to telling the truth (which will be lifted when she graduates). Although she is a Royal and looking forward to her destiny, she feels for the Rebels and believes they have the right to choose their own destiny.

Cerise Hood, the daughter of Little Red Riding Hood and The Big Bad Wolf (can only happen in cartoons) conceals the fact of who her father actually is. She wears a red hood to cover her wolf ears, has a strong craving for meat and wolf-like instincts. Her red hood also gives her the ability to secretly travel through shadows.

Dexter Charming, the son of King Charming and the brother of Daring Charming, is a Royal and more down-to-earth-than his older brother. He likes Raven but is unaware that Cupid has a crush on him. Daring is the first son of King Charming and is destined to become the prince who will save Apple White.

Other Characters: Hopper Croakington (son of the Frog Prince), Lizzie Hearts (daughter of the Queen of Hearts), Kitty Cheshire (daughter of the Cheshire Cat), Tiny (the son of the Giant from *Jack and the Beanstalk*), Duchess Swan (daughter of Odette, the Swan Princess from *Swan Lake*), Sparrow Hood (the son of Robin Hood and Maid Marian), Milton Grimm (the founder and Headmaster of Ever After High. He and his brother, Giles are named after the Brothers Grimm).

Voice Cast: Erin Fitzgerald (Raven Queen/C.A. Cupid), Jonquil Goode (Apple White/Cedar Wood), Kate Higgins (Briar Beauty), Cindy Robinson (Madeline Hatter), Laura Bailey (Ashlynn Ella), Grant George (Hunter Huntsman), Julie Maddalena (Blondie Locks), Rena S. Mandel (Cerise Hood), Evan Smith (Dexter Charming), Cam Clarke (Hopper/Giles Grimm), Wendee Lee (Lizzie Hearts), Bekks Prewitt (Kitty Cheshire), Malcolm Danare (Tiny), Stephanie Sheh (Duchess Swan), Todd Haberkorn (Sparrow Hood), Jamieson Price (Milton Grimm), Valerie Arem, Joe Sanfelipo (Narrators).

Comment: Based on the series of dolls released by Mattel, the program is well animated and the voice cast well chosen. The episodes are rather short (under 3 minutes) and the stories quick and right to the point.

Episode List:

1. The World of Ever After High.
2. Apple's Tale: The Story of a Royal.
3. Raven's Tale: The Story of a Rebel.
4. Stark Raven Mad.
5. True Reflections.
6. Maddie-in-Chief.
7. Here Comes Cupid.
8. Briar's Study Party.
9. The Shoe Must Go On.

10. The Cat Who Cried Wolf.
11. Cedar Wood Would Love to Lie.
12. Catching Raven.
13. The Tale of Legacy Day.
14. The Day Ever After.
15. Replacing Raven.
16. Blondie's Just Right.
17–19. True Hearts Day.
20. Class Confusion.
21. Apple's Birthday Bake-Off.
22. The Beautiful Truth.
23. MirrorNet Down.
24. Rebel's Got Talent.
25. Upon a Table.
26. Blondie Branches Out.
27. Poppy the Roybel.
28. O'Hare's Split Ends.
29. Maddie's Hat-tastic Party.
30. Lizzie Heart's Fairy Tale First Date.
31. Apple's Princess Practice.
32. Lizzie Shuffles the Deck.
33. Duchess Swan's Lake.
34. Cerise's Picnic Panic.
35. Kitty's Curious Tale.
36. And the Throne-Coming Queen Is…
37. Best Feather Forward.
38. Ginger in the Bread House.
39. Ashlynn's Fashion Frolic.
40. An Hexclusive Invitation.
41. Chosen with Care.
42. Just Sweet.
43. Through the Woods.

86 *Experiment 42. youtube.com.* 2014 (Dolls).

At one point in the history of the world, two races of people, the Extraordinary and the Ordinary lived peacefully with one another. One day, however, a wedge divided the two groups and the Extraordinary were banished. They were not defeated as they found a mysterious gateway to a secret kingdom where they could live in peace and not fear the Ordinaries.

As the kingdom prospered, many experiments were conducted to make life more enjoyable. Unfortunately, most were failures and stored in the lower depths of a basement. One such failure was Experiment 42, an attempt to teleport people to various dimensions located within the kingdom. For four "people" (Lydia, Noah, Perry and Katie), finding Experiment 42 has changed the course of their lives. When Noah pushed a red button it activated the machine and sent them into a dimension where something needs to be fixed or it will destroy all dimensions located within the kingdom. Once a solution is found to remedy the problem, travelers are returned to their own dimension. The program charts the travels of Lydia, Noah, Perry and Katie as they transport to various dimensions to get the kingdom's history back on track.

Voices (as credited): Ace. **Comment:** Ace is a very talented young girl who not only created an intriguing series but provides good voices, photography and character movement of the LPS (Littlest Pet Shop) dolls.

Episode List: *1.* Fairies in Danger. *2.* Lets Save the City. *3.* Halloween. *4.* Legend of the Whisperer. *5.* Curse of the Seven Sins. *6.* The Maze of the Seven Sins. *7.* Guardian of the Seven Sins. *8.* Ninja's Burning Past. *9.* The Phoenix and the Dragon. *10.* Play the Game. *11.* The City of Flames.

87 *Faeries of the Fae. youtube.com.* 2013 (Fantasy).

Marlo is a young woman who has felt, since she was a child, that the stories told to her about faeries were only myths, passed down from generation to generation. Recently, however, she has been encountering unexplained situations that have led her to believe that those childhood stories were not myths and that she may be more than just an ordinary female. The program begins with a mystery (just who or what Marlo is) and slowly proceeds to reveal that she is a Faerie, descended from the Fae, a collective of Faeries based on the folklore of England, that are usually friendly toward mankind and remain neutral in their conflicts. But with the good comes the evil: Hunters (here vampire-like beings) who are out to destroy all Faeries. The battle between the Fae and Hunters for supremacy had raged on for untold centuries until the Hunters won and drove the Fae into hiding. Marlo, it is learned, was born of the light and pure blood and is the Blood Key, a being that can re-open a portal to reunite all Faeries and continue their battle against the Hunters. The Hunters now fear a resurgence of war and it is presumed Marlo will become their target as destroying her will keep the Fae from once again becoming powerful enough to pose a threat (the program ends with Marlo just about to discover what she really is and what actually happens is unknown).

Voice Cast (as credited): Voiceychic (Marlo), LilGusher15 (Leona), The DepartedCry (Salem), Bpoiipnoi (Dennis), Enigma7597 (Marana), Paige Michal (Sirus), KotoriChan 1994 (Julia), VoiceActor 12 (Xavier), HarmanyStriker (Zera), Luana6972 (Narissa), Lady Serena: HappyNisa (Lady Serena).

Credits (as listed): *Director-Writer:* MoreSims3 Productions. **Comment:** Computer animated program that is dark at times and thus its characters appear frightening during those scenes. The animation is a bit stiff and the mouth movement is not truly synchronized with voices (which also range from low and difficult to hear to loud). The story, however, is good but the series appears to have been abandoned after the third episode.

Episode List: *1.* Beginnings. *2.* Recruiting. *3.* The Hunt.

88 The Fairy Forest. *youtube.com.* 2014 (Dolls).

A look at three fairies (Plomette, Diamond Rose and Daisy Dreams), two Wizards (Rarity and Twilight) and a Guardian (Fluttashy) as they experience life in a magical fairy land.

Voices (as credited): Aquamarine. **Comment:** The dolls used are not identified but the voices, photography and doll manipulation is excellent.

Episode List: *1.* How It Began. *2.* The Start of a Plan. *3.* The Tale of the Pony and the Siren. *4.* The Plan.

89 Fairy Tale High. *fairytalehigh.com.* 2013 (Cartoon).

Fairy Tale High School is, like its name implies, an educational institution for future fairy tale princesses. Three teenage girls, Cinderella, Sleeping Beauty (Rose) and Snow White are three such students taking classes with such soon-to-become famous characters as Rapunzel, Tinker Bell, Alice (in Wonderland) and Belle (Beauty and the Beast). The program follows the lives of three princesses-in-training as they experience life as ordinary teenage girls before becoming the lovable, immortal characters fate had intended them to be.

Comment: The program contains excellent computer animation but a cast or credits are not given (not on screen or on the website). It also appears that after the second episode, the project was just abandoned.

Episode List: 2 untitled episodes, labeled "Episode 1" and "Episode 2" have been produced.

90 The Fairy Tales. *youtube.com.* 2011–2012 (Fantasy).

Fairy tale princesses Snow White, Sleeping Beauty and Cinderella have been taken out of their storybook element and placed in a large, modern-day home in the Hollywood Hills where they must learn to live together in a reality-like TV show experiment to see if the princesses can live together (without killing each other) and find their happily ever after.

Cast: Karyn Nesbit (Snow White), Jessica Gardner (Cinderella), Bethy Poluikis (Rose, a.k.a. Sleeping Beauty), Shana Davis (Alice; from *Alice in Wonderland*), Pippa Hinchley (Evil Stepmother), Landon Ashworth (Prince Charming), Hunter McKeever (Hansel), Olivia Lauletta (Gretel). *Narrator:* Stephen Israel. **Credits:** *Producer:* Betty Cleland, John Cleland, Brian Normoyle, Katie Piel. *Director:* Joey Schow. **Comment:** With all the formats of televised reality shows, it is a wonder that this concept was only thought up for the Internet. The program is very well done with excellent acting and production values. The only real complaint would be with the low volume of the narration which makes it difficult to understand. Incorporating other fairy tale characters associated with the main cast also makes for more conflict to test the patience of the three princesses.

Episode List: 3 untitled episodes, labeled "Episode 1," "Episode 2" and "Episode 3" have been produced.

91 Fairytale Secrets. *youtube.com.* 2015 (Dolls).

The LPS (Littlest Pet Shop) series of dolls are used to recreate animal versions of classic fairy tales.

Voices (as credited): Faith. **Comment:** Although some liberties have been taken with the stories, the voices, doll manipulation and photography are very good.

Episode List: *1.* Little Red Riding Hood. *2.* Snow White. *3.* The Prince and the Pauper. *4.* The Ugly Duckling.

92 The Fin Trials. *youtube.com.* 2014 (Fantasy).

To relieve the anxiety of just having gotten their flu shots, two girls (Alice and Piper) decide to go for a swim in the local public pool. Immediately, upon entering the pool, contact with the water transforms them into Mermaids. Alice and Piper are stunned and wonder if the flu shots had anything to do with what just happened. Luckily for them, they were the only ones at the pool and their secret is safe. As Alice and Piper begin to adjust to what has happened they learn that their friend Ashley has had the same experience following her flu shot. Although the girls cannot figure out how the flu shots changed their lives, they must now keep secret what happened, learn how to control their developing powers and pretend to be ordinary school girls.

Cast (as credited): Heidi (Piper), Clara (Alice), Joanna (Ashley), Kenzie (Flora), Gina (Greed), Brianna (Revenge), Remy (Jealousy). **Comment:** The sound is hard to understand at times, especially when the girls discuss what they believe turned them into Mermaids. The acting however, is good and the photography acceptable.

Season 1 Episode List: *1.* Discovery. *2.* Found Out. *3.* Don't Tell. *4.* Is This Real Life? *5.* Test Subjects. *6.* The Reveal. *7.* Controlled. *8.* Chase. *9.* Memories. *10.* The Light. *11.* Finale.

Season 2 Episode List: *1.* Not Again. *2.* Life and Death. *3.* The Sins. *4.* S.O.S. *5.* In the Woods. *6.* Perspective. *7.* Twisted. *8.* Jealousy. *9.* Flora. *10.* The Last Battle.

Season 3 Episode List: *1.* New and Improved. *2.* Switched.

93 The Fins. *youtube.com.* 2012 (Fantasy).

Brookes, Sky and Twilight are three very special young girls. Sky and Twilight have received a strange necklace (a Mermaid holding a pearl) from their mothers while Brookes has received an identical necklace from her grandmother. Each of the girls also shares a secret: when they come in contact with water they transform into Mermaids. Brookes' grandmother was a Mermaid and the mothers of Sky and Twilight were also Mermaids. The necklaces retain their abilities which have now been passed onto the next generation. The program follows Brookes, Sky and Twilight as they learn how to control their developing powers yet appear as ordinary girls. **Cast (as credited):** Hannah (Brookes), Victoria (Sky), Isabelle (Twilight). **Comment:** While the picture is a bit unsteady at times, it is nicely photographed and the three young leads do a good job of presenting their story. **Episode List:** *1–2.* Pilot. *3.* Power Surge. *4.* New Discoveries. *5.* Fishy Hide-Outs. *6.* Potions and Fish Heritage. *7.* Adventure and Limited Power. *8.* Necklaces.

94 Fins and Flippers. *youtube.com.* 2013 (Fantasy).

While walking through the woods two young girls (Tracy and Skyeia) discover a hidden pond with water that appears to be bubbling. As the girls watch, the water produces a magic mist that encompasses them and transforms them into Mermaids. While Tracy and Skyeia quickly adjust to what has happened they also know they must be careful around water (as it can cause them to change) and not reveal to anyone what has happened to them. The program relates their mishaps as they struggle to hide their secret while attempting to live lives as normal girls even though they are plagued by mysterious changes in their appearances (like their hair changing color) while not in their Mermaid state. **Cast (as credited):** Isabella (Skyeia), Sara (Tracy), Gabrielle (Serena). **Comment:** The program is nicely photographed, well acted and even incorporates well done special effects. **Episode List:** *1.* The Beginning of a New Life. *2.* Have a Tail, Now You Don't. *3–4:* Unknown titles. *5.* Um, Your Hair Is Green.

95 Fins of Twins. *youtube.com.* 2013 (Fantasy).

When they become bored just watching TV, sisters Skyler and Dakota perform a spell to summon Mermaid ghosts. As they chant "Wins of Fins" something bites each of the girls on the hand and the girls quickly stop what they are doing. The following day, when Skyler and Dakota each come in contact with water they are transformed into Mermaids. They realize that the bite each suffered was from a Mermaid ghost and they are also developing the powers of the four elements (Rain, Wind, Earth and Fire). Shortly after, the ghost of a Mermaid named Annie appears to them to warn them about the dangers they now face and to be aware of Mermaid Hunters, who seek to cap-

ture Mermaids and steal their powers. The program follows Skyler and Dakota as they learn to control their powers and keep secret the life they now lead. **Cast:** Nikki Crawford (Dakota Fins), L.J. Cleave (Skyler Fins), Simone Doggett (Lexi Watson). **Comment:** It is difficult to tell, but the program is either a British or Australian production by Skyler and Dakota's accents. The transformation idea is original and although Mermaid ghosts are not seen, it is well presented through voice only sequences with the sisters. The acting is good and the overall production is well done. **Episode List:** *1.* Something Bit Me. *2.* Phase 2 Mermaids. *3.* Something Fishy.

96 Fire Ice: A Mermaid's Tail. *youtube.com.* 2011 (Fantasy).

As a young girl (Christy) returns home from shopping, she spies a necklace in the waterfall that adorns the courtyard of the hotel in which she is staying while on vacation. While retrieving the necklace, she sees that there is also another one and takes both of them with her. She has decided to give one to her best friend, Lily. The following morning, Christy meets with Lily and presents her with the necklace. Shortly after, when each girl comes in contact with water, they are transformed into Mermaids and stories follow their mishaps as they try to conceal their secret while at the same time learning how to control their magical powers. Also known as *Fire and Ice: A Mermaid Life.* **Cast (as credited):** Erica (Christy), Jody (Lily). **Comment:** While the girls handle their roles well, the picture is not clear and there is an annoying clicking-like sound that persists throughout the episodes. **Episode List:** *1.* The Find. *2.* Revealed. *3.* Boiled.

97 Fire Ice: Just Add Water. *youtube.com.* 2010 (Original); 2015 (Revised).

Original Story Line: Three friends (Bailey, Nikki and Tetra) are hiking when they take a wrong turn and become lost. As they wander they come across a cave and enter it. Curious to see where it leads they begin exploring and soon find themselves near a pool where strange lights engulf them. Suddenly, the girls are propelled back home and appear to be unharmed. Shortly after, however, each girl is transformed into a Mermaid when she comes in contact with water. Bailey, Nikki and Tetra must now keep secret what has happened and attempt to lead ordinary lives. *Revised Version:* Bailey, Nikki and Tetra, from the prior version, are now high school girls and while walking along a California coast line stumble across a mysterious cave and enter. As they begin to explore it they wander deeper and deeper into it and, with the tide coming in, feel it is safer to continue and find another exit rather than go back. Several minutes later it appears they have reached a dead end as there is nothing but water ahead of them. Suddenly, a light from a full moon illuminates the water and engulfs them, leading them to the sea and safety but with one big difference: they are now Mermaids. Like the prior version, the program follows the girls as they struggle to adjust to their newly acquired powers and conceal their secret identities.

Cast (as credited; both versions): Brooke (Tetra Chadwick), Shannon (Bailey Boudy), Mariah (Nikki Leawood). **Comment:** The original version is well done with acceptable photography and acting and is typical of most Mermaid series that feature young girls. Although only one episode has been produced for the revised version, it features the same three girls and in a much more sophisticated presentation. The cave sequences are suspenseful and very well done. The acting is very good and, based on what has been released, appears to be one of the better Mermaid series produced for the Internet.

Original Series Episode List: *1.* A Strange Night. *2.* A Special Secret. *3.* Power Hour. *4.* A Change in the Tail. *5.* Moonlight Madness.

Revised Series Episode List: *1.* A Change in the Tides.

98 *First Day.* *alloyentertainment.com.* 2010–2011 (Comedy).

Cassie is a teenage girl just starting her first day of high school. From what to wear and how to present herself has been carefully planned and now all Cassie has to do is make that good first impression. Unfortunately, for Cassie, everything that can go wrong does as she tries to impress a boy (Ryan) and her first day becomes a total disaster. That night, while talking to her plush dog Max, Cassie wishes that what happened today never did—"I just wish I could erase today and start over." The following morning Cassie finds that her idle wish has come true as she begins to relive events of the prior day all over again. Cassie had humiliated herself in front of the perfect guy but now she has been given a second chance. But can she undo what already happened? Cassie believes that knowing in advance what will happen and avoiding those hazards to impress Ryan will be the key that ends her repeating each day as that first day. The program chronicles what happens each day that Cassie relives and how, even when knowing the future, one cannot change what has already happened.

Cast: Tracey Fairaway (Cassie Mitchell), Elizabeth McLaughlin (Sasha), Jesse Kove (Ryan), Erik Stocklin (Gregg), Martha Brigham (Curly Haired Girl), Jazz Raycole (Paige), Alanna Masterson (Abby), Bailey Noble (Rosie Rovello), Ron Butler (Vice Principal Lewis), Kara Crane (Taylor Weller), Alexandra Rodriquez (Whitney), Brandon Jones (JT Fox), Molly McAleer (Miss Harvey). **Credits:** *Producer:* Tripp Reed, Joshua Bank, Bob Levy, Leslie Morgenstein. *Director:* Sandy Smolan. *Writer:* Alyssa Embree, Jessica Koosed Etting, Benjamin Oren, Melissa Sadoff Oren. **Comment:** Although the idea

has been done before, it is very well presented here in a different take with excellent acting and production values. It shows just how awkward life can be for a young girl when she makes that move from grammar school to the next level of her education.

Season 1 Episode List: *1.* The Boyfriend Plan. *2.* If at First You Don't Succeed. *3.* Wherefore Art Thou Romeo? *4.* Must Love Punk and Pets. *5.* Sister Act. *6.* Repeat Offender. *7.* Kiss Me You Fool. *8.* I Want to Love.

Season 2 Episode List: *1.* First Dance: Totes Adorbs. *2.* First Dance: Deja Boo. *3.* First Dance: Friending the Enemy. *4.* First Dance: More Like Honesty. *5* First Dance: Pretending Sucks Way More. *6.* First Dance: Never Saw It Coming.

99 *Fish Out of Water (2004).* 2004 (Fantasy).

Unknown to three young girls (Madison, Tabitha and Nicole) who are about to enter a public pool, the water has been treated with an unusual chemical by a mysterious person. The girls are alone in the pool when a shooting star passes over them and the water begins to bubble. Rather than be afraid, each girl wishes she could become a Mermaid. Within seconds their wishes are granted and now each girl must not only learn to control her Mermaid abilities, but keep their identities secret while navigating life as ordinary girls.

Cast (as credited): Madison, Tabitha and Sabrina (Themselves). **Comment:** With good photography, limited special effects and acceptable acting by the girls, a nicely presented (and the earliest known) Mermaid series has evolved. The program has since been taken offline.

Episode List: *1.* About to Experience the Unknown. *2.* Strange Things Are Happening. *3.* Powers. *4.* Adjusting.

100 *Fish Out of Water (2011).* 2011 (Fantasy).

A young girl named Ashley is swimming in the ocean when she encounters a disturbance that initially does not affect her. Later, however, when she first comes in contact with water, she transforms into a Mermaid. Now Ashley must keep secret what happened as she attempts to live life as a normal girl.

Cast (as credited): Hannah (Ashley), Carolyn (Brit), Madison (Kate). **Comment:** Acceptable acting and pretty girls but the sound and photography are only fair. The program has been taken offline.

Episode List: *1.* Pilot. *2.* Hidden Powers. *3–5.* Untitled. *6.* A Close Call. *7.* A New Secret.

101 *Fish Out of Water (2012).* *youtube.com.* 2012 (Fantasy).

Kelly, Kaity and Christy are young girls who are also Mermaids. There is no introductory episode explaining how they became creatures of the sea (although black magic is mentioned and could be the source). As the girls attempt to accept what has happened to them, they must also learn how to encompass their developing powers and pretend to be ordinary school girls.

Cast (as credited): Kelly Gomez, Kaity and Christy (Themselves). **Comment:** Failure to establish how the girls became Mermaids is disappointing while the acting and photography are only just acceptable.

Episode List: *1.* Unknown Title. *2.* Kelly's Powers. *3.* Evil Twin. *4.* Roller Coaster.

102 Fish Out of Water (2014). *youtube. com.* 2014 (Dolls).

LPS (Littlest Pet Shop) dolls are encompassed to tell the story of Maria Waters, a teenage "girl" who was born a Mermaid and possesses a blue tail (which can only be seen when she comes in contact with water). Maria's efforts to keep her secret while attending school are the principal focus of stories.

Voices (as credited): MacKenzie. **Comment:** Maria, represented by an LPS dog does have a tail and swimming sequences are shown. The voices, doll manipulation and photography are excellent.

Episode List: *1.* First Day of School. *2.* The New Guy.

103 Fish Scales. *youtube.com.* 2011 (Fantasy).

A unknown young girl is seen writing a note and placing it in a green bottle: "A young girl has a wish to be different. With one touch of water she will change. I hope the girl who reads this will know what will happen next." Two girls, Cece and Rickey, stumble across that green bottle and open it. Accompanying the note is a spell that so intrigues them that they decide to read it. Nothing happens at first; however, when Cece and Rickey come in contact with water, they transform into Mermaids. In the only two episodes that were produced, the girls are only seen from the waist up in their bikini tops; no Mermaid tails are seen (YouTube comments show that viewers were disappointed). The program does follow their efforts to keep secret what happened while adjusting to their Mermaid powers.

Cast (as credited): Katie (Cece), Lexi (Rickey). **Comment:** While the overall production and acting are acceptable, the program appears to have been abandoned (perhaps due to the lack of Mermaid tails and further viewer complaints).

Episode List: 2 untitled episodes, labeled "Episode 1" and "Episode 2" have been produced.

104 Fishy Friendship. *youtube.com.* 2011 (Fantasy).

While in her living room, a young girl (Elizabeth) finds an unusual bracelet on a shelf. Fascinated with it, she places it on her wrist, goes for a drink of water and is transformed into a Mermaid. Elizabeth must now learn to lead a double life but most importantly, keep her secret from her sister, Katie, who has become suspicious of her actions and has set her goal to find out why Elizabeth is suddenly acting differently.

Cast (as credited): Carolyn (Elizabeth), Hannah (Katie). **Comment:** The girls are pretty and the idea is good but the pacing is very slow and cries out for editing to speed things along.

Season 1 Episode List: *1,2,3.* Untitled Episodes. *4.* Sleep Over. *5.* Untitled. *6.* Exploring. *7.* Secrets Found. *8.* A New Tail. *9.* Travel Time. *10.* Season Finale.

Season 2 Episode List: *1.* Untitled. *2.* The Notes. *3.* Christmas Special. *4.* The Craziest Day. *5.* Newer Powers. *6.* How the Fourth Came to Be. *7.* We're Under Attack. *8.* It's Coming. *9.* Oh, No. *10.* Finale. *11.* Epilogue.

105 Fizzy's Lunch Lab. *youtube.com.* 2009– 2011 (Cartoon).

Professor Fizzy is a very eccentric culinary genius who believes children need not only physical activity but good nutritional habits. With the assist of Mixie Bot ("the best kitchen gadget ever"), Corporal Cup ("the ingredient leader") and Sully the Cell ("the personal guide to human anatomy"), Fizzy attempts to relate health aspects to children and reduce obesity while battling Fast Food Freddy, "a grease monger" who is opposed to children abandoning fast food for healthy food.

Voice Cast: Larry Murphy (Professor Fizzy), Miya Duffy (Avril), Magena Goltermann (Corporal Cup), Veronica Taylor (Mixie Bot), Jackson Tolliver (Henry), Bobby Smithney (Fast Food Freddy). **Credits:** *Producer:* David Schlafman, Evan Sussman, Matty Moore. *Director:* Mike Annear, Evan Sussman. *Writer:* Dave Schlafman, Evan Sussman. **Comment:** Acceptable animation (for adults) that combines music, songs and light comedy to stress the benefits of healthy eating to children.

Episode List: *1.* Unclogging the Pipes. *2.* Summer Treatwave. *3.* Happy Harvest. *4.* Bob Lazy's Boffo Bargain. *5.* Shopping the U. *6.* Hoagie Throw Down. *7.* Tummy Trauma. *8.* Food Camp: Mighty Molasses Cookies. *9.* Jinormous Juicer. *10.* Protein Power Up. *11.* The Lazy Hazy. *12.* RoboFizz 2000. *13.* Family Dinner Team. *14.* Fast Food Franny. *15.* Kid Critic. *16.* Breakfast Boost. *17.* Attack of the Pizzantors.

106 Forever Scales. 2012 (Fantasy).

Layla and Krystal appear to be just ordinary school girls until an unexplained event changes their lives forever. They are together when two necklaces fall from the sky and land before them. The necklaces reveal that when the girls first wear them, they are true

Mermaids and the reincarnations of Mermaid princesses (now spirits) who lived centuries ago. They also learn, through those Mermaid spirits, that they have been chosen to become their true selves to save the world from the evil Dark King and his minions. To do so, however, they must find eight magic pearls, which when placed together, will grant them the ability to defeat the Dark King. **Cast:** Katie Ashley (Layla Searis), Alex Gillian (Krystal Flare). **Comment:** An intriguing premise that is adequately acted but the program has since been taken offline.

Episode List: *1.* Mermaid Necklace. *2.* Mermaid Princesses. *3.* The Dark King's Minion. *4.* The Winter Pearl. *5.* The Unknown Visitor.

107 *Four Tails.* 2012 (Fantasy).

While walking their dogs, four young girls (Bree, Claire, Skyler and Lauren) find a strange bottle which they believe contains soda. Without really thinking first, they each take a sip, unaware that it is a magic Mermaid potion. Later that day, when the girls go swimming, they discover the effects of the "soda" when each of them becomes a Mermaid and now must keep their abilities a secret—while still trying to be ordinary young girls. **Cast (as credited):** RunningLuver-4Ever (Bree), Sillygal4Ever (Claire), 04ever (Skyler), Friend 1 (Lauren). **Comment:** Poorly presented Mermaid series due to unexplained reasons why most of the girls do not show their faces on camera and are seen from the back only; it has since been taken offline.

Episode List: *1.* Mermaids? *2.* The Powers. *3.* The Necklaces. *4.* Bad Luck. *5.* Necklace. *6.* Mermaid. *7.* Rose. *8.* New Tail.

108 *The Four Tails in the Water. youtube. com.* 2012 (Fantasy).

An Italian produced Mermaid series that begins when four girls (Emma, Regina, Rikki and Bella) meet on a beach and become instant friends. As they walk along the shore they stumble upon a mysterious portal that beckons them to enter. As they enter, the girls are engulfed in rays from a full moon that illuminates the water surrounding them. The scene then jumps to the girls at their homes and shows that, as each comes in contact with water, they are transformed into Mermaids. The program charts their adventures as they use their Mermaid abilities to battle a group of evil Sirens. **Cast (as credited):** Bianca P. (Regina, Cleo, Cristina), Valentina P. (Rikki), Chiara (Bella), Marta (Emma), S. Severa (Paesaggi). **Comment:** The program is presented in Italian without English captions or subtitles. While it can be figured out what is happening just through the presentation, there are sound problems (like wind blowing into the microphone) but good acting by the cast as well as acceptable pho-

tography (on the same lines as those Mermaid series produced in America).

Season 1 Episode List: *1.* Metamorphosi. *2.* Un Invito Isolito. *3.* I Ciondoli. *4.* Le Sirene Origianli. *5.* Stregate Dalla Luna. *6.* La 4 Sirena.

Season 2 Episode List: *1.* Il Ritorno. *2.* Scoperte Magiche. *3.* Partenza Par Il Mare. *4–5.* Attrazione Magnetica. *6.* The Movie.

109 *Fresh Water Fantasy. youtube.com.* 2015 (Fantasy).

Two sisters (Anastasia and Aurora) are by a lake playing a game of Frisbee catch when they find two tiaras near the shore. The girls take the tiaras home and wash them off. They appear fine until Aurora notices a rash on her leg that looks like fish scales. She tells her sister about the rash and that she does not feel well. Believing that Aurora just needs some rest, Anastasia suggests that she take a bath and then go to bed. Aurora is seen stepping into the bath water when she screams. The screen turns to black and the series just ends there. There is no doubt Aurora will become a Mermaid with Anastasia to follow had the program produced more episodes. **Cast (as credited):** Samantha (Anastasia). Rachel (Aurora). **Comment:** Very pretty girls and good photography but the program is slow-moving and just drags a situation out before getting to where it needs to be.

Episode List: *1.* Mermaids Aren't Real. *2.* Sea Sick.

110 *From Skater to Part Fish. youtube.com.* 2013 (Fantasy).

Shortly after she returns home from skate boarding, a young girl (Logan) sees a glass with a red liquid with a note attached: "Home made smoothie. Mom." Believing it was made by her mother Logan takes a sip but finds it unpleasant and dumps the remainder of the drink in the sink. As she runs the water to flush the contents down the drain, water splashes on her hand and she experiences a metamorphosis when she becomes a Mermaid. But this is only the beginning of her troubles. Shortly after, Logan finds a box with a necklace and a note (from the Queen of the Sea) telling her that the necklace will give her Mermaid Powers when she wears it. Logan slowly adjusts to what is happening to her and believes that she is successfully keeping her secret until she and her friend, Melody, meet for a smoothie and Logan accidentally spills the drink on Melody, transferring her into a Mermaid. The program ends here and appears to have been abandoned as no additional text or video information appears. **Cast (as credited):** Emily (Logan), Jessica (Melody), Marta (Adriana). **Comment:** Even though the third and fourth episodes are not available for viewing the story can still be followed. Overall, the production is acceptable.

Episode List: *1.* Skater to Fish Freak. *2.* Time Stops. *3.* Episode taken offline. *4.* Then There Were Two.

111 *Fun with Kate and Chloe.* youtube.com. 2015 (Variety).

Two very pretty sisters, 11-year-old Kate and 8-year-old Chloe, present comical videos in which they present topics of interest to children. See also *Club Kate.*

Host (as credited): Kate and Chloe. **Comment:** Wholesome fun for children with excellent acting and production values.

Episode List: *1.* Candy Testing with Kate and Chloe. *2.* Candy Eating Contest. *3.* Coolest Item Challenge. *4.* "Annie" (2014) Movie Review. *5.* Cake Decorating Contest. *6.* Chloe and Kate Find a Snake. *7.* Atomic Fireball Candy Challenge—Super Hot. *8.* Trampoline Gymnastics.

112 *Fur Your Information.* youtube.com. 2013 (Children).

An interview program geared to children with a furry puppet (Puppet Sloth) conducting interviews with Internet celebrities and their charitable endeavors.

Cast: Aaron Schachter (Puppet Sloth). **Credits:** *Producer*: Brad Mathias. **Comment:** Although geared to the small fry, many may not understand what transpires between the host and his guests as it all centers on charitable work. Puppet Sloth takes on the role of a late night talk show host and simply talks to his guests about their activities.

Episode List: *1.* Interview with Michael Buckley and Project for Awesome. *2.* Interview with Jake Bley and It Gets Better. *3.* Interview with Nic Foti and Project for Awesome.

113 *The Ghost Girl.* youtube.com. 2011 (Dolls).

Claira, her sister, Genevieve and their friends Mary Jane and Kiley are watching a zombie horror movie on TV when they hear a strange noise but are unable to figure out its source. The girls theorize that the house is haunted and ban together to uncover the source of the mysterious noise. The program follows their investigation to uncover what they believe is a ghost.

Cast (as credited): Hailey Walber (Claira Howard), Clarissa Maxwell (Genevieve Howard), Elizabeth Cole (Mary Jane), Kanani Akina (Kiley), Libby Montoya (Mrs. Howard). **Comment:** Not as spooky as it sounds, but well done with good voices, doll manipulation and photography (but the program ends without a conclusion).

Episode List: 3 untitled episodes, labeled "Episode 1," "Episode 2" and "Episode 3" have been produced.

114 *The Girl with the Long Blonde Hair.* 1997 (Drama).

She appears to be an 11-year-old girl. She has long blonde hair and can take on the appearance of a pretty girl or a plain Jane depending on the circumstances that surround her. She has no official name and when she becomes a part of someone's life it can be felt that she is not an ordinary girl. The girl, an Angel from above, has been assigned a very special mission: help children overcome their problems. The program, presented as an anthology, begins with the girl receiving an assignment then follows her activities as she becomes a part of each child's life.

Cast: Nicole Galiardo (The Girl). **Comment:** The earliest Internet series specifically designed for children. While the dramatic approach was encompassed, it plays well and gets a message across on how to solve a problem or at least deal with it. The program, which has good video quality for the time, has been taken offline. There are no credits or other cast listed except for The Girl.

Episode List: *1.* Madison: A Child Lost. *2.* Nicole: A Child Alone. *3.* Tabitha: A Child Bullied. *4.* Sabrina: A Child Unloved. *5.* Joshua: A Latch Key Child. *6.* George: The Wrong Direction. *7.* Stacey: A Child Thief. *8.* Amber: A Child's Sadness. *9.* Tammy: A Child's Imaginary World. *10.* Hailey and Megan: Separated Twins.

115 *Girls with Sharp Fins.* youtube.com. 2014–2015 (Fantasy).

Grace, Rachel and Julia are in a backyard swimming pool when Grace finds a strange pink plastic-like tube that appears to be harmless. Later that day Grace receives a phone call from an unknown person telling her that she and her friends have special powers. The girls experiment and find they do have the powers of a Mermaid but have not physically changed. They surmise it was the pink tube that granted them their powers, but unknown to them, a spell has been cast upon them by an unknown presence that enables them to become Mermaids when they touch water. As Grace, Rachel and Julia try to accept what is happening to them they encounter a mysterious man who is seeking to absorb their powers. The program follows the girls as they battle a powerful enemy that could destroy them if he should succeed in his quest.

Cast (as credited): Grace, Rachel as Julia as Themselves. **Comment:** Acceptable acting and photography combine with an intriguing storyline and a slight twist on how young girls become Mermaids.

Season 1 Episode List: *1.* Pilot. *2.* A New Enemy. *3.* Episode 3. *4.* The Agent. *5.* Season Finale.

Season 2 Episode List: *1.* The Start. *2.* Stupid Technology. *3.* Jail Birds. *4.* Episode 4.

Season 3 Episode List: *1.* What's Up with Grace? *2.* Bloopers.

116 The Godzilla Bros. *youtube.com.* 2010; 2015 (Cartoon).

Godzilla, the Japanese-created movie monster, is asleep in his cave when he is awakened by Angurius, his estranged brother, who has returned seeking a place to stay. Godzilla appears to be angry but allows his trouble-prone brother to share his cave. The brothers are once again together and the program charts their experiences in a prehistoric-like world where their efforts to live peaceably are often interrupted by other monsters seeking to destroy them. **Comment:** A cast and credits are not given. In the 2010 version, the animation is a bit crude and the actual *Godzilla* movie roars are used (each roar is accompanied with English dialogue). The 2015 reboot uses what appears to be simple computer animation which produces much better-looking monsters. The original Godzilla roaring sound has been replaced by different roaring effects but continues to use English dialogue to translate the sounds. Both versions can still be seen and is quite an intriguing series to watch. **Episode List:** *1.* Godzilla. *2–3.* MechaGodzilla. *4.* The Lost Pilot.

117 Goldie Blox Saves the Day. *youtube. com.* 2015 (Dolls).

Goldie Blox was once an ordinary doll leading an ordinary life. But her desire to help people has changed her from ordinary to extraordinary when she came into the possession of a real girl (unnamed) and now performs heroic deeds for her. Goldie Blox, with her bright yellow hair, lives in a Sears Craftsman tool box and has a mission to help those who are unable to help themselves. The program chronicles her adventures as she risks her life to perform good deeds (as in the pilot where she attempts to rescue a dog from a raging river). **Cast:** Aria Ekholm (Girl/Voices). **Comment:** A well done program with good voices and photography. When the girl sees that help is needed she opens the tool box and removes Goldie Blox. Goldie then becomes "alive" to do what is needed. **Episode List:** *1.* Pilot: Barbie's Lost Puppy.

118 Gone. 2015 (Dolls).

A newspaper headline has stated that a young girl has been kidnapped and the police are doing everything they can to find her. Posy and Cora are young girls who are aware of the situation but Posy is a bit shocked to hear Cora say that she wishes she could be kidnapped as it would be fun to fight for her life. At the time of publication the series appeared to be active but had only reached this point in the story. It could be assumed that Cora will either become a victim or pretend to be kidnapped (to see how her friends and family respond). **Cast (as credited):** Niomi Rose (Posy Daniels), Becca Reynolds (Cora Night). Voices by Liz. **Comment:** The photography is excellent as are the voice characterizations and doll manipulation (American Girl dolls are used) but the series has since been taken offline. **Episode List:** 2 untitled episodes, labeled "Episode 1" and "Episode 2" have been produced.

119 Gortimer Gibbon's Life on Normal Street. *youtube.com.* 2014–2015 (Comedy).

Captain Normal was an unusual man with unusual secrets and strange powers. To conceal his secrets he created Normal Street, a supposedly ordinary city suburb that is anything but ordinary. Three friends, Gortimer, Melanie (Mel) and Ranger attend Normal Street Middle School but believe because of all the strange situations they encounter, that their city is anything but normal. The program follows their experiences as they attempt to deal with all the weird "stuff" that seems to only happen to them. **Cast:** Sloane Morgan Siegel (Gortimer Gibbon), Ashley Boettcher (Mel Fuller), Drew Justice (Ranger Bowen), Robyn Lively (Claire Gibbon), David Bloom (Stanley Zielinski), Chandler Kinney (Catherine Dillman), Paula Marshall (Lora Fuller), Coco Grayson (Abigail), Kim Rhodes (Vicki Bowen), Ryder Cohen (Gardner Gibbon), Bart Johnson (Will Fuller). **Credits:** *Producer:* Luke Matheny, David Anaxagoras, Laurie Parres, Ann Lewis Hamilton, Eric D. Wasserman. *Director:* Luke Matheny, Ryan Shiraki, Steven K. Tsuchid, Sasie Sealy, Alethea Jones, Joe Nussbaum, J.J. Johnson. *Writer:* Gretchen Enders, Garrett Frawley, David Anaxagoras, Brian Turner, Amimta Goyel, Laurie Parres, Ann Lewis Hamilton, Levi Abrino, May Chan, Eric D. Wasserman. **Comment:** Shades of the TV series *Eerie, Indiana* can be seen as it too dealt with kids encountering unusual happenings in their seemingly normal town. Although geared to children the program is very well produced and acted and can easily appeal to adults as well as it combines comedy, mystery and adventure in an entertaining manner. An original series produced for Amazon Prime (a pay service) that can be viewed for free on YouTube.

Season 1 Episode List:
1. Pilot.
2. Gortimer vs. the Frog of Ultimate Doom.
3. Gortimer vs. the Mobile of Misfortune.
4. Mel vs. the Mel-o-dramatic Robot.
5. Gortimer and the Mystical Mind Reader.
6. Gortimer Gets Shushed.
7. Ranger and the Legend of Pendragon's Gavel.
8. Gortimer and the Leaky Dream Catcher.
9. The Mystery of the Blood Moon Eclipse.
10. Ranger and the Mysterious Metamorphosis.
11. Mel vs. the Fickle Fortune Teller of Fate.
12. Gortimer and the Surprise Signature.
13. Gortimer and the Lost Treasure of Normal Street.
14. Gortimer vs. the Relentless Rainbow of Joy.

Season 2 Episode List:
1. Gortimer and the Blazer of Glory.
2. Ranger and the Super Charged Championship.
3. Gortimer vs. the Terrible Touch-Up.
4. Ranger and the Very Real Imaginary Friend.
5. Gortimer and the Vengeful Violinist.
6. Mel vs. the Hidden Herstory of Normal Street.
7. Gortimer vs. the Friendship Bro-celet.
8. Mel and the Mel-Functioning Brain.
9. Stanley and the Tattoo of Tall Tales.
10. Gortimer vs. Gortimer vs. Gortimer.
11. Ranger and the Fabled Flower of Normal Street.
12. Mel vs. the Future.
13. Gortimer, Ranger and Mel vs. the Endless Night.

120 Gotham Girls. *youtube.com.* 2000–2002 (Cartoon).

Characters from the DC Comics universe are seen in animated form as they uphold the peace, battle crime and deal with their own personal lives most notably, the super hero Batgirl and the villains Catwoman, Poison Ivy and Harley Quinn.

Voice Cast: Adrienne Barbeau (Selina Kyle/Catwoman/Renee Montoya), Tara Strong (Barbara Gordon/Batgirl/Elizabeth Styles), Arleen Sorkin (Dr. Helena Quinzel/Harley Quinn), Diane Pershing (Dr. Pamela Lillian Isley/Poison Ivy), Stacie Randall (Zatanna Zatara), Jennifer Hale (Det. Selma Reesedale/Dora Smitty/Caroline Greenway), Bob Hastings (Commissioner James Gordon). **Credits:** *Producer:* Alan Bruckner. **Comment:** The original web site at the WB.com no longer exists. Aspects associated with the original presentation have also been discontinued (like trailers, screensavers and games). Episodes 21 through 31 have been restructured from the prior comedy-like episodes to a more dramatic approach (especially with the introduction of the transsexual Det. Selma Reesedale).

Episode List:
1. The Vault.
2. Lap Bat in a Rooftop Chase.
3. Trick or Trick.
4. A Little Night Magic.
5. More Than One Way.
6. Precious Birthstones.
7. The Three Babies.
8. Pave Paradise.
9. The Gardener's Apprentice.
10. Lady X.
11. Hold That Tiger.
12. Miss Un-Congeniality.
13. Strategy.
14. Baby Boom.
15. Cat-n-Mouse, Cat-n-Mouse.
16. Bat'ing Cleanup.
17. Cat Sitter.
18. Gotham Noir.
19. Scout's Dishonor.
20. I'm Batgirl.
21. Missing in Action.
22. Gotham in Pink.
23. Hear Me Roar.
24. Ms.-ing in Action.
25. Gotham in Blue.
26. A Cat in the Hand.
27. Jailhouse Wreck.
28. Honor among Thieves.
29. No, I'm Batgirl.
30. Signal Fires.
31. Cold Hands, Cold Heart.

121 H2O Magic. 2012 (Fantasy).

While walking through the woods two young girls (Macy and Isabella) discover a strange cave near a river. While exploring it, they are exposed to strange moon-like beams they later discover have endowed them with Mermaid abilities (or as they call themselves, "Merfreaks"). Now, when they make contact with water, they are transformed into Mermaids and must learn to live a normal life while accepting the fact that they are also creatures of the ocean.

Cast (as credited): Emmie (Isabella), Emme (Macy). **Comment:** An obvious inspiration based on the TV series *H20: Just Add Water* that has poor sound, capable acting and acceptable photography. The program has since been taken offline. **Episode List:** *1.* Merfreaks. *2.* Power Surge. *3.* Sea Jewelry. *4.* Shaking the Truth. *5.* A New Fin. *6.* Bella's Dying of Boredom.

122 H2O: Mermaid Adventures. *youtube. com.* 2015 (Cartoon).

An animated adaptation of the live action Australian series *H20: Just Add Water.* In the original series, three girls (Cleo Sertori, Emma Gilbert and Rikki Chadwick) are enjoying an ocean outing when their boat's motor stalls and strands them near the mysterious Mako Island. The girls swim to the island and feel safe for the moment. Everything changes when they find a cave filled with water and decide to swim in it. The water, affected by the moon's rays, engulfs them and transforms them into Mermaids. For the animated version, the city in which Emma, Cleo and Rikki live has become Dolphin City (not Gold Coast in Australia). New to the program are Bernie, the Hermit Crab; Zita, the curious Eel; Teddy the Turtle; Carlotta the Jelly Fish; and Sue, the enchanted Manta Ray. While the girls can live both in the sea and on land, their adventures with their ocean friends as well as their land-bound friends are the focal point of stories.

Voice Cast: Sonja Ball, Holly G. Frankel, Angela Galuppo, Thor Bishopric, Sara Braden, Pauline Little, Danny Brochu, Matthew McKay, Sara Camacho, Robert Naylor, Eleanor Noble, Bruce Dinsmore.

Credits: *Producer*: Denis Olivieri. *Director*: Tian Xiao Zhang. **Comment:** Excellent animation that is a compliment to the original series. The animated version needed to make the changes described above to distinguish itself from the live-action series and not become just a repetitive retelling of that series. The program, originally produced for pay service Netflix can be viewed for free on YouTube.

Season 1 Episode List: *1.* The Secret of Mako Island. *2.* Caught in the Net. *3.* The White Mermaid. *4.* A Stormy Party. *5.* Mako Island Hotel. *6.* The Mysterious Seaweed. *7.* It's in the Bag. *8.* Dolphin City Triangle. *9.* Poseidon's Daughter. *10.* Dolphin City Mascot. *11.* Bad Waves. *12.* Jaws-ache. *13.* The Lost Ring.

Season 2 Episode List: *1.* Reported Missing. *2.* Memory Lapse. *3.* Valentine's Day. *4.* Kidnapped. *5.* Strange Phenomenon. *6.* Handle with Care. *7.* The Return of the White Mermaid. *8.* Three Days Underwater. *9.* Robot Duel. *10.* The Creature from the Bay. *11.* Underwater Takeover. *12.* Imminent Danger. *13.* Trapped.

123 *H2O Mermaids*. youtube.com. 2014 (Fantasy).

Three very young girls (Finlay, Dylan and Ella) walking along the beach suddenly fall into what they believe is an inactive volcano crater. As they seek to find a way out, they enter a pool of water that begins to bubble and immediately transforms them into Mermaids. The program ends here but it is assumed that if additional episodes are produced it will follow their efforts to keep secret what happened as they adjust to becoming Mermaids.

Cast: Finlay Ross (Finlay), Dylan Herford (Dylan), Ella Janes (Ella), Phoenix Vinar (Phoenix). **Credits:** *Producer-Director*: Ella Janes. **Comment:** The girls appear to be between six and seven years old and considering their age they do a very good job. The program has over 896,000 views on You Tube but it appears to have been abandoned.

Episode List: *1.* The Change.

124 *Half Blood Vampire*. 2015 (Dolls).

Ivy is a girl with a secret: she is half-human and half-vampire and, because of her flawed nature, has been banned from the undead world and sentenced to live life as a school girl in the human world. Ivy, although 1600 years old, appears as a young girl and must, as part of her punishment, transform the children of her school into vampires. Ivy faces termination if she should reveal what she really is and the program chronicles her experiences as she interacts with human children and the conflicts that arise as she struggles to carry out her sentence.

Voices (as credited): Amber. **Comment:** Although the program has adult-like themes, the dolls remove that aspect and make it more kid-like. It has

good doll manipulation and photography but has since been taken offline.

Episode List: *1.* Close Encounters. *2.* Friend or Foe. *3.* Mortal Enemies. *4.* Unknown title. *5.* Claws Unleashed. *6.* It's Time.

125 *The Happy Family Show*. youtube.com. 2011–2015 (Dolls).

Barbie dolls are encompassed in a simple program where incidents in the lives of the Sherwood family are comically explored: parents Alan and Midge and their children, Jenny, Ryan, Nikki, Hannah and Nathan. Also known as *The Barbie Happy Family Show.*

Voices (as credited): Kevin, Christine and Josh. **Comment:** Although hands can be seen manipulating the dolls, it, along with the voices and photography, is well done.

Season 1 Episode List: *1.* Happy Robbery. *2.* Baby Sitter Mayhem. *3.* The Not So Happy Accident. *4.* Staring Contest. *5.* Back in Time. *6.* Alan's Happy Birthday. *7.* Halloween Pranks. *8.* A Very Merry Christmas.

Season 2 Episode List: *1.* Baby, Baby. *2.* Justin Bieber. *3.* Frankie from "Monster High." *4.* Halloween Pranks. *5.* Christmas Special.

Season 3 Episode List: *1.* Midge and Alan's Wedding Day. *2.* Nikki's New Dog. *3.* Haunted Cabin. *4.* One Direction, Come Over.

126 *A Hard Mer-Life*. 2010 (Fantasy).

A day at the beach for a young girl (Amanda) is anything but enjoyable when she finds that her contact with the water has transformed her into a Mermaid. She fears discovery (especially from her family) and now struggles to keep secret what happened while pretending to be an ordinary girl.

Cast (as credited): Destiny J. (Amanda), Ilsa (Elise), Felicia (Matilda), Faith (Hope), Kara J. (Amanda's sister), Julia A. (Julia). **Comment:** Pretty girls cannot always save a Mermaid series; it needs to also have what is lacking here: better sound and photography. The program has since been taken offline.

Season 1 Episode List: *1.* A Mermaid Dream. *2.* Tail Change. *3.* Research. *4.* The Meeting. *5.* Secret's Out.

Season 2 Episode List: *1.* Discovered. *2.* Concussion. *3.* Julia Returns. *4.* Freeze Potion. *5.* One More Mermaid.

Season 3 Episode List: *1.* The Heart-Shaped Stone. *2.* Moonstruck. *3.* A Wizardly Visit. *4.* Mean Girl. *5.* Can We Be Friends? *6.* Goodbye.

Season 4 Episode List: *1.* Water. *2.* My Sister's a Mermaid. *3.* The End.

127 *Harry the Bunny*. babyfirsttv.com. 2009–2015 (Educational).

Harry is a three-year-old rabbit whose one ambition is to explore the world that surrounds him. He delights in discovering anything that is new but must stay within the parameters of his environment (like his bedroom, his backyard). Through Harry the Bunny's simplistic adventures (like identifying colors, counting and letter identification) children learn the basics of the world in which they live.

Comment: While the format is very pleasing and it will appeal to preschool children, cast and credits are not given (on screen or anywhere else). Why this was decided is unknown as credit should be seen for a program that truly attempts to help toddlers learn various aspects of life. For adults, however, the program can become a chore to watch as it is rather monotone. Each thirty minute episode is divided into multiple segments that give parents the option of monitoring what is being seen and limit watching to what they seem fit.

Episode List: *1.* Shapes, Numbers and More! *2.* What Is It? Hat. *3.* What Is It? Drum. *4.* What Is It? Singing. *5.* Green/Learning Colors. *6.* What Is Cereal? *7.* What Is It? Bottle. *8.* Big and Small/Opposites. *9.* Yellow: Learning Colors. *10.* Introducing Opposites. *11.* Wheels on a Bus. *12.* Red: Learning Colors. *13.* Twinkle, Twinkle Little Star. *14.* Four: Learning Numbers. *15.* What Is It? Cup. *16.* Loud and Quiet. *17.* Three: Counting. *18.* Long and Short. *19.* Was Is It? Orange Juice. *20.* Two: Learning to Count. *21.* What Is It? A Carrot. *22.* Blue: Learning Colors. *23.* What Is It? Water. *24.* What Is It? Milk. *25.* What Is It? Coloring. *26.* One: Learning Numbers.

128 Haunted Visions. *youtube.com.* 2013 (Dolls).

Aislinn is a 16-year-old girl who died young but never moved on. She is an Eternal (half ghost, half human) and can live forever but must always remain on Earth. She fears, that because she never ages her true being will be discovered if she remains in one place for too long a time, thus she must constantly assume new identities. Season 1 episodes follow Aislinn as she enrolls in a boarding school (St. Jude Academy) and reacts with the other students. In season 2, Aislinn is uncovered to be a ghost by Diana and Missouri, ghost hunters who soon realize what she actually is and ask her to join them in their quest to debunk supernatural occurrences.

Cast (as credited): Ms. Flanclan (Voices). **Comment:** Although the plot does read like a live action series, it is not and is not as scary as it could normally be. The photography, voices and doll manipulation are excellent but the sound leaves a lot to be desired. Crucial explanation segments are over-powered by music making it difficult to figure out what is happening.

Episode List: Season 1 contains 6 untitled episodes while the second season has produced 2 untitled episodes.

129 The Haunting of Sunshine Girl. *you tube.com.* 2010–2012 (Horror).

A daughter (Sunshine) and mother (Kat) ghost hunting team attempt to help people who are threatened by paranormal activity. It begins when Sunshine, a teenage girl interested in the paranormal (having experienced a ghostly occurrence when she was four years old) and Kat move to a new home in a new town and Sunshine soon discovers that her home is not only haunted but has given her the ability to hear and feel what others cannot. It takes time to convince her mother what has happened, but with her own mysterious past (disappearing for two years, supposedly abducted by aliens, and returning with a child named Sunshine) Kat soon becomes a believer. With the assist of the mysterious Victoria, the girl who befriends Sunshine (and who possesses psychic abilities—and may be a ghost) and Sunshine's friend, Nolan (who had a near-death experience and can now see spirits), their adventures are explored as they deal with and attempt to debunk unnatural occurrences.

Cast: Paige McKenzie (Sunshine Girl), Mercedes Rose (Kat), Adrienne Vogel (Victoria), Maxwell James Arnold (Nolan), Seth Renne (Uncle Tommy), Christopher Toyne (Alister Turnbull), Tabitha Knight (Goth Girl), Rhyan Schwartz (Bailey). **Credits:** *Producer-Writer-Director*: Nicholas J. Hagen. **Comment:** Although a bit scary at times, the program has been called a paranormal version of the TV series *Gilmore Girls* for the close mother-daughter relationship and sharing of experiences. It is well acted and produced and although geared to a teenage audience, Sunshine does refer to her audience as kids on occasion. The overall presentation resembles that of a video vlog and the horror stems more from what is said as opposed to actual encounters with the unnatural, especially in first season episodes.

Season 1 Episode List:
 1. We Moved Into a Haunted House.
 2. Showing You My Haunted House.
 3. Meet My Mom at the Haunted House.
 4. The "Breaking Bad" Meth Lab.
 5. The First Real Ghost Activity Caught on Tape.
 6. I Hear a Ghost ... Or Do I?
 7. Catching a Ghost on Camera Is Hard Work.
 8. Almost Caught a Ghost on Film! Almost.
 9. Meeting Creepy Lady.
 10. My Mad Guitar Skills. Not.
 11. Ghost Shuts Door on Me.
 12. Mom Makes a Video. Ugh!
 13. Ghost Activity Scares Me and Mom.
 14. Trying to Hear a Ghost.
 15. Just Me Being a Dork.
 16. Update on Creepy Lady. Is She a Witch?
 17. Caught on Tape and I'm Freaked Out!
 18. Mom Makes Another Video.
 19. My Thoughts on the Ghost Activity.

20. Using the Baby Monitors to Hear Ghosts.
21. Even More Dedicated to Catch a Ghost Now!
22. Creepy Lady Speaks.
23. Follow Up to Creepy Lady Encounter.
24. Ghost Activity Sets Baby Monitor Off.
25. About My Research Into the Ghost in This House.
26. Ghost Outside My Door.
27. Why We Moved Into This Haunted House.
28. Waiting for Ghosts.
29. Scary Ghost Activity Caught on Tape.
30. Demon Image and Audio Recording?
31. I Can Keep Hunting Ghosts.
32. Researching the Paranormal.
33. Ghost Moves Objects around the Room.
34. Ten Random Facts about Me.
35. Ghost Moves Object and Scares Me.
36. Ghost at Old Fort.
37. Mom Gives an Update about the Creepy Witch Lady.
38. Ghost Moves Object on Video.
39. What's Happening with YouTube Friends!
40. Haunted House Information from Landlord.
41. Mom Has a Weird Accident.
42. Mom's Thoughts on Her Accident.
43. Field Trip to a Ruin.
44. Should I Stop Doing Videos?
45. Ghost in House.
46. Ghost Child Caught on Tape.
47. Update Video After Ghost Child Video.
48. Ten Random Facts about Me, Part Deux.
49. Creepy Lady Enters My House.
50. Looking at the Box Creepy Lady Gave Me.
51. More on the Box from the Creepy Lady.
52. Is This Pandora's Box?
53. I Kind of Miss the Ghosts.
54. We Open the Box…
55. Scary Ghost Activity Caught on Tape.
56. My Mom Is Ok … I Hope.
57. Last Video—I Just Wanted to Say Goodbye Properly.
58. I Need to Track Down the Creepy Lady.
59. Mysterious Photos of Ghosts.
60. Using a Ouija Board to Contact Ghosts?
61. Info on My New Friend.
62. Title Unknown (Video deleted).
63. Update to Scary Ghost Child Caught on Tape Video.
64. Creepy Lady Finally Spotted.
65. Ghost Caught on Tape.
66. Are the Ghosts Stronger?
67. Mom and I Get Into a Small Fight.
68. I Apologize for My Mom and the Last Video.
69. I'm Leaving Mom out of It.
70. Are We Moving?
71. Creepy Lady Is Going to Help Me with My Haunted House.
72. Mom Has Set a Move Out Date.
73. Girl Attacked by Ghost.
74. Update to Ghost Attack.
75. Still at a Friend's House.
76. Creepy Lady to the Rescue.
77. The Ghost Activity Seems to Have Left.

Season 2 Episode List:
1. My Mom and I Head Out on a Road Trip.
2. On the Road to Find Ghosts.
3. A Haunted Hotel.
4. We Arrive at the Haunted Hotel.
5. Checking Out the Historic Anchor Inn.
6. Our Haunted Hotel Room.
7. Exploring the Haunted Hotel.
8. The Story of the Hotel Haunting.
9. EVP of a Ghost Recorded at the Haunted Hotel.
10. Poltergeist Activity at the Haunted Hotel.
11. Ghost Voice Recording: EVP Caught on Tape.
12. A New Day Full of Excitement.
13. We Visit a Book Store on the Oregon Coast.
14. Driving Down the Coast and Arriving at Newport, Oregon.
15. Creepy Furry Scares Me!
16. Getting Lunch and Being Teased.
17. We Arrived at the Haunted Lighthouse.
18. Checking Out the Haunted Lighthouse.
19. Ghost Story of a Haunted Lighthouse.
20. Mom Gets Upset at Haunted Lighthouse.
21. About My Dad.
22. Legend of the Black Eyed Kids.
23. Ghost Lights Candle.
24. Real Ghost EVP Recorded.
25. Visiting a Surprise Haunted Location.
26. A Mortuary with a Disturbing Past.
27. Wrapping up the Road Trip.

Season 3 Episode List:
1. Back Home with the Ghosts?
2. Who Are the Ghosts?
3. I Think the Ghosts Are Back.
4. I'm Being Followed.
5. Paranormal Activity Caught on Tape.
6. Best Ghost Video Ever!
7. Smudging Again.
8. Telling Mom the Ghosts Are Back.
9. Calling an Occult Expert.
10. Danger of the Ouija Board.
11. Mom Explains Why She Used the Ouija Board.
12. Being Followed Again.
13. My Mom Won't Be Ok Forever.
14. I'm Going to See My Dad.
15. That Was the Worst Day Ever.
16. Follow Up to Last Video.
17. I Have Decided…
18–24. Worst Day Ever.
25. Follow Up to Worst Day Ever.
26. We're Going Back to the House.
27. About to Go to the Scary House.
28. At the Scary House.
29. Unanswered Questions.
30. Quick Update on Things.
31. What Is Wrong with Mom?

32. A Ghost Expert?
33. Creepy Lady and Mom.
34. Don't Trust Her.
35. Scary Ghost Noise.
36. The Morning After.
37. In Case I Vanish.
38. A Spiritual Medium Is Coming.
39. A Worrisome Call.
40–42. Visit from the Medium.
43. Paranormal Medium Hurt by Ghost.
44. Update on the Paranormal Expert.
45. A Cult? What?
46. Leaving the Occult Expert.
47. Asking Mom about the Cult.
48. Last Resort … The Ouija Board.
49. Where Are We?
50. Asking Creepy Lady Questions.
51. The Sacrifice Site.
52. Thinking about Things.
53. Asking the Medium for Help Again.
54. Demon Test.
55. Possessed by Demon Test.
56. Took Mom to the Doctor.
57. Poltergeist Activity.
58. Mom Is Possessed by the Demon.
59. Going to Sacrifice Myself to the Demon.
60. About to Do the Sacrifice.
61. Recovering.
62. Uncle Tommy Tells Mom's Secrets.
63. Demon Sacrifice Filmed.
64. YouTube and P.O. Info.
65. Shout Outs! Because I Can!
66. Thoughts on the Sacrifice.
67. Ok, I've Decided to Change.
68. Is Mom Still Possessed?
69. Last Video of This Play List.

Season 4 Episode List:
1. What Happens Now?
2. Should I Try to Contact Dad?
3. Weird Thing Happened Today.
4. Random Guy Has Info on the Paranormal.
5. The Legend of the Luiseach.
6. Ten Random Facts about Nolan.
7. Thoughts on Nolan?
8. Something in the Mail.
9. Nolan and the Note.
10. Special Paranormal Powers.
11. It's Not Me.
12. Stalker Weirdo?
13. A Mysterious Photo.
14. On the Way to the Warehouse.
15. At the Warehouse.
16. Visit a Haunted House?
17. Guess Who's Back?
18. I Want to Go to the Haunted House.
19. Can We Go to the Haunted House?
20–26. The Haunted House Visit.
27. Back from the Haunted House.
28. I Heard the Ghost.
29. Halloween Special! Yay!

30. Crazy Paranormal Activity.
31. EMF Ghost Evidence Videos.
32. What's Wrong with Nolan?
33. Demon Possession Test for Nolan.
34. Nolan's Confusing Past.
35. Nolan Is Coming Back Over.
36. Paranormal Videos—Documentary.
37. Nolan Possessed by Demon?
38. I'm So Confused.
39. Returning to Haunted Warehouse.
40. Uncle Tommy the Protector.
41. Ghostly Experience—Black Eyed Kids?
42. Residual Haunting.
43. A Letter with Helpful Information?
44. Back to Nolan's Grandma's House.
45. Insane Paranormal Activity.
46. Paranormal Reality TV Show.
47. Getting It Tested.
48. Ghost Documentary—Astral Projection.
49. Communicating with Ghost Séance.
50. I'm Doing the Right Thing to Get More Answers.
51. A Ghost under the Stairs.
52. The Warehouse at 3:00 a.m.
53. Searching for Nolan in the Warehouse.
54. Finding Nolan.
55. Evil Ghost Groundlings—Haunted Places.
56. Ghost Ectoplasm Forensics—Results!
57. Grave Encounter with Little Girl Ghost Caught on Tape.
58. Scary Cult Films Found–Shocking Satanic Worship Exposed!
59. Analyzing the 8mm Cult Film Found in My Back Yard—Terrifying!
60. Occult Film.
61. I've been on YouTube for One Year!
62. Ghost Activity EVP of Girl Screaming and Crying.

Season 5 Episode List:
1. I've Had Some Time to Think.
2. The Paranormal World of Sunshine.
3. Psycho-kinesis Ghosts Caught on Camera.
4. Discussing Victoria's Return.
5. Haunting Evidence.
6. Ghost Girl Caught on Video Tape: EVP.
7. Haunting of Sunshine Girl: Teen Vlog Series.
8. Discussing Occult Poltergeist and My Dad.
9. Haunting of Sunshine Updates.
10. Erie Evil Screaming Noises.
11. Victoria's Haunted Poltergeist Activity Revealed.
12. Ghostly Activity in House: Nolan's Return.
13. Paranormal Activity—Spirit Sound EVP.
14. Teen Ghost Hunters—Supernatural Activity.
15. Poltergeist Activity: Spirits Haunting House.
16. Ghost Spirit Calls from the Afterlife.
17. Poltergeist Paranormal Activity Caught on Tape.
18. Reviewing the Last Paranormal Activity.
19. Ghost Stories: Nolan's Dreams.

20. Scary Ghost Attack.
21. Real Paranormal Activity.
22. Scary Phone Calls, Haunting Experience.
23. Ghost: Lessons from My Mentor.
24. Strange Poltergeist Activity.
25. Update from My Last Ghost Video.

Season 6 Episode List:
1. On the Road with Haunted Sunshine Girl.
2. Paranormal Activity in Creepy Cabin in Woods?
3. Sighting in Creepy Cabin.
4. Unknown Visitor in Creepy Cabin in the Woods.
5. Following Ghost Sounds in the Creepy Cabin.
6. Hearing Sounds in the Creepy Cabin.
7. Creepy Ghost Footage Captured.
8. Creepy Ghost Footage Captured Continued.
9. First Morning in the Creepy Cabin.
10. Creepy Secrets of the Guest Book.
11. Looking for the Ghost in the Creepy Cabin.
12. A Break to Ask You a Question.
13. Ghost Writes on Mirror.
14. Ghost Footage Captured on Video.
15. Ghost Captured on Video!
16. We Go Looking for the Ghost and Find Something Interesting.
17. Opening the Mysterious Box.
18. How to Deal with the Ghost.
19. Getting Away from the Ghost a Bit.
20. Returning to the Ghost…
21. It's Not Over…
22. Why Do Ghosts Like the Dark So Much? Seriously.
23. The Ghost Touched Me! Ahhhhhhhh!!!
24. The Morning after Our Ghostly Encounter.
25. Saying Goodbye to Our Ghost and the Cabin in the Woods.

Season 7 Episode List:
1. Nolan's Mom Knows of a Haunted House.
2. They Keep Calling.
3. Meeting with the "Real Paranormal Investigators."
4. Filling in the Scooby-Doo Gang on the Next Haunted Adventure.
5. Checking Out the Haunted River House (During the Day When It Is Safe).
6. So I Trespassed.
7. Going Back to the Haunted (?) River House.
8. The Scooby Gang Explore the Haunted River House.
9. Giving the Homeowner the Bad News about Her Haunted House.
10. Picking up the Scooby Gang.
11. We Have Arrived.
12. The Day at the Haunted River House Continues.
13. Internet at the House Is Spotty.
14. Should We Use the Ouija Board?
15. Ouija Board Antics in the Attic.
16. The "Professional Ghost Hunters" Do Their Thing.

17. Nolan Reveals a Secret.
18. These Silly Boys.
19. Killing Time at the Haunted River House.
20. The Guys Have Specific Ideas about Ghost Hunting.
21. We Heard a Noise!
22. Is That a Ghost?
23. What Was That?
24. Trying the Ouija Board at Night.
25. Now What?
26. The Ghost Makes an Appearance … Sort Of.
27. The Best Haunted Slumber Party Ever.

Season 8 Episode List:
1. Breaking the Rules.
2. I Can't Get the Haunted Dream Out of My Mind.
3. Freaking Out. Just Saw Creepy Lady.
4. Ghost Slams Door.
5. Convincing Mom There Are Ghosts.
6. Scary Ghost Videos.
7. Is It Me Who's Haunted?
8. Ghost Talks and Moves Object.
9. Horrible Dream about Ghost Girl Anna.
10. Creepy Lady Is Back.
11. Calling Victoria (But Not on a Phone).
12. Nolan's Haunted (?) Apartment.
13. I Don't Attract Ghosts … Do I?
14. Scary Ghost Attack.
15. An Update after Our Buffy "Hush" Adventure.
16. The Latin Ghost.
17. Strange Haunted House Event.

Season 9 Episode List:
1. Worried about Nolan.
2. A Surprise about Nolan.
3. Random Video Monday #17.
4. Uncle Tommy Made Me Tell Mom About Nolan.
5. I Heard from Nolan.
6. Checking in with Nolan's Mom … Or Not.
7. Checking Out the Address … Wait, I Know This Place.
8. Random Video Monday #18.
9. Victoria Talks of Nolan.
10. Gobble Gobble.
11. Random Video Monday #19.
12. Getting Rid of the Ghost.
13. Victoria Sniffs out Nolan.
14. Random Video Monday #20.
15. Victoria Talks of Anna.
16. Random Video Monday #21.
17. An Update That Really Isn't an Update.
18. Screw Ups.
19. Favor Time! Help Me Be "On the Rise."
20. Random Video Monday #22.
21. Victoria Helps with a Missing Nolan.
22. So, I Have a Confession.
23. 30 Minutes after My Confession.
24. Nolan Is Jealous.
25. Tonight Is the Night: My Movie Premiere!
26. My Movie Is Available!

27. The Brothers Fight—About Me!
28. Random Video Monday Christmas Eve Special #28.
29. Merry Holidays.
30. So Nolan, How Jealous Are You?
31. Victoria Talks about Anna, the Girl Ghost.
32. Nolan Bans Me.
33. Nolan the Thief?
34. I Get My Camera Back.
35. Random Video Monday New Year's Eve Special #29.
36. New Year's Day Adventure with My Boys.
37. Why Are You Always Here?
38. Could I Be Haunted?
39. Creepy Reads a Book.
40. Victoria Just Hangs Out.
41. Ghost Apps Work! OMG!
42. Random Video Monday #23.
43. Don't Hang Out with Nolan.
44. Telling Nolan.
45. Nolan Says Goodbye … For Now.
46. Random Video Monday #24.
47. Is Everywhere I Go Haunted?
48. Recap Video.
49. Ghost Hunting Clothes.
50. How to Watch My Channel—The Haunting of Ghost Girl.
51. Random Video Monday #25.
52. Haunted Valley—Yacolt, WA: Finding Ghosts.
53–56. Return to the Cabin in the Woods.
57. Ghost Caught on Camera at Night!
58. Scary Slenderman Cult Film.
59. Random Video Monday #27.
60. Poltergeist Moves Object Right in Front of Us!
61–66. Real Life Paranormal Activity.
67–81. Return to the Cabin the Woods Again.
82. Scary Don't Watch! Zombie Attack.
83. How to Be a Great Boyfriend.
84. Ghost Caught in a Reflection.
85. Random Video Monday #31.
86. Real Ectoplasm Ghost Video.
87–88. Random Video Monday #32.
89. Do You Feel Like You Have No Friends?
90. Ghost Slams Door!
91. Random Video Monday—Book Club.

Season 10 Episode List:
1. It's Time to Focus.
2. Real Ghost Haunting.
3. Paranormal Activity in My House.
4. Ghost Intervention.
5. Strange Things Happen at Night.
6. Uncle Tommy Is Gone.
7. Paranormal Activity.
8. Scary Ghost Encounter.
9. Anna's Dad Is Back.
10. Paranormal Activity House.
11. Mom and I Discuss Missing Uncle Tommy.
12–20. Visiting Real Life Paranormal Activity House.

21. What Happened at the Real Paranormal Activity House?
22. Nolan Wants Something.
23. Evil Ghost Presence Captured on Video!
24. Nolan Reacts the Morning after the Last Video.
25. A Mysterious Ghost Recording.
26. Violent Intruder in Real Life.
27. What Next?
28. Ghost Audio Recording.
29. EVP Captured.
30. Real Life EVP in Sound Booth.
31. Recording Ghost Sounds.
32. Real Ghost Sounds in the Ceiling.
33. Paranormal Evidence.
34. Crazy! Ghost Footage.
35. The Ghost of a Dead Man Appears.
36. Mom Freaking Out about Dad Calling.
37. Trying to Get Info from Mom.
38. Pondering the Ghost Similarities.
39. Ghost Caught in Mirror.
40. Pondering the Underworld.
41. Nolan's Apartment Has a Ghost.
42. Nolan Has a Few Things He'd Like to Say.
43. All Right Mom, Spill It!
44. Ghost at Nolan's.
45. Whose House Is the Ghost In?
46. Victoria Saves the Day.
47. We Ask Mom More After Talking to Victoria.
48. Victoria Is Back Again.
49. I Move an Object Just by Thinking.
50. Ghost Enters the House—Violently.
51. Victoria Tells Us Who Is After Me.
52. The Hunter Is Here.
53. Nolan Is Attacked.
54. Nolan Is Missing, I am Going to His Place.
55. I Am Attacked.
56. Victoria Needs to Train Me.
57. Victoria Takes Me to the House for Training.
58. Ghost Spotted in Training House.
59. Ghost Heard in Training House.
60. Ghost Attacks Us in Training House.
61. Ghost Attacks Woman.
62. Girl Scares Off Ghost.
63. Nolan Finally Called Last Night and Now I'm Here.
64. Looking for Nolan and I Found Victoria.
65. Nolan Appears and He's Acting Weird Again!
66. Victoria Says Some Weird Things.
67. So Nolan Brings Back the Info on Dad.
68. Victoria Gives Me One Last Piece of Advice.
69. Reacting to the Ghost Sounds.
70. Is That a Demon at My Door?
71. Ghost Man in My House.
72. Following the GPS Coordinates.
73. Nolan Wants to Go Now!
74. Off We Go!
75. Nolan Is Not a Good Road Tripper!
76. What's in This Abandoned Building?
77. We Find Something Creepy.

78. Who Is This Man Watching Us?
79. What the Heck Are We Doing?
80. Going Deeper and Deeper Into the Woods.
81. They Stole Our Jeep.
82. The End Is Near. My Dad Reveals Himself.
83. The Death of Nolan (Warning Graphic!).
84. A Letter from Nolan.

Season 11 Episode List:
1. So What's Going On?
2. Well It Figures, Talk About a Ghost, See a Ghost.
3. The Shadowy Figure Spotted.
4. Something Wakes Me Up in the Middle of the Night.
5. Girl Spots Ghost and Video Captures Its Voice.
6. Taking Another Look at the Last Clip.
7. Ghost Caught on Camera in Kitchen.
8. Time to Get Serious.
9. I Am Ceffly Dwr Incarnate.
10. What's Happening to Her Face?
11. Reaction to the Face Melt Video.
12. Myles Brings Me to a Haunted House.
13. Things Get Creepy Fast in the Haunted House.
14. Ghost Activity! You Won't Believe Who Shows Up.
15. Victoria Is Back and She Has Something to Say.
16. His Face Is Melting! So Scary!
17. Is Myles Real?
18. Mom Is Gone and the Ghost Is Back.
19. Weekend Alone Is Getting Interesting.
20. Did You Hear That? EVP Caught on Camera.
21. Calling Mom to Get Her to Come Home.
22. Saturday Night Movie Night Is Interrupted.
23. My Thoughts on What Happened This Weekend.
24. The Ghost Is Behind Me.
25. The Ghost Is Angry.
26. Ghost Seen!
27. Ghost Slams Door.
28. Watch Out Behind You.
29. The Ghost Is Close.
30. Angry Ghost.
31. Ghost Heard on Tape As I Talk to It.
32. I Visit a Haunted Farmhouse.
33. Ghost Down Hall.
34. Ghost Heard Walking and Spotted in Basement.
35. Scary! Ghost Rocking in Chair.
36. Ghost in the Room. Listen!
37. What's in the Basement? A Ghost?
38. Back to the Ghosts!
39. The Ghost Is Messing with Me.
40. Shape Shifting Ghost.
41. The Ghost Is Behind Me.
42. Ghost Appears at the Top of the Stairs.
43. The Ghost Is Talking to Me.
44. The Ghost Is Back! My Mom Saw It Too!

45. Ghost Gives a Warning.
46. Something Is at My Door.
47. Voice Coming from My Closet.
48. Uncle Tommy Is Back.
49. Uncle Tommy Heard Something Upstairs.
50. Something at the Bottom of the Stairs.
51. Ghost Waiting Outside My Room.
52. The Ghost Was Right Behind Me.
53. Saw the Ghost in the Middle of the Night.
54. Victoria Has a Message for Me.
55. Uncle Tommy Saw the Ghost Too.
56. Ghost Crawling Up the Stairs. Scary!
57. Victoria Is Locked in My Room, Screaming!

Season 12 Episode List:
1. Door Moving Behind Me.
2. New Information on the Creepy Ghost.
3. Ghost Crawling Down the Stairs!
4. Victoria Gets Serious about the Ghost.
5. Who Slammed My Door? The Ghost?
6. Ghost Sighting in the Middle of the Day.
7. Why Is the Door Moving?
8. The Ghost Snuck Up on Me.
9. Ghost Follows Me Into My Room.
10. I Need Your Advice.
11. Ghost Watching Us!
12. Doors Slamming All Around Me. Why?
13. Something Trying to Get Into My Room.
14. Ghost Drags Me Down the Stairs.
15. The Ghost Is Getting Aggressive.
16. Was the Ghost Trying to Communicate with Us?
17. Power Went Out. Then the Noises Started.
18. Maybe I Should Move?
19. I Think I Made the Ghost Mad.
20. The Ghost Has Bloody Hands.
21. One of Us Might Actually Get Hurt.
22. The Ghost Came Out of Nowhere.
23. Mom Thinks We Have to Move.
24. Ouija Board Caught on Fire.
25. My New, Brilliant Idea.
26. Chicken Heart to Banish the Ghost?
27. Success! Is the Ghost Finally Gone?

130 Hellbenders. *youtube.com.* 2012–2013 (Cartoon).

Zach and Chris are not only roommates but rather dense friends who always try to do the right thing—but what they think is right is never so. The mischief they create and their efforts to fix what they broke are chronicled.

Cast: Zach Hadel (Zach), Chris O'Neil (Chris). **Credits:** *Writer-Creator*: Zach Hadel, Chris O'Neill. **Comment:** The animation is a bit off center as characters have large round heads with small eyes and mouths. Stories are also highly exaggerated as the situations Zach and Chris encounter can only happen in a cartoon.

Episode List: *1.* Ice Cream. *2.* Appaloosa. *3.* A Hellbenders Christmas.

131 Hidden by the Scales. *youtube.com.* 2012 (Fantasy).

Friends Alyssa and Tori are hanging out together when Alyssa receives a text message: "If you do not forward this to 100 people in the next 10 hours you will become a part of the ocean." Alyssa ignores it. Later Alyssa and Tori discover the results of not forwarding that text: spilled bottled water transforms them into Mermaids. Now, with new identities, Alyssa and Tori must lead dual lives—publicly as ordinary school girls and secretly as Mermaids. **Cast (as credited):** Madisyn (Alyssa), Lindsey (Tori). **Comment:** A slightly different twist on Mermaid mythology but the program suffers from poor sound. **Episode List:** *1.* Pilot: The Forward.

132 Hidden Spirits. *youtube.com.* 2014–2015 (Dolls).

It is a time when the spirits of the four elements (Earth, Wind, Water and Fire) need to attach themselves to mortals to help continue their mission of controlling Mother Nature. Four pets (Cody, Kiara, Alice and Penelope) are chosen, one for each element and the program, using LPS (Littlest Pet Shop) dolls explores what happens as each learns how to control his or her power and use it for the benefit of all mankind. **Voices (as credited):** Christian. **Comment:** Good voices coupled with good doll manipulation and photography. **Episode List:** *1.* The Escape. *2.* Spirits and Dragons. *3.* Planning the Rescue. *4.* The Cave Tribe. *5.* New Friendship. *6.* Wanted. *7.* Miniature. *8.* Dragon Fire. *9.* Unknown Title. *10.* Thieves. *11.* Jax. *12.* Royal Encounter.

133 Hipster Mermaid. *youtube.com.* 2013 (Advice).

A beautiful, red-haired woman named Traci appears to tell her audience that she was once a Mermaid but has temporarily relinquished that ability to live on land as a human. She has, as she says, "gotten so good at it" that she now feels she needs to help "you guys get out of the mainstream" and become better humans. **Cast:** Traci Hines (Hipster Mermaid). **Credits:** *Producer:* Hali Ducote. *Director:* Chase Friday. **Comment:** At times it feels like Traci is addressing other Mermaids who have chosen to live on land as humans. Although the program is geared to teenagers and young women, tween girls will easily become attracted to Traci by the program's title and how astonishing she appears when she is seen as a Mermaid. Overall, though, it is a program of advice on how to deal with certain aspects of life. See also *A Day in the Life* and *Traci Hines, Mermaid.* **Episode List:** *1.* Wear This, Look Awesome. *2.* Snag a Roommate; Score a Sweet Pad. *3.* Go for Coffee, Stay for the Band. *4.* Grab an App, Date some Humans. *5.* Roomie Problems, Basic Solutions. *6.* Beauty Guru? I Woke Up Like This.

134 A History of Radness. *youtube.com.* 2015 (Musical Comedy).

Jack and Tessie are a brother and sister who attend middle school and with some friends have formed their own band. Their band formation has made them appear like outsiders to their fellow classmates but each believes they can achieve a dream: become a success in the music world. The program charts their experiences—from the band's formation to the harsh realities associated with the music industry. **Cast:** Marlhy Murphy (Tessie), Isaak Presley (Jack), Cecilia Balagot (Portia), Dalton Cyr (Judd), Alexis Sky (Cindy), Blesson Yates (Tom), Jaden Martin (Roop), Megan Truong (Janelle), Bethany Cosentino (Older Tessie), Dan Reynolds (Older Jack). **Credits:** *Producer:* Skot Bright, Andrew Green, Alethea Jones. *Director:* Alethea Jones. *Writer:* Andrew Green. **Comment:** Produced by Amazon Prime but only select music scenes are available for free on YouTube. It is well produced and acted but the pilot only establishes the premise (as of April 2016 additional episodes have not appeared). By coincidence, a 2016 Nickelodeon series called *School of Rock* has a similar premise. **Episode List:** *1.* Pilot.

135 HitStreak. *youtube.com.* 2013–2014 (Musical Comedy).

HitStreak is a Miami-based, legendary music recording studio (owned by Ray) that is facing challenging times and could close its doors forever. Four talented young people, Noah (age 16), Crystal (15), Brian (13) and Mariangeli (10) have formed a musical group (HitStreak) in an effort to save the company. They are managed by a former Latina pop star (Isabel) and the program interweaves songs, music videos and comedy as the group attempts to make a name for themselves in the recording world and save Ray's company. **Cast:** Noah Schnacky (Noah), Crystal Shannon (Crystal), Mariangeli Collado (Mariangeli), Brian Inerfeld (Brian), Chiqui Delgado (Isabel), Howard Hesseman (Ray). **Credits:** *Producer:* Erin Foster White. **Comment:** Television quality production with an excellent story, acting and photography. The program, however, has an annoying laugh track and, because it was originally an interactive and mobile series, it is also plagued by numerous pop ups (relating to the interactive aspect) that are even more annoying than the fake laughter. There is also no introduction as to how the group was formed or how Isabel became their manager; it begins with the group performing a song and assumes the viewer will know who they are and what plans they have.

Episode List: 45 untitled episodes, labeled "Episode 1" through "Episode 45" have been produced.

136 *Humperstash and Stinkyfats. youtube. com.* 2010 (Comedy).

Humperstash and Stinkyfats are pre-teenage boys with only one thing in common: they are, as they call themselves, arch enemies. Exactly why is not clearly stated but it appears to stem from the fact that Humperstash envisions himself as a hero and out to right wrongs; Stinkyfats, however, sees Humperstash as a loser and despises his heroics. Thus Humperstash has set out to prove what he believes while Stinkyfats is out to prove him wrong. As stories progress a supposed evil alien (Lumpy Cheese) enters their domain and the boys end their feud to join forces and defeat Lumpy Cheese and his plan to end daylight.

Cast: Talan Hutto (Humperstash), Connor Bitner (Stinkyfats), Dallas Hokanson (Snuffles), Boomer Morgan (Lumpy Cheese), Jim Stulting (Troll), Tessa Wolfe (Village of Oh! Person), Katrina Blackwell (Female Lumpy Cheese). Credits: *Producer-Director*: Jim Stulting. *Writer*: Connor Bitner, Dallas Hokanson, Talan Hutto, Jim Stulting. Comment: At first glance the program will appear strange to adults as it just seems to be two boys chasing each other then becoming friends in a disjointed concept. A lot of what is seen can be explained by the producer as the show "was filmed with no scripts, no planning or props and mostly developed on the fly." That being established, the lead characters do quite well portraying arch enemies and accepting that fact, things like the boys becoming lost in the woods (when there are only a few trees and homes all around) can be accepted. For what it is, it is surprisingly well done.

Episode List: *1*. WTF? *2*. I Don't Speak English. *3*. Zombie Blues. *4*. Dance Off. *5*. You Can't See the Forest from the Cheese. *6*. Tolls and Trolls. *7*. Berries and Buddies. *8*. Frozen Snuffles. *9*. Too Many Snuffles. *10*. Oh? *11–12*. The Savior of Stinky Woods.

137 *I Am a Mermaid.* 2012 (Fantasy).

A young girl (unnamed) finds a strange box in her room that she has never noticed before. Upon opening it, she finds items she believes are related to Mermaids and one in particular, a flower-like necklace, fascinates her. She places it around her neck before going to bed and that night transforms into a Mermaid without touching water. The girl assumes it was the necklace that caused the transformation and the program follows her efforts to keep secret what happened as she learns to adjust to her developing powers.

Cast (as credited): A. Reid (The Girl). Comment: It is basically the unnamed girl talking about what happens to her. Her Mermaid tail is not shown and the program is rather slow-moving and uninteresting.

Episode List: 3 untitled episodes, labeled "Episode 1," "Episode 2" and "Episode 3" have been produced. It has since been taken offline.

138 *I Can't Believe I'm a Mermaid. you tube.com.* 2014 (Fantasy).

It is early morning and as a young girl (Ella) awakens she finds a mysterious, heart-shaped box under her pillow. She opens it and finds it is from her grandmother on the occasion of her 13th birthday. The box contains a butterfly-like pendant and a sea shell with a note attached that tells her to read the chant (on the accompanying piece of paper). Out of curiosity, Ella recites the chant but nothing happens. Shortly after, however, when Ella comes in contact with water she transforms into a Mermaid. Unsure as what to do, Ella consults her older sister, 15-year-old Emma and learns that her family is descended from Mermaids and that she has come of age to assume her role (it appears that during the American Revolution, an ancestor rescued and married a Mermaid. The Mermaid's genes prevailed and have been passed down from generation to generation). Ella, like Emma, must keep her ancestry a secret and protect it by pretending to be just an ordinary girl.

Cast (as credited): Grace (Ella), Kaiya (Emma/Mom). Comment: The idea is good but the program suffers from a fuzzy picture and unsteady camera movement.

Episode List: *1*. The Beginning. *2*. Episode 2.

139 *I'm a Mermaid.* 2015 (Fantasy).

As a young girl (Alexa) returns home from school she finds a note on her bedroom door and reads it. It appears to have been a spell as she is immediately transformed into a Mermaid. Based on the only episode produced, it is assumed contact with water will cause future transformations and how she learns to adjust to her developing powers and keep them secret will be the focus of stories.

Cast: Brianna McIntosh (Alexa). Comment: It is hinted on the web page that there will be more adventures for Alexa. However, poor sound and photography dominate the pilot episode and if further episodes are posted, hopefully this will be corrected. The series has since been taken offline.

Episode List: *1*. Pilot.

140 *In Too Deep. youtube.com.* 2010 (Fantasy).

When Cheyenne and Skyler learn that their friend Tarah is returning to San Francisco for a visit after moving to L.A., they plan to surprise her with an evening picnic. As the picnic gets underway, a mysterious waterfall appears opposite them. Tarah and Cheyenne become fascinated and run into it but nothing happens. The next day, when Tarah and Cheyenne each come in contact with water they transform into Mermaids. Although the program ends unresolved, it does establish that Tarah and Cheyenne must act like normal girls while concealing the fact that they are Mermaids.

Cast: Claire Wewerka (Cheyenne), Mara McDonald (Tarah), Katie Wewerka (Skyler), Macie McDonald (Alex), Rebekah Wewerka (Amber), Madi McDonald (Ashley), Gabriel Wewerka (Zale). **Comment:** An overall well done production with good acting, pretty girls and decent photography.

Episode List: *1.* Disaster Picnic. *2–3.* Untitled.

141 *Infinite. youtube.com.* 2015 (Dolls).

On a warm night in June of 2008 as a mother reads a bedtime story to her daughters (Ember and Kira) she hears a rumbling noise and mutters "They know." The mother attempts to get her children to safety but is unsuccessful as she and Kira are killed. Ember wakes up in a hospital, unsure as to what happened and remembers only one thing—that her mother gave her a necklace before disaster struck. Feeling that she needs to just disappear, Ember sneaks out of the hospital and vanishes into the night.

Seven years later, Ember, who has taken the name Emma, appears to be the same. She has not aged and has come to realize she is an Infinite, an eternal person who must keep her identity and the powers she possesses a secret. She is being sought by persons unknown (to her) who want to capture her and encompasses her powers. Ember must also be careful to not stay in one place for too long as she does not age and thus she could expose herself. The program follows Ember, now as Emma, as she attempts to live a life as normal as possible while at the same time avoid the hunters who are seeking to capture her.

Cast (as credited): Ruby Matthews (Ember Shaffer), Porter Owens (Greyson Dyer), Florence Carter (Jade Ruleau), Olivia Owens (Lucy Dyer), Leia Coleman (Missy). Voices by Christina. **Comment:** Although the program is a bit hard to comprehend (especially for young children) it is very well done with good voices, doll manipulation and photography.

Episode List: 5 untitled episodes, labeled "Episode 1" through "Episode 5" have been produced.

142 *Into the Blue. youtube.com.* 2014 (Fantasy).

Maddie, Tris and Mia are friends who, while swimming in enchanted pool waters, experience a transformation into Mermaids. While they quickly learn to accept what has happened, they must now struggle to control their powers but most importantly, maintain their secret. The program was originally titled *Into the Deep.*

Cast (as credited): Stephanie (Maddie), Paulina (Tris), Augustine (Mia). **Comment:** The program starts off on the wrong foot with extreme facial close-ups coupled with difficult to understand dialogue.

Maddie is already a Mermaid when the story begins and no real effort is made to explain how. The sound is lost at times although the picture is often steady and the photography clear. Overall, the production needed some fine tuning to establish things.

Episode List: *1.* Aunts, Cousins and Pools. *2.* The Change. *3.* Lost and Found. *4.* The Flashback. *5.* It Is Here. *6.* A Magic Pool and a Mermaid's Tail. *7.* Then There Were Three. *8.* The Last Swim.

143 *Iron Man Extremis. youtube.com.* 2010 (Cartoon).

An animated update of the original Iron Man comic book character that now finds Tony Stark, a wealthy industrialist, as a weapons designer whose creations are being used in the war against Al Qaeda in Afghanistan. During an inspection tour, one of Tony's bombs explodes, and sends a piece of shrapnel into his chest that nearly kills him. He is able to save himself when he develops a special suit of armor that allows him to function without the shrapnel moving and piercing his heart. It also provides him with special abilities that will enable him to battle evil and continue with his original goal: use the profits from his weapons dealings to benefit humanitarian causes. The series itself deals with Tony, as Iron Man, as he attempts to stop Mallen, a government-hating terrorist that has been transformed into a killing machine by a stolen experimental serum called Extremis.

Voice Cast: Jason Griffith (Tony Stark/Iron Man), Therese Spurrier (Maya Hansen), Ted Lewis (Mallen). **Credits:** *Producer:* Dan Buckley, Alan Fine, Ruwan Jayatilleke. *Director:* Dan Green, Mike Halsey, Joel Gibbs. *Writer:* Stan Lee, Warren Ellis, Don Heck, Ruwan Jayatilleke, Jack Kirby, Larry Lieber. **Comment:** Excellent animation coupled with good voice characterizations and a fast-moving, action-themed story.

Episode List: 6 untitled episodes, labeled "Episode 1" Through "Episode 6" have been produced.

144 *The Italian Mermaids. youtube.com.* 2012 (Fantasy).

Melissa and Danny are friends hanging out at Danny's house when they spot two cups, filled with what looks like water, on the kitchen counter. The girls, believing they were placed there by Melissa's mother, take a drink. The liquid is bitter and they just dismiss it. A short time later, when each girl comes in contact with water, she transforms into a Mermaid. While the program does follow their efforts to keep secret what has happened, they find their secret at risk when an unknown person (dressed as an alien) is aware that they are Mermaids, snaps a picture of Danny in her Mermaid state and reports back to his superior—an unknown person who has plans for both Melissa and Danny.

Cast (as credited): Sophie (Melissa), Chloe

(Danny). **Comment:** While it is not explained why the program has the title it has, it is well done with acceptable acting and photography.

Episode List: *1*. Mermaids Exist. *2*. Power Potion. *3*. Taken. *4*. Psycho Boy.

145 *It's My Mermaid Life.* *youtube.com.* 2010 (Dolls).

A day at the beach turns magical for a girl named Emily when she finds stones that have been washed ashore by the ocean's waves. Unknown to Emily, the stones are sacred and have what could be called a curse as "who ever finds them will be turned into a Mermaid." Emily, having touched the stones, transforms into a Mermaid and must now keep a secret while not only adjusting to her developing powers, but pretend to be an ordinary girl.

Cast: A girl listed only as Zoe provides the voices. **Comment:** Although the girl (Zoe) handling the dolls can be seen manipulating them, it is still well done and enjoyable.

Episode List: *1*. Washed Up.

146 *Jedi Camp.* *youtube.com.* 2012–2013 (Adventure).

As the visual in the opening theme explains, the setting is "a short time ago in a galaxy not so far away." Here a man named Paul Powell (the Chancellor) has established Jedi Camp, basing his training program on the Jedi troopers from the film *Star Wars*. The troopers here, however, are middle school children who attend classes during summer school breaks to learn the way of the Jedi. Leia, who, like Paul, appears to be something other than she is, is the main instructor; and a camper, Lucas, may also be something more than just a young boy. The campers attend a six week course wherein they learn the skills and the ways of "The Force." It is during the last week of training that each camper must enter the Tournament of Champions and prove their abilities to be crowned a Jedi Knight—but only one such camper will win that honor. While the program does chart Lucas's journey to become a Jedi Knight, it also focuses on bullying and how kids handle it (here Lucas being bullied by a fellow camper named Andy).

Cast: Stuart Allan (Lucas), Amanda Ward (Leia), Keith Szarabajka (Paul), Andy Scott Harris (Andy), Hunter Cudini (Hunter), Gabe Eggerling (Gabe), Morgan Bertsch (Morgan), Maya Rush (Maya), Andrew Bowen (Harry), Korbyn Hawk Hanan (Korbyn), Raevan Lee Hanan (Raevan). **Credits:** *Producer*: William Ostroff, Scott Cronan, Tai Fauci, Jack Monroe. *Writer-Director*: William Ostroff. **Comment:** The program is very well done (compares to a network TV production) with excellent acting and production values. It also encompasses the original *Star Wars* theme and music.

Episode List: *1*. A New Camper. *2*. The Bully Strikes Back. *3*. Rebound of the Jedi. *4*. The Camp Menace. *5*. Attack of the Bullies. *6*. Rise of the Jedi.

147 *The Jolly Rogers Case Files.* *orsothestory goes.com.* 2015 (Comedy).

A spin off from the "Happy Thoughts" episode of *Or So the Story Goes* (see entry). "Happy Thoughts" told the story of a ghost hunting team (Jane Hook, Ronnie, Percy and Julian) as they attempt to rid the Darling home of an evil ghost that has attached himself to the daughter, Wendy.

Jane Hook, the team leader, was drawn into the world of the supernatural when she encountered the ghost of a young boy that destroyed her world and eventually led her to form a paranormal team (The Jolly Rogers) to help people threatened by supernatural forces (and in a way, to hopefully end her own nightmare). Episodes follow the cases Jane tackles with an overall goal to become famous by appearing on the reality television series *Paranormal Uncovered* (but questioning whether she has the credentials to prove her worthiness).

Cast: Melissa Malone (Jane Hook), Diann Gogerty (Percy Ames), Christopher Michael Christiana (Julian), Bryan Civitarese (Ronnie). **Credits:** *Producer*: Outtake Productions. *Director*: Theresa Labreglio. *Writer*: Theresa Labreglio, Melissa Malone. **Comment:** The program, like *The Haunting of Sunshine Girl* (see entry), is not as frightening as ghost-related series seen on the cable channel Destination American but its subject matter does draw children to them. The producers of both shows took into consideration that children may be watching. It is somewhat like the TV series *Goosebumps* in that suspense is presented but not in manner that will upset children. The acting and production values are very good and the story flows smoothly from episode to episode.

Episode List: *1*. The Interview. *2*. Case 21D. *3*. Case 6C. *4*. 9L. *5*. Case 42G. *6*. Case 13F. *7*. Case 88E. *8*. Case 85B. *9*. Case 88F. *10*. Case 66P. *11*. Case 31M. *12*. PU Audition.

148 *Just Add Magic.* *youtube.com.* 2015 (Comedy).

While in the attic of her home, Kelly and her two best friends, Darbie and Hannah find a mysterious cookbook hidden many years ago by her grandmother. As the girls look through the book they find such recipes as Healing Hazelnut Tarts, Shut-Up Strawberry Shortcake, Chipper Chocolate Chip Cookies and Lazy Lasagna. While it is not made exactly clear in the free snippet episodes, Kelly believes that the book is somehow cursed and her grandmother is under a spell. She feels that the only way to break the curse is to prepare the recipes and hope to find the one concoction that will do the trick. The book also comes with a warning: "Whenever adding cedronian spice, whatever results will come with a price." The program follows Kelly, Darbie and Hannah as they experiment with the various recipes and how their use can become more troublesome than helpful (eating Lazy Lasagna, for example, causes one to become lazy; Strawberry Shut-Up Cake causes one to lose their ability to talk).

Cast: Olivia Sanabia (Kelly Quinn), Abby Donnelly (Darbie), Aubrey K. Miller (Hannah), Judah Bellamy (Jake), Amy Hill (Mama P), Brady Reiter (Charlotte), Matt Knudsen (Coach Richards), Aiden Lovekamp (Buddy Quinn), Jama Williamson (Mrs. Quinn), Andrew Burlinson (Mr. Quinn). **Credits:** *Producer*: Andrew Cholerton, Frank Merwald, Kim Tushinsky. *Director*: Joe Nussbau. *Writer*: Nancy Cohen, Joanna Lewis, Kristine Songco. **Comment:** A very well produced and acted program on which only brief segments can be seen on YouTube for free (it can be seen in full for a fee on Amazon Prime). It is a bit like the Nickelodeon series *Talia in the Kitchen* which uses the same situation as a teenage girl experiments with supposedly cursed spices once used by her father, a chef.

Episode List: *1.* Grandma's Cookbook. *2.* Keep Cooking. *3.* First Cake. *4.* Basketball Practice. *5.* Buddy Can't Talk; the Team Captain Is…

149 Justice League Gods and Monsters Chronicles. *youtube.com.* 2015 (Cartoon).

Batman, Superman and Wonder Woman, members of the DC Comics Justice League of America, are given new lives in an alternate reality where each character, now a member of the Justice League Gods and Monsters, battles the evil that also exists there. Here Kirk Langstrom is Batman (not Bruce Gordon); Hernan Guerra is Superman (not Clark Kent) and Bekka of the New Gods (not Diana Prince) is Wonder Woman.

In the first episode, "Twisted," Batman battles Harlequin, a deranged woman who not only enjoys killing people but delights in either mutilating their bodies or turning them into taxidermy-like figures with freakish grins. The twist here: When Batman finally captures Harlequin, he is seen with retractile wings, and like a vampire bat, bites Harlequin on the neck to satisfy his thirst for blood.

The second episode, "Bomb," focuses on Superman (here the son of Zod, not Jor-El) and his battle against Brainiac, who is threatening to not only destroy Metropolis, but the entire East Coast with a red energy field. It is shown that Superman also kills, destroying Brainiac when he confronts him.

"Big," the third episode finds Wonder Woman coming to the aid of Steve Trevor to stop the evil organization, Kobra from unleashing a destructive super weapon on the world. While they appear to achieve their goal, Wonder Woman's killing of the Kobra leader with her sword causes a chain reaction that unleashes Giganta, a towering blue female-shaped robot that is actually a super weapon and appears to be unstoppable (until Wonder Woman teleports into Giganta's head and destroys the wiring to her brain to disable her).

Twisted Voice Cast: Michael C. Hall (Batman), Tara Strong (Harlequin).

Bomb Voice Cast: Benjamin Bratt (Superman), Paget Brewster (Lois Lane), Daniel Hagen (Dr. Sivana), Penny Johnson Jerald (Amanda Waller), Tara Strong (Brainiac).

Big Voice Cast: Tamara Taylor (Wonder Woman), Tahmoh Penikett (Steve Trevor), Bruce Thomas (Kobra).

Credits: *Producer*: Sam Register, Bruce Timm, Alan Burnett. *Voice Director*: Wes Gleason. *Director*: Bruce Timm; *Writer*: Alan Burnett, J.M. DeMatteis. **Comment:** The three episode first season serves as a companion to the animated film *Justice League: Gods and Monsters*. A second season of ten episodes was announced beginning in 2016. The animation is excellent but the stories are a bit violent especially since the main super heroes are seen in a different light (like all three killing their enemies). It is unknown at the time of publication if the second season will follow the tradition previously set or revert the characters to their less violent ways.

Episode List: *1.* Twisted. *2.* Bomb. *3.* Big.

150 Keeping a Mermaid Secret. *youtube. com.* 2011 (Fantasy).

While in the backyard of her home a young girl (Taylor) becomes fascinated by a necklace that she finds on the ground. She places it around her neck and returns to the house for a drink of water. As she touches the water she transforms into a Mermaid. The program, which appears to have been abandoned, just ends here with no text or video information as to what will occur next.

Cast (as credited): Ariana (Taylor). **Comment:** The program would no doubt follow Taylor's efforts to keep her secret; it has acceptable acting and photography but the sound becomes poor toward the end of the episode.

Episode List: *1.* Pilot.

151 The Kicks. *youtube.com.* 2015 (Comedy-Drama).

Nickelodeon's series *Bella and the Bulldogs* follows a girl (Bella) who becomes a member of her school's football team, the Bulldogs. *The Kicks* follows a girl (Devin Burke) who, after moving to California, becomes a member of her school's soccer team. Like Bella, Devin becomes the hope of her team and the program charts Devin's experience as she attempts to turn a losing team into a winning team.

Cast: Sixx Orange (Devin Burke), Emyri Crutchfield (Zoe Knox), Gabe Eggerling (Bailey Burke), Sophia Mitri Schloss (Emma Gelbaum), Monica

Lacy (Sharon Burke), Tim Martin Gleason (Tom Burke), Isabella Acres (Mirabelle Harris), Madison Hu (Kara), Noah Urrea (Cody McBride), Noemi Gonzalez (Coach Flores), Alex Morgan (Herself). **Credits:** *Producer:* David Babcock, Todd Cohen, James Frey. *Director:* Elizabeth Allen Rosenbaum. *Writer:* David Babcock. **Comment:** The program is based on the book by Olympic gold medalist (U.S. Women's Soccer Team) Alex Morgan. It is well acted and produced but only previews are available for free on YouTube (it is produced for Amazon Prime and a fee is required to watch). Madison Hu co-stars on the Disney Channel series *Best Friends Whenever* as Marci.

Episode List: *1.* Pilot.

152 *Kid's Town. youtube.com.* 2013 (Comedy).

Brian Russell is the 12-year-old son of Paul Russell, a peace officer who constantly uproots Brian as the demands of his job make it necessary to move from one location to another. The town of Bailey's Path (where Paul is now the Deputy Police Chief) has become their current home and Brian again finds himself the new kid in town. This time, however, he discovers that Bailey's Path is not like any other town for here children are equal to adults and have just as much "power, culture and intelligence" (for example, the Mayor's son is king of the playground). Brian also finds that at school he has become a part of "small town playground politics" and his experiences, as he encounters a first love, small town civics and power struggles, while struggling to figure out his place in the world, are depicted.

Keith Lightfoot is a paperboy (for the *Daily Bailey*) who aspires to become a journalist; Jamie Redshaw is the Mayor's son and the leader of the town's kids; Vanessa Boyd is the smartest girl in school (and the object of affection for both Brian and Jamie); Brian Smith, Jr., is Brian's newest friend; Lynn Boyd is Vanessa's mother, the librarian and town council woman; Beth Pilly is Vanessa's best friend; Eric Gregory is the schoolyard bully; Travis Redshaw is the Mayor; Jarvis Lightfoot is the newspaper editor; Jessica Lightfoot is Keith's sister; Justine is the local store owner. **Cast:** David Knoll (Brian Russell), David Dodsley (Paul Russell), Jeni Ross (Vanessa Boyd), Emilia McCarthy (Beth Pilly), Noah Ryan Scott (Jamie Redshaw), Jacob Ewanuik (Keith Lightfoot), Richard Davis (Brian Smith, Jr.), Ryan Manning (Eric Gregory), Darrin Baker (Travis Redshaw), David Schaap (Jarvis Lightfoot), Raven Adamson (Jessica Lightfoot), Merle Matheson (Justine). **Credits:** *Producer:* Jeff Knoll, Michael Heuthe. *Director:* Mikelle Virey. *Writer:* Tomas Street. **Comment:** The program is produced in Canada with very good acting and production values. While the series is aimed at children, it can be enjoyed by adults also. It is literally a look at how children navigate life when everything appears so confusing.

Episode List: *1.* New Kid in Town. *2.* Friend or Foe. *3.* Drive Thru. *4.* Face to Face. *5.* Speak and Be Heard. *6.* It's Not a Date. *7.* A Night at the Movies. *8.* Align Yourself. *9.* The Fake Article. *10.* Your File. *11.* Reason to Stay. *12.* Who's in Charge Here?

153 *Kira the Mermaid. youtube.com.* 2013 (Fantasy).

Kira is a young girl who constantly dreams about becoming a Mermaid. One day, after a nap, she awakens feeling that something is just not right. As she goes for a drink of water, she accidentally spills some on herself and magically transforms into a Mermaid. Or has she? It was, as she discovers, just another dream, when she actually awakens. The dreams continue and unknown to Kira, they are actually an omen of what is to come. Several days later Kira's dream becomes a reality when contact with water transforms her into a Mermaid. Kira must now keep secret what happened and pretend to be an ordinary girl while adjusting to and learning to use her Mermaid powers.

Cast: Kira Manning (Kira). **Comment:** Kira is very pretty and the program moves right along with good acting and photography. It is also different than other Mermaid series in that Kira's father (Rikk) is part of the program (adults are just not seen in others) as is her younger sister Lily. This does add a different feel but only two episodes have been produced and the story remains unresolved.

Episode List: *2* untitled episodes, labeled "Episode 1" and "Episode 2" have been produced.

154 *Krogzilla. youtube.com.* 2012 (Cartoon).

Krogzilla is a variation of the Japanese monster Godzilla. He lives among humans and despite his prehistoric-like lizard appearance, is accepted as a part of society. He also held down a job but has recently been downsized (by 200 feet). He lists his job skills as smashing cars, sinking oil tankers and fire-breathing and only wants a new job so he can pay the rent. Krogzilla is green, now stands about six feet tall and the program charts his mishaps as he seeks to find suitable employment that fit his skills (all of which are compromised by Marcus, the barnacle that lives with him).

Voice Cast: Cory Edwards (Krogzilla), Josh Greene (Marcus). **Credits:** *Producer-Writer-Director:* Cory Edwards. **Comment:** Krogzilla doesn't resemble any of the feature film versions of Godzilla and has his own unique green appearance. The animation is acceptable with good voices and stories.

Episode List: *1.* The Interview. *2.* Big Dogs. *3.* Attack of the Kiosk. *4.* Tiny Buildings. *5.* Regurgitated. *6.* Party Marty. *7.* Pet Store. *8.* The Sub. *9.* Price Bombers. *10.* Deconstruction.

155 *The Language of the Waves. youtube. com.* 2015 (Fantasy).

At Nika Island, Maldives, a young girl (Alexia) is swimming in the ocean when she finds and necklace and places it around her neck. The necklace transforms Alexia into a Mermaid, but that is only part of a new life she must now lead. Shortly after, she finds an old journal ("The Journal of Emily Rate") and learns that the ocean's waters also turned that girl into a Mermaid. With her vacation ended, Alexia and her family return to their home in America. Upon entering her bedroom Alexia finds a note: "Hello. This is the Mermaid Government. Say this magic spell: 'Human on land, fish in the sea will be forever united with me.'" Alexia complies and is again transformed into a Mermaid—but this time on dry land. Suddenly, a girl, her Mermaid Government Agent, appears as a Guardian Angel of sorts to help Alexia learn how to be a good Mermaid and embark on a dangerous quest that could cost Alexia her life.

Many centuries ago Mermaids and (what are now considered evil) Sirens lived together in peace and harmony. Their sea world was ruled by the Mermaid Government which was composed of both Mermaids and Sirens. One day Mermaids decided they wanted to rule and destroyed the Siren officials. When the Mermaids created a new government the Sirens revolted and a war was begun that still rages today. The Mermaids, in essence, turned the once peaceful Sirens evil and Alexia, considered the Chosen One, must somehow use her abilities as a Mermaid to stop the Sirens from overthrowing the Mermaid Government and once again restore the peace.

Cast (as credited): The Little Mermaid (Alexa/Calyssa/Aqua/Lydia), Hanna (Herself), Kay (Herself). **Comment:** The program has excellent underwater photography but the overall production is hampered by very poor sound (to compensate for this, the characters' dialogue appears on screen as they speak).

Episode List: *1.* A Foamy Secret. *2.* A Family Secret. *3.* The More the Merrier … Or Not. *4.* Tentative n*2. *5.* The Destiny Necklace. *6.* Consequences. *7.* A Significant Dream.

156 *The Last Mermaids. youtube.com.* 2010 (Fantasy).

Evelyn and Vanessa are young girls who find what appear to be just ordinary heart necklaces. However, after placing them around their necks they are transformed into Mermaids when they come in contact with water. Now with a secret they must share, Evelyn and Vanessa begin their lives as Mermaids while pretending to be ordinary school girls.

Cast (as credited): Evelyn and Vanessa (Themselves). **Comment:** The program is rather slow-moving but has acceptable acting and photography.

Episode List: *1.* Freeze, Stop, Go. *2.* Flopped. *3.* Ring Equals More Powers? *4.* Falling Over. *5.* Snow Tails. *6.* Bad Dream. *7.* The Lost Mermaids Grave.

157 *The Last Splash. youtube.com.* 2013 (Fantasy).

Avery is a young girl who finds an unknown liquid, and without thinking first, drinks it. She realizes, the following day, that what she did was a mistake as she has been transformed into a Mermaid. Avery's adventures, as she tries to adjust to being a Mermaid while also living the life of an ordinary girl are chronicled.

Cast: Kira Brown (Avery). **Comment:** Avery is pretty but the production is very poor. Background voices interrupt the flow of the program and the sound is very low at times

Episode List: *1.* What's New? *2.* I Still Have a Tail. *3–4.* Captured.

158 *Legend of the Animal Healer. youtube. com.* 2012 (Cartoon).

Martine is a teenage girl who, after the death of her parents in a fire, is sent to live with her only known relative, her grandmother Gwyn Thomas, who operates a game reserve in South Africa. As Martine settles into her new life she begins to hear stories about a white giraffe, a mythical creature that no one has ever seen but is said to leave footprints as it wanders. Gwyn dismisses the story, telling Martine it is nothing but local native superstition. One stormy night however, Martine is startled to see the white giraffe when she looks out of her bedroom window. The following day Martine begins a quest to see if the white giraffe really exists or if it was a figment of her imagination. As Martine begins her search, she encounters a deadly cobra and is saved when the white giraffe intervenes. The white giraffe (named Gemmy by Martine), and Martine quickly become friends. Gemmy is not the only secret hidden in the jungle. At the cave in which Gemmy lives, Martine meets Grace, a medicine woman who protects the white giraffe and realizes that Martine "has the power" (to help animals). Grace gives Martine a special a bag of vials that contain ancient medicines that can heal. The story follows what happens when Gemmy is stolen by poachers and Martine, assisted by her schoolmate Ben, attempt to save Gemmy and return her to her native land. (Martine learns that she can heal when Gemmy is wounded and she administers the special medicines to save her.)

Voice Cast: Sabrina Amran (Martine). **Comment:** The series is based on the children's book *The White Giraffe* by Lauren St. Jhon and is animated by a young girl (Shoshana Hetherington). The animation is stiff (very little movement) but well done for this type of project.

Episode List: 7 untitled episodes, labeled "Episode 1" through "Episode 7" have been produced.

159 Legend of the Mermaid. 2012 (Fantasy).

Two girls (Aeryn and Kathy) are in a boat on the ocean when they venture out a bit further than they had intended and find themselves drifting toward an unknown island. As they begin exploring the island they stumble across a pool of water that looks harmless. As they venture in for a swim, rays from a full moon shine down and engulf the girls in a swirl of bubbling water. While they are not immediately affected, Aeryn and Kathy later experience a transformation into Mermaids when they return home and come in contact with water. Their efforts to keep secret what happened, adjust to their developing Mermaid powers and pretend to be ordinary girls is the focal point of stories.

Cast (as credited): Rikki Fox (Aeryn), Suzette (Kathy), Cristelle (Girl on Beach). **Comment:** The program which has since been taken offline, features pretty girls but only fair sound and photography.

Season 1 Episode List: *1.* The Beginning. *2.* Powers. *3.* Water Troubles. *4.* Beginning or the End? *5.* Just in Time. *6.* Heat Everything. *7.* Memories.

Season 2 Episode List: *1.* A New Discovery. *2.* Journey to the Past. *3.* Overdose Fishiness.

160 Life as Dolls. *youtube.com.* 2014 (Dolls).

Barbie dolls apparently have the same problems as humans and the program charts the experiences of one such doll family, the Wilson's: Bridget, Lexi, Katie, Cosette and Jayn.

Voices (as credited): Hodappk71. **Comment:** While the doll manipulation and photography are good, the young girl providing the voices speaks softly at times making it a bit hard to hear.

Episode List: *1.* Our New Home. *2.* The Selfie Experience.

161 Life at Westmount. *youtube.com.* 2011 (Dolls).

American Girl dolls become "real" to relate life at Westmount Academy, a school for young ladies. Because only a pilot film was produced, it introduces the two main girls, Bella and Sophie as they acquire jobs at Starbucks.

Voices (as credited): Sydney and Summer. **Comment:** The camera work is a bit shaky and Sydney and Summer do show their arms and hands while manipulating the dolls. Other American Girl series do not have this aspect and perhaps the mean comments listed on YouTube bringing out this fault may have led the girls to abandoning their project. Despite what happened, the girls do deserve credit for doing a good job in presenting their idea.

Episode List: *1.* Pilot.

162 Life of a Mermaid. 2011 (Fantasy).

What appears to be a typical summer day turns into a magical surprise for two young girls (Katie and Rikki) when the pool in which they are swimming is engulfed by light from a crescent moon and transforms them into Mermaids. Realizing that they must keep secret what has happened to them, Katie and Rikki attempt to conceal their Mermaid life while pretending to be ordinary girls.

Cast as Credited: Macy (Rikki and Emily), Kensley (Katie), Emma (Kylie), Charlie (Rose). **Comment:** The program does feature pretty girls but the sound is a bit low at times. It has since been taken offline.

Episode List: *1.* The Cave. *2.* Getting Wet, Part 1. *3.* Getting Wet, Part 2. *4.* No Fish. *5.* Changing Waters. *6.* Power Play/New Neighbor. *7.* The Sun. *8.* The Crystal's Power. *9.* No Tail. *10.* Finding Out Why. *11.* Green?

163 The Life of a Secret Mermaid. 2011 (Fantasy).

Two girls, Amy and Blare, are seen as being Mermaids, but there is no explanation as to how their transformation occurred. In fact, nothing much of anything is established as the girls are just seen talking to each other; it ends with a rain storm approaching and the girls rushing into a house to avoid getting wet.

Cast (as credited): Katie (Amy), Chloe (Blair). **Comment:** The program, which contains poor sound and picture quality, just has no substance. It opens in the middle of nowhere and ends the same way. It has since been taken offline.

Episode List: *1.* Heat Wave. *2.* Briny Dilemma.

164 Life of a Teenage Werewolf. *youtube. com.* 2013 (Dolls).

A simple trip to the mailbox by a young girl (Brianna Roberts) turns frightening when she finds a note telling her that something is out to get her. Seconds later an unknown beast attacks her and scratches her face. Another note appears and informs her that she has been inducted into the Twilight School of Werewolves. Although Brianna does not understand why she has been chosen, she accepts what happened and enrolls in the school. The program follows Brianna as she attempts to adjust to her new life as a werewolf.

Voices (as credited): Victoria. **Comment:** The LPS (Littlest Pet Shop) dolls are used and here a white dog represents Brianna when she is normal; and brown dog shows her in her werewolf state. Good photography, voice characterizations and doll manipulation highlight the program.

Episode List: 12 untitled episodes, labeled "Episode 1" through "Episode 12" have been produced.

165 The Life of Bratz. *youtube.com.* 2010 (Dolls).

The Bratz Dolls are incorporated to tell the story of a group of teenage girls living in Chicago. Particular focus is on Amy and Brittney, rivals for a boy named Cole.

Voices (as credited): Cutiechick 74. **Comment:** Acceptable production with good voices, doll manipulation and photography.

Episode List: 3 untitled episodes, labeled "Episode 1," "Episode 2" and "Episode 3" have been produced.

166 *The Life of 2 Mermaids.* 2013 (Fantasy).

April and Kelly are friends who, while in the backyard of April's home, find a bottle filled with a liquid left by persons unknown. Foolishly, the girls take a sip and appear to find that it was only distasteful. Later, however, when April and Kelly come in contact with water, they are transformed into Mermaids. The program appears to have been abandoned and just ends here. It is assumed it would have followed the format of other such program with the girls struggling to keep secret what happened to them.

Cast (as credited): Alana (April), Grace (Kelly), Roxy, Leo, Adam. **Comment:** Only April and Kelly appear in the episode. It appears more episodes were planned but for unexplained reasons, only a pilot aired. The acting and photography are acceptable but the program has since been taken offline.

Episode List: *1.* Pilot.

167 *Life with Barbie.* *youtube.com.* 2013 (Dolls).

The Mattel line of Barbie Dolls are encompassed in a story wherein Barbie, just moving into a new home, must also contend with the antics of her sisters, Bethany, Skipper, Stacey and Chelsea, who have taken it upon themselves to move in with her.

Voices (as credited): Kelsey. **Comment:** Kelsey not only handles the dolls well, but her voice characterizations (as well as the photography) are very good.

Episode List: *1.* Sister Madness. *2.* Too Much Coffee. *3.* That Single Guy. *4.* Fall Fever. *5.* Halloween Havoc. *6.* Christmas Chaos. *7.* Jealousy Cheese. *8.* Trapped Turkeys. *9.* Too Much Tea. *10.* Movie Theater Mayhem. *11.* Ambush at Rosebush.

168 *Lily the Unicorn.* *youtube.com.* 2015 (Cartoon).

In a world within our world there is a land where unicorns exist and through the magic they possess they can make the impossible happen. Lily is one such unicorn and her experiences as she interacts with her friends and simply seeks to spread happiness are depicted.

Voice Cast: Marieve Herington (Lily), Amanda Philipson (Doris/Djuna), Phil LaMarr (Roger), Jess

Harnell (Graham/Guru). **Credits:** *Producer:* Dallas Clayton, Lisa Henson, Halle Stanford. *Writer:* Jackie Buscarino, Dallas Clayton. **Comment:** The program, based on the book by Dallas Clayton, is produced in association with the Jim Henson Company and Amazon Prime; select episodes can be viewed for free on YouTube. The animation is a bit crude but acceptable for its prime audience—young children.

Episode List: *1.* Falafel Waffle Song. *2.* Food Stand Friends. *3.* The Guru.

169 *The Lives of the Secret Mermaids.* 2009 (Fantasy).

As the program begins an unknown person is seen pouring something (fish oil) into the water of a pool. Later that day two young girls, Bella and Alyssa, are enjoying themselves in that pool when they notice a fishy smell emanating from the water and decide to leave and return home. Shortly after, when they come in contact with water they transform into Mermaids. Now, with a secret to share and developing powers that they must learn to control, the program relates their efforts to conceal what has happened and pretend to be ordinary girls.

Cast (as credited): Teeniepup 989 (Bella), Bumpoo 34 (Alyssa). **Comment:** Acceptable production with good photography, pretty girls and an interesting take on how two girls become Mermaids. The program, however, has since been taken offline.

Episode List: *1.* The First Splash. *2.* The Mishap. *3.* The Power Within. *4.* Pool Party. *5.* The Hidden Secret.

170 *L.J.'s Trip.* *vimeo.com.* 2013 (Fantasy).

L.J. is the host of an educational television series wherein he relates historical facts to children. But unlike any other such host, L.J. possesses a time machine that allows him to return to a specific era and report first hand on what happened. Accompanied by his robot (and photographer) Cambot, the program charts L.J.'s mishaps in various time periods as a time traveler who can't quite adjust to time travel.

Cast: Joel Stigliano (L.J.). **Credits:** *Producer:* Ben Guenther. *Writer-Director:* Mike Gray, Matt Brunson. **Comment:** Comedy blends with fantasy in a concept that was presented in a more serious side on the TV series *You Are There* and *Captain Z-Ro* in the 1950s. The program has possibilities as there is a lot to explore—whether it is by comedy or drama.

Episode List: *1.* The Salem Sisters. *2.* The Origin of Tools. *3.* Magic. *4.* To the Future.

171 *Lost in Oz.* *youtube.com.* 2015 (Cartoon).

Dorothy Gale, the 12-year-old daughter of Evelyn Gale (the daughter of the original Dorothy from *The Wizard of Oz*) accidentally stumbles upon her grandmother's journal that details her adventures as a child in the magical land of Oz. As Dorothy opens the book she sees a page with a message that reads "Say Go Forth." Dorothy reads the message aloud and suddenly finds herself trapped in her room in a tornado-like wind. Dorothy is able to contact her mother by phone but learns there is no way to stop what is happening and she will be transported from her Kansas home to Emerald City in the Land of Oz. Before she and her dog Toto are swept away, Evelyn tells Dorothy to follow the Yellow Brick Line and find an address (41 and Infinity). While Dorothy's house does not land on a witch (as in the movie), it is seen that Oz has been transformed into a modern city with a citizenship other than Munchkins. As Dorothy tries to find the address her mother gave her, she meets West, a young witch who has been sent to find her (West's mother is a friend of Evelyn and Evelyn had contacted her to help Dorothy). At the address she is seeking Dorothy discovers that in order for her to return home she must find one of each of the 100 magical elements that are common in Oz. The program charts Dorothy's journey, accompanied by West and West's friend, Ojo, a giant Munchkin, as they seek the magic elements.

Cast: Landry Bender (Dorothy Gale), Nika Futterman (West/Triplets), Jorge Diaz (Ojo), Chris Cox (Toto/Winged Monkeys), Alexander Polinsky (Fitz), Allison Mack (Evelyn Gale). **Credits:** *Producer:* Abram Makowka, Darin Mark, Jared Mark, Richard Scott, Mark D. Warshaw. *Director:* Paul Stodolny.

Comment: Although the program, which can be viewed in full for a fee on Amazon Prime, a snippet can be viewed for free on YouTube. It is computer animated and very well done. Landry Bender co-stars with Lauren Taylor on the Disney Channel TV series *Best Friends Whenever.*

Episode List: *1.* Pilot.

172 The Lost Tails. *youtube.com.* 2012 (Fantasy).

Although she has had her plush panda for a number of years, a young girl (Saffire) notices a necklace on it that she has never seen before. Curious, Saffire takes the necklace off the panda and places it around her neck. Moments later, when she goes for a drink of water, she transforms into a Mermaid. Now, with a secret to keep, Saffire must also learn how to adjust to her developing powers and pretend to be an ordinary girl.

Cast: Saffire Strong (Saffire). **Comment:** The program suffers from poor video quality as well as blackout scenes and low sound that make it just difficult to watch.

Episode List: *1.* The Mermaid Dream. *2.* He Found Out.

173 A Luxurious Bratz Life. *youtube.com.* 2011 (Dolls).

A look at a group of high school freshmen (Bratz dolls Victoria, Meghan, Jessie, Summer, Kinsey, Chris, Austin and Jeremiah) "all new to this jazz" as they embark on the first stage of their adult lives.

Voices (as credited): TMGB (themightyguppybear). **Comment:** Good doll manipulation coupled good voices and photography.

Episode List: 10 untitled episodes, labeled "Episode 1" Through "Episode 10" have been produced.

174 The Mad Life. *youtube.com.* 2014 (Dolls).

Events in the lives of a group of teenagers: Skittles ("The Cute One"), Mickey (a girl, "The Bad One"), Johanna ("The Rebel"), Michael ("The Nerdy One"), Kurt ("The Rapper"), Maddie ("The Heartbreaker") and Steve ("The Nice Guy").

Comment: Other than the creator, "Generator 12," there is no cast listed. The doll movement is okay but the picture is a bit shaky at times.

Episode List: 4 untitled episodes, labeled "Episode 1" through "Episode 4" have been produced.

175 MadLo Show. *webserieschannel.com.* 2012 (Children).

A variety show geared to children with interviews, guest performances, talent contests and games. But it also comes with a warning that it is "a comedy for kids by kids for entertainment purposes only. It is intended for the minds of mindless individuals. Do not try to do any of the stunts you may see ... as we are not responsible for any injuries that might occur or places you may get thrown out of ... in that case you would be one of the mindless individuals that we are talking about."

Cast: Ashley Lonardo, Jessica Lonardo, Alex Madera. **Credits:** *Producer:* Jennifer Lonardo. *Director:* Ashley Lonardo. *Writer:* Jessica Lonardo, Alex Madera. **Comment:** Immediately you will be struck as to how natural the child hosts are; it is like they are just being themselves and not acting. Overall the program is well done and presented but on-location scenes suffer from very poor camera work (images are very shaky, sometimes blurry and, while this can be seen as acceptable as approaching unsuspecting people for interviews does not always go as planned and the camera operator must follow the hosts).

Episode List: 8 untitled episodes, labeled "Episode 1" Through "Episode 8" have been produced.

176 Magic in the Water. 2015 (Fantasy).

Alex, Samantha and Tess are young girls who stumble across a strange recipe for a drink that so intrigues them that they decide to make it. The end result (a potion) looks appealing and each girl takes a sip. Alex, Samantha and Tess transform into Mermaids and must now keep secret what happened while pretending to be ordinary girls.

Cast (as credited): Sammi (Alex/Samantha/Tess/Marceline), Jordan (Ivan). **Comment:** Sammi does a good job portraying four characters with a well produced program that has since been taken offline.

Episode List: *1.* The Magic Begins. *2.* Marceline and Ivan's New Life. *3.* Found. *4.* Sirens. *5.* Mermaids vs. Sirens. *6.* The Siren's Potion.

177 *Magic Island.* 2015 (Fantasy).

Rosie and River are best friends who do everything together, no matter how much trouble they get into. One day, while contemplating what to do for a science project, Rosie suggests they go to the stream (that is near their home) and gather various rocks for a presentation. Although the stream is active (and deep), its shore is quite muddy and the girls manage to get their legs covered in mud while searching for rocks. To wash the mud off, Rosie and River elect to go swimming in the stream. It appears that the mud, when combined with the stream water, activates a recessed gene each carries that transforms them into Mermaids. Rosie and River must now keep secret what happened as they pretend to be ordinary girls while adjusting to their developing powers.

Cast (as credited): Kayla (Rosie), Poppy (River). **Comment:** The story and acting are good but the filming is below par. Not only are some scenes shaky but the fingers of the person filming can be seen over the lens. It has since been taken offline.

Episode List: *1.* Is It a Dream? *2.* Powers.

178 *The Magic Shell Mermaids. youtube. com.* 2011–2013 (Fantasy).

A day at the beach turns into more than just swimming when two young girls (Lexi and Sofia) stumble across magical sea shells that endow them with the ability to become Mermaids when they come in contact with water. While the program does chronicle their efforts to keep their abilities secret it also focuses on Lexi and Sofia's encounter with an evil Siren and decision they must make: whether or not to join King Neptune in the undersea kingdom and assist him in keeping the oceans safe.

Cast (as credited): Taylor (Sofia), Bella (Lexi). **Comment:** One of the longer-running Mermaid series that, despite its sometimes poor sound and questionable photography, does present an intriguing story as the girls adjust to becoming Mermaids.

Episodes, 1–20:
1. The Magic Shell.
2. A Fishy Secret.
3. Investigation and Teleportation.
4. Power Showers.
5. A Lake Date.
6. Bubbles Bring Best Friends.
7. A Siren's Tale.
8. A Mermaid's Gift.
9. Neptune's Honor.
10. Treasure Hunt.
11. Mermaid's Necklace.
12. More Powers.
13. Potion Commotion.
14. Mysterious Voice.
15. Cave Conniption.
16. River's Tail.
17. Kidnapped.
18. Found.
19. Half-Scaled.
20. Dream Chased.

Episodes, 21–37:
21. Moon Stones.
22. Best Friend For-Never.
23. Dayna's Secret.
24. Frenemies?
25. Siren's Trinket.
26. Rained Out.
27. Which Witch Is Which?
28. Amethyst's Voice.
29. Intruder.
30. Taken.
31. Moon Blinded.
32. Message in a Bottle.
33. Siren Sofia.
34. New Mermaid?!?!
35. Time Travel Tails.
36. Hurricane of MerPowers.
37. Concluding Episode.

179 *Magic Tails (2011). youtube.com.* 2011–2012 (Fantasy).

As a young girl (Lela) walks along the beach shore she finds a dolphin necklace and a mysterious liquid (Magic Mio) that she is compelled to drink (possibly from possession of the necklace). The liquid not only transforms her into a Mermaid, but her friends Taylor and May, when they become jealous and yearn to become Mermaids. The program chronicles what happens as the girls attempt to keep their abilities a secret while trying to lead a normal life.

Cast (as credited): Ellie L., Katie T., Gracie W. **Comment:** Good idea, pretty girls, capable acting but the production suffers from poor sound.

Episode List: *1.* Wonderstruck. *2.* Amazement. *3.* The Crazy Side of Taylor. *4.* Control May. *5.* We're More Powerful Then We Think. *6.* Watch Out. *7.* Halloween House of Horror. *8.* Who's Future? *9.* Kidnapped. *10.* Give Us Answers. *11.* Sneaking In. *12.* Saved at Last. *13.* Leila, Taylor and May. *14–15.* The Mermaid Christmas. *16.* A Witch or a Mermaid. *17.* The Time Is Limited.

180 *Magic Tails (2014).* 2014 (Fantasy).

While walking on the beach, a young girl (Sydney) finds a magic ring that when placed on her finger transforms her into a Mermaid. Excited and not realizing she should keep it a secret, she tells her friends (Maggie, Cassie, Emma, Lily, Zoe and Samantha) about the magic ring. Intrigued and also wanting to become Mermaids, the girls head to the beach, where, like magic, they each find a ring—and are granted their wishes. Seven girls, seven Mermaids and how each adjusts to her new life is the focal point of stories.

Cast (as credited): Maggie, Cassie, Emma, Lily Zoe, Samantha, Zac, Ryan. **Comment:** While the program does encompass a large cast (including a rarity in Mermaid series—boys) it suffers from poor sound and sometimes poor camera angles. It has since been taken offline.

Episode List: *1.* Mermaid Magic. *2.* Zac and Cam. *3.* Merman. *4.* Friends. *5.* Party Tails. *6.* Mermaid vs. Mermen. *7.* Missing Tails. *8.* New Mermaid and New Merman. *9.* Paranormal Mertivity. *10.* Bath Bomb. *11.* New Story. *12.* New Life. *13.* New Water Hits. *14.* New Tails. *15.* Magic Tails. *16.* Magic Hits. *17.* Happy Times. *18.* Rick's Return. *19.* Frozen. *20.* Sad Times. *21.* New Times.

181 *The Magical Scarecrow's Garden.* 2008 (Educational).

Scarecrows serve only one purpose: to protect a farmer's fruits and vegetables from predators like birds and rabbits. *The Magical Scarecrows Garden* is a book written by Catherine Chapman about an imaginary world of fruits and vegetables, protected by Magical Scarecrows who tell children how to eat healthy. Mother Earth has given the Scarecrows "life" but they become upset when they learn children are not eating the healthy crops they protect. Each chapter of the book is meant to stress good nutrition by the experiences the Scarecrows encounter when they call Mother Earth to learn why certain things happen and how they can change it.

Reader: Katy Manning. **Comment:** Episodes have been taken offline and it appears that only two episodes were produced. While the idea does sound intriguing, an evaluation based on viewing cannot be made.

Episode List: *Chapter 1*: Rosy Apple. *Chapter 2.* Cool Potato.

182 *Make Waves.* youtube.com. 2013 (Fantasy).

Two girls (Hope and Ky), strangers to each other, are swimming in the ocean when a sudden storm engulfs them and transports them to a strange pool. Hope and Ky become quick friends and are mysteriously transported back to the ocean when the storm subsides. The following day, when Hope and Ky come in contact with water, they are transformed into Mermaids. Two girls, literally strangers to each other, now share a secret which they must keep as they struggle to adjust to their developing powers, battle evil Sirens and live lives as ordinary school girls.

Cast (as credited): Olivia (Hope), Haley (Ky), Lindsay (April). Ella (Aria), Michaela (Anzu). **Comment:** The program is well acted and has good photography but it suffers from poor sound at times (wind blowing into the microphone).

Episode List: *1.* Into the Water. *2.* The Ocean's Gift. *3.* April and Aria. *4.* Hope's Birthday. *5.* Trust. *6.* Trick or Tail. *7.* Sirens.

183 *Man of the House.* youtube.com. 2014–2015 (Children).

Victor is the eight-year-old son of a single mother (Kathy) who has taken on the responsibilities of becoming the man of the house. Kathy accepts Victor's quest and stories follow Victor as he attempts to look out for his mother, including his efforts to find her a husband and father for him.

Cast: Devin Brown (Victor), Sherri Perry (Kathy), Bobbie Lee (Michael), Sofea Watkins (Lacey), Carolyn Mitchell (Angel), Dashiell Brooks (Jacob). **Credits:** *Producer-Writer-Director:* Kameishia Wooten. **Comment:** A somewhat slow-moving comedy that should focus more on Victor than on his mother's love life (dating habits). Aspects of the film and TV series *The Courtship of Eddie's Father* can be seen with Victor reacting to his mother's (as opposed to the film's father's) dates. The acting and production values are good.

Episode List: *1.* Pilot: It's Your Birthday. *2.* Episode 2. *3.* Movie Night.

184 *Mari-Kari.* shannen-doherty.net 2010–2012 (Cartoon).

Mari and Kari are twin sisters who attend the Gilles de Rais Elementary School. Mari is shy and sweet while Kari is just the opposite, a girl who is considered evil. While what happens to Kari is not shown, a newspaper article reveals the following: "Creepy Local Girl's Gruesome Death Delights Community." A flashback shows that "gruesome death" and reveals that Kari was disliked by her teacher and her schoolmates and some unknown person chose to kill her (she is seen tied to a telephone pole and bloody; how she died is not mentioned).

It has been several weeks after the unfortunate demise of Kari, and Mari is struggling to get along without her sister when she is startled to see that Kari has returned to her—in the form of a human spirit. Kari has a mission: to watch over Mari and extract revenge on anyone who taunts her. Mari now has a ghostly guardian and the program follows her efforts to live as normal a life as possible despite all the strange things that happen as Kari looks out for her (especially protecting her from Shari, the school's Prima Dona and the Cool Girls, who despise Mari for her cheery demeanor and naturally adorable fashion style). Larry is the dead kid who "lives" in the shed in the back of the sisters' home.

Voice Cast: Shannen Doherty (Mari and Kari), Steve Blum (Larry), Georgette Perna (Shari). **Credits:** *Producer-Director:* Jody Schaeffer, Austin Redding, Jim Burns. *Writer:* Keith Fay. **Comment:** Well animated series that is as much for kids as it is for adults. Mari is a cute blonde with an enchanting smile and wide blue eyes; Kari is seen in a ghostly bluish image and stories, which are presented like a serial, are amusing and well done.

Episode List: *1*. She's Back. *2*. Kill Them with Kindness. *3*. Hey Dead Girl. *4*. Unsatisfactory Diva. *5*. Hang This. *6*. A Fate for the Dance, Part 1. *7*. A Fate for the Dance, Part 2. *8*. The Super Fantastic Mari-Kari Season Finale Sadie Hawkins Day Dance Mega Bloodbath Finale. *9*. Mari-Kari Special Report.

185 *Masters of the Universe.* 2012–2013 (Adventure).

A trilogy based on the comic book *He Man and the Masters of the Universe* which relates the heroics of He-Man, the protector of the Castle Greyskull. In actuality He-Man is Prince Adam, the son of King Randor and Queen Marlena, the rulers of the planet Eternia. The Sorceress of the Castle Greyskull has given Adam special powers and his weapon, the Sword of Greyskull, to defend the castle from Skeletor—an evil sorcerer "from another dimension" with a skull for a head who operates from Snake Mountain and seeks the powers of the Castle Greyskull.

Cast: David McCullars (He-Man), John F. Carroll (Malik), Bridget Farias (Kareen), Chris Romani (Evil-Lyn), Bethany Harbaugh (Teela), Russell Minton (Kothos), Andrew Brett (Skeletor), Elisabeth Raine (Rayna), Lee Wilson (King Greyskull), Bjorn Korthof (Prince Adam), Juli Dearrington (Sorceress), Javier Smith (Keldor/Zodac), John Athin (General Blade), Darwin Miller (Eldor), Emily Hampton (Princess Adora/She-Ra), Joseph Fontinos (King Randor), Joseph Gouldthrope (Stratos), LeRoy Beck (Melaktha). **Credits:** *Producer-Writer*: John F. Carroll. *Director*: John F. Carroll, Russell Minton. **Comment:** Could be considered a live-action version of the animated TV series *He-Man and the Masters of the Universe* with good acting and production values. The program has since been taken offline.

Episode List: *1*. Wizard of Stone Mountain. *2*. The Fountain of Life. *3*. The Trials of Darksmoke.

186 *Maui Mermaids. youtube.com.* 2015 (Fantasy).

It is sunset when two girls (Brooklyn and Hazel) decide to check out Trident Bay, an area near their home in Hawaii that people just avoid. As they enter the bay, a light emerges from the water and engulfs them, but they appear to be unaffected. The following day, when Brooklyn and Hazel come in contact with water, they are transformed into Mermaids. Encompassing what they have become, Brooklyn and Hazel must now navigate lives as both Mermaids and ordinary school girls.

Cast (as credited): Nikki (Brooklyn), Nicole (Hazel). **Comment:** Nicole is also credited as both

Hazel and Taylor in the opening theme although she is called Hazel in the program. The program has good photography and capable acting.

Episode List: *1*. Trident Bay. *2*. The Discovery. *3*. First Swim.

187 *Mayfes Mermaids. youtube.com.* 2015 (Fantasy).

Three girls (Hazel, Ella and Stella) are walking when they stumble across what appears to be an old book. As they look through it they believe it is a book of spells and decide to recite one. Nothing happens until later that day, when each comes in contact with water that they become Mermaids. But that is not their only problem as a mysterious man has begun pursuing them, seeking their blood (which is blue) for what appears to be an experiment to change any girl into a Mermaid. The program follows Hazel, Ella and Stella as they attempt to avoid capture and defeat the Mystery Man (as he is called).

Cast (as credited): Hazel, Ella and Stella as Themselves. **Comment:** The title is not explained in the episodes or on the website. The program begins quite badly with very poor photography (very unsteady picture) but does improve as the story progresses.

Episode List: *1*. The Spell. *2*. Stranded. *3*. Mystery Man, Part 1. *4*. Mystery Man, Part 2.

188 *Mean Girls. youtube.com.* 2013 (Dolls).

A rather dramatic approach for a doll series that tackles the subject of bullying as it occurs in a school catering to girls and how they cope and deal with it. The program does come with a warning (that, unfortunately only appears in the program's text information) stating that it is not recommended for young children.

Cast (as credited): Natalie Wood (Natalie Squires), Noelle Raske (Emma Rose), Autumn Wood (Stacy Johnson), Lanie Holland (Cassidy Sparrow). **Comment:** Very good photography and doll manipulation is coupled with excellent voice characterizations.

Episode List: 2 untitled episodes, labeled "Episode 1" and "Episode 2" have been produced.

189 *Merfreak. youtube.com.* 2013 (Fantasy).

Three young children (Zapper, Katelin and Lucas) become lost while walking through the woods and stumble across a mysterious waterfall. As Zapper and Katelin become curious they enter its waters. While nothing happens, they feel they should return home and somehow manage to find their way back. Later, when Zapper touches water, he becomes a Merman and Katelin, when she comes in contact with water, becomes a Mermaid—all to the astonishment of Lucas, who has remained normal (as he didn't enter the waterfall). With Lucas vowing to keep their secret, Zapper and Katelin must now learn to live lives as both "Merfreaks" (as Zapper says) and ordinary grammar school kids.

Cast (as credited): Andrew (Zapper), Grace (Katelin), Aaron (Lucas). **Comment:** Although the picture is very fuzzy, the stars are quite young and do a decent job with an inexpensive camera and no experience.

Episode List: *1.* I'm a What!

190 MerGirls. *youtube.com.* 2013 (Fantasy).

One day a young girl (Amy) is surprised to find a hand-held mirror and a piece of paper that contains what appears to be a spell. As Amy picks up the mirror and reads the spell (difficult to hear what she is saying) she transforms into a Mermaid (without touching water) when she finishes. The program focuses mainly on Amy as she now must keep secret what has happened while pretending to be just an ordinary girl.

Cast (as credited): Grace (Amy), Taylor (Frankie), Braiden (Bella). **Comment:** Rather slow-moving program (too much focus on Amy as she takes her sweet time about everything) although the photography is good.

Episode List: *1.* The Magic Mirror. *2.* Power Hour. *3.* A New Book. *4.* New Powers, New Spells. *5.* The Bad Spell. *6.* New Mermaid.

191 Mermaid at Heart. *youtube.com.* 2013–2014 (Fantasy).

While walking along the beach a ten-year-old girl (Riki) stumbles upon something she had never noticed before: a cave. A bit nervous, but intrigued, Riki decides to explore the cave and is doused by water when a wave comes crashing into the shore. Unknown to Riki, the water was magically enhanced and its effects become evident when she returns home, comes in contact with water and is transformed into a Mermaid. Now, with newly acquired abilities, Riki must learn to keep a secret while attempting to live a normal life and fulfill a destiny that could affect the oceans of the world (as her developing powers will enable her to defeat The Evil Ones who are seeking to destroy Mermaids and their goodness). Amber is a reporter who has suspicions about Riki and has vowed to reveal what she really is.

Cast (as credited): Emily (Riki and Amber). **Comment:** Emily is a pretty girl and handles her roles well although the production has poor sound and only acceptable photography.

Episode List: *1–2.* Shoreline. *3.* Exposed. *4.* The Journey Begins. *5.* She's Back.

192 Mermaid at Midnight. *youtube.com.* 2012 (Fantasy).

While swimming at the beach, a young girl (Brinn) stumbles across a secret cave, becomes intrigued and

enters it. As she begins to explore it she blacks out then awakens to find herself back home and unsure as to how she got there. Passing it off as just a weird dream, Brinn becomes thirsty and, after taking a drink of water, magically transforms into a Mermaid. She must now learn how to control her Mermaid abilities (like freezing and heating water) and also live her life as a normal school girl. Complicating her life are two necklaces: one that she found in the cave (that when worn creates a duplicate of herself) and one, found in a mysterious box in her backyard, that turns its wearer into an evil being. The program ends unresolved with Brinn appearing to become a pawn in a good vs. evil situation.

Cast (as credited): Weibits (Brinn). **Comment:** The sequence with Brinn "swimming in the ocean" can clearly be seen as being shot in a swimming pool and "the cave" [with tile walls] is apparently her home's bathroom. Weibits is the only performer and the overall production is acceptable although it does suffer from poor sound at times.

Episode List: *1.* The Moon Shell. *2.* Weird Waves. *3.* An Evil Presence. *4.* Just the Beginning.

193 Mermaid Bay. *youtube.com.* 2013 (Fantasy).

While walking through the woods three girls (Marina, Ally and Sophie) find a small box near a stream of water. When they return home and open the box they find it contains three necklaces. Each girl takes one and each becomes a Mermaid when she comes in contact with water. Three girls, a shared secret and their efforts to help each other adjust to the life they must now keep secret.

Cast (as credited): Grace (Marina Haven), Anna (Ally Dillard), Mariah (Sophie Moore). **Comment:** An overall well done program with good acting and photography and pleasing background music. However, when the episode ends and the blooper portion begins, over-powering music obstructs the dialogue.

Episode List: *1.* Fish Out of Water.

194 The Mermaid Diaries. *youtube.com.* 2014 (Fantasy).

Cousins Nerissa and Oceana are walking through a park when a sudden storm approaches. While seeking shelter, they come across a cave and enter it. As it continues to rain and the girls become bored, they fall asleep and awaken a short time later to see a girl (Vivienne) standing opposite them. Vivienne tells them, "You shouldn't have come here. Go now and do not come back. This cave is not safe." Vivienne then dives into water that appears to be in the cave. As the rain begins to stop, Nerissa and Oceana leave. But, as Nerissa and Oceana learn when they return home, they should have heeded Vivienne's warning as now, when they come in contact with water, they transform into Mermaids. The following day Nerissa and Oceana return to the cave and again encounter

Vivienne. They learn they were destined to become Mermaids and that she has been assigned to teach them how to use and control their powers. The program follows Nerissa and Oceana as they, along with Vivienne, seek to protect their secret while pretending to be ordinary girls.

Cast (as credited): Alexa J., Rebecca R., Marianna R. **Comment:** The program has nice photography and acceptable acting (although it can be seen that Vivienne is reading her lines during long speeches).

Episode List: *1.* Pilot. *2.* Vivienne. *3.* The Learning Curve.

195 *Mermaid Fantasy (2011). youtube. com.* 2011 (Dolls).

The Mattel line of Barbie Mermaid dolls are incorporated to tell the story of a group of beautiful Mermaids (Violet, Posie, Shelly, Merissa, Wisteria, Lily, Sunflower, Lilac and Victoria) and what life is like for them living in a magical world beneath the sea—a world much like teenagers encounter in the human world.

Voice Cast (as credited): Sweetie and Cutie. **Comment:** Very well done program with a good story line and manipulation of the dolls against believable backgrounds.

Episode List: *1.* Power Party (Pilot).

196 *Mermaid Fantasy (2014). youtube. com.* 2014 (Fantasy).

Gerda and Rebecka are friends who are looking through a box of items when they find a folder containing papers. As they examine the papers they see one that intrigues them—a recipe for a drink. Venturing into the kitchen, the girls make the drink but find it rather unpleasant after they taste it. The following day, as each of the girls first comes in contact with water they are transformed into Mermaids. The program, produced in Russia, follows Gerda and Rebecka as they attempt to deal with what has happened to them while pretending to be ordinary girls and not reveal their secret.

Cast: Karolin Gerda (Greda Valk), Maria Rebecka (Rebecka Romb). **Comment:** The program uses both the English and Slovak languages and is somewhat difficult to follow. The girls are very pretty and the photography is acceptable (better scene framing should have been considered).

Episode List: *1.* Something Fishy. *2.* Moon Pool.

197 *Mermaid Forever. youtube.com.* 2012 (Fantasy).

Alexsandra is a young girl who, while in her family's hot tub, is engulfed by bubbling water that emits blue-like waves. Alexsandra is apparently unaffected but when she first comes in contact with water she is transformed into a Mermaid. Mystical forces have ac-

tually caused Alexsandra's transformation for a specific reason: to battle an evil Siren that is seeking to destroy Mermaids and rule the seas. The program follows Alexsandra as she attempts to lead a normal life while also dealing with all the problems associated with what she has now become.

Cast (as credited): Katariina (Alexsandra), Marta (Siren), Kertu (Getter), Leenue (Leenu), George (Jack), Assu (Alexander), Lila (Lola), Natali (Emily). **Comment:** The program is produced in Estonia (a country in the Baltic region of Northern Europe) and presented in the Estonian language. Although the photography is very good, the program has no English subtitles and it is nearly impossible to totally follow the program. There are also noticeable sound losses and, surprisingly, the program has a very high number of YouTube hits (the first episode, for example, has over seven million views). Katariina is a very pretty girl and if pretty can get views, then *Mermaid Forever* has found the key to success.

Season 1 Episode List: *1.* I Am a Mer … Mer … Mer… *2.* Two Mermaids Forever. *3.* Full Moon. *4.* In a Holiday. *5.* Attack from the Moon. *6.* Just Keep Swimming.

Season 2 Episode List: *1.* Attack. *2.* She Is Killing Me. *3.* Not Ready. *4.* War. *5.* Finale.

Season 3 Episode List: *1.* Comeback

198 *Mermaid Girl. youtube.com.* 2014 (Fantasy).

It appears to be summertime and a young girl (Natalie) is bored and just doesn't know what to do. After sitting around for a while she decides to go for a walk and meets a girl (Emilee) whom she tries to befriend. Emilee is a bit shy and the two do become friendly. As they agree to meet again the following day, Natalie spies something (not clearly shown) in a wicker basket. The scene begins to spin and the program ends. It appears that the program has been abandoned and whatever Natalie saw will eventually turn her (and possibly even Emilee) into Mermaids. It is unknown what will occur next.

Cast (as credited): Natalie and Emilee as Themselves. **Comment:** Although the camera work is a bit shoddy, especially in Natalie's walking scenes, the acting is good.

Episode List: *1.* Pilot.

199 *Mermaid in the Water.* 2013 (Fantasy).

As a young girl (Katriel) is playing outside, she loses her balance and falls, hitting her head on the ground. She wanders back into her house, where she sees a pink liquid and drinks it. A thunderstorm is approaching and the drink puts Katriel to sleep. She awakens shortly after to find herself in the bathtub and transformed into a Mermaid. The program follows a young girl as she struggles to hide her new identity while pretending to be an ordinary girl.

Cast (as credited): Katriel Tori (Katriel), Buddy

(Himself). **Comment:** The program is a bit sketchy as to why Katriel's fall contributed to her becoming a Mermaid. There are some sound and video issues (like an unsteady picture) but Katriel does her best to make it a good production. The program has since been taken offline.

Episode List: *1.* New Beginnings. *2.* Daughter of the Deep. *3.* Friends in Unexpected Places. *4.* Finding Out.

200 *Mermaid Island.* 2010 (Fantasy). The program has two distinct story lines.

Story Line 1: Two friends, Isabella and Ally are walking when they spot two paper cups filled with a red liquid. There is a note attached that says, "To you. Drink me." Intrigued, but not really thinking, they decide to taste the liquid. It appears to be unpleasant but nothing happens. Later that day they find a treasure chest hidden in grass and open it to find pictures of them mixed in with assorted potions and two necklaces. The girls do question how their pictures could have gotten into the chest but sort of just shrug it off when they become fascinated by the necklaces and try them on. It is now seven episodes into the series. With the eighth episode Isabella and Ally come in contact with water and it appears the necklaces are magical as they are transformed into Mermaids. The girls must now keep secret what has happened and, as they adjust to their developing powers, they must also battle the evil—ghosts and zombies.

Story Line 2: A typical day for two girls (Isabella and Ally) at the beach turns into a nightmare when they are captured by persons unknown brought to a mysterious island and put through a series of weird experiments. With the experiments completed, the girls are returned to the beach but they are not as they were before: they are now Mermaids. As Isabella and Ally set their goals to find out who captured them and why they were chosen to become Mermaids, the program also charts their adventures as they attempt to keep secret what happened and adjust to their developing powers.

Cast (as credited): Savannah (Isabella), Ciera (Ally). **Comment:** The program has acceptable acting and photography but has since been taken offline.

Episode List: Season 1 consists of 8 untitled episodes; Season 2, 6 untitled episodes; Season 3, 11 untitled episodes; Season 4, 13 untitled episodes; and Season 5, 1 untitled episode.

201 *Mermaid Madness. youtube.com.* 2015 (Fantasy).

McKenna and McKenzie are friends who possess magical necklaces (assumed to have been found at the beach as there is no explanation as to how they acquired them. The girls are just seen together talking about the necklaces when the series begins). Shortly after the program begins, the girls place the necklaces around their necks. However, when they each come in contact with water, a transformation occurs and they become Mermaids. Their mishaps are followed as they struggle to keep their secret, adjust to their powers and pretend to be ordinary girls

Cast (as credited): McKenna and McKenzie as Themselves. **Comment:** As previously stated, there is no introduction. It is also slow-moving as nothing much of anything happens.

Episode List: 3 untitled episodes, labeled "Episode 1," "Episode 2" and "Episode 3" have been produced.

202 *Mermaid Magic. youtube.com.* 2012 (Fantasy).

A young girl (Caroline) is in the backyard of her home when she finds a bottle with a light blue liquid in it and an inscription that reads "For Ice Cream." Curious, Caroline takes the bottle into the kitchen and begins wondering about it—"Could it be a Mermaid potion? Could it be poisonous?" When her curiosity gets the best of her, she opens the bottle and pours its contents into a glass and sips it. When she discards what remains in the glass, a bracelet appears. The bracelet looks to be normal but when Ashley accidentally spills water on herself she is magically transformed into a Mermaid. She is not startled, however, and after drying her purple tail (to return her legs) she finds that she also has the power to make wishes come true. Her adventures as she adjusts to her Mermaid life are chronicled. Also known as *The Magic of Mermaids.*

Cast (as credited): Pianopup210 (Caroline and Serena). **Comment:** As the first episode plays, the following message will appear over the picture: "This is my first episode and is very bad quality. Like really, really bad quality. I promise it gets better eventually and the plot gets more interesting. Please excuse this horrible episode" (to delete the message, click on the text image, then click the "x" in the upper right corner). Caroline is a very pretty girl and she acts naturally. Simple plot, pretty girl and the episode does not play as bad as indicated. The sound is poor and does require an extra effort to hopefully understand. The production values do improve in succeeding episodes.

Season 1 Episode List: *1.* Magic Potion. *2.* Powers and Disasters. *3.* Troubled Waters. *4.* Full Moon. *5.* Random Potion. *6.* Discovered. *7.* Season Finale.

Season 2 Episode List: *8.* Crisis. *9.* Return of the Sirens. *10.* Consequences. *11.* Reactions. *12.* Siren Rebellion. *13–14.* Season Finale.

203 *Mermaid Masquerade (2013).* 2013 (Dolls).

Harmony, Cole and Faith are ordinary girls who attend a seemingly prestigious high school called Silver Springs. Their lives, however, change from ordinary to extraordinary when they buy some jewelry, later come in contact with water and transform into Mermaids. The program, which uses LPS (Littlest Pet Shop) dolls, charts their adventures as they attend classes but pretend to be ordinary girls.

Voices (as credited): Harmony. **Comment:** The program encompasses good voice characterizations, doll manipulation and photography. It has since been taken offline.

Episode List: *1.* Changes. *2.* Invitations. *3.* Dates and Drama.

204 Mermaid Masquerade (2014). *you tube.com.* 2014 (Fantasy).

Two sisters, Maya and Hailey are playing in the snow in their backyard and appear to be having a good time. However, when they return indoors and come in contact with water, they transform into Mermaids. But how? Maya acquires the power to heat water while Hailey can freeze it. As Maya and Hailey analyze what happened they believe that it may be lined to a birthmark they each have that is somehow related to Mermaids. As the story progresses, the girls find rings and necklaces and learn that they, plus the birthmarks, are all related to becoming Mermaids and acquiring powers. They must now keep a secret while pretending to be ordinary girls.

Cast: Maddy Grace (Maya Smith), Addie Rose (Hailey Smith). **Comment:** Nice photography, pretty girls and good acting. There is a sound problem in the first episode wherein it is rather difficult to hear what the girls are saying as they are talking against the background of running water.

Episode List: *1.* The Start of Something New. *2.* Just a Dream? *3.* Changes. *4.* Moms, Dads and Aunts. *5.* Jewels. *6.* Power Practice. *7.* Uncle Phil. *8.* New Powers. *9.* Can't Control It. *10.* Apocalypse.

205 Mermaid Masters. 2013 (Fantasy).

As a 13-year-old girl (Annya) begins swimming in the ocean, a magical scanner records who she is and it is determined that she is no ordinary girl. Moments later an unknown mystical force transforms Annya into a Mermaid (her true being) and the program follows Annya as she struggles to keep secret what happened while pretending to be an ordinary girl.

Cast: Michaela Parker (Annya). **Comment:** Annya is pretty and the story good, but the production suffers at times from poor sound and video quality. The program has since been taken offline.

Season 1 Episode List:
1. Metamorphosis.
2. I Found My Power.
3. Get Off My Tail.
4. Missing Child and Hospital Surgery.
5. MerSick.
Season 2 Episode List:
1. The Awakening.

2. Keep Your Enemies Behind You.
3. Sick Again.
4. Cold Front.
5. MerBirthday.
Season 3 Episode List:
1. The Mix-up.
2. Birthday Bash.
3. Reckless Child.
Season 4 Episode List:
1. Finding Out.
2. Rescued.
3. Christmas.
Season 5 Episode List:
1. New Mermaid.
2. The Twins Are Missing.
3. The Locket.
4. Party Mermaid.
5. The E-mail.
6. Lonely Mermaid.
7. Powerful Necklaces.
8. Bizarre Dreams.
Season 6 Episode List:
1. Ghost Napped.
2. Twists and Turns.
3. Mermaid Flu.

206 Mermaid Minute. *youtube.com.* 2012–2015 (Information).

Various aspects of the undersea world are explored through minute long videos hosted by a pretty Mermaid named Linden.

Host: Linden Wolbert (Mermaid Linden). **Credits:** *Producer:* Virginia Addison, Grace Addison, Neil Andrea, Heidi Fogo. **Comment:** Excellent underwater photography is combined with interesting aspects of sea life in a program that is simply too short. Adding several additional minutes to each topic would play even better than the condensed version that evolved. However, with the short attention span most Internet users have when it comes to certain types of programs, perhaps the right decision was made here.

Season 1 Episode List: *1.* Meet a Real Mermaid. *2.* Starfish. *3.* Crabs. *4.* The Remora (Sucker) Fish. *5.* Trumpet Fish. *6.* Barnacles. *7.* Cute Seals of the Pacific. *8.* Ocean Currents. *9.* Caribbean Reef Sharks. *10.* Season 1 Finale.

Season 2 Episode List: *1.* Lion Fish. *2.* Kelp.

207 Mermaid Miracles. *youtube.com.* 2013 (Fantasy).

During the early 18th century a young couple walking along the beach found a nest and what appeared to be an abandoned baby Mermaid. With no one else in sight they took the baby home and chose to raise her as their own child (whom they named Ana). Unknown to the couple, fate had intended for them to find Ana and thus create a legacy that would carry

Ana's mission of protecting the oceans for the future through her children and her children's children.

It is the year 2013 and sisters Inga and Ilsa, the great, great grandchildren of Ana, have also been endowed with Mermaid abilities, but have kept it secret from their children, Maya (Inga's 13-year-old daughter) and Ashley (Ilsa's daughter). While Inga appears to be living a normal life with Maya, Ashley's life is quite different as her mother mysteriously disappeared several years ago but she has hope that her mother will return to her.

One day, while on the beach with Ashley, Maya finds a bottle that apparently washed up on shore and opens it. Inside is a note, somewhat aged over time, that reads, "You are at the age when your powers come. Don't be alarmed. Don't run." Maya and Ashley are unable to make sense of it and ignore it, although Maya elects to keep the note. Suddenly, an unexpected wave washes upon the shore and splashes Maya and Ashley with water. Immediately, they are transformed into Mermaids. Although a bit shocked, they are quite rational and when their mermaid tails dry, they return to normal.

Ashley is a bit reluctant to accept what has happened and wonders why, while Maya is eager to embrace her metamorphosis. Their questions are answered by Inga, when she tells them that she too is a Mermaid and they have reached the age when they too must embrace their heritage. They also learn why: to love, respect and protect the oceans at all times. It is also learned through Inga that "when the tide is high be open to help others; when the tide is low, be open to receiving help from others." She concludes with, "Be careful to whom you give your heart" (as a Mermaid has only one chance to truly fall in love). As Maya and Ashley begin to embrace what they have become, they also learn that Isla was kidnapped by Sirens, evil sea creatures who are seeking the Tempest, a mysterious object that can destroy mankind, and must keep them from ever finding it. The program follows Maya and Ashley as they attempt to live the lives of normal teenage girls while embracing a destiny that could cost them their lives.

Cast: Maya Tritt (Maya), Ashley Harmon (Ashley), Inga Tritt (Inga), David Tritt (David, Maya's father), Chad Rush (Chad), Hanna Formica (Roxy), James Cooney (Ricky), Abby Oliver (Isla), Chloe Hightower (Chloe), Kias Porter (Kias). **Credits:** *Producer*: David Tritt, Maya Tritt. *Director*: Brett Mazurek. *Writer*: Maya Tritt. **Comment:** Charming Mermaid tale with good acting and production qualities. The underwater sequences are well done and comedy (with Mermaid hunters) mixes with light drama. The series, written by star Maya Tritt when she was 12 years old, has a very large world-wide following (Over 3 million views on YouTube alone) and is really unique when one so young not only encompasses Mermaid mythology but respect for the oceans and ecology as well. While it is aimed at children and teens, it is easily enjoyed by any age group. If you have

seen the movie *Aquamarine* and/or the TV series *H2O, Just Add Water* you will also enjoy *Mermaid Miracles.*

Season 1 Episode List: *1.* Pilot. *2.* True Self. *3.* Shiny Things. *4.* The Golden Rules. *5.* The Chase. *6.* Mermaid Party. *7.* I Dream of Mermaids. *8.* The Siren's Song.

Season 2 Episode List: *9.* Heart's Desire. *10.* Sirens vs. Mermaids. *11.* Follow Your Heart (the program concludes unresolved).

208 *Mermaid Mishaps.* 2012 (Fantasy).

How do young girls and even teenage girls become Mermaids? There are apparently many ways and the program was set to explore those ways (called mishaps) through short exploratory videos (as in the only episode presented, by a teenage girl watering her plants, touching the plant leafs and transforming into a Mermaid).

Cast: Holly Benison (Mermaid). **Comment:** Just based on the pilot, the program did show potential for becoming an enjoyable series. Holly is petty and can act and the program has very good photography. It has since been taken offline.

Episode List: *1.* Plant Watering: A Nightmare.

209 *Mermaid Pearls.* 2014 (Fantasy).

Two young girls (Emily and Gea) are at the beach (apparently by themselves) when a storm begins developing. With no other choice but to swim to an island for safety, the girls seek shelter in a cave they find there. As the girls wait out the storm, the light from a full moon shines down on them. A caption "Let's leave" is seen on the screen. It is assumed the girls swam back to the beach and safely made it home as the next scene opens with the caption "The Next Day." Emily and Gea appear to be fine until they come in contact with water and are transformed into Mermaids. Their lives have changed and they must now learn how to be Mermaids while also pretending to be ordinary girls.

Cast (as credited): Emily M. (Emily), Gea A. (Gea). **Comment:** The program is spoken in Albanian with English subtitles. All the underwater and Mermaid swimming scenes are simulated giving those particular scenes a cartoon-like look. It is the only Mermaid series created by two Albanian girls and while it is amateurish, the simulated aspects make it interesting to watch. The program has since been taken offline.

Episode List: *1.* A Waters Change. *2.* Water Power. *3.* Moon Eyes. *4.* Friend or Foe? *5.* Voice in the Dark.

210 *The Mermaid Portal.* *youtube.com.* 2011 (Fantasy).

On a distant, unnamed planet a very pretty Mermaid (Pandora) is in her ocean home when a mysterious mist engulfs her and transports her to Earth, where she emerges in a small spring that appears to run through the property of the parents of a girl named Alisha. Alisha immediately spots Pandora and, after learning what has happened, offers to let her live in her home. Pandora, who can acquire her legs when she is not in contact with water, accepts the offer and the two become immediate friends (Pandora also acquires clothes by sharing Alisha's wardrobe). The program explores an alien Mermaid's experiences on Earth and her attempts to keep her secret while seeking a way to return to her own world.

Cast (as credited): Julia Alexa (Pandora), Hanna (Alisha), Quinn (Kevin), Judith (Charlotte), Robert (Vincent). **Comment:** Pandora adjusts much too quickly to what has happened (as does Alisha to Pandora). Pandora also has no trouble speaking and understanding English and appears to be familiar with Earth customs, hinting that there may be some sort of connection between her world and Alisha's. The acting and photography are good and the limited special effects are also well done.

Episode List: 5 untitled episodes, labeled "Episode 1" through "Episode 5" have been produced.

211 Mermaid Powers (Series 1). 2013 (Fantasy).

Two sisters (Belle and Coral) are playing outdoors when they find a necklace. While examining it, they find their lives changing forever when they touch water and transform into Mermaids. Their efforts to keep secret what happened as they pretend to be ordinary girls is the focal point of the program (which appears to have been abandoned after the first episode).

Cast (as credited): Belle and Coral as Themselves. **Comment:** A slow-moving, uninteresting program with poor acting and photography; it has since been taken offline.

Episode List: *1.* The Beginning.

212 Mermaid Powers (Series 2). 2013 (Fantasy).

A young girl (Emily) is playing in her backyard when she finds a necklace in a glass jar. She removes the necklace from the jar and places it around her neck. When she goes to wash her hands she transforms into a Mermaid and slowly begins to develop powers. As Emily struggles to cope with what has happened, she learns that her friends, Emma and Layla are also Mermaids (through magic necklaces) and must join together and use their powers (Emily, water; Emma, fire and Layla, love) to defeat an unknown person who has discovered what they are and now seeks to steal their powers.

Cast (as credited): Dwat (Emily), Brak (Layla), Bawi (Emma). **Comment:** The program begins rather poorly as it is slow-moving and not very interesting (especially episode 5, which is totally devoted to teenagers singing). It does improve a bit after the fifth episode but it has since been taken offline.

Season 1 Episode List: *1.* Awaken. *2.* Revealed. *3.* Birthday Tail. *4.* Answers Found. *5.* A Whole Day of Magic. *6.* Decisions. *7.* In Deep Trouble. *8.* Halloween Magic.

Season 2 Episode List: *1.* Truth Again. *2.* Truth. *3.* Christmas Love. *4.* Fish Surprise. *5.* Battle On. *6.* The Book. *7.* The Attack. *8.* The Final Battle.

213 Mermaid Scales (2012). youtube.com. 2012–2015 (Fantasy).

An unknown person (seen only by the arms) is filling a green bucket with water and placing a sign that reads "Danger" on it. Two young girls, friends Tiffany and Jessie, are returning home after spending a day at the lake and find the bucket. Although they do not see the danger sign, Tiffany tells Jessie not to touch it. Jessie ignores her and splashes her with its water; Tiffany retaliates and splashes water on Jessie. Shortly after, when the girls enter Jessie's home and come in contact with water, they are transformed into Mermaids. As Tiffany and Jessie attempt to adjust to what has happened to them, they find their secret in danger of exposure when Jessie's younger sister, Kelly, becomes suspicious of their actions and sets out to find out why they are suddenly acting differently (later, their secret is threatened by their friend Britney when she becomes curious about them). The program follows Tiffany and Jessie as they struggle to conceal who they really are while not only attempting to adjust to their Mermaid abilities, but live lives as ordinary girls.

Cast (as credited): Eloisa de Farias (Tiffany), Elena de Farias (Jessie), Emanuela de Farias (Kelly), Camila (Britney), Natalia (Goddess), Dana (Lindsey). **Comment:** Eloisa de Farias is a very pretty young girl who has an amazing talent to not only act but create (with her sisters Elena and Kelly) a series that is well done with good acting, a well-thought story and nice photography.

Season 1 Episode List:
1. The Start of Everything.
2. Swimming Far.
3. Don't Touch the Book.
4. Want a Piece of Me?
5. Power Makes Perfect.
6. Say Cheese.
7. The Lost.
8. Kidnapped.
9. Happy Birthday Jessie.
10. Power Necklace.
11. Season Finale.
Season 2 Episode List:
1. I'm Back!
2. Keep Trying.
3. Plastic Baby Dolls.

4. The Move.
5. Goodbye.
6. Hello Miami.
7. The Potion.
8. Miami Sequarium.
9. Welcome to the Bahamas.
10. Love Again.
Season 3 Episode List:
1. Tiffany's Birthday.
2. A Little Sneak.
3. Magical Cup.
4. Lost and Found.
5. What the Tail.
6. Disaster Date.
7. Is It the End?
8. Necklace Again?
9. Eggs.
Season 4 Episode List:
1. Mackenzie the Fish.
2. There's a Bird on My Window.
3. Bored Mermaid.
4. Even Mermaids Have Talent.
5. County Side.
6. Season Finale.

214 *Mermaid Scales (2013). youtube.com.* 2013 (Dolls).

Evelyn Rose is a young girl, alone at the beach when she becomes bored and decides to go for a swim. As she swims she spies a cave and enters it. She exits the water and begins walking in a stream-like path that appears to run the entire length of the cave. Feeling that she has ventured too far, Evelyn begins her journey back when the water begins to bubble but nothing happens. The next day, when Evelyn comes in contact with water she transforms into a Mermaid. She soon discovers she has the power to control water and the program relates her efforts to conceal who she really is while pretending to be an ordinary girl. **Cast (as credited):** Noelle Raske (Evelyn Rose), Autumn Wood (Evelyn's mother). **Comment:** Nice photography, voices and doll movement but the program appears to have been abandoned. **Episode List:** *1.* Pilot.

215 *The Mermaid Secret.* 2014 (Fantasy).

While out for a walk a young girl (Crystal) finds a strange round object in the grass and picks it up. She thinks nothing of it and returns home. Shortly after, when she comes in contact with water she transforms into a Mermaid. Crystal confides in her friend Alia, who agrees to help her adjust to what has happened and help her keep secret the fact that she is a real Mermaid. **Cast (as credited):** Syd (Crystal), Riss (Alia). **Comment:** Although the girls are pretty, the program suffers from poor sound and video quality; it has since been taken offline.

Episode List: 8 untitled episodes, labeled "Episode 1" through "Episode 8" have been produced.

216 *Mermaid Secrets (2013). youtube.com.* 2013 (Dolls).

Marina, a young girl attending boarding school, elects to go for a hike but neglects to tell her roommates Sam and Danny. As Marina strolls through the woods she suddenly finds herself encompassed by a strong wind that transports her to the branch of a large tree. Unable to explain what happened and seeing that she is only a short distance from the ground, Marina jumps off but becomes frightened when the ground opens and she falls into a cave with a mysterious pool of water. Enticed by the sparkling water, Marina, who apparently had her bathing suit under her clothes, goes swimming. When it is heard that Marina believes it is time to return home, she magically reappears in her dorm room but keeps secret what happened to her. Shortly after, when Marina comes in contact with water she transforms into a Mermaid, luckily with no one around when it happened. The program follows Marina's efforts to avoid situations that could expose her and her battle against Nelli, an evil Sea Demon who has discovered her secret and seeks to acquire her powers. **Voices:** Marina Gylinder, Sam Marina, Danny Shaw. **Comment:** Very good voice characterizations and doll movement coupled with a good story and intriguing twists. **Season 1 Episode List:** *1.* The Hike. *2–4:* Unknown; taken offline. *5.* Drew.

Season 2 Episode List: *1.* An Intense Sleepover. *2.* Sushi Wakes Up. *3.* Love Is Discovered. *4.* Going to South Carolina. *5.* Adriana and Claire. *6.* Sirens. *7.* The Trouble Has Just Begun. *8.* One Girl Revolution. *9.* Second Chances, Dangerous Games and Lovers. *10.* The Truth Comes Out. *11.* Nelli Did It. *12.* And So It Begins.

217 *Mermaid Secrets (2014). youtube.com.* 2014 (Fantasy).

Faith, Wendy and Autumn are best friends who do everything together. One day, while Faith and Autumn wait for Wendy to join them at the local park, they begin to wonder why Wendy is late. As Wendy approaches the park she spies Faith and Autumn and somehow manages to hear what they are saying from a distance. Misinterpreting what is being said (believing they are talking about her in a bad way) she becomes jealous, approaches Faith and Autumn and throws them to the ground with energy blasts emitted from her hands. Suddenly a dark gray smoke emerges from the ground and encircles the girls. The smoke makes them realize they have powers and something else—the ability to transform into Mermaids when they come in contact with water. The girls now share a secret and, as they attempt to learn more about what they have become and how to use and control their powers, they also face a threat from Brittany, Faith's cousin who has become suspicious of them and who could soon expose them.

Cast (as credited): Kennedy (Wendy), Tatianna (Faith), Kenzie (Autumn), Brittany (Brittany). **Comment:** The acting and photography is good but the sound is quite bad at times with wind blowing into the microphone (creating a crackling noise) and making it virtually impossible to understand what is being said.

Episode List: 5 untitled episodes, labeled "Episode 1" through "Episode 5" have been produced.

218　A Mermaid Tail (Series 1). 2013 (Fantasy).

Three hundred years ago, a Mermaid recited a spell from a scroll to carry her spirit over time and ensure that her heritage would live on. It is the 21st century when on the anniversary of the night the spell was cast, that two girls are born: Brooke and Chelsea. The girls are unknown to each other until fate brings them together and they became best friends. Brooke and Chelsea are now attending school and one day, while at the beach, they stumble across that ancient scroll and recite the spell that it contains. Brooke and Chelsea are transformed into Mermaids and, according to the scroll, "must take their destiny into their own hands." The program follows Brooke and Chelsea as they attempt to adjust to what has happened, learn to control their developing powers and keep secret what they have become.

Cast (as credited): Jordan (Brooke), Megan (Chelsea). **Comment:** Jordan not only acts but does the filming. It is a well done presentation with good acting and an intriguing story; it has since been taken offline.

Episode List: 3 untitled episodes were produced, labeled "Episode 1," "Episode 2" and "Episode 3."

219　A Mermaid Tail (Series 2). youtube.com. 2013 (Fantasy).

It is the night of a full moon when three friends (Eleanor, Jessica and Lorissa) decide to go swimming. But before they enter the water, a sizzling-like sound is heard that frightens them and they run back into Lorissa's house. There, they magically transform into Mermaids and must now not only live with and protect their secret, but learn how to control their developing powers.

Cast (as credited): Autumn (Eleanor), Zoe (Jessica), Chloe (Lorissa). **Comment:** Overall, the acting and production are good although a further exploration of how a sizzling sound changed the girls into Mermaids would have helped the story.

Episode List: 5 untitled episodes were produced, labeled "Episode 1" through "Episode 5."

220　A Mermaid Tale (2013). youtube.com. 2013 (Dolls).

Four teenage girls (Rosie, Serena, Rachel and Cayleigh) are at the beach when the sea water, combined with the rays from the sun, causes a metamorphosis and transforms them into Mermaids. The girls, acknowledging the fact that they are now different, agree to help each other understand what has happened and keep each other's secret while learning to adjust to their developing powers.

Cast (as credited): MerGirl 3196 (Voices). **Comment:** The dolls appear to be from Mattel's Barbie line (although no specific doll identification is given). Two girls appear to be manipulating the dolls and providing the voices but only MerGirl 3196 is listed on her YouTube channel page. The camera work is a bit shaky at times and captures glimpses of that second girl in some scenes.

Episode List: Season 1 contains 8 untitled episodes while Season 2 consists of 6 untitled episodes.

221　A Mermaid Tale (2014). youtube.com. 2014 (Fantasy).

Alex and Nicole are friends looking for sea shells at the beach when they become separated and Alex finds a strange shell with a ribbon next to it. She places the ribbon through a hole in the shell, makes a necklace and places it around her neck. She then hears a voice say, "Mermaid when wet; human when dry. The curse will last until the end of time." Alex seems a bit unnerved and heads for home, leaving Nicole at the beach alone. Later, Nicole appears at Alex's door, upset that she had to walk home alone. Alex tries to avoid explaining why until she accidentally spills water on herself and transforms into a Mermaid in front of Nicole. Alex tells her about the necklace she made and believes that is what caused her to become a Mermaid. Nicole agrees to keep Alex's secret and help her adjust to what has happened. But doing so becomes more difficult and dangerous when an evil Siren appears and seeks to destroy Alex to acquire her powers.

Cast (as credited): Ella S. (Alex), Ella G. (Nicole). **Comment:** Pretty girls coupled with good photography makes for a pleasing story about Mermaids.

Episode List: *1. What the Heck. 2. Discovering Much More. 3. The Dark Side of Me.*

222　A Mermaid Tale (2015). 2015 (Fantasy).

While preparing a science experiment for school, a mishap occurs wherein Emma and her friend Cambree are splashed with the mixture Emma was preparing. The chemical causes the girls to fall asleep but when they awaken they discover they have been transformed into mermaids. Emma and Cambree learn that by holding their hand over their tails they can reverse the process and regain their legs. They also discover that any contact with water, as well as nights of a full moon can transform them back into Mermaids. The program relates their efforts to keep secret what happened while pretending to be ordinary girls.

Cast (as credited): Cambree and Emma as Themselves. **Comment:** While the girls are pretty and the overall production acceptable, the program has since been taken offline.

Episode List: *1*. A "Fin" Adventure. *2*. Ice Skating Lessons. *3*. Is It Open Yet?

223 *Mermaid Tales (2011)*. *youtube.com*. 2011 (Fantasy).

While preparing to take a bath, a young girl (Brenna) finds a charm that she places on her necklace. The following day, when she comes in contact with water, she is magically transformed into a Mermaid. She realizes that it was her necklace that caused the metamorphosis and that by simply saying "Go away tail," she can regain her human legs (normally a girl's legs would return after her tail dries). Brenna must now learn how to keep her secret while attempting to live the life of an ordinary girl.

Cast (as credited): Bailey (Brenna). **Comment:** An overall good production with acceptable acting, sound and photography.

Episode List: *1*. Something Fishy. *2*. Power to the Mermaids. *3*. Tails and Scales.

224 *Mermaid Tales (2014)*. *youtube.com*. 2014 (Dolls).

A young girl (Lila) receives an unexpected package in the mail and, after opening it, finds it contains a plastic drinking cup and an assortment of packets containing what appear to be various cooking spices. Lila begins experimenting with the spices and mixes them together in the cup. She adds water and what appears to be an appealing drink occurs. Amy is reluctant to taste the drink until curiosity gets the best of her and she consumes it. While it has no immediate effect on her, her life does change when she comes in contact with water and she is transformed into a Mermaid. With only a pilot episode produced it is difficult to predict what will happen in Amy's life, but it would have most likely followed the format of other Mermaid series and relate her efforts to keep what happened a secret.

Cast (as credited): Melanie McConneled (Lila Greans), Skylar Jackson (Jenny Reese), Saige Copeland (Sarah Sea). **Comment:** The program, which encompasses American Girl dolls, appears to have been abandoned. While Jenny and Sarah are listed in the cast, they do not appear. The doll movement and voice characterizations are good.

Episode List: *1*. Pilot.

225 *A Mermaid Treasure*. *youtube.com*. 2011 (Fantasy).

Millie is a 13-year-old girl who believes it is time she became a Mermaid—like her mother. Her mother, however, feels Millie is not adult enough to assume such a responsibility and refuses to grant her the power to do so. Millie believing differently has her mind set on becoming a Mermaid and elects to do it on her own. At a bookstore Millie finds a history of Mermaid mythology and buys it. As she looks through the pages at home she finds a spell that she believes will grant her desire: "O Guardian of the Deep Sea, may you grant me this one plea. I'll forever be your nightingale so long as you turn my legs into a tail." An unknown force grants Millie her wish and, through the only two episodes that were produced, it appears it would have followed Millie as she safeguards her secret (especially from her mother) while pretending to be an ordinary girl.

Cast (as credited): Cassandra (Millie). **Comment:** Thus far the only Mermaid series to focus on an Asian girl. The overall production is acceptable.

Episode List: *1*. A Fishy Discovery, Part 1. *2*. A Fishy Discovery, Part 2.

226 *Mermaid Waters*. 2013–2015 (Fantasy).

While preparing to attend a party, a young girl (Emma) notices a necklace in her bathroom sink and places it around her neck. Immediately thereafter, when she comes in contact with water she is transformed into a Mermaid. The program follows Emma as she attempts to keep her Mermaid abilities a secret while pretending to be an ordinary girl.

Cast (as credited): Lauren (Emma), Ashlie (Claire), Savannah. **Comment:** A simplistic story with pretty girls and an acceptable production; it has since been taken offline.

Season 1 Episode List: *1*. I'm a Mer ... Mer ... Mer ... Mermaid! *2*. Power Outage. *3*. Mermaid Splashin.' *4*. Stressed to Water. *5*. The Missing Story. *6*. Different Ways. *7*. Finale.

Season 2 Episode List: *1*. Moonlight. *2*. New Power. *3*. Where is Mike? *4*. A New Fish in the Sea. *5*. Thunder No Storm. *6*. I Found It. *7*. Crazy Skyping. *8*. Final Crazy Skyping.

227 *Mermaid Wonders*. *youtube.com*. 2014 (Fantasy).

While on vacation, a young girl (Zira) stumbles across a strange pool at the same time there is a full moon. Zira enters the pool and, as she finds a necklace, the water begins to bubble. Suddenly she finds herself back home and in her bed. Was it a dream? Zira believes so until she sees the necklace she found beside her and begins to wonder just what happened. Intrigued by the necklace, Zira places it around her neck and, while taking a shower, is transformed into a Mermaid. Zira's experiences as she attempts to adjust to what she has become are the focal point of stories.

Cast (as credited): Jaida (Zira), Sofia (Chelsy). **Comment:** The program is rare in that it features a young African-American girl as the lead. Unfortunately, it has very bad photography, poor sound and uses numerous filler material that slows the pace (for example, Zira doesn't become a Mermaid until the third episode).

Episode List: *1.* Packing Away. *2.* Vacation, Necklace and a Strange Place. *3.* Finding Out. *4.* The Potion That Changed Everything. *5.* The New Girl in Town.

228 *Mermaid World. youtube.com.* 2011 (Dolls).

It has to be assumed that two girlfriends, Jessica and Jade have come in contact with some sort of mystical waters as they are already Mermaids when the program begins. It is also established that their friend Jake is aware of their secret. Because the program ends unresolved, it has to be assumed Jade and Jessica will, with Jake's help, learn how to understand and control their developing powers while keeping their true identity secret from the rest of the world.

Cast (as credited): Jessica, Jade, Amber and Jake. **Comment:** The camera is a bit shaky at times but the doll movement and voices are good.

Episode List: *1.* At the Beach. *2.* At Amber's House. *3.* Untitled.

229 *Mermaids.* 2012 (Fantasy).

Liz, a young girl recently relocating to Texas with her family, meets and befriends a girl named Kenna. Unknowingly, the girls have something in common (a recessed Mermaid gene) that becomes activated when they come in contact with a strange stone pendant found by Liz. Now, with both Liz and Kenna possessing the same attributes, they must learn to embrace their Mermaid heritage while at the same time live life as ordinary young girls.

Comment: A cast and credits are not given. Even crediting the girls with first names (as has been done on other Mermaid series) should have been done as the program is a bit better than others like it. The girls are good but the sound is poor at times. The program has since been taken offline.

Season 1 Episode List: *1.* Mermaids. *2.* Power Surge. *3.* Tail of Halloween. *4.* The Deep End. *5.* Dreams (Power Hour). *6.* Unknown title. *7.* Stone Trouble. *8.* Season Finale.

Season 2 Episode List: *9.* The Uninvited Guest. *10.* Two of the Same. *11.* Bubbly Message. *12.* A Splashtastic Problem. *13.* The Siren's Tower. *14.* Finale.

Season 3 Episode List: *15.* MER (begins and ends the Third Season).

230 *Mermaids Charm. youtube.com.* 2014 (Fantasy).

Two young girls (Gabby and Violet) are enjoying themselves in a backyard pool when the water suddenly becomes very warm and magically changes them into Mermaids. This occurs in the only episode, the pilot, and presumably, Gabby and Violet will have to figure out how to live as both Mermaids and ordinary school girls (no hint of what is to follow is presented).

Cast (as credited): Gabby, Violet. **Comment:** Rather bad presentation as it looks like two girls just frolicking in a pool. It is also mostly one stationary shot as the camera is placed near the pool and what it sees is what you see. It also appears that the younger sister of one of the girls has decided to make unannounced appearance as she waves one of her plush animals in front of the camera. It can be seen that no effort has gone into the project as even what causes the metamorphosis was not well thought out.

Episode List: *1.* Pilot.

231 *Mermaids 4 Life. youtube.com.* 2013 (Fantasy).

After enjoying the day swimming at the local pool, friends Taylor and Erica find a mysterious rock with a ring and necklace that are beside it. Rather than just pass it by, they decide to take the jewelry. Nothing happens at first, but when they return to the water, they are transformed into Mermaids. Now, faced with new challenges, Taylor and Erica must keep secret their abilities while at the same time lead normal lives.

Cast (as credited): Mariella (Taylor Brooke), Charlie (Erica Wilson). **Comment:** Acceptable production (although the sound is poor at times). The girls are pretty and handle their roles well.

Episode List: *1.* Pilot. *2.* Jellyfish and Swimming. *3.* New Tail Way. *4.* Sico. *5 and 6.* Hard Tails. *7.* Serious People. *8 and 9.* Untitled. *10.* School Episode. *11.* Season Finale.

232 *Mermaids from Land. youtube.com* 2015 (Fantasy).

While watching a Mermaid video on YouTube, a young girl (Chloe) believes it contains a hidden message about a specific tree in the woods that surround her home. Intrigued, Chloe, with the help of her friend Stacy, begins a quest to find that tree. After a brief search, Chloe believes she has found the tree and discovers that it has a tent-like opening. As she and Stacy enter the tree and begin exploring, they find themselves in an apparently abandoned house and discover two bracelets. Chloe and Stacy each take a bracelet and appear to be okay until they exit the house and are transformed into Mermaids without the assist of water (although, it is later discovered that water can also cause the transformation). By manipulating their hands across their Mermaid tails, Chloe and Stacy discover they can return their legs to normal. Two young girls and the adventures they encounter as they try to conceal what they have become and lead normal lives as school girls.

Cast (as credited): Chloe (Chloe), Stacy (Stacy). **Comment:** The sound is very poor and difficult to understand making it a chore to follow the story. The program is nicely photographed and it can be seen as two girls just having fun and being themselves as they are filmed.

Episode List: *1.* I have a New Secret. *2.* Now You Know My Secret. *3.* It's Cold Outside. *4.* Mermaids Can Have Bad Dreams To. *5.* I Don't Like Secrets. *6.* I Forgot. *7.* Oops!

233 *Mermaids in the Deep Blue.* youtube. com 2014 (Fantasy).

Kathryn and Katie Dowdy are twin teenage sisters who share one secret: they are both Mermaids. It was while snorkeling in the ocean that a recessive Mermaid gene was activated and transformed the sisters into creatures of the deep. Kathryn and Katie must now keep secret what has happened and adjust to their developing powers while pretending to be normal, everyday teenage girls.

Cast: Cassidy Lewis (Kathryn and Katie Dowdy). **Credits:** *Producer:* Lidia Flish. *Director:* David Shore. *Writer:* Cassidy Lewis. **Comment:** If you did not know in advance that Cassidy Lewis plays Kathryn and Katie you would swear they were two different girls. The effects are that good for an amateur production (especially in a trampoline sequence where both girls are seen jumping at the same time). The acting and photography are also very good.

Episode List: *1.* The Deep Blue (3 parts). *2.* The Magic Hole (3 parts). *3.* The First Spell (3 parts). *4.* A 12-Year-Lie (3 parts). *5.* First Full Moon (5 parts).

234 *The Mermaid's Island.* 2013–2014 (Fantasy).

A British produced program wherein a young girl (Cleo) is magically transported to a beach where she is engulfed by strange lights, transformed into a Mermaid then magically transported back home. Cleo is followed as she struggles to conceal the fact that she is now a real life Mermaid.

Cast (as credited): Hellen Gardoord (Cleo), Madison Sallyder (Kelsey), Kaitlin Mindow (Amy), Pink Moxie Girlz (Lily), Yellow Moxie Girlz (Nixie), Rose Moxie Girlz (Sirena), Purple Moxie Girlz (Cindy). **Comment:** The girls are pretty, the dialogue easy to understand (no thick accents) but the program has since been taken offline.

Episode List: *1.* A Special Chance. *2.* The New Girl, Part 1. *3.* The New Girl, Part 2. *4.* The Potion. *5.* Untitled. *6.* The Wrong Tail. *7.* Song of the Full Moon. *8.* A Special Dream.

235 *A Mermaid's Journey.* youtube.com. 2015–2016 (Fantasy).

Paige is a young girl who lives with her grandmother, Cora. Over the past few nights Paige has had a recurring dream about having the ability to breathe underwater and swimming with a beautiful Mermaid. As Paige finds she is unable to dismiss the dreams, she approaches her grandmother about them. Cora tells her "We must talk." Cora hands Paige a star shaped necklace and explains that she was meant to be a Mermaid as Cora was also a Mermaid in her youth. Cora grew up in a magical world called Siren Springs and was best friends with a Mermaid named Joella. But Cora yearned to live among humans and abandoned Joella and her immortality; Joella resented this and grew bitter, vowing to one day destroy Cora.

Paige is taken by Cora to a hidden doorway that leads to Siren Springs. Although Paige is reluctant to open the door, Cora tells her it is time; she must encompass her destiny. Cora cannot accompany Paige as she has grown old and is not capable of making the journey. Cora is also unaware of Joella seeking revenge and believes that Joella will help Paige adjust to her new world. Paige is given the bracelet by Cora and instructed to find Joella and give it to her; Joella will then know that Cora sent her.

The secret doorway is opened and Paige enters the waters beneath it. She follows a light and emerges in Siren Springs where she meets a girl who calls herself Morgan. When Morgan spies the necklace Paige is wearing she realizes that she has some sort of connection to Cora. Unknown to Paige, Morgan is actually Joella who sees Paige as the key to her achieving her vow of revenge. Meanwhile, Cora has become uneasy and fears that Paige's journey to find Joella may be more dangerous than she thought and brings Paige's friend, Desiree, into her confidence. She tells Desiree what has happened and asks her to help Paige in Siren Springs. Desiree agrees and through magic Desiree is transported to Siren Springs. The story follows Paige and Desiree as they attempts to defeat Morgan when Paige learns who she really is and what her intentions are.

Cast (as credited): Paige, Joella, Desiree and Cora (Themselves). **Comment:** Care was taken to produce the series. The acting, story and photography are very good and *A Mermaid's Journey* is one of the best of all the Mermaid series.

Episode List: *1.* The Secret Door. *2.* A New World. *3.* A Dangerous Quest. *4.* The Hidden Past. *5.* The Betrayal.

236 *A Mermaid's Life.* youtube.com. 2011 (Fantasy).

Two girls (Alex and Lauren) are walking through the woods when they spot a waterfall that empties into a small stream. Fascinated by the falling water, the girls place their hands under it. As the water touches their skin it secretly unlocks their recessed Mermaid genes. Although nothing happens at first, the following morning their lives are changed forever when they first come in contact with water and they transform into Mermaids. Alex and Lauren must now keep secret what happened, adjust to their developing powers and pretend to be ordinary girls.

Cast (as credited): Catherine (Lauren), Heather (Alex). **Comment:** Two pretty girls, good acting and nice photography.

Episode List: *1.* The First Sight. *2.* I've Got a Secret.

237 *Mermaids on the Wave.* 2014 (Fantasy).

Cassadee and Alex are friends who, while swimming, suddenly find themselves transported to a strange pool and engulfed in bubbling water. The water transforms them into Mermaids and now Cassadee and Alex must keep secret what happened to them while trying to live their lives as ordinary girls.

Cast: Mary Frances (Alex), Anna Claire (Cassadee). **Comment:** Like most Mermaid series, the girls are pretty but the sound and photography leave a lot to be desired; it has since been taken offline.

Episode List: 2 untitled episodes, labeled "Episode 1" and "Episode 2" were produced.

238 *Mermaids Rule 101.* *youtube.com.* 2014 (Fantasy).

Emma and Serena, roommates and friends at a boarding school, are studying for an upcoming science test when they come across a strange formula and decide to experiment with it. The result has no immediate effect on them until they come in contact with water and are transformed into Mermaids. The program not only charts their adventures as they attempt to keep their secret and adjust to their developing powers, but how they use their abilities to battle evil Sirens who are seeking to absorb their powers.

Cast (as credited): Lannise (Emma/Siren Caterina), Audrey (Serena/Siren Theresa), Sadie (Melissa), Savannah (Siren). **Comment:** Very slow moving program that simply takes too long to establish things. The acting and photography, however, are acceptable.

Original Episode List: *1.* The Beginning. *2.* Shopping. *3.* The Mountain Trip. *4.* Drink Up. After these episodes the program was revised with the same cast.

Revised Episode List: *1.* The Beginning. *2.* Serena and Her House Break. *3.* School Flood. *4.* Parade and Sirens. *5.* A Trip to Kansas. *6.* Tails and Strikes. *7.* Melissa and Books. *8.* Missing. *9.* Running. *10.* Broken. *11.* Mountains.

239 *Mermaids: Secrets from the Deep.* *you tube.com.* 2014 (Fantasy).

As she walks along the street a young girl (Melody) falls through a hole and finds herself in a strange place next to a pool of water. As she looks into the water, she loses her balance and falls in. The water begins to bubble and Melody finds herself in her bed and awakening from what she believes was just a weird dream. Shortly after, when she comes in contact with water Melody transforms into a Mermaid and realizes it was no dream. The program follows Melody as she attempts to conceal her secret while pretending to lead the life of an ordinary girl.

Cast (as credited): Mermaid 101 (Melody). **Comment:** Acceptable acting and photography but the program appears to have been abandoned or cancelled.

Episode List: *1.* Something Smells Fishy (the original first episode that is not watch-able due to a faulty 3D effect). *2.* I'm a Fish (a remake of the prior episode). *3.* Powers. *4.* Lunar Eclipse.

240 *A Mermaids Story.* *youtube.com.* 2015 (Fantasy).

As two young girls (Kenya and Grace) are swimming in a pool, they find a bottle with a note inside. The girls open the bottle and read the note: "You are old enough to see what is truly inside of you." The girls are puzzled until they suddenly feel a strange sensation and are transferred into Mermaids. Kenya and Grace must now keep secret what happened and pretend to be ordinary girls while attempting to adjust to their powers of control over water.

Cast (as credited): Kenya Oliver (Kenya), Grace (Grace), Oliver (Oliver), Seth (Seth). **Comment:** The girls are pretty and, with the exception of poor sound in the first episode, the overall production is well done.

Episode List: *1.* Pilot. *2.* Boys. *3.* Dry Land. *4.* Trip to Elba Island.

241 *A Mermaid's Tail.* *youtube.com.* 2013 (Fantasy).

Three young girls (Jenny, Lela and Tiffany) are walking through a forest when they stumble across an enchanted pool. Intrigued, the girls enter its waters and are transformed into Mermaids. Each must now keep a secret while pretending to be ordinary school girls.

Cast: Kai Krasnansky (Lela), Patti Swimley (Jenny), Camilla Jensen (Tiffany). **Comment:** The girls are very pretty and perform their roles well. The photography is also good and the story typical of virtually all other Mermaid series.

Episode List: *1.* Pilot.

242 A Mermaid's World. *youtube.com.* 2012 (Fantasy).

Many decades ago a young Mermaid named Alyssa hid two star-shaped necklaces near a rock at a lake. It is 2012 when two girls (Dylan and Sadie) stumble across the rock and find the hidden necklaces. Thinking nothing of it, the girls take the necklaces and place them around their necks. The following day, when the girls use the local swimming pool, everything is normal. However, when they return home and shower, the necklaces transform them into Mermaids—secrets they must keep while leading ordinary lives. Season 2 involves the girls in a mystery when they find, while swimming in the ocean, a strange and mysterious marble and seek to uncover its origins.

Cast: Micah Cornor (Dylan King), Kinley Miller (Sadie Collins), Mikayla Welsh (Paige). **Comment:** Poor sound quality hampers an interesting production based on Mermaid mythology.

Season 1 Episode List: *1.* A Whole New World. *2.* Power Practice. *3.* Sick Days. *4.* The Eclipse. *5.* Three's a Crowd. *6.* Season Finale.

Season 2 Episode List: *1.* Season 2 Ep. 1. *2.* Rainy Day Searches. *3.* Lake Adventures.

243 MerSisters. *youtube.com.* 2013 (Fantasy).

Jessica has just returned from the library with what she believes is a book about Mermaids. When she opens it with her sister Erica they discover that it is a box disguised as a book and contains a large sea shell and a necklace. Both girls examine the items and place them back in the book. Shortly after, when Jessica and Erica come in contact with water, they are transformed into Mermaids. Shocked, but accepting what happened, they vow to keep it a secret. In a strange twist on all other Mermaid series, Jessica and Erica place the necklace around their mother's neck and the shell beside her as she sleeps. The program concludes with their mother awakening to find that she too has become a Mermaid.

Cast (as credited): Jessica (Jessica, the Blue Mermaid), Erica (Erica, the Green Mermaid), Mom (Herself). **Comment:** The program appears to have been abandoned after one episode. Jessica and Erica are very pretty and the acting and photography quite good. The twist does make for an intriguing story line but why Jessica and Erica chose to make their mother a Mermaid remains a mystery.

Episode List: *1.* Episode 1 (Pilot).

244 Midnight Mermaids. *youtube.com.* 2013 (Fantasy).

Serena and Madison are young girls who wish they were Mermaids. One day, while the girls are in the local public swimming pool, something is about to happen when a message appears on the screen saying "After this the camera broke so it's getting fixed." It apparently never did get repaired as the episode ends just there and nothing else has appeared since.

Cast (as credited): Luci (Serena), Tegan (Madison). **Comment:** The sound is low, the photography is okay but the project appears to have been abandoned and should have been taken offline as it just goes nowhere with no text information stating what the story line would be.

Episode List: *1.* Season 1, Episode 1.

245 Minnesota Magic. *youtube.com.* 2013 (Fantasy).

Chloe is a very pretty girl who is intrigued by Mermaids but strongly believes they do not exist. While walking through a park Chloe sees an unusual rock that grabs her attention. She picks up the rock and brings it home with her. As she studies the rock she becomes curious to find out more about it and turns to a book on Mermaids that she possesses. She finds a picture of the rock and reads the accompanying text, which is actually a spell. The following day, when Chloe comes in contact with water she transforms into a Mermaid and finds that what she never believed in actually exists. Although the program ends at this point, it can be assumed it would have focused on her efforts to keep secret what happened had additional episodes been produced.

Cast: Julie Rood (Chloe). **Comment:** The program has good acting and production values and no information appears as to why it was just stopped after the first episode.

Episode List: *1.* Surprises and Mysteries.

246 Modern Mermaids. *youtube.com.* 2014 (Fantasy).

Two girls (Chelsea and Persephone) are at the beach when a storm begins to develop. As they seek cover in a cave that they see, Chelsea finds a strange-looking sea shell that transforms her into a Mermaid. Persephone, however, does not see the change (in a different part of the cave) and Chelsea keeps secret what happened to her when she reverts to her normal self. As the storm lets up the girls return home. The following day when Chelsea goes for a swim she transforms into a Mermaid. Her friends (Brooke, Oceana and Persephone) witness the transformation and through Chelsea's inability to control her powers she accidentally transforms Brooke, Oceana and Persephone into Mermaids. The program follows four girls and their efforts to keep secret what they have become while pretending to lead ordinary lives.

Cast (as credited): Adeline (Chelsea), Delany (Brooke), Peyton (Persephone), Jess (Oceana).

Comment: Pretty girls, good acting and nice photography combine to make for an enjoyable series.

Episode List: *1.* The Beginning (web site title; "The Change" is the screen title). *2.* Discovery. *3.*

Misunderstood. *4.* The Secret. *5.* I Can't Live Like This. *6.* The First Day. *7.* Swimming Away. *8.* Christmas.

247 *Monster High.* monsterhigh.com 2010–2011 (Cartoon).

Monster High is a school that caters to the children (ghouls) of monsters that have survived the centuries. A look at the lives of those ghouls is presented as they simply try to live lives that are normal to them but perceived as being weird to others.

Characters:

Frankie Stein, the daughter of Frankenstein and his bride, is 15 days old, but suffers from clumsiness as her body parts have a tendency to fall off.

Draculaura is the daughter of Count Dracula but does not drink blood. She thrives on vegetables and is 1,599 years old.

Clawdeen Wolf, the daughter of the Werewolf, is covered in fur and outgoing and sweet.

Lagoona Blue, the daughter of the Creature from the Black Lagoon, is sweet and sensitive and carries her pet piranha, Neptune, with her in a fishbowl purse.

Abbey Bominble is the offspring of the Abominable Snowman of the Himalayas.

Cleo De Nile is the daughter of the Mummy and considered the mean girl of the ghouls.

Deuce Gorgon, the son of the Gorgon Medusa, is friendly but must wear sunglasses to prevent his turning people into stone.

Ghoulia Yelps is a zombie offspring and the smartest girl at school (although she only speaks zombie—moans and groans).

Holt Hyde and Jackson Jekyll are the offspring of Dr. Jekyll and Mr. Hyde.

Gill, a child of Aquaman, must wear a bubble of water over his head to survive.

The New Guy is the student whose head catches fire when he becomes excited.

Ramona is a member of the Ghoul Squad Fearleading Team.

Voice Cast: Kate Higgins (Frankie Stein), Laura Bailey (Lagoona Blue/Headmistress Bloodgood), Ogie Banks (Clawd Wolf), Cameron Clarke (Heath/Mr. Rotter), Erin Fitzgerald (Abbey Bominable/Spectra), Dee Dee Green (Draculaura), Julie Maddalena (Rebecca Seam/Venus McFlytrap), Mark Mercado (Gargoyle), Audu Paden (Ghoulia Yelps), Cindy Robinson (Holt Hyde/Jackson Jekyll), Salli Saffioti (Clawdeen Wolf), Evan Smith (Deuce Gorgon/Gil Webber), America Young (Howleen Wolf), Wendee Lee (Nefera De Nile), Andrew Duncan (Narrator). **Credits:** *Producer:* Ken Faier, Asaph Fipke, Chuck Johnson, Audu Paden. *Director:* Steve Sacks, Mike Fetterly. *Writer:* Mike Montesano, Ted Zizak. **Comment:** The animation is standard and the situations creepy enough for any fan of animated horror series. The program is presented as a tie in with Mattel Toys who distribute dolls based on the characters.

Episodes List:

1. New Ghoul in School.
2. Jaundice Brothers.
3. The Talon Show.
4. Fear Squad.
5. Substitute Creature.
6. Party Planners.
7. Blue Lagoona.
8. Copy Canine.
9. The Hot Boy.
10. Bad Scare Day.
11. Photo Finish.
12. Cyrano De Ghoulia.
13. Bad Zituation.
14. Clawditions.
15. Freedom Fight.
16. Totally Busted.
17. Freakout Friday.
18. Mad Science Fair.
19. Sock and Awesome.
20. The Good, the Bat and the Fabulous.
21. Rumor Run Wild.
22. Fur Will Fly.
23. Horroscope.
24. Idol Threat.
25. Hatch Me If You Can.
26. Date of the Dead.
27–29. Scream Building.
30. Why We Fright.
31. Fear-a-Mid Power.
32. Beast Friends.
33. Varsity Boos.
34. Gloomsday.
35. Falling Spirits.
36. Fatal Error.
37. Screech to the Beach.
38. Witch Trials.
39. Don't Cheer the Reaper.
40. Road to Monster Mashionals.
41. Queen of the Scammed.
42–43. HooDoo You.
44. Fear Pressure.
45. Fear the Book.
46. Desperate Hours.
47. Miss Infearmation.
48. Hyde and Shriek.
49. Daydream of the Dead.
50. Nefera Again.
51. Back to Ghoul.
52. Abominable Impression.
53. Frost Friends.
54. Hyde Your Heart.
55. Ghostly Gossip.
56. Hiss-teria.
57. Phantom of the Opry.
58. The Bermuda Love Triangle.
59. Here Comes Treble.
60. Dueling Personality.

61. Neferamore.
62. Rising from the Dead.
63–64. Monster Mashionals.
65. Dodgeskull.
66. Game of DeNile.
67. Uncommon Cold.
68. Ghosts with Dirty Faces.
69. Hickmayleeun.
70. No Place Like Nome.
71. Sibling Rivalry.
72. The Nine Lives of Toralei.
73. Unlife to Live.
74. Abyss Adventure.
75. Unearthed Day.
76. Creepfast Club.
77. HooDoo That, VooDoo That You Do.
78. I Know What You Did Last Fright.
79. Honey, I Shrunk the Ghouls.
80. HooDude Voodoo.
81. Undo the Voodoo.
82. Night of a Thousand Dots.
83. Beast Ghoulfriend.
84. Aba-Kiss Me Deadly.
85. Bean Scare Done That.
86. A Perfect Match.
87. His-toria.
88. The Need for Speed.
89. The Halls Have Eyes.
90. Mauled.
91. Scare-Born Infection.
92. Boo Year's Eve.
93. Franken-Styled.
94. Defending Your Lagoona.
95. Freaky Fridate.
96. The Ghoulest Season.
97. Fright Dance.
98. Scare-Itage.
99. Tough As Scales.
100. Tree of Unlife.
101. No Ghouls Allowed.
102. I Scream You Scream.
103. Frankie's Joltin' Juice.
104. Tortoise and the Scare.
105. Fierce Crush.
106. Invasion of the Ghoul Snatchers.
107. Flowers for Slo-Mo.
108. Ready, Wheeling and Able.
109. Creature of the Year.
110. Party Undead.
111. Student Disembodied President.
112. Clawbacks.
113. Field of Screams.
114. Angry Ghouls.

248 Monster Tails. *youtube.com.* 2013 (Dolls).

Claire, Taylor, Madison and Faith are friends who are looking forward to a boat cruise when they are approached by a group of girls who believe they are uninvited guests and push them overboard. The girls

spot a cave and swim toward it as a full moon begins to appear in the sky. While not shown, the Coast Guard apparently spots them and rescues them. The following day as the girls come in contact with water, they are transformed into Mermaids. The girls believe it was a combination of the sea water and the full moon that caused the metamorphosis and each must now help the other keep their secret while pretending to be ordinary teenage girls.

Voices (as credited): Chrissy and Hillary. **Comment:** Although the girls' hands can be seen manipulating the dolls, it is well done and one of the longest of the doll series.

Season 1 Episode List: *1.* The Start of Something Amazing. *2.* Power Hour. *3.* A Strange Beach Day. *4.* Moon Possession. *5.* Into the Pool. *6.* A New Monster Comes to Town. *7.* Trapped. *8.* A Change in Tail. *9.* Season 1 Finale.

Season 2 Episode List: *1.* The Other Merfish. *2.* Power Upgrade. *3.* Time Spell. *4.* Solutions. *5.* Rainy Day. *6.* Love Struck. *7.* Wishes Come True. *8.* The New Guy. *9.* Conflicts and Answers. *10.* Evil Nymph. *11.* Trouble in the Water. *12.* Controlled. *13.* Friendship. *14.* Getting Necklaces.

Season 3 Episode List: *1.* New Discoveries.

249 Moon Mermaids. *youtube.com.* 2013 (Fantasy).

While swimming in what appears to be a man-made lake, a young girl (Aqua) finds a necklace that she later shows to her friend Angel. The necklace apparently has no effect on Aqua, but it does transform Angel into a Mermaid when she comes in contact with water. Problems arise when Aqua's brother, Noah, becomes suspicious of his sister and sets his goal to find out what she is hiding. Stories follow Aqua as she attempts to help Angel adjust to her Mermaid abilities while at the same time protect her from her brother whose discovery could reveal to the world what she has become.

Cast (as credited): Jenna (Angel), Kenzi (Aqua), Maddie (Crystal), Noah (Noah). **Comment:** While the girls are cute, the sound is poor and the picture suffers from unsteady movement.

Episode List: 4 untitled episodes, labeled "Episode 1" through "Episode 4" have been produced.

250 Moon Tails. 2014 (Fantasy).

One day Jess and her sister, Tessa, find a pair of rings lying on the grass. Although Tessa knows they are magical moon rings and should not be worn, they each place one on their finger. Their first contact with water transforms them into Mermaids and Jess and Tessa must now not only keep their identities a secret but use their abilities to defeat a group of evil Sirens who have become a threat to humans.

Cast (as credited): Sarah, Jessica, Oceane. **Comment:** The program, since taken offline, has pretty girls but poor sound and video quality. It uses the theme song to the Disney Channel series *Girl Meets World* ("Take on the World" as sung by Rowan Blanchard and Sabrina Carpenter) as its theme song.

Episode List: *1.* The Rings. *2.* Situations and Books. *3.* Powers. *4.* Sleepovers. *5.* Sirens in Summer. *6.* Siren's Message.

251 *Moonlit Mermaids of the Lagoon.* you tube.com. 2012 (Fantasy).

It is established that a young girl (Oceana) has been a Mermaid for quite some time and has kept her secret from everyone, including her parents and best friend Cordelia. One day, as Oceana and Cordelia walk alongside the shore line of a lagoon, Cordelia spots a rock formation, attempts to climb it but loses her balance and falls into the water. Oceana immediately jumps into the lagoon and saves Cordelia's life but she reveals the fact that she is a Mermaid. While Cordelia attempts to adjust to what has just happened, her life changes forever when she transforms into a Mermaid (the water released Oceana's essence which was absorbed by Cordelia's body, causing her metamorphous). The program, which appears to have been abandoned, just ends here with the assumption that the girls will have to conceal who they are while pretending to be ordinary girls.

Cast (as credited): Katie (Oceana), Bethany (Cordelia). **Comment:** Although it is not established how Oceana became a Mermaid, the program is well acted and photographed. No reason is given as to why additional episodes were not made.

Episode List: *1.* Episode 1 (Pilot).

252 *Mountain Mermaids.* youtube.com. 2013 (Fantasy).

The lives of two girls, Kylie and Elizabeth, change forever when they find what appears to be a note (not shown) that leads to a hidden treasure. As they follow the map, it leads them to a strange necklace but nothing else. Is the necklace the treasure? The following day, as Kylie and Elizabeth go for a hike, they take a wrong turn and find themselves on the wrong side of a mountain trail. Suddenly, the ground opens and the girls fall into a water pool in a cave. The water begins to bubble and its effects transform them into Mermaids. Kylie and Elizabeth exit the water and when their tails dry their human legs reappear. They manage to find their way out of the cave and back home but each must now pretend to be ordinary girls while concealing the fact that they are actually Mermaids.

Cast (as credited): Dani (Kylie), Kate (Elizabeth). **Comment:** The girls are pretty, the premise a bit stretched at times, but the acting and photography are good.

Episode List: *1.* The Treasure Hunt. *2.* The Discovery. *3.* Research. *4.* The Test. *5.* The Secret Door. *6.* Phone Call.

253 *Mrs. P. Presents.* youtube.com. 2009– 2011 (Children).

Stories selected by children from "The Magic Library" (via the program's website) and read by Mrs. P., a kindly middle-aged woman whose readings are interspersed with static drawings that illustrate various aspects of each story.

Host: Kathy Kinney (as Mrs. P.). **Credits:** *Producer:* Clay Graham, Kathy Kinney. *Illustrations:* Jacob Herring. **Comment:** Pleasant program for children with a matron-like host that, in most cases, are presented in a reasonable amount of time (under 15 min.). Kathy Kinney's name may be familiar as she played Mimi on *The Drew Carey Show.*

Episode List:
1. Billy's New Plant.
2. The Big Yellow Cat.
3. The Magic Baseball Poster.
4. Rumpelstilkskin.
5. The Little Match Girl.
6. Jack and the Beanstalk.
7. Goldilocks and the Three Bears.
8. The Emperor's New Clothes.
9. Wanda's Wart.
10. Aladdin.
11. The Brave Little Tailor.
12. The Little Mermaid.
13. Thumbelina.
14. The Butterfly.
15. The Fir Tree.
16. The Inexperienced Ghost.
17. Faithful John.
18. The Little Brother and Sister.
19. The Gold Children.
20. Rikki Tikki Tavi.
21. The Cat That Walked By Himself.
22. The Elephant's Child.
23. The Magic Piano.
24. Home Perfect Home.
25. The Ugly Duckling.
26. The Goose Girl.
27. The Nightingale.
28. Bad Little Boy.
29. A Pair of Silk Stockings.
30. The Monkey's Paw.
31. The Hand.
32. The Tell Tale Heart.
33. Nightmare.
34. The Velveteen Rabbit.
35. The Gift of the Magi.
36. Hand and the Nightmare.
37. The Snow Man.
38. The Brave Tin Soldier.
39. Alice in Wonderland.
40. Snow White.
41. The Six Swans.

42. Sally's Poor Brain.
43. The Three Little Pigs.
44. Eugene Fitz and the Impish Gnome.
45. Tom Thumb.
46. Hansel and Gretel.
47. Little Red Riding Hood.
48. Androcles and the Lion.
49. Cinderella.
50. Rapunzel.
51. The Princess and the Pea.
52. Sleeping Beauty.
53. The Frog Prince.
54. The Treasure Decision.
55. Thinking Cap.
56. Ramona and the Fire.
57. Lucky the Bamboo Chopper.
58. Mountain Dog.
59. Pretty Princess and Funky Frog.
60. Spattered Mud and Crushed Petals.
61. The Peanut Butter and Jelly Hotdog.
62. The Tale of Squirrel Nutkin.
63. The Walrus and the Carpenter.
64. The City Mouse and the Country Mouse.
65. Puss 'n' Boots.
66. The Tale of Peter Rabbit.
67. The Cat That Walked By Himself.
68. The Goose Girl.
69. The Six Swans.
70. The Gold Children.
71. The Hand and the Nightmare.

254 *Ms. Vampy's Tween Tawk, Teen Tawk & In Between Tawk.* msvampy.net. 2011 (Talk).

Ms. Vampy, a vampire from Brooklyn, New York, molded in the style of Cassandra Peterson and her Elvira, Mistress of the Dark character, presents information to girls that cover topics such as body image, peer pressure, self-esteem, facing one's fears and the opposite sex.

Host: Brooke Lewis (Ms. Vampy). **Credits:** *Producer;* Brooke Lewis, Alison B. Buck. *Writer-Director:* Brooke Lewis. **Comment:** Brooke Lewis is a very sexy vampire and she presents her conversations well with references to current teen idols, movies and TV series that also fall into a topic of discussion.

Episode List: *1.* In Between Tawk, Part 1. *2.* In Between Tawk, Part 2. *3.* Tween Tawk, Part 1. *4.* Tween Tawk, Part 2. *5.* Teen Tawk, Part 1. *6.* Teen Tawk, Part 2.

255 *My Best Friend Is a Mermaid.* youtube.com. 2012 (Fantasy).

Hoping to be like her slightly older friend, Kristina, a young girl (Emma) begins by trying to emulate her. One day, when Kristina stumbles across a gate that leads to a lake, she becomes compelled to go swimming; unknown to Kristina she has been followed by Emma. Although it appears that Kristina has been unaffected by the water, she later discovers that when she comes in contact with water, she transforms into a Mermaid. Emma, drawn to the magical lake, also swims in it, and she too becomes a Mermaid when water touches her skin. Now, with Mermaid abilities in common, Kristina and Emma must conceal their secret and try to live normal lives.

Cast (as credited): Brianna (Kristina), Elizabeth (Emma), Sky (Sophie), Bree (Jordan). **Comment:** The girls handle their roles quite well and overall a good production although some scenes are a bit blurry and jumpy.

Season 1 Episode List: *1.* The Fall That Changed Everything. *2.* True Friends. *3.* Secret Revealed … Again. *4.* Fish'd. *5.* Power Point. *6.* Cursed Shell. *7.* Season 1 Finale.

Season 2 Episode List: *8.* Promises. *9.* Untrusted. *10.* Moonlight Dreams. *11.* The Potion. *12.* Transformed. *13.* The Sleepover. *14.* Season 2 Finale.

Season 3 Episode List: *15.* The New Beginning. *16.* New Moon. *17.* Wet Works. *18.* The Missing. *19.* Closed Doors. *20.* Bucket List.

256 *My BFFs a Mermaid.* youtube.com. 2013 (Fantasy).

The program begins with a young girl (Crystal) swimming in a pool with a clear indication that she is a Mermaid. Her friend, Christina unexpectedly arrives to visit her and discovers her secret. But Christina is more upset than Crystal as Crystal never told her that she was a Mermaid. The following day Christina confronts Crystal and learns from her that she was born a Mermaid and that her parents were creatures of the sea and used their abilities as Protectors (special MerFolk assigned to protect Mermaids from Hunters). The program just ends here with no real hint as what to expect next.

Cast (as credited): Crystal and Christina as Themselves. **Comment:** The program is rather slow moving and editing would have helped to tighten scenes. The acting and photography are acceptable and in a separate "Update Video," Crystal and Christina appear on camera to explain that, although they have been lax, they do plan to continue the series. But, being that much time has passed, it appears unlikely.

Episode List: *1.* Something Fishy.

257 *My Big, Big Friend.* youtube.com. 2012–2014 (Cartoon).

Lili, Matt and Yuri are six-year-old friends with one thing in common: an imaginary big blue elephant named Golias. As the children experience a problem and seek answers on how to solve them, Golias becomes real to them and takes them on exciting but imaginary adventures that he feels will present them with the solutions they are seeking.

Voice Cast: Addison Holley (Lili), Nissae Isen

(Yuri), Tajja Isen (Nessa), Scott McCord (Golias). **Credits:** *Producer*: Peter Williamson, Kevin Gillis. **Comment:** Very good animation and charming stories in a well produced series geared to very young children. Each program consists of two episodes.

Season 1 Episode List:
1. Brickle Pickle/All the Way Up.
2. Hippolicious/Clowning Around.
3. Air Buddies/The Good Sneakers.
4. Skipping Stones/No Kid Is an Island.
5. Show and Tell/Perfect Princess.
6. Count Glerm/Hair Brained Idea.
7. Accident's Happen/Lili's Tea Party.
8. Tell Me a Story/Food's Up.
9. A Chance of Tomatoes/Time Out.
10. Missing Miss Puffy/Descent to the Downstairs.
11. Faeries of the Forest/Diggin' a Hole.
12. Fort Messy/Beach Blast.
13. Finders Keepers/Everyone's a Critic.
14. King of the Monkeys/That's My Spot.
15. Music Man/Dream On.
16. It's My Party/Doggie Duty.
17. Derailed/Something Special.
18. Sleepover/I Didn't Think of That.
19. The New Farmer/Perfect Picnic.
20. Lili Bee/Flower Power.
21. No, My Game/Manly Matt.
22. Stickers/Matt's Fun Park.
23. Big and Small/Valentine's Day.
24. The Boat Ride/Hot and Cold.
25. Super Lili/Holding It In.
26. You Can't Me/Toy Drive.

Season 2 Episode List:
1. Harold the Hamster/The Caterpillar Dance.
2. Toy Breaker/Stuck.
3. Ready, Set, No!/Orange and Purple.
4. Hooray for You/No Way, Karate.
5. Teacher Trouble/A Knightly Thing to Do.
6. One and Only/Sand and Flowers.
7. Love Potion/The Pink Princess Nightgown.
8. Let's Play Forever/Can't Wait.
9. Toughen Up, Nessa/More Like Matt.
10. The Amazing Matt/Don't Give Up.
11. Into the Dragon's Den/What About Me?
12. What's the Big Idea?/Ice Cream and Bananas.
13. Musical Chairs/Who Did It?
14. Helpless/Taste Test.
15. Leader Lili/The Incredible Shrinking Matt.
16. I Can Do That/Where Are You?
17. Santa Lost His Sleigh.

258 *My Boyfriend's a Vampire.* youtube.com. 2013 (Dolls).

Samantha is a teenage girl who is dating a boy named Cory. All seemed well with Samantha until Cory's strange behavior has her believing that he is hiding something from her. While it is revealed that Cory is a vampire, the program just ends in the middle of nowhere with Samantha having a dream that Cory is a creature of the undead but not sure if it was just a dream or a vision.

Cast (as credited): Claire Vernon (Samantha), Ryan Singer (Cory), Hallie Portman (Meg), Kittie Reese (Rita), Elizabeth Fisher (Debby). **Comment:** The program appears to have been abandoned. It does have some sound problems (noticeable dead air) but the voices, doll manipulation and photography are good (there are even neck biting scenes).

Episode List: 2 untitled episodes, labeled "Episode 1" and "Episode 2" have been produced.

259 *My Ghost Sister and Me.* youtube.com. 2010 (Drama).

Rosie Jenkins is a 14-year-old girl living in England with her mother following her parents (Nick and Susan) divorce, who feels that something is missing from her life. One day fate intervenes and Rosie discovers that element: her younger sister, Amy, who has returned from the dead as ghost, first to be a sister to Rosie then to warn Rosie and protect her from a demon (The Dark One) who is seeking her soul. (Amy was killed in a tragic accident that so traumatized Rosie that she created a mental block to conceal all memories of Amy). As Rosie and Amy become close, Rosie learns that she is a Seer (can communicate with the dead) and that The Dark One seeks to bring her to his side (evil) by stealing her soul. Amy's efforts to protect Rosie from The Dark One form the basis of second season episodes. The first season relates Rosie's efforts to convince her disbelieving mother that Amy has come back as a ghost while the concluding third season explores Rosie's efforts to help people with her newly discovered abilities.

Cast: Heather O'Connell (Rosie Jenkins/Amy Jenkins/Kate Evans), Jason O'Connell (Susan Jenkins/Nick Jenkins), Brianna Lynn (Alison Gemmerson), Dominic O'Connell (The Dark One), Leon Ward (Justin Jenkins), Jack Elm (Jacob Tyler), Ann O'Connell (Mary Smith), Hannah Wilson (Young Susan), Nicola O'Connell (Julie Burkins). **Credits:** *Producer-Writer-Director*: Jason O'Connell.

Comment: Heather O'Connell is delightful and convincing in her dual role as Rosie and Amy. Although the program is produced in England, it is not hampered by thick British accents and is easily understandable. The production values are good even though the split screen effect is not used for the sisters (Amy and Rosie do not appear together or side by side in the same scene; the camera instead focuses on the individual character as she speaks. This is understandable as limited budget programs cannot encompass stand-ins and the cost involved in creating the illusion of one actress appearing as two people in one scene). It works here and the program, which has a man playing the role of the mother, is enjoyable and worth watching for the ghostly aspect it presents.

Episode List: *1.* The Meeting. *2.* A Plan Is Formed. *3.* Guilty. *4.* Goodbye. *5.* Ouija Boo, Part 1. *6.* Ouija Boo, Part 2. *7.* Gone but Not Forgotten. *8.* The Seeer. *9.* A Haunting Revelation. *10.* Something Suspicious. *11.* Paranormal Activity. *12.* Protect Me Not. *13.* Crossover. *14.* Surprise. *15.* What Was Then. *16.* A Visit from the Past. *17.* The Sleepover. *18.* Spirit Away. *19.* Truth. *20.* The Christmas Episode (Although not a part of the series, it is a special episode that has Rosie and Amy celebrating their first holiday together).

260 *My Immortal: The Web Series.* *myim mortalseries.com.* 2013 (Musical Comedy).

Enoby Darkness Dementia Raven Way is a student at Hogsmeade, a magical high school that teaches future wizards how to embrace their special abilities. Enoby is not the brightest of girls and while she has trouble pronouncing her own name, she believes she is the number one Goth girl and will stop at nothing to prove it. Students like Harry Potter, Hermione Granger and Ron Weasley have become victims of her misguided efforts and stories follow Enoby as she turns the fantasy world of Harry Potter, including the Hogwarts School, upside down.

Cast: Justine Cargo (Enoby Darkness Dementia Raven Way), Joseph Bradley (Harry Potter), Eli Terlson (Draco Malfoy), Justin Kosi (Ron Weasley), Jennah Foster-Catlack (Hermione Granger), Jen Matotek (Bellatrix Lestrange), Tanya Casole-Gouveia (Narcissus), Richard Chuang (Yaxley), Jeff Stone (Snap), Brian McLellan (Loopin), Dani Alon (Millicent Bulstrode), Amie Everett (Pansy Parkinson), Michael Demski (Viktor Krum), Gabriel Mansour (Vlad). **Comment:** If you like a heroine who has trouble pronouncing her own name (although she is pretty), dancing (maybe attempting to dance) Goths, satanic faith and a confused Harry Potter then *My Immortal* is your cup of tea.

Season 1 Episode List: *1.* Prepz. *2.* Tear Up the Night. *3.* Episode 3. *4.* The Yule Ball. *5.* Dumbledore Dies.

Season 2 Episode List: *1.* Episode 1 Improved. *2.* Queen of Cups. *3.* House Show. *4.* Battle of the Bands. *5.* Ron's Day. *6.* The Authority. *7.* Queen of Pentacles. *8.* Queen of Wands. *9.* Final Battle.

261 *My Life as a Mermaid.* *youtube.com.* 2015 (Fantasy).

It is a moon-lit night when mysterious balls, made of blue glass, appear in the bedroom of a girl named Clare. Curious, Clare begins examining the balls and is mystified as to what they are or how they just appeared in her room. Shortly after when Clare washes her hands, the water transforms her into a Mermaid—the effect of touching the blue glass balls. Although Clare quickly adjusts to what has just happened, she is shocked to learn that she is considered "The Chosen One" (also called "The Special One") and must use her abilities as a Mermaid to save mankind by finding a mystical ball that is also being sought by evil Sirens who plan to use its power to destroy the world above the seas.

Cast (as credited): Isabel Peterson (Clare), Maddie (Kiki), Clara (Niomie), Faith (Shawa), Dixie (Merissa). **Comment:** Nice photography, capable acting by the cast but the sound is a bit hard to understand at times.

Season 1 Episode List: *1.* The Moon's Gift. *2.* An Important Dream. *3.* Kiki's Letter. *4.* Lalala. *5.* Who Is Niomie? *6.* The Ankle Anchor Bracelet. *7.* Spell Book. *8.* Powers. *9.* Power Glitch. *10.* Niomie's Return. *11.* Showing the Tail.

Season 2 Episode List: *1.* The First Tail. *2.* Sick Days. *3.* The Moonlight Trance. *4.* The Moon's Care Package. *5.* Kiki's Love Life. *6.* Reading Minds. *7.* Cinco de Mayo—Par-Tay! *8.* The Truth. *9.* The Magic Amulet. *10.* The Power of the Magic Amulet. *11.* The Visions.

Season 3 Episode List: *1.* The Shell Switch.

262 *My Life as a Vampire.* *youtube.com.* 2012 (Dolls).

Annabelle and Rosie Blackwood are sisters that live in LPS (Littlest Pet Shop) City (also representing the dolls used). Annabelle is in the ninth grade while Rosie is a sixth grader. One day after school Rosie makes a horrifying discovery: Annabelle is a vampire (when she sees her feeding on her latest victim). Annabelle does not harm Rosie but the program mostly veers off the vampire theme after the first episode to become more of a doll's-eye view of life in school.

Cast (as credited): Jay (a 15-year-old boy who does all the voices and doll movements). **Comment:** Interesting when you consider it is a teenage boy providing the voices and not a girl. Overall the doll manipulation is well done and no reason is given why the format strayed away from the vampire theme.

Episode List: *1.* Hard Times. *2.* At First Glance. *3.* Broken Love. *4.* Harsh Winter, Part 1. *5.* Harsh Winter, Part 2. *6.* Guess Who's Back? *7.* Captured.

263 *My Little Mermaid Secret.* *youtube. com.* 2012 (Fantasy).

While in the backyard of her home, a young girl (Cadence) spies a blue cup on a table. As she picks up the cup she finds a note attached that reads "Drink Me." Curious, but without really thinking first, Cadence takes a sip. Immediately, she is transformed into a Mermaid and now, with developing powers, she must keep her new identity a secret while pretending to be an ordinary girl.

Cast: Cadence Amudson (Cadence). **Comment:** Young girls who attempt to make their own series all fall into one basic category: an inability to properly use a camera. Here, while Cadence tries to do a good job, her framing of scenes is bad and some scenes are quite unsteady.

Episode List: *1*. The Drink. *2*. I'm a Mer.... *3*. The Power.

264 *My Living Doll. youtube.com.* 2013 (Fantasy).

While in the backyard of her home, a young girl (Amy Kingston) finds what appears to be an abandoned, beat-up doll. She shows it to her friend, Katie, who tells her it is just trash and to discard it. Amy, however, feels a strange attraction to the doll and elects to keep it. Amy names the doll Maisy and proceeds to clean her and provide new clothes for her. All is progressing well until Maisy becomes real and a possible threat to Amy (and Katie) as it appears Maisy needs to possess Amy to remain alive. The British produced program ends in a cliff hanger-like situation with everything left unresolved but it can be assumed Amy will somehow overcome Maisy (most likely with the help of Katie) and return her life to normal.

Cast: Amy Kingston (Herself), Sophie Kent (Katie Ciffield), Molly Lucas (Maisy). **Comment:** Like the series *Doppelganger* (see entry) it is a horror-themed show aimed here, however, at both boys and girls. While the story and acting are acceptable, a very shaky camera makes it difficult to watch.

Episode List: *1*. How We Found Her. *2*. She's Alive. *3*. The Threat.

265 *My Magical Mermaid Life.* 2012 (Fantasy).

During their swim in a public pool, two girls (Jessie and Emma) find ankle bracelets on the pool floor. The girls exit the pool, place the bracelets on their ankles and return to the water. Magically they are transformed into Mermaids (by coincidence, there are no other swimmers and their secret is not exposed). Later, the girls each discover they have a power: Jessie can freeze water, Emma can heat it. The program follows Emma and Jessie as they must learn to accept what they have become.

Cast (as credited): Emma (Herself), Jessie (Herself). **Comment:** Pretty girls but a very badly presented pilot with an unsteady camera and a splashed water drop on the camera lens that blurs images. The program has since been taken offline.

Episode List: The Pilot.

266 *My Magical Secret Mermaid Life. you tube.com.* 2013 (Fantasy).

Jessica is a teenage girl who returns from school to find a bracelet in a cup of water in her room. Why is it in water? Who put it there and why? Not having the answer to any of the questions, Jessica places the bracelet on her wrist and is suddenly endowed with dual abilities: those of a Mermaid and those of a wizard. In a twist on normal Mermaid stories, Jessica must now learn to not only control her transformations into a Mermaid but also adapt to her life as a magical wizard.

Cast (as credited): Sarah (Jessica, Brenna, Mom and Brittany). **Comment:** Sarah plays all the roles (even sings the theme) but all hope for the series is lost with bad filming and equally bad sound. While used, special effects are very poorly done. Sarah appears to be having a good time, but her enthusiasm does not spill over to attract viewers. If some care had been taken to script the program and incorporate one or two other girls to play roles, it might have come off better than it now plays.

Episode List: *1*. Bracelet in Water. *2*. Tail Wizard and Friend. *3*. Enemy Plus Powers. *4*. Pool Party Mayhem. *5*. The Rock. *6*. Scavenger Hunt to Save a Secret. *7*. The Cave. *8*. Brittany's Heroes Are Not Heroes.

267 *My Mermaid Life.* 2013 (Fantasy).

Tess is a young girl who stumbles across a mysterious bottle containing an unknown liquid. As she examines the bottle she becomes overwhelmed and takes a sip. Nothing happens at first but when she comes in contact with water she transforms into a Mermaid. The program, produced in Germany, follows Tess as she struggles to keep secret what happened and as she adjusts to living life as a Mermaid.

Cast (as credited): Laura Verstraelen (Tess), Daan (Niels), Emma (Jolijn), Lucky (Himself). **Comment:** The format of a young girl finding a mysterious liquid has been done several times before but it is seen from a different perspective being produced in a foreign country. The acting is good and the girls pretty but like American Mermaid series, the sound and photography are only acceptable. The program has since been taken offline.

Episode List: 9 untitled episodes, labeled "Episode 1" through "Episode 9" have been produced.

268 *My Mermaid World.* 2015 (Fantasy).

Jade is a young girl whose dreams constantly revolve around Mermaids. She has no explanation as to why until she finds a note from her mother, who mysteriously disappeared years ago, that explains the reason: she left to escape Mermaid Hunters who were seeking her and protect Jade (who, when she becomes of age, will transform into a Mermaid). Jade disbelieves the note, thinking her friend Kinsey played a trick on her. However, when Jade enters the kitchen and comes in contact with water, she transforms into a Mermaid but the situation does not seem to faze her (it's like nothing even happened). The next day, when Jade invites her friend Derek over, and attempts to get him a glass of water, she accidentally spills some on herself and, knowing what is about to happen, attempts to run off but transforms in front of Derek before she is able to do so. As Derek promises to keep her secret Jade realizes that her mother was actually a Mermaid and fled to protect her. She must now, with Derek's help, keep her secret, learn to adjust to her developing powers and pretend to be an ordinary girl.

Cast (as credited): Isabelle N. (Jade), Yoshi Y. (Derek), Madelyne (Alice). **Comment:** Overall, a nicely filmed program with good acting; it has since been taken offline.

Season 1 Episode List: *1.* The Weird Note. *2.* I Know Your Secret. *3.* Power Freak. *4.* New Tail. *5.* Full Moon Magic. *6.* The Chase.

Season 2 Episode List: *1.* The Chase Continues. *2.* Kidnapped. *3.* New Powers.

269 *My Mysterious Life. youtube.com.* 2011 (Dolls).

A teenage girl (Jessica) has just moved into a new home and immediately becomes unsettled when she begins hearing strange noises and cannot figure out where they are coming from. Having just made new friends (Nicole and Rebecca), Jessica invites them over and confides in them what she has been experiencing (why she didn't tell her parents is not explained). Adding to the mystery is a note that the girls find that tells Jessica "To get out of the house or else." Although episode 2 is missing (and perhaps established a story line) it has to be assumed that Jessica, with the help of Nicole and Rebecca, will become detectives and attempt to solve the mystery of what (or who) is haunting Jessica's home (as determined by the remaining episodes).

Cast (as credited): Jenny (Jessica), Renee (Nicole), Rachel (Rebecca). **Comment:** Interesting story, good doll manipulation and voices but the sound is obstructed at times in outdoor scenes by wind blowing into the microphone.

Episode List: *1.* The Beginning. *2.* Unknown. *3.* Rebecca's Accident. *4.* What's Wrong Sky? *5.* A Mysterious Person. *6.* A New Friend. *7.* Nicole's Powers. *8.* Jessica's Powers.

270 *My Secret Mermaid Life (2012). youtube.com.* 2012 (Fantasy).

While out for a swim a young girl (Samantha) encounters a magic fountain that sprays her with water then mysteriously transports her back home. Although she is unable to figure out what happened, Samantha appears to be fine until she comes in contact with water and transforms into a Mermaid with a pink tail. Realizing that it was her encounter with the fountain that caused the metamorphosis, Samantha finds that she must now encompass her Mermaid abilities while at the same time conceal her secret and resume her life as an ordinary school girl.

Cast: Samantha Pape (Samantha). **Comment:** Capable acting by Samantha but the program is flawed

by poor sound (resulting from only using the camera microphone) and a very unsteady picture at times.

Episode List: *1.* Metamorphosis. *2.* Surprise Tail. *3.* The Weird Change. *4.* Splash of Legs and Tail. *5.* Bath Tail. *6.* Finding 2 Powers. *7.* Finding Another Power and Tail. *8.* Tail Trouble. *9.* The Crescent Moon Light. *10.* Washing and Water Tail. *11.* Powers, Water, Tail. *12.* Tail and Powers. *13.* Beach Tail. *14.* Tail, Powers, Water and Natalie—What Next? *15.* Treadmill Tail + Drawing Tail. *16.* Tail and Searching. *17.* Pool, One Wish Plus Magic Bath. *18.* Ring and Strange Water Craving. *19.* Full Moon, Magic Fountains and Spilling Water. *20.* Grandma and Trouble. *21.* Powers, Natalie's Tail. *22.* Uh-Oh. *23.* My Secret Slipped. *24.* Dream, Pass Out, Shower.

271 *My Secret Mermaid Life (2013). youtube.com.* 2013 (Fantasy).

As a young girl (Ashley) begins swimming at the beach her eye catches a shiny object that draws her to it and magically transports her into The Moon Cave. At that exact moment, the water, affected by the moon's rays, begins to bubble and appears to trap Ashley. Ashley, keeping a cool head, manages to find her way back to the ocean and safety. Although unnerved, she appears to be unharmed. The following day, however, when Ashley comes in contact with water, she transforms into a Mermaid and must now navigate life as a creature of the sea and a normal young girl.

Cast (as credited): Ashley (Herself). **Comment:** Underwater scenes are well done, Ashley is good but the program suffers from poor sound.

Episode List: *1.* Pilot.

272 *My Splash Side. youtube.com.* 2015 (Fantasy).

An earthquake, deep within the Pacific Ocean, unleashes a tsunami that washes ashore two Mermaids (Veronica and Finley). The girls (in their human-like state) are found and raised by a human family with two young daughters, Piper and Zoey. Veronica and Finely, hoping to one day return to their realm in the sea, keep their abilities secret and sneak out of the house each night to energize themselves in the ocean. Piper and Zoey, however, have become suspicious of their actions and have set their goal to figure out what Veronica and Finley are hiding. Realizing that their secret is in danger, Veronica mixes a potion that she believes is harmless and will just deter Piper and Zoey from continuing their probe. The potion makes Piper and Zoey sick and backfires when Piper and Zoey come in contact with water and are transformed into Mermaids. Veronica and Finley reveal their secret to Piper and Zoey and the four girls must now learn to keep each other's secret and pretend to be ordinary girls while learning how to encompass their Mermaid abilities.

Cast (as credited): Gabby K. (Veronica), Maci H. (Finley), Julia K. (Piper), Hannah H. (Zoey). **Comment:** Very pretty girls, good acting and nice photography highlight a series that shows potential if further episodes are produced.
Episode List: *1.* Scale Tails. *2.* Double Trouble.

273 *Mysterious Murders.* youtube.com. 2013 (Dolls).

The LPS (Littlest Pet Shop) dolls are incorporated to tell the story of the search for a killer who preys on teenage "children."
Voices (as credited): Trudy. **Comment:** Although the topic sounds somewhat out of the range of children, comments posted on YouTube show that kids love this kind of stuff. There are scenes of "graphic violence" (a doll laying on its side and fake blood placed near it) and because animal dolls are used, it is much tamer than adult live-action series that deal with the same topic. The voices, music, doll manipulation and photography are good.
Episode List: *1.* How It All Started. *2.* The Dream.

274 *Mystery Mermaids.* youtube.com. 2013 (Fantasy).

While on the beach, a teenage girl (Fay) sees a young girl lying on the sand (a Mermaid washed up from the sea and with her human legs). The girl (Willow) is struggling to adjust to her "land legs" (after spending much time as a Mermaid) and is wearing a strange bracelet—a bracelet that is identical to the one Fay is wearing. The program ends here and it can be assumed that the bracelets are linked to each other and Fay is also a Mermaid.
Cast (as credited): Maija (Willow), Laura (Fay). **Comment:** *Mystery Mermaids* could be considered the second worst Mermaid series as *Mystical Magical Tails* (see entry) holds the record as being the worst. Fay is not very like-able and a bit overweight to become an attractive Mermaid. She is also very unsympathetic—as Willow struggles to get to her feet and is asking for help, Fay just stands there and watches. It is only when Willow does manage to get to her feet that Fay shows any signs of compassion when she notices the bracelet.
Episode List: *1.* Pilot.

275 *The Mystic Tails.* youtube.com. 2012 (Fantasy).

While walking through the woods, two young girls (Izzy and Maya) are attracted to a river's memorizing waterfall and find two necklaces sparkling in the water. The girls retrieve the jewelry and place them around their necks. Everything appears to be normal. That night, when the girls come in contact with water, they transform into Mermaids—a secret they soon discover is also possessed by a school mate (Kylie) who also found a necklace in that river. Three girls drawn together by a secret and their abilities to guard that secret form the bases of the series.
Cast (as credited): Hannah H. (Izzy), Kaylan Y. (Maya), Kaylynn K. (Kylie), Candice R. (Morgan), Becky K. (Kahea). **Comment:** Acceptable Mermaid series although using camera microphones presents sound that is quite poor at times.
Episode List: *1.* Beginning Through Trouble Waters. *2.* And Then There Were 3. *3.* A Book Can Say a Thousand Words. *4.* Frozen in Fear. *5.* The Acceptance of Something Great. *6.* Unraveled Mysteries. *7.* The Bigger Picture. *8.* Decisions, Decisions. *9.* Dreams of Danger. *10.* Abducted. *11.* Game On.

276 *Mystical Magical Tails.* 2015 (Fantasy).

A cave, with magical powers has remained hidden for an untold amount of time, until two girls (Rikki and Katey) and a young boy (Tyler) discover it and are transformed into Merfish. Now as creatures of the sea, Rikki, Katey and Tyler must keep secret their metamorphosis while at the same time pretending to be ordinary children.
Cast (as credited): Rikki, Katey and Tyler as Themselves. **Comment:** Absolutely the worst of the Mermaid series (even viewer comments on YouTube complain about it—and these are from kids!). Not only is the sound hard to understand but it has terrible camera work: upside down and side scenes; shaky out-of-frame scenes and scenes with the camera searching for something to film. The program has since been taken offline.
Season 1 Episode List: *1.* Pilot. *2.* Scales. *3.* Powers. *4.* Untitled. *5.* The Moon's Power. *6.* The Key. *7–9.* Untitled. *10.* Magic. *11.* Fever. *12.* Swim.
Season 2 Episode List: *1.* Untitled. *2.* Episode 2. *3.* Uh Oh.

277 *Mystical Mermaid Magic.* youtube.com. 2012 (Fantasy).

Three girls (Courtney, Caroline and Nicole) are swimming in a lake when they are magically transported to a cave and placed in knee deep water. It has to be assumed the water is enchanted as the next scene shows the girls back home. As the only produced episode ends, each of the girls comes in contact with water and is transformed into a Mermaid. It also has to be assumed that the program will follow their efforts to keep secret what happened as they adjust to their Mermaid powers.
Cast (as credited): Katelyn (Courtney), Beth (Caroline), Taylor (Nicole). **Comment:** The program has low sound and just ends in the middle of nowhere. The acting is good but it appears the program has just been abandoned.
Episode List: *1.* Season 1, Episode 1.

278 *Myths.* youtube.com. 2013–2014 (Dolls).

Aine is a young girl who believes she does not

exist. She is 14 years old and is living in secret with Nana Wisdom, a woman who took her in when she found her 12 years ago wandering the streets. Aine only reveals that she ran away from her home due to "an injustice." She has never attended school, has no friends and no one even knows she exists. Or so she thinks. It is on the occasion of her 14th birthday that Aine's life changes forever. Nana reveals to her that from the day she was born she has been special but was not of age to encompass what she really is—a Fairy (like Nana). But there are those who seek to capture and imprison Fairies and Aine must realize that her life is in constant danger from those who seek to harness her powers. The program relates what happens when Nana is captured by evil Fairies and Aine must risk her life to save her.

Cast (as credited): Kae (Alice), Henry (Leo). **Comment:** Well done and intriguing program with good doll movement. A problem does exist, however, with music over powering certain scenes and making it difficult to understand what is being said.

Episode List: 11 untitled episodes, labeled "Episode 1" through "Episode 11" have been produced.

279 Namaka (Mermaid Show). *youtube. com.* 2013 (Fantasy).

It is the night of a full moon when three girls (Blaze, Nikki and Alex) enter a backyard pool. The rays from the moon cause the water to bubble and affect the girls by transforming them into Mermaids. Three girls, a shared secret and their efforts to adjust to their developing powers while pretending to be ordinary school girls.

Cast: Emma Petrelli (Blaze Hildon), Krystal Black (Nikki Mendez), Lydia Blue (Alex Smith). **Comment:** The girls are very pretty and perform their roles well but the photography is horrible with a picture that is very unsteady (bobs in and out). The girls realize this and in YouTube comments mentioned that they chose a very bad cameraman and hoped to replace him if future episodes were made.

Season 1 Episode List: *1.* Pilot. *2.* Meet Kate. *3.* Testing. *4.* Dark Moon. *5.* Revealed. *6.* Powers. *7.* Birth Day. *8.* Pink Moon.

Season 2 Episode List: *1.* Halloween Special, Part 1. *2.* Halloween Special, Part 2. *3.* News from Namaka.

280 Neptune's Mermaid. *youtube.com.* 2013 (Fantasy).

Kristie is a young girl who has kept a secret her whole life: her late mother was a Mermaid. Kristie had been influenced by her mother and her greatest desire is to also become a Mermaid. One day, unknown forces grant Kristie her desire and she is transformed into a Mermaid. Kristie must now encompass the abilities of a Mermaid while attempting to lead an ordinary life.

Cast (as credited): Brianna (Kristie and Alyssa). **Comment:** Acceptable photography but the production suffers poor sound at times.

Season 1 Episode List: *1.* Changes. *2.* Adjustments. *3.* New Girl. *4.* A Fishy Birthday. *5.* Ashley. *6.* The Abduction. *7.* Phase 2 of the Mermaids. *8.* Season 1 Finale.

Season 2 Episode List: *9.* Caves and Sirens. *10.* Mer-Hunt. *11.* Tied Up and Everything. *12.* The Siren's Realm (series finale).

281 The Nerdy Journal. *youtube.com.* 2013 (Dolls).

Hailey is a preteen girl and just entering the sixth grade. She dresses like what she calls "a nerd" but is anything but. She has friends, is bright and feels she needs to record her life as it unfolds through a video journal. The program simply relates Hailey's activities as she navigates life at school and at home.

Cast (as credited): Hannah (Voices). **Comment:** A simple premise that is well done with good doll manipulation and voices.

Episode List: 4 untitled episodes, labeled "Episode 1" through "Episode 4" have been produced.

282 New Life as a Mermaid. 2015 (Fantasy).

Aqua is a young girl who, while swimming, discovers a strange shell that magically transforms her into a Mermaid. Rather than keep secret what has happened, Aqua tells her best friend, Serena, and upon showing her the shell, she too is transformed into a Mermaid. The girls must now share a secret and not only figure out how to live dual lives, but cope with their developing powers.

Cast (as credited): Aqua and Serena as Themselves. **Comment:** As with several other such series, pretty girls cannot always save a program. While the acting is acceptable, the sound and photography are faulty at times. The program has since been taken offline.

Episode List: *1–4.* Untitled. *5.* Siren's Warning. *6.* Moon Struck Tragedy.

283 The New Mr. Peabody and Sherman Show. *youtube.com.* 2015 (Cartoon).

Peabody's Improbable History was a segment of the 1959 TV series *Rocky and His Friends* about a young boy named Sherman and his friend, Mr. Peabody, a wise dog that created a device (the Way Back Machine) that enabled them to travel back in time to witness historical events. In 2014 the segment was made into the feature film *Mr. Peabody and Sherman.* In the closing segment of the film Mr. Peabody and Sherman decide to begin a television series hosting historical figures from their penthouse. It is from this point that the Internet series picks up and through its episodes, present not only time travel but conversations with the historical figures they elect to visit and help (like advising Cleopatra on how to get a date; helping Wilbur and Orville Wright find their missing air plane; helping Queen Isabella recoup the money she lost to a scam artist so she can finance Christopher Columbus's trip; taking Galileo into outer space so he can see that the world is round, not flat).

Voice Cast: Chris Parnell (Mr. Peabody), Max Charles (Sherman). **Credits:** *Producer:* David P. Smith, Tiffany Ward. *Director:* John Sanford, Greg Miller, Mike Bell. **Comment:** Although not an exact duplicate of the original TV segment, the characters closely resemble them. The animation is a bit disappointing to anyone who recalls the original version. The program can be seen for free on YouTube or for a fee on Netflix, for which it was produced.

Episode List: The Perfect Show/Napoleon. 2. Stuck/Mozart. 3. Sherman's Pet/Marco Polo. 4. Handcuffs for a Song/Wright Brothers. 5. New Sponsor/Cleopatra. 6. Black Hole/Winston Churchill. 7. Big Boy/Blackbeard. 8. Biggest Fan/Queen Isabella. 9. Peabody's Parents/Galileo. 10. Patch Games/Mark Twain. 11. Favor for Christine/Lady Godvia. 12. Medieval Fest/John Sutter. 13. Outbreak/Greek Games.

284 *No Ordinary Girl (2013). youtube.com.* 2013–2015 (Fantasy).

While searching for her lost cat Annie, a young girl (Mia) wanders into the woods and finds herself in a strange area that she has never seen before. As she attempts to cross a running stream her foot touches the foam that sometimes forms in the water near the shore line. Mia feels it is best to leave and manages to find her way back home (without her cat). Later, when she begins changing the water in her aquarium, the water touches her hand and she transforms into a Mermaid. The program follows Mia's adventures (and later with Peyton when she too becomes a Mermaid through a spell) as she attempts to adjust to her Mermaid powers while at the same time hoping to keep secret what has happened to her.

Cast (as credited): Kathryn (Mia), Sarah (Hailey), Amber (Peyton), Charlie (Zach). **Comment:** A quality production with good acting and photography.

Season 1 Episode List: *1.* Change. *2.* Zach. *3.* A New Light. *4.* Powers. *5.* Fail. *6.* Mind. *7.* Ocean Potion. *8.* Prank. *9.* Science Fair. *10.* Friends/Enemies. *11.* Lonely. *12.* Two Mermaids. *13.* Edmonton. *14.* Forgiven. *15.* Kidnapped.

Season 2 Episode List: *1.* Miserable Hero. *2.* Saving the Day. *3.* No Ordinary Powers. *4.* Discovering Powers. *5.* Sea Monsters. *6.* Mermaid Magic. *7.* Great, It's Jayden. *8.* Never Again. *9.* The Haunting. *10.* Turtle Madness. *11.* Fish Fever. *12.* The Book. *13.* Escape. *14.* Research. *15.* Goodbye.

285 *No Ordinary Girl (2014).* 2014 (Fantasy).

Two sisters (Ahavah and Eloise) are in a forest-like area when a mysterious force engulfs them and transforms them into Mermaids (but they are not seen as Mermaids but have their associated powers). The program, produced in France, follows the girls as they learn to accept what has happened to them and keep it secret.

Cast: Ahavah Huart (Ahavah), Eloise Huart (Eloise). **Comment:** A well acted and photographed program but there is no English translation or available sub titles. The program has since been taken offline.

Episode List: 3 untitled episodes, labeled "Episode 1," through "Episode 3" have been produced.

286 *No Ordinary Girls. youtube.com.* 2011 (Fantasy).

Angelica and Alex are at a café when their waitress friend (Amber) serves them a meal with water. Amber, as well as Angelica and Alex drink the water and moments later transform into Mermaids. The program just ends at this point with no text or video information relating what will happen next (other than assuming the girls will keep secret what happened as they adjust to becoming Mermaids).

Cast (as credited): Angelica, Alec and Amber as Themselves. **Comment:** A rather poor production in story, video and acting.

Episode List: 2 untitled episodes, labeled "Episode 1" and "Episode 2" have been produced.

287 *Not So Normal.* 2011 (Fantasy).

Kristen and Danielle are sisters who, while walking together stumble upon a strange, apparently abandoned house and enter it. Spotting a bowl of an unknown liquid the girls dare each other to drink from it. The dare is taken and, after consuming the liquid, it appears each girl is fine. Later, however, when they return home and come in contact with water, they are transformed into Mermaids. Now, with a secret they must keep the program charts their efforts to do just that while attempting to be ordinary young girls.

Cast as Credited: Kristen, Danielle, Megan. **Comment:** An Australian produced series with pretty girls but only acceptable sound and photography; it has since been taken offline.

Episode List: *1.* Lost for Miles. *2.* Transformation. *3.* Another Tail. *4.* Dreams Come True. *5.* Going Wild. *6.* The Loud Mouth. *7.* When Water Strikes. *8.* Tentacle Trouble.

288 *Ocean Destiny. youtube.com.* 2015 (Fantasy).

It appears to be just another typical day for a girl named Bella until she goes to wash her hands and finds a strange necklace in the sink. Intrigued, she places it around her neck and is transformed into a Mermaid. Her efforts to figure out what happened (how the necklace got in the sink and who put it there) and keep her secret are the focal point of stories.

Cast: Micaella Constandinou (Bella). **Comment:** The program starts off rocky with very bad camera work, poor sound (hard to understand at times) and a slow-moving plot. It gradually improves but getting through those first episodes is a major problem.

Season 1 Episode List: *1.* Metamorphosis. *2.* Powers. *3.* Full Moon Starts. *4.* New Power. *5.* Rikki or Bella.

Season 2 Episode List: *1.* All Just a Dream. *2.* The Loosing. *3.* The Talking Olivia. *4.* I'll Help You. *5.* Guardians.

Season 3 Episode List: *1 and 2.* Untitled. *3.* Back to School.

289 Ocean Heart Mermaids. youtube.com. 2009–2014 (Fantasy).

While home alone a young girl (Rizu) finds a strange heart-shaped stone on her front porch. Although puzzled as to how it got there, Rizu picks up the stone and brings it inside. Shortly after, when Rizu washes her hands, the water transforms her into a Mermaid; when she dries herself off, she regains her human legs. Rizu theorizes that the stone is magic and she must now encompass the life of a Mermaid (a member of the Sisterhood of Mermaids) while also trying to keep her secret and retain her identity as a normal school girl.

Cast (as credited): Lizzie (Rizu), Abby (Michi, Rizu's sister). **Comment:** One of the longer Internet Mermaid series that has good underwater photography but suffers at times from poor sound.

Season 1 Episode List:
1. The Stone.
2. And Then There Were Two.
3. Testing the Waters.
4. Christmas Special.
5. Visiting Yia Yia.
6. The Musical.
7. Hurricane Brittani.
8. Virtual Reality.
9. Our Fishy Cousin.
10. Hector the Pest.
11. Disturbance in the Air.
12. Interesting Neighbors.
13. Getting Mono.
14. The Return of Cousin Waldorf.
15. The Merman.
16. Dancing on Water.
17. The Discovery.
18. Powers.
19. The Dangerous Boyfriend.
20. Mysteries Abound.
21. Deep Freeze.
22. Season Finale.

Season 2 Episode List:
23. Rizu Come Home.
24. Got Hunger.
25. Mermaid Dungeon.
26. Christmas Special.
27. Clarence the Tutor.
28. Alter Egos.
29. Halloween Special.
30. Shellfish Secret.
31. Fat Camp.
32. She's a Robin Egg.

290 Ocean Mermaid. 2013 (Fantasy).

After visiting an area called Moon Falls Island, a young girl (Reeva) finds that it has activated a recessed gene and transformed her into a Mermaid. Now with a secret she must keep, Reeva struggles to adjust to her developing powers while pretending to be an ordinary girl.

Cast (as credited): Phoebe as Reeva. **Comment:** The program, with acceptable acting and production values, has since been taken offline.

Episode List: Six untitled episodes, labeled "Episode 1" through "Episode 6" have been produced.

291 Ocean of Dreams. youtube.com. 2013 (Fantasy).

Emma and Kylee are young girls who are strangers to each other until they accidentally bump into each other one afternoon. They decide to hang out together even though Emma feels "there is something fishy" about Kylee and Kylee has the same feelings about Emma. As they talk, Emma tells Kylee she knows the location of a secret pool; intrigued, Kylee asks Emma to take her there. As the girls enter the water, a ball of changing colors mysteriously appears. The water becomes warm and begins to bubble, activating a recessed gene each carries that transforms them into Mermaids. Now, with developing powers and a secret they must keep between themselves, Emma and Kylee struggle to also live their lives as ordinary girls.

Cast (as credited): Brooke (Emma Jones), Peyton (Kylee Geller). **Comment:** The girls perform their roles well and the photography is acceptable.

Episode List: *1.* The Secret Pool. *2.* Powers before the Change. *3.* Something More Powerful. *4.* New Powers. *5.* Number 4. *6.* Potion Book.

292 Ocean of Glass. youtube.com. 2013 (Animated Fantasy).

Marissa is a young girl who prefers her own dream world as opposed to living in the real world. Her mother wants her to be "normal" and she has a half-sister who is "perfect." One day, while swimming in the ocean and doing what she enjoys most—finding "treasures" on the ocean floor, Marissa spies a strange sea shell, made into a necklace that magically attaches itself to her and allows her to breathe underwater. That night Marissa has a dream wherein she meets a Mermaid (Blank) who tells her she is no longer a "full human" but a "Mer" and has been given Mermaid ears that can only be seen by "Mers" but not a tail ("That will change in good time"). The program follows Marissa as she struggles to accept what she has (and will) become while attempting to keep her new life secret.

Voice Cast: Shashona Hetherington (Marissa), Rachel Davis (Blank). **Comment:** The program encompasses still-like animation with only slight mouth movements. It is a bit strange at first, but once you adjust to it the program becomes quite enjoyable. The voices actors are very good and do a great job making the whole concept work.

Episode List: *1.* Eternal Blue (Pilot).

293 The Ocean Potion. *youtube.com.* 2011 (Fantasy).

Based on the only video information that appears on line (a trailer), it appears to tell the story of a young girl who finds a magic potion, drinks it and not only transforms into a Mermaid, but inherits ancient powers as well.

Cast (as credited): Grace, Morgan, Will and Matt. **Comment:** The trailer is basically all of season 1 seen in a sped-up recap (that runs 2 minutes and 29 seconds). The series cannot be followed by this although it can be seen that the girls are pretty and the photography good. It is also impossible to evaluate the overall series based on this remnant.

294 Ocean Secrets. *youtube.com.* 2014 (Fantasy).

It is a warm summer day when two girls (Piper and Oceana) walking along the beach shore come across strange sea shells. The girls become intrigued by the shells and take them home with them. Later, while examining her shell, Oceana cuts her finger on it. After treating her wound, she decides to take a shower. Her contact with the water transforms her into a Mermaid. Meanwhile, Piper, who also possesses a sea shell, becomes a Mermaid when she first comes in contact with water. Piper and Oceana now share a secret and, as they attempt to adjust to their developing powers must also pretend to be ordinary school girls.

Cast: Hannah Jenkins (Oceana and Clover), Megan Wakefield (Piper), Sarah Jenkins (Regina). **Credits:** *Producer-Director*: Hannah Jenkins, Megan Wakefield. **Comment:** Although a notice appears that the first episode is "really bad" it is better than some other Mermaid series. The acting and production does improve as the series progresses.

Episode List: *1.* The Magic Shell. *2.* The Not-So Secret. *3.* The Magic Bracelets.

295 Ocean Sisters. *youtube.com.* 2014 (Fantasy).

Kim and Tori are friends who, while walking along the street spot two necklaces sitting atop a tree stump. They pick them up, examine them and, thinking nothing about it, place them around their necks. Shortly after when Kim and Tori come in contact with water they transform into Mermaids and must now conceal what they have become while pretending to be ordinary girls.

Cast (as credited): Emma (Kim), Michelle (Tori), Elena (Olivia). **Comment:** A good story coupled with pretty girls, good acting and nice photography.

Episode List: *1.* A Change. *2.* Tori's Nightmare. *3.* Friendship Is No Day at the Beach. *4.* Into the Tide.

296 Ocean Tails. *youtube.com.* 2011 (Fantasy).

A young girl (Kat) is standing by a pool when her brother pushes her and she falls into the water. Angered, she storms out of the pool but is mysteriously transported to a strange area where she finds herself in another pool. Here, when the water begins to bubble, she is transformed into a Mermaid. Although shocked, Kat quickly adjusts to what has happened but finds that what she was able to do before, especially with her best friend Lilly, is no longer possible as any contact with water will cause her to change into a Mermaid. The program follows Kat as she tries to keep secret what happened and reconnect with Lilly, who is bitter with Kat for neglecting her.

Cast (as credited): Erika (Kat), Jodi (Lilly/Tessla), Brooke (Amity). **Comment:** There is an annoying background clicking noise that can be heard in each episode. The photography is acceptable, the girls are very pretty but the story just ends abruptly after the third episode.

Episode List: *1.* The Change. *2.* Old and New. *3.* Untitled.

297 Oh Noah! *youtube.com.* 2011 (Cartoon).

Noah is a very curious nine-year-old boy whose life suddenly changes when he visits his grandmother, Abuela, in a Spanish-speaking section of Mexico and finds that his inability to speak the language places him in an awkward situation: he cannot communicate with her (or anyone else) and must take it upon himself to learn Spanish. Noah's efforts to learn simple words and phrases are meant to help young children also learn and understand simple Spanish. The program was originally titled *Noah Comprende.*

Voice Cast: Jorge Diaz, Vanesa Tomasino, Omar Avila, Danny Katiana, Katie Leigh, Ricardo Nunez, Alicyn Packard. **Credits:** *Producer*: Jill Peters, Ashley Postlewaite, Reggy Regan, Sandra Sheppard, Darrell Van Citters, Miao Chen. *Director*: Darrell Van Citters.

Writer: David Matthew Feldman, Louise Gikow. **Comment**: Produced in association with the digital PBS Kids channel, the animation is typical of such shows and, through the mishaps Noah encounters through a language barrier, does manage to achieve its goal of teaching children basic Spanish.

Episode List: *1*. A Wale Tale. *2*. Breaking the Ice. *3*. Down the Drain. *4*. Goodbye Kitty. *5*. Hammer Away. *6*. Hop, Look and Listen. *7*. I Say Tomato. *8*. Monkey Business. *9*. Not Milk. *10*. Out on a Limb. *11*. The Red Balloon. *12*. Making a Splash.

298 The Old Mermaid from Key West. *you tube.com*. 2013 (Fantasy).

A legendary Mermaid named Marina, the daughter of the King of the Seas (Neptune) is sunning herself on a supposedly deserted beach when she is spotted by a young girl (Zoe). Zoe possesses a net and sneaks up upon Marina and captures her. Zoe takes Marina, who has become weak without water, to her home and locks her in the garage. Zoe has managed to keep Marina hidden from her parents but Marina is growing weaker and must return to the ocean and to her home on Australia's Great Barrier Reef or she will lose her powers forever. Although only one episode has been produced, it shows Marina's desperate efforts to escape from Zoe and return to the sea. Additional episodes appear to have been planned as two other characters are seen in the opening theme ("Mom" as Queen Isabella and "Gabbi" as Siren Sister) but do not appear in the first episode.

Cast (as credited): Maria Valladares (Marina), Verena (Zoe). **Comment**: The program, though easily explained above, is a bit confusing to figure out as there is a lack of continuity. The acting is acceptable but the photography is quite bad (jerky and shaky camera).

Episode List: *1*. Pilot.

299 On Top of Witches. 2015 (Fantasy).

Emma is a young girl who has just moved into a new home with her family. The house appears to be quite old and Emma is adjusting to her new surroundings when she hears a voice (her invisible guide) tell her that she is a witch and that she must learn to use her powers for good. The program basically follows Emma as she begins her apprenticeship while at the same time concealing the fact that she is a witch.

Cast (as credited): Micalla (Emma). **Comment**: There are limited and good special effects but the program is slow moving and has poor sound and poorly framed scenes. It has since been taken offline.

Episode List: *1*. New Home. *2*. Bad Magic Hair Day. *3*. First Day of School.

300 Once Upon a Mermaid. *youtube.com*. 2014 (Fantasy).

Friends Mary and Sarah are in Mary's home when Mary reaches in the kitchen cabinet for a glass and finds a piece of paper that turns out to be a recipe. Curious, the girls decide to make the drink called for by the recipe. Shortly after drinking the mixture they are transformed into Mermaids. They must now help each other adjust to what has happened and attempt to keep it secret while pretending to be ordinary girls.

Cast (as credited): Emma De La Paz (Mary), Hannah De La Paz (Sarah). **Credits**: *Writer-Director*: Hannah De La Paz. **Comment**: Acceptable acting and production although it does drag a bit at times.

Episode List: *1*. Fish Out of Water. *2*. Powers. *3*. Stalker. *4*. Vengeance. *5*. Way Too Close.

301 Once Upon a Zombie. *facebook.com*. 2013 (Cartoon).

An evil curse has been placed on the lovable characters of Fairy Tale Land and turned their world upside down. Once adored by children, Cinderella, Snow White, Sleeping Beauty, Ariel (The Little Mermaid), Rapunzel and Belle (from "Beauty and the Beast") have become Zombie Princesses and the program follows their efforts to reverse the curse before they become evil and are unable to return to their former selves.

Comment: It appears that only the two episodes listed were produced. It is stated that a series "is coming in the fall of 2013" and based on "the children's book and frightfully fabulous doll line coming fall 2013"; but for unknown reasons it appears to have never occurred. It is a very well done computer animated series but unfortunately there are no voice or production credits listed on the screen, YouTube or IMDb.

Episode List: *1*. Once Upon a Zombie Preview. *2*. Once Upon a Zombie Sizzle.

302 One Different Secret. *youtube.com*. 2012 (Fantasy).

While swimming in the ocean two young girls (Aly and Serena) see a mysterious white rock (which they touch), hear hypnotic-like music and see the splash of what appears to be the tail of a fish (actually the tail of a Mermaid). It is the following morning and the girls, at Serena's home, have no idea as to how they got there or whether what they saw in the ocean was real or just a dream. Their mystery is solved when Serena accidentally spills a glass of water on herself and she transforms into a Mermaid (with a gold tail). Aly is unbelieving until Serena throws water on her and she too transforms into a Mermaid (with a blue tail). Minutes later they transform back into normal girls when the water evaporates and their legs reappear. Aly and Serena, however, are no longer normal girls; they have been endowed with Mermaid abilities through contact with the white rock and must now learn to encompass their abilities as Mermaids to protect the oceans while at the same time resume their lives as average American girls.

The plot also has the girls encountering two Shape Shifter sisters: Marlowe and Talie. When they were children Marlowe and Talie found a black and white rock in their backyard and touched it. Marlowe, touching the white side, became good [life and air] and Talie, touching the black side became evil [death and Earth]). Aly (the sun) and Serena (the moon) also have elements but are unable to defend themselves when Talie appears and must now join with Marlowe and defeat Talie (who seeks to destroy them and acquire their powers).

Cast (as credited): Claire (Aly Fisher), Avery (Serena Watchmen), Sophie (Talie Kresh), Olivia (Marlowe Kresh), Laura (Laura Star). **Comment:** For a program that is apparently run by a young girl (Avery) it is a remarkable achievement. While not as professional as other such programs about Mermaids (but on the level with *A Splashy Tale*, which is also done by a young girl) it does show that with a good idea a program can be developed—and turn out better than you would think being done by someone so young (and obviously talented).

Episode List: *1.* Ocean Swim. *2.* Element Change. *3.* Shape Shifter's Trick. *4.* Bad News. *5.* The Unexpected. *6.* The Missing Mermaid. *7.* Forgotten Memories. *8.* Answers Lead to Questions. *9.* A Half for a Whole. *10.* Old Age Magic. *11.* How About an Upgrade. *12.* Call of the Sirens. *13.* Laura's Potion. *14.* The Beginning of Something New. *15.* Life with Talie.

303 One Mermaid Tail. *youtube.com.* 2013 (Fantasy).

A young girl (Ashley) is alone at the beach when she finds a series of unusual sea shells. She gathers them up and takes them home with her. When she takes them out of her bag she discovers that some of the shells have transformed into a necklace. Ashley places the necklace around her neck but becomes light headed and faints. As she awakens, she finds two notes and hears a voice: "We are the Mermaid Guardian. We are here to protect you." Ashley is then told to get "The book on Mermaids" that her grandmother gave her when she was a young girl. As Ashley looks over the book she learns she is destined to become a Mermaid. The program, however, ends at this point and it is assumed Ashley will be guided in her actions by the mysterious Mermaid Guardian (the voice) as she adjusts to her new life.

Cast (as credited): Alex as Ashley. **Comment:** Alex is very pretty and can keep one watching but very low sound (even with the volume up full) is a problem. It is just too difficult to understand what the soft-spoken Alex is saying. The acting and photography, however, are very good.

Episode List: 3 untitled episodes, labeled "Episode 1" through "Episode 3" have been produced.

304 One Minnesota Mermaid. 2013 (Fantasy).

Sapphire is a young girl who wishes for only one thing: more excitement in her boring life. One day, when she goes into the kitchen of her home she sees a necklace on the counter with a note (from "The Sea") telling her to wear the necklace. Sapphire does so and when she goes for a drink of water she transforms into a Mermaid. Now, with the excitement she wanted, she must also pretend to be an ordinary girl and keep secret what happened.

Cast (as credited): Erin (Sapphire). **Comment:** The program needs to better establish how the necklace came to be on the counter and that she is the only family member to notice it. The sound and photography are only adequate and the program has since been taken offline.

Episode List: *1.* New Mermaid. *2.* Finding Treasure. *3.* Thanksgiving Mermaid. *4.* New Powers. *5.* The Day after Christmas.

305 One Tail, One Secret. *youtube.com.* 2014 (Fantasy).

After a strange dream in which a girl (Luna) envisions three keys, she awakens to find those keys by her side. The keys are to a chest Luna has in her bedroom that once belonged to her late mother. Luna opens the chest and finds what she calls "Mermaidy stuff." As she looks over the items she discovers a bottle with a blue liquid and a diary that reveals her mother was a Mermaid. She learns through the diary that it is now her turn to carry on her family's Mermaid tradition and instructions to rub the blue liquid on her legs and look into a magic sea shell mirror (from the chest) on the eve of a full moon. As Luna proceeds to follow the instructions, she hears a voice emanate from the mirror that tells her to place a necklace from the chest around her neck. She does so but nothing happens. The following day, the effects of the procedure become evident when she goes swimming and transforms into a Mermaid. Luna's efforts to keep secret what happened as she adjusts to her developing powers are the focal point of stories.

Cast (as credited): Sasha (Luna), Vivian (Emily). **Comment:** Surprisingly well done program with pretty girls, very good acting, story and photography.

Episode List: *1.* Something Fishy. *2.* Halloween. *3.* New Girl in Town. *4.* Broken. *5.* Back and Forth.

306 Or So the Story Goes. *orsothestorygoes. com.* 2014–2016 (Anthology).

Modern, multi-part adaptations of classic fairy tales presented in a darker retelling of each fable.

Condensed stories are presented on the first spin off *Or So the Story Goes: One Shots* (see title) while a paranormal comedy was presented in a second spin off (from the episode "Happy Thoughts") called *The Jolly Rogers Case Files* (also see for information).

Comment: The production values are well above many other Internet series with acting that is also exceptional. There are numerous fairy tales from which to adapt material and encompassing the same child performers in various roles could make the program more kid friendly as certain performers will become favorites to viewers. Although comparisons could be made to the television series *Goosebumps* and *Shelley Duvall's Faerie Tale Theater*, *Or So the Story Goes* is a totally different take on what has been done before and entertaining to watch. For its 2016 season, *Or So the Story Goes* takes a bold step forward with a slasher production of *Rumplestiltskin* that is rated PG and geared to an older teenage audience. At the time of publication the project had only just begun production.

Episodes:

1. *Little Rosemary.* A three-part retelling of *Little Red Riding Hood* that begins when a ten-year-old girl (Rosemary) mysteriously vanishes and her friend, twelve-year-old Hazel Leonard, sets out to discover what happened to her.

Cast: Rainni Moran (Hazel), Rayna Loos (Lilah), Lilla Cabrera (Rosemary), Blake Weissman (Matty), Christopher Michael Christiana (Simon), Noah Dunton (Rich), Penelope Hinds (Seana), Melissa Malone (Rachel), Diann Gogerty (Lexi), Anais Fifer (Charlene), Edward Nolan (John). **Credits:** *Producer*: Melissa Malone, Jackie Moran, Outtake Productions. *Director*: Melissa Malone, Theresa Labreglio. *Writer-Creator*: Melissa Malone.

Episode List: Three episodes, titled "Little Rosemary, Part 1," "Little Rosemary, Part 2" and "Little Rosemary, Part 3."

2. *Happy Thoughts.* A ghost hunting team attempts to help a family (the Darlings) whose home is haunted by the ghost of a homicidal teenage boy (Peter) that has set his sights on the family's daughter (Wendy).

Cast: Noah Dunton (Peter), Rayna Loos (Wendy Darling), Joe Lenihan (John Darling), Abigail Friend (Michelle), Jerry Scaglione (Sam), Syd Livingston (Nana Lorraine), Hank Morris (Lindsay Darling). *The Ghost Hunters*: Melissa Malone (Jane Hook), Bryan Civitarese (Ronnie), Diann Gogerty (Percy), Christopher Michael Christiana (Julian). *The Lost Children*: Rainni Moran (Lea), Tristan Moran (James), Penelope Hinds (Miranda), Blake Weissman (Tootles), Amelia Osborne (Tina). **Credits:** *Producer*: Jackie Wheeler-Moran, Outtake Productions. *Director*: Theresa Labreglio. *Writer*: Melissa Malone, Theresa Labreglio. *Assistant Director*: Rainni Moran. *Composer-Musical Director*: Judith Avers.

Episode List: 1. Welcome to Neverland. 2. You Know How Rabbits Are. 3. Tick Tock. 4. Will C. 5. Nothing to Lose. 6. Get Up. 7. Two Sides of the Coin.

3. *Sweet Truth.* Gretel Marin is a 15-year-old girl obsessed with getting the most views for her video vlog, "Sweet Truth." One night, while out with her tech-savvy friend, Hansel seeking a story, Gretel crosses the path of a seemingly kind woman (Gwendolyn) who offers them refuge when they become lost in the woods. Gretel and Hansel soon discover that they, along with two sisters (Emmeline and Aveline) are being held captive in Gwendolyn's home. Gretel's efforts to escape by joining forces with Emmeline and Aveline to defeat Gwendolyn form the basis of the story. Based on the Grimm's Brothers story "Hansel and Gretel."

Cast: Julia Bushman (Gretel), John Elliott Pickel (Hansel), Heather Girardi (Gwendolyn, the Witch), William Day (Lance), Hank Morris (Cecilia, the Evil Stepmother), Rainni Moran (Emmeline), Abigail Friend (Aveline), Edward Smucygz (Officer Jim).

Credits: *Producer*: Jackie Wheeler-Moran, Outtake Productions. *Director*: Theresa Labreglio. *Writer*: Theresa Labreglio, Melissa Malone. *Musical Director/Composer*: Judith Avers.

Episode List: 1. You're in or You're Out. 2. The Last Straw. 3. We're Lost. 4. Straight from the Oven. 5. Don't Forget to Subscribe.

307 *Or So the Story Goes: One Shots.* *orso thestorygoes.com.* 2014 (Anthology).

A spin off from *Or So the Story Goes* that presents short, dark stories of people's encounter with the unknown.

Cast: Rainni Moran (Lauren), Melissa Malone, Diann Gogerry. **Comment:** Although only one episode was produced, it is well acted, written and directed. It is suspenseful but geared to children and does not delve into the realms that would unnecessarily frighten them.

Episode List:

1. The Box. Following the death of her mother, a 14-year-old girl (Lauren) receives a box as an inheritance with a stipulation that she never open it. The story focuses on Lauren as her curiosity grows and temptation beckons her to open the box.

308 *The Other Side of Me: A Mermaid Story.* *youtube.com.* 2013 (Fantasy).

As Leah and her younger sister, Rosa Lin are playing in their backyard they find a bottle containing a blue liquid. Curiosity gets the best of them and they each take a sip. Other than being foul-tasting, nothing appears to happen. Minutes later, however, when they come in contact with water, they transform into Mermaids. The program follows two sisters and how they adapt to becoming Mermaids while pretending that nothing ever happened.

Cast (as credited): Ava (Leah), Lily (Rosa Lin) Natalie (Skyler). **Comment:** Standard Mermaid series with acceptable photography and acting.

Episode List: 1. A New Life. 2. A Magical Mistake.

309 Our Crazy Mermaid Life. *youtube.com.* 2011 (Fantasy).

While swimming in the ocean a young girl (Nikki) fears for her life when it begins to thunder. Spotting what appears to be a sea cave (said to be an underwater volcano), Nikki seeks shelter and swims into it. The waters that encircle the volcano, however, are magical and begin to bubble. The scene immediately switches to Nikki in her bedroom and reaching for a water bottle. Her first drink of the water transforms her into a Mermaid. With a secret she must keep and with powers she must learn to control, Nikki must now pretend to be an ordinary girl. **Cast (as credited):** Alahna (Nikki), Madison (Ally), Haley (Mikala), Olivia (Lexi). **Comment:** The swift shift from the cave to the bedroom sort of ruins the program as no explanation is given as to how that happened. The sound is very poor and the program also suffers from an unsteady picture. **Season 1 Episode List:** *1.* The Switch. *2.* Something's Fishy. *3.* Unsafe Waters. *4.* Nikki's Not Alone. *5.* Finding Out Ally's Powers. *6.* The Test. *7.* The Problem with Nikki. **Season 2 Episode List:** *1.* Who Is Nikki? *2.* A Wave of Excitement.

310 Our Little Scaly Secret. *youtube.com.* 2012 (Fantasy).

It is the night of a full moon and three friends (Clare, Amber and Rose) decide to sleep outdoors. As they sleep the moon's rays encompass them and, unknown to them, activate a recessed Mermaid gene each possesses. The following day, when each girl comes in contact with water she is transformed into a Mermaid. The program follows their efforts to protect their secret while pretending to be ordinary girls. **Cast (as credited):** Megan (Claire), Juliet (Amber), Crystal (Rose). **Comment:** The girls are pretty and the photography is good but the episodes are a bit slow-moving. **Episode List:** *1.* A Wish Come True. *2.* Breakfast and Moon Wash. *3.* Sea Shells and Candles. *4.* Eating Lunch Is Dangerous.

311 Our Mermaid Adventure. *youtube.com.* 2012 (Fantasy).

One day two sisters (Saraphina and Lizzie) find a strange note that tells them they are about to embark on an adventure: "On a day of the month when the moon is visible during the day, take a bath as if you were dry." Saraphina and Lizzie follow the instructions but shrug it off as nonsense when nothing happens. Later that day, however, when the girls come in contact with water, they transform into Mermaids—and must now guard their secret while also pretending to be normal girls. **Cast (as credited):** Saraphina, Lizzie, Alyssa.

Comment: Enjoyable Mermaid adventure with good acting and underwater photography but the use of camera microphones makes it difficult to understand the dialogue at times. **Episode List:** *1.* The Book. *2.* The Secret. *3.* Do the Mermaid. *4.* Well That Didn't Last Long. *5.* Cousin Alyssa. *6.* Being a Mermaid Is Not Always Easy. *7.* Shopping Weekend.

312 Our Mermaid Tails. *youtube.com.* 2013 (Fantasy).

While digging in an ancient (said to be 1,000 years old) garden on the side of her home, a young girl (Aquamarine) finds something in the dirt and takes it into her house to wash it off. The water reveals that what she found was a necklace, which she promptly puts around her neck. Fifteen minutes later, when she takes a drink of water, she transforms into a Mermaid. Aquamarine quickly adjusts to what happened and realizes it was the necklace that changed her life. Later that day, when Aquamarine is with her friend Anastasia, she accidentally spills water on her and is shocked to see that Anastasia is also a Mermaid— but not one in the normal sense as Anastasia was born a Mermaid. Two young girls with a secret and their efforts to embrace their Mermaid abilities while pretending to be ordinary girls. **Cast (as credited):** Angel W. (Aquamarine), Keira A. (Anastasia). **Comment:** The picture quality is a bit fuzzy but the acting and overall production is good. **Episode List:** *1.* Pilot.

313 Our Ocean Dream. *youtube.com.* 2014– 2015 (Fantasy).

When they feel they need some excitement to liven up a boring day, four friends (Alex, Scarlet, Samantha and Savanna) elect to go for a boat ride. The sequences that follow all take place in a backyard pool. A huge wave strikes the boat and strands the girls in the middle of the ocean. Somehow Samantha manages to find a cave where they feel they will be safe until they are rescued. It is the night of a full moon, however, and the water that is in the cave, begins to bubble and magically transforms them into Mermaids. The scene then switches to a house where the girls have gathered to talk about what has happened and how they must now keep a secret while attempting to live ordinary lives. **Cast (as credited):** Maikeala (Scarlet), Trinity (Alex), Courtney (Samantha), Kadence (Savanna) Rayne (Addie). **Comment:** Being that the program was made by a group of young girls, allowances have to be made. Although only a pool was used to simulate what happened to them, the idea is good and it would have been impossible for them to do it any other way. The girls are pretty, the picture quality is good (although jumpy at times) but the sound is occasionally poor due to wind blowing in the microphone.

Episode List: *1.* Magical Moon Pool. *2.* Episode 2. *3.* I Know You're a Mermaid.

314 *Our Scaly Secret. youtube.com.* 2011 (Fantasy).

Three girls (Chelsey, Tatum and Sierra) are enjoying themselves in a pool when the sky darkens and the water that surrounds them begins to bubble. They all make a wish to become Mermaids but nothing happens. The following day, when each comes in contact with water, they find that their wish has been granted by unknown forces when each transforms into a Mermaid. The girls now share a secret and must not only learn how to encompass their Mermaid abilities but pretend to be ordinary girls.

Cast (as credited): Jackie (Chelsey), Abigail (Tatum), Cassidy (Sierra). **Comment:** Although the sound is a bit difficult to understand in the first episode, the overall production has acceptable acting and photography.

Episode List: *1.* A Wish Come True. *2.* Trouble with a Tail. *3.* A New Girl.

315 *Our Secret Tail. youtube.com.* 2013 (Fantasy).

Emerald and her friend Lily are walking Emerald's dog when it breaks lose and leads the pursuing girls to a strange place that they have never seen before. After bringing the dog home, Emerald and Lily return to the site and begin to explore it. It is early evening and a full moon is beginning to appear when they find what appears to be a pool of sea water. Now lost and believing the water is the way back home they jump in. While swimming the water begins to bubble and the girls are magically transported to safety. They appear to be unharmed but the next morning, when they come in contact with water each is transformed into a Mermaid. The program follows Emerald and Lily as they struggle to keep secret what has happened while pretending to be ordinary school girls.

Cast (as credited): Emily Claire (Lily), Sadie (Emerald). **Comment:** It is often difficult to judge a series by the only episode produced as assumptions have to be made as to where it is headed and will the same qualities apply. Based on the pilot, the overall production contains good acting and nice photography.

Episode List: *1.* Fish Out of Water, Parts 1 and 2.

316 *Our Special Power.* 2013 (Fantasy).

Bailey and Izzy are best friends who do everything together. One day, while walking they stumble across what they call a "rock pool" and foolishly decide to swim in it. The water appears to be normal but when it begins to bubble it transforms them into Mermaids.

Their efforts to keep secret what happened while pretending to be ordinary girls are related.

Cast (as credited): Bella (Bailey), Katie (Izzy), Devisha (Seianna), Emma (Amy), Sharon (Mother's voice). **Comment:** While the girls are pretty and the idea good, the sound and photography are poor. The program has since been taken offline.

Season 1 Episode List: *1.* The Transformation. *2.* Elementals. *3.* Practice Makes Perfect. *4.* Chemical Action. *5.* Wet and Wild. *6.* Alert. *7.* Follow the Clues. *8.* Birthday Tail. *9.* Izzy's Revenge. *10.* Halloween Special. *11.* Season Finale.

Season 2 Episode List: *1.* Questions Answered. *2.* The Mermaid Book.

317 *Our Vampire Life. youtube.com.* 2012 (Fantasy).

Hazel and Aoife are young girls who lead a boring life. They are best friends but stuck in the same mundane routine each day. It appears, by the only episode released (the pilot) that the girls are seeking a way to change their lives and, although not specifically stated (but based on the title) becoming something else would solve all their problems. The program just ends with that thought with a second episode promised (as related in the closing theme) but nothing else has appeared.

Cast: Aisling Finnegan (Hazel Smith), Saoirse Mcguinness (Aoife Watters). **Comment:** The girls are pretty, the photography, although a bit jumpy at times is acceptable and the idea may have played out well (young girls becoming vampires) had the series continued; it now just appears to have been abandoned.

Episode List: *1.* Boring Day (Pilot).

318 *The Palace Wall. youtube.com.* 2013 (Dolls).

The life of Britta Kinglsey, the newly crowned Princess of the mythical country of Camden, and the members of her Royal Court are chronicled.

Cast (as credited): Lynlea Hollow (Britta Kingsley), Harper Dayleya (Samantha Alfred), Jessa McConnell (Willa Westley), Kate Kittredge (Lillian Kingsley). **Comment:** Good stop motion photography opens each episode with good voices and doll manipulation comprising the balance of episodes.

Episode List: *1.* The Coronation. *2.* Royal for a Day. *3.* The Coronation Ball. *4.* The Equestrian Adventure.

319 *Past Meets the Future. webserieschannel.com.* 2013 (Mystery).

One hundred years ago a man uncovered a strange treasure (not stated what) that he buried hoping to keep others from finding it. The man and his teenage daughter, Victoria, lived in a shack in the woods and felt they were safe until rival treasure hunters tracked him down. Victoria, alone in the shack, is accosted by the treasure hunters and killed when she refuses to betray her father and reveal the location of the treasure.

It is the present when a teenage girl (Bonnie) stumbles onto that shack in the woods (in the middle of nowhere) and brings her friend Eliza to search it with her. While doing so, Bonnie knocks a candle off a table and both she and Eliza are startled to see the ghost of a girl—Victoria—appear before them. Victoria tells them that she needs their help to move on but the only way that can happen is if they uncover the treasure that was stolen by her father. Victoria is unable to tell them where the treasure is buried, but she can provide the clues she composed 100 years ago to help them. She also tells them that others (Scarlet and Clare) have become aware of the treasure and are also seeking it. Before disappearing, Victoria gives Bonnie an Eliza their first clue: "On the opposite side of an artist's expression you will find the key." Feeling that she needs help, Bonnie asks her friend Daniel to assist her. He deciphers the clue to mean the back of a painting. As Bonnie looks around the shack, she sees a painting, checks the back and finds the key of which Victoria spoke. But what does it open? The program charts Bonnie, Eliza and Daniel's search to unravel clues and find the treasure so Victoria can move on.

Cast: Sarah Peterson (Eliza), Tunji Wolfe (Bonnie), Rhett Davis (Daniel), Isabella Minter (Scarlet), Abby Miller (Clare), Elinor Hudson (Victoria). **Credits:** *Producer-Writer-Director*: Rhett Davis. **Comment:** An all teenage cast and a surprisingly well produced and acted series. Story line wise, there are some problems (which are easily overlooked to enjoy the program). These include Victoria's history (which is not really explained) and the treasure (it is unknown how her father acquired it and what it is). The shack, being in the woods for 100 years is in remarkable condition (with all its furnishings still intact) and for some unknown reason, never before discovered. Scarlet and Clare, the rival treasure hunters, are nasty and get away with everything they do, even kidnapping Bonnie, Eliza and Daniel (who, for unknown reasons, do not seek help from the police or anyone else). *Past Meets the Future* is the type of web series that would make a good transformation to cable TV on either Nickelodeon's Teen Nick or its regular Nickelodeon channel.

Episode List: *1*. The Mysterious Shack. *2*. Trapped in Confrontation. *3*. The Secret Revealed. *4*. Help Wanted. *5*. Double-Cross. *6*. The Meeting. *7*. Breaking and Entering. *8*. Coming Clean. *9*. Kidnapped. *10*. Pure Hearts.

320 *Peanuts Motion Comics*. *youtube.com*. 2008 (Cartoon).

The original Charles Schulz Peanuts characters are seen for the first time in a web adaptation of stories originally created for the comic strip (which began in 1964). Like the holiday "Peanuts" TV specials, it is simply a look at very brief incidents in the everyday lives of Charlie Brown, his dog, Snoopy and the other Peanuts characters (as listed in the cast).

Voice Cast: Alex Farris (Charlie Brown), Leigh Bourke (Patty), Taya Calocetto (Violet), Alison Cohen (Frieda), Claire Corlett (Sally), Michelle Creber (Lucy), Quinn Lord (Linus), Jake D. Smith (Schroeder), Bill Melendez (Snoopy). **Credits:** *Producer*: Chris Bartleman, Blair Peters. *Director*: Brad Gibson, Jayson Thiessen. *Writer*: Charles Schulz. **Comment:** Retains all the charm of the TV specials with good animation and excellent voices. Bill Melendez, who voices Snoopy, also voiced the character for the TV specials that air annually on ABC and CBS.

Episode List: *1*. Linus for President/The Election. *2*. The Sore Arm/Independence Day. *3*. Eraserophagia/The Great Pumpkin (the first half of the title refers to a condition Charlie Brown develops from nibbling on pencil erasers). *4*. A Fall Rain/Some Advice. *5*. Ready to Pitch/Back on the Mound. *6*. Dear Santa/I'm New At It. *7*. Science Project/April Fool. *8*. Crabby Little Girl/Mother's Day. *9*. All Your Faults/Service Rendered. *10*. The Good Brother/Valentine's Day.

321 *Pop Star Life*. 2011 (Dolls).

Kasi is a 13-year-old girl with an unrelenting fascination for a famous pop star named Cindy Sparkle. Kasi is so obsessed with Cindy and her own dream of becoming a famous recording star that her whole life now revolves around that one ambition. The program follows Kasi, talented as she is, as he attempts to pursue a dream that few achieve.

Cast (as credited): Cici (Cindy Sparkle), Kit (Kasi), Julie (Lizzy), Ivy (McKenzie). **Comment:** The stop motion opening theme sequence is nicely done. The photography and voices given to the dolls are also very well executed. The program, however, has since been taken offline.

Episode List: 6 untitled episodes, labeled "Episode 1" through "Episode 6" have been produced (although a 7th episode was promised to conclude the series but it never appeared).

322 *The Possibility Shop*. *youtube.com*. 2009–2011 (Variety).

The program, sponsored by The Clorox Company and produced through The Jim Henson Company (but not encompassing Muppets) is simply a how-to-like presentation wherein a charming craft shop owner (Courtney) presents ideas through which mothers and their children can work together and create unique items while at the same time gaining new perspectives through which to see the world (especially during holidays or special events. The episode "Thanksgiving," for example, features Courtney showing parents how to keep the kids entertained until dinner; "Time Machine" shows how to relive favorite family moments; and "Sick Day," wherein keeping a sick child occupied is explored).

Cast: Courtney Watkins (Herself), Danielle Bessler (Ivy, the Girl Scout), Felix Ryan (Mix), Bonnie Burroughs (Super Working Mom), Suzan Brittan (Stay-at-Home Mom), Justin Galluccio (Spy Boy).

Credits: *Producer*: Lisa O'Brien, Chris Thomes. *Director*: David Gumpel. *Writer*: Elise Allen. **Comment:** The program is also known as *Jim Henson's Possibility Shop* and incorporates simple hand-made puppets. The overall production is excellent and can compare with most programs produced for television.

Season 1 Episode List:
1. Thanksgiving.
2. Holidays.
3. Time Machine.
4. The Big Game.
5. Rock the House.
6. Valentine's Day.
7. Love Your Pet Day.
8. St. Patrick's Day.
9. April Fools Day.
10. Sick Day.
11. The Birds Are Back in Town.
12. Mother's Day.

Season 2 Episode List:
1. 4th of July Parade.
2. Carnival Block Party.
3. Father's Day.
4. Lemonade Stand.
5. Drive-In Movie Night.
6. Pen Pals.
7. Spring Surprise Baskets.
8. Host a Spring Swap Party.
9. Field Trip to the Museum.
10. Lucky Token Box.
11. Leadership Election.
12. Tree Bloomin' with Love.
13. YOU-nique Talent Show.
14. New Year's Board Game.
15. A Handmade Heart.
16. Thanksgiving Table Creation.
17. Chalkboard Vases.
18. Mini Haunted House.
19. Clever Costume Ideas.
20. Friendship Party.

Season 3 Episode List:
1. Adventure in a Snap Sack.
2. Wooden Car Racing.
3. Power Play Symbols.
4. A New Twist on Recess.
5. Slumber Party Camp-In Kit.
6. Transformation Costumes.
7. Monsters Be Gone.
8. Boomerang Society.

9. How to Throw a Fun-draiser!
10. Flying Angel Holiday Portraits.
11. Make and Take Party Favors.
12. Nightly News.
13. The Great Valentine Paper Make-Over.
14. Fresh Air Trekking.
15. Pet S'paw.
16. Bird Necklaces.
17. Lei Day.
18. Family Game Night.

323 *Pretty Little Liars—American Girl Style*. *youtube.com.* 2010 (Dolls).

An adaptation of the book series by Sara Shepard and featuring American Girls dolls as the "performers." The book was also adapted to television as *Pretty Little Liars* (ABC Family Channel) and tells the story of five best friends (Alison DiLaurentis, Aria Montgomery, Emily Fields, Hanna Marin and Spencer Hastings), members of a clique known as both the Pretty Little Liars and Liars. The girls rule the school they attend but their lives change for the worse when Alison, their leader, disappears and is later found dead. Suddenly, the remaining girls begin receiving text messages from an unknown source that uses the name "A." The program, like the TV series, relates the events that befall the four friends as they try to figure out who "A" is—the ghost of Alison? Or someone who knows their deep dark secrets and threatens to expose them.

Voice Cast (as credited): Rachel Kassie. **Comment:** Even though the program is aimed at young girls (who have no doubt seen the TV series), it can get a bit creepy at times, especially with its eerie theme song and background music. The doll manipulation and voices are very good and for a series using dolls, it is exceptionally good.

Episode List: 4 untitled episodes, labeled "Episode 1" through "Episode 4" have been produced.

324 *Puffin Rock*. *youtube.com.* 2015 (Cartoon).

Oona (blue) and her younger brother, Baba (white), are puffin birds that live on a colorful but mythical Irish island. The program follows the adventures they share with their friends and family: Mossy, Oona's best friend (a brown pygmy shrew); May (a rabbit), Silky (a gray seal pup); Otto (a green owl); Bernie (an elderly hermit crab); and Flynn (A fox).

Voice Cast: Kate McCafferty (Oona), Sally McDaid (Baba), Anna McDaid (May), Darragh Gargan (Mossy), Laura McCallan (Silky), Brenn Doherty (Otto), Jim Craig (Bernie), Orna Canning (Flynn), Caitlin McGinness (Pip and Pop), Geraldine Cole (Grandma). *Narrator*: Chris O'Dowd. **Credits:** *Producer*: Fionnuala Deane, Francesca Dow, Laura Campbell. *Director*: Maurice Joyce. **Comment:** Simple story telling is mixed with simple flash animation that presents facts about puffins (and other animals) to pre-school children in an interesting manner. The program, originally produced for pay service Netflix, can be viewed for free on YouTube.

Episode List:
1. Puffin Practice.
2. The Mystery Egg.
3. To See the Moon.
4. The Shiny Shell.
5. Friendly Flynne.
6. A Feather Bed.
7. Beach Rescue.
8. Lost Berries.
9. Night Lights.
10. Pond Life.
11. Bird Detective.
12. Bernie's Shell.
13. Hop, Skip and Bump.
14. Bouncing Back.
15. A Noisy Neighbor.
16. Stormy Weather.
17. Rock Music.
18. Baba's Adventure.
19. The Burrow Race.
20. Silky's Slide.
21. Ruffled Feathers.
22. Finding Bernie.
23. The Foggy Day.
24. Run, Flap, Fly.
25. Spot the Puffin.
26. The Sad Whale.
27. The Fast Day.
28. Baba's Friend.
29. Flying High.
30. Silky's Sea Horses.
31. Keeping Cozy.
32. Baba's Picnic.
33. The Empty Shell.
34. Cave Camping.
35. Mossy Goes Solo.
36. Flooded Burrow.
37. Daytime Sleepover.
38. Bird Detective.
39. Three's a Crowd.

325 Puppatics. *youtube.com.* 2013 (Puppets).

Quackers, Furball and Teddy are puppets with one common goal: create a web series. With no talent, no writing skills and no real idea as to what goes into making a series, the program charts their efforts to accomplish that goal while trying to overcome one additional problem: their individual personality flaws that also threaten any chances they have to succeed. **Voice Cast:** Sean Jo Arcand (Quackers/Furball/Goofball), Brian Arcand (Teddy), Josh Mercure (Block Head/King Slug/The Wizard). **Credits:** *Director:* Chris Esper. *Writer:* Sean Jo Arcand. **Com-**

ment: Although not an original idea (*The Muppet Show* and *The Shari Show* [with Shari Lewis] used a similar concept with puppets producing TV shows) the program is well done with enjoyable stories but a premise that may be too difficult for younger children to comprehend.

Episode List: Ten untitled episodes, labeled "Episode 1," through "Episode 10" have been produced.

326 The Puppets in the Park. 2006 (Puppets).

A spin off from *Waterman* (see entry) that incorporates the characters from that series (Waterman, Ice Cream Girl, Pal and Roybot) to tell nursery rhymes for children in a park setting. **Voice Cast:** Bryan Waterman, Chris Barnhill, Katie Yorra, Devin Farmer. **Credits:** *Producer-Writer-Director:* Bryan Waterman. **Comment:** The program adapts mostly well-known fairytales and nursery rhymes that children can easily identify with. The amusing, well-produced program has since been taken offline.

Episode List: *1.* The 3 Little Pigs. *2.* Humpty Dumpty. *3.* Mr. Slippy Fist. *4.* Gingerbread Man. *5.* Jack and the Beanstalk. *6.* The Old Woman Who Lives in a Shoe. *7.* Hansel and Gretel. *8.* The Boy Who Cried Wolf. *9.* Jack and Jill. *10.* Resurrection of the Easter Bunny. *11.* Three Billy Goats Gruffafied.

327 Pur Aqua Mermaids. *youtube.com.* 2013 (Fantasy).

After returning home from vacation, a young girl (Siara) comes in contact with water and is magically transformed into a Mermaid. While unsure at first as to what happened she removes a stone from her pants pocket and theorizes that the stone is magical (found while swimming in a place called Pur Aqua) and caused her to become a Mermaid when she touched water. Now, accepting what she has become, Siara must learn to live two lives—ordinary girl and Mermaid.

Cast (as credited): Sydney Peterson (Siara), Aimee (Ariana). **Comment:** Sydney is charming as is Ariana (the Mermaid she later befriends). The underwater photography is good but the program suffers from poor sound at times as well as sometimes unsteady images.

Episode List: *1.* A Mermaid!? *2.* My Tail Is Not for Show. *3.* An Un-Forgotten Place. *4.* The Call. *5.* Ariana. *6.* Episode Taken Offline. *7.* Cursed Island. *8.* Home Again. *9.* A Full Moon. *10.* One Strange Vacation (an introduction video to the series).

328 Pure Water. 2014 (Fantasy).

It appears to be an ordinary, normal day for friends Elianah and Samantha until they stumble across two necklaces and decide to keep them. Unknown to them the jewelry is magical and transforms them into Mermaids when they come in contact with water. Elianah and Samantha realize that their lives have been changed forever and now must learn to keep secret what has happened to them while living lives as ordinary girls.

Cast (as credited): Elianah, Samantha. **Comment:** While the overall production is satisfactory, the crucial first episode (which explains how the girls became Mermaids) has no sound, making it difficult to fully understand what is happening. The program has since been taken offline.

Episode List: *1.* The Splash. *2.* The Change. *3.* The Sleepover. *4.* The Tail Thief. *5.* Switched Tails.

329 Rachel Likes to Read. *youtube.com.* 2013 (Children).

"Hi, I'm Rachel and I like to read" opens each program as a young woman named Rachel selects a children's book and proceeds to explore it by first by familiarizing her audience with its characters then reading it.

Cast: Rachel Geistfeld (Rachel). **Credits:** *Producer-Director:* Rachel Geistfeld. **Comment:** The program is quite entertaining as Rachel does not simply read a book, but expresses emotion in her words, performs mini skits relating to the text and has simplistic drawings illustrating the story.

Episode List: *1.* Rainbow Fish. *2.* Three Little Dinosaurs. *3.* Ping and Pong Are Best Friends (Mostly). *4.* Time for a Hug. *5.* Knuffle Bunny. *6.* The Saggy Baggy Elephant. *7.* Polly's Pet. *8.* The Very Hungry Caterpillar. *9.* The Gruffalo. *10.* Each Peach Pear Plum.

330 The Realm of Arragara. *youtube.com.* 2014 (Dolls).

Arragara is a strange world inhabited by about 200 people that is located within the inner core of the Earth. There is also an outer core, but it is dangerous as thought-to-be mythical creatures (such as demons, Cyclops, sirens and vampires) actually do exist. It is here that two teenagers, Lena and Seth have become trapped, having fallen through a black hole that appeared on the grounds of their school. Their adventures in the mysterious Arragara are chronicled as they seek a way to return to their own realm of Earth.

Cast (as credited): Felicity Merriman (Lena Green), Will Harrison (Seth Owens), Josie Montoya (Ashleigh Wells), Mia St. Claire (Layla Green), Julie Albright (Erin Green). Voices by Alexis. **Comment:** Considering the fact that dolls are used and an adventure format has been established, the program is well done with good doll manipulation and photography.

Episode List: 8 untitled episodes, labeled "Episode 1" Through "Episode 8" have been produced.

331 Richie Rich. *youtube.com.* 2015 (Comedy).

As a younger child Richie Rich would not eat his vegetables and apparently placed them in some sort of "storage box." As the years passed and that vegetable box grew it morphed into an incredible power source that not only made Richie, now 12 years old, rich, but supplied the world with an alternate power source when he sold it. Now Richie is not only the world's richest kid (said to have over a trillion dollars) but lives in a fabulous mansion built especially for him, his father (Cliff) and sister (Harper). The grounds also contain an amusement park and Richie has his own race car. Murray is Richie's 12-year-old accountant; Irona is his gorgeous robotic maid and Darcy is his best friend. The program, based on the comic book of the same name, relates events in the life of a super rich kid as he tries be an "ordinary" kid (although producing a major motion picture as his book report on *The Wizard of Oz* is, for example, his idea of being an ordinary kid. Harper, on the other hand, tries not to be influenced by her brother or idiotic father; she is however, portrayed in one aspect as being normal [like striving for "A's" in school so she can get into Harvard] and a bit "extra" ordinary by helping the environment by hosting a telethon for homeless turtles).

Cast: Jake Brennan (Richie Rich), Lauren Taylor (Harper Rich), Joshua Carlon (Murray), Jenna Ortega (Darcy), Kiff VandenHeuvel (Cliff Rich), Brooke Wexler (Irona). **Credits:** *Producer:* Joe Davola, Jeff Hodsden, Shauna Phelan, Tim Pollock, Brian Robbins. *Director:* Adam Weissman, Phill Lewis, Joel Zwick, Sean K. Lambert. *Writer:* Jeff Hodsden, Tim Pollock, Bo Belanger, Sidney Jacobson, Jeny Quine. **Comment:** Simply put, the program is unbelievably bad. With the exception of Lauren Taylor as Richie's sister, the acting and stories are truly awful. How the show was green lit and why the producers chose to literally make kids and adults look like idiots is the mystery. Irona dresses in a sexy French maid outfit. But why did Richie hire such a sexy "girl" at his age (it appears by early episodes he hasn't yet hit puberty; and why did his father approve of his hiring her?). How can Murray manage such huge amounts of money being only 12? And why would Richie keep a friend like Darcy when all she does is spend his money (and act like a "trophy wife") while Harper has to beg and scheme to get money from Richie? And worst of all is Richie's totally immature and idiotic father, Cliff (even worse than a man-child). How did he ever hold down a job or even find a woman to marry him? (It appears that Cliff is a widower or else Richie's mother would have re-entered his life to claim some of that wealth). It's also a "nice" touch in the opening theme that the producers emphasize that children not eating their vegetables is a good thing (look what it did for Richie). While the above are "kind" words about the show, much more negative comments can be found on IMDb.com in the "Explore More" User Reviews section. The program can be seen for free on YouTube or for a fee on Netflix, for which it was produced. Lauren Taylor "escaped" *Richie Rich* and currently stars with Landry Bender on the Disney Channel series *Best Friends Whenever*.

Season 1 Episode List: *1.* Man$ion Warning. *2.* Royal Flu$h. *3.* The $et Up. *4.* The Wonderful Thing$ He Doe$. *5.* The Madne$$ of Queen Harper. *6.* More or Le$$. *7.* $nowball Effect. *8.* Good Deed$. *9.* $pooky $tuff. *10.* Fir$t Love.

Season 2 Episode List: *1.* Rapper'$ Delight. *2.* Briti$h Rich. *3.* $uper Heroe$. *4.* $tockholm Cowboy. *5.* Plu$ One. *6.* Back to the Pre$ent. *7.* Fun and Game$. *8.* Wa$hed Up. *9.* Meet the Camper$. *10.* Ladie$ Man. *11.* Family Tie$.

332 *Riptide Mermaids.* *youtube.com.* 2015 (Fantasy).

Ella Kail is a young girl who stumbles across an old recipe written by her grandmother. Believing it would be fun to follow the recipe's directions, Ella produces what appears to be an ordinary liquid drink. Curious to what it may taste like, Ella sips it through a straw and stops when she finds it distasteful. Seconds later she transforms into a Mermaid. Although only a pilot episode had been released at the time of publication, it appears that any contact with water will transform Ella into a Mermaid and the program will relate her efforts to conceal her secret (and abilities) while pretending to be an ordinary girl.

Cast (as credited): Anna F. (Ella Kail). **Comment:** A typical Mermaid series with acceptable acting and photography.

Episode List: *1.* Season 1, Episode 1.

333 *Rock Stars.* 2012 (Dolls).

The LPS (Littlest Pet Shop) dolls are encompassed to follow the life of a young girl (Chloe) as she follows her childhood dream and, with the help of her friends Alex and Jade, seeks to become a rock music star.

Voices (as credited): Shannah. **Comment:** If adults and teens have attempted to become rock stars, why not doll pets? The program is very well done with good voices, doll manipulation and photography. The program, however, has since been taken offline.

Episode List: 3 untitled episodes, labeled "Episode 1," "Episode 2" and "Episode 3" have been produced.

334 *Roommate (Mermaid Series).* *youtube.com.* 2014 (Fantasy).

Penelope is a teenage girl attending boarding school and presently living in a dorm room by herself.

Suddenly, a girl named Annabelle appears and announces that she is her new roommate. Penelope and Annabelle have noting in common and it appears the two simply do not like each other. The situation changes dramatically when Penelope, drinking water she finds unpleasant, spits it out and sprays Annabelle, turning her into a Mermaid. Penelope is shocked ("That girl is strange") but can't figure out if Annabelle is good or evil. She does, however, agree not to reveal her secret. Episodes 1 through 7 are set at the school with the remaining two episodes being set at Penelope's summer home with Penelope and Annabelle as its residents ("Because roommates have to be together"). It is here where Luna, a girl who claims to be Annabelle's twin sister, appears. At first glance Luna appears sinister (possibly a Siren) and just up to no good. As the series winds down (and concludes in a cliff hanger) it is learned that Luna is evil and that Annabelle, despite her attitude, is good and seeking to protect Penelope from Luna, who has tricked Penelope into helping her defeat her sister.

Cast (as credited): Anuka (Penelope), Sophie (Annabelle and Luna). **Comment:** The well-produced program is more of a suspense and mystery drama than a typical Mermaid series. The Mermaid aspect is not presented until the third episode and such sequences are limited. It is more of a focus on Annabelle and Penelope and later Luna and what transpires between the three girls. Anuka and Sophie are good but, for a kids' show are quite nasty to each other and do have potty mouths (even the children who watched the show have noted that on the YouTube comment posts). Adding "Mermaid Series" to the title may have been a gimmick by Anuka and Sophie to attract kids to their show as "Roommate" by itself would not have done the trick.

Episode List: 9 untitled episodes, labeled "Episode 1" through "Episode 9" have been produced.

335 *Ruby Skye, P.I.* *rubyskyepi.com.* 2013 (Mystery).

"There are a few things that every detective needs: sharp senses, intuition, curiosity, determination, an understanding of human nature and the ability to put the clues together to tell a story. There are millions of mysteries in the big city—and I'm gonna solve all of them" says Ruby Skye, a modern-day Nancy Drew. Ruby has a knack for stumbling upon mysteries and is blessed with an insatiable curiosity to solve them. Ruby is stubborn, smart and determined. Once she feels something is not right she will pursue it until she uncovers what is troubling her. The program follows Ruby as she solves mysteries—most often finding mishap as she rarely has a plan and plunges head first into a situation. Assisting Ruby is her younger sister Hailey, a girl who is not as outgoing as Ruby but apparently joins her for the adventure she encounters; foiling Ruby is Diana Noughton, a girl who for "highly mysterious reasons," dislikes Ruby and does everything in her power to annoy her. "And there is this other thing that every detective needs," says Ruby, "and that is my sidekick, Griffin" (who is also her best friend).

Cast: Madison Cheeatow (Ruby Skye), Marlee Maslove (Hailey Skye), Elena Gorgevska (Diana Noughton), Kevin Gutierrez (Griffin Lane), Ali Adatia (Vinnie), Scott Beaudin (Edmund O'Fyne), Nawa Nicole Simon (Ms. Springer), Kirklynne Garrett (Mrs. Gooje), Rodrigo Fernandez-Stoll (Griffin's father), Rosemary Dunsmore (Ava O'Deary), Samantha Wan (Ophelia Bedelia), Laura Decarteret (Lillian O'Shyte), Jordan Prentice (Henry O'Henry), Shaun Shetty (Finch). **Credits:** *Producer*: Jill Golick, Steve Golick. *Director*: Kelly Harms. *Writer*: Jill Golick, Julie Strassman. **Comment:** Madison Cheeatow is delightful as Ruby in a fast-moving, enjoyable series. The production values are excellent with good writing and story direction. The mysteries presented are well paced and allow the viewer to follow the clues and uncover the culprit at the same time or perhaps even before Ruby. The mystery of "The Spam Scam" (Episodes 1–12, wherein Ruby tries to uncover a thief who scammed her neighbor out of great deal of money) and "The Haunted Library" (Episodes 13–21, Ruby attempts to see that the rightful heir to a library is found) are the mysteries presented.

Episode List: *1*. Animal Farm. *2*. Kay Eye Ess Ess. *3*. Break-In. *4*. A Real Green Dress. *5*. Caught Ruby Red Handed. *6*. Sister Act. *7*. Stalled. *8*. Scissor Sandwich. *9*. Tossed. *10*. Seven Minutes in Heaven. *11*. Best Served Cold. *12*. Dunh Dunh Dunh. *13*. A Well-Read Poltergeist. *14*. Ava's Last Puzzle. *15*. Where There's No Will, There's a Way. *16*. Creepy. *17*. Edmund. *18*. A Regular Sherlock. *19*. On the Trail of a Thief. *20*. The Final Clue. *21*. Apparently the Heir.

336 *Sage the Mage.* sagethemage.com. 2013 (Comedy).

Los Angeles is home to Sage, an adorable eight-year-old girl who is also very special. She is a magician and, with her magic chicken bone (wand), she can bend the laws of nature and explore mystical realms. Sage is in the third grade and is known as Elementary Sage to her neighbor Simon, a galaxy-hoping Ultra Magician (Level 23) who has established a vacation home on Earth (or to his people, Planet MW6371). Simon is a member of the Arcane Order of the Great Sapphire Atom, an outer space society of magicians and has become sort of a mentor to Sage as he oversees her progression into a first-class magician. Sage, however, is very curious and constantly experiments with the abilities she already has, causing her numerous misadventures as she tries to undo the mischief she creates. Stories follow Sage as she works her way from Young Elementary Class Mage to an Ultra Magician like Simon.

Cast: Grace Goodell (Sage), Georgia Goodell (Rosemary), Milo Goodell (Parsley), Sean O'Don-nell (Simon). **Credits:** *Producer-Writer-Director*: Sean O'Donnell. **Comment:** A program worthy of cable's Nickelodeon channel as it has qualities that match any of its programs. Grace Goodell is captivating as Sage and stories do not lack for humor or action. There are numerous, well executed special effects as Sage creates magic and stories are well constructed so as not to become tiresome. Network TV producers could take some lessons on how to produce a quality program on a limited budget from *Sage*.

Episode List: *1*. Sage Rocks. *2*. Parsley's Perplexation. *3*. Let It Snow … Indeed! *4*. Push Echo. *5*. Sage on the Evil English Ivy. *6*. Sage's Most Awesomest Ever Show. *7*. Trick or Donut? *8*. Out of the Frying Pan. *9*. Into the Fire.

337 *Salt Life.* youtube.com. 2013–2015 (Fantasy).

Samantha is a young girl who finds a necklace in a most unusual place: a tree. Intrigued, she decides to keep it. Unknown to her it has magical powers that transform her into a Mermaid when she comes in contact with water. The program follows Samantha as she attempts to adjust to her new life style while at the same time pretending to be just an ordinary girl. Season three finds Samantha moving to a new city and having to leave behind the magic tree that held the Mermaid necklace and granted her the ability to become a Mermaid. As she settles into her new home, Samantha, no longer a Mermaid finds a bracelet that appears in her bathroom sink. Fascinated by the bracelet she places it on her wrist and with her first contact with water transforms into a Mermaid.

Cast (as credited): Samantha N. (Samantha), Juliana (Juliana), Madison (Madi), Debbie (Debbie). **Comment:** Only Season 3 episodes remain on line and based on that, the sound is low at times, the picture is not only unsteady but some scenes are badly framed. The acting, however, is good.

Season 1 Episode List: *1*. I'm a Mermaid. *2*. Heat Wave. *3*. Ice Age. *4*. Whirlpool. *5*. Swimming. *6*. Untitled. *7*. The New Mermaid. *8*. Untitled. *9*. Moonstruck Mermaid. *10*. Untitled.

Season 2 Episode List: *1*. Mermaid Madi. *2*. Untitled. *3*. The Potion. *4*. Untitled. *5*. Random Potion. *6*. Swimming. *7*. The Mysterious Bottle. *8*. The End of the Tree.

Season 3 Episode List: *1*. It's Back. *2*. Two Transformations. *3*. Fire and Water.

338 *Scale Tails.* youtube.com. 2014 (Fantasy).

While walking through the woods, three girls (Kelsey, Brianna and Crystal) spy a mysterious blue liquid in a Mason jar and take it. At Kelsey's home, curiosity gets the best of them and they each decide to sip the liquid. Other than an apparent unpleasant taste nothing happens—at first. Shortly after, when each girl comes in contact with water she is transformed into a Mermaid. The program follows their efforts to help each other adjust to what has happened while pretending to be ordinary girls to keep their secret.

Cast (as credited): Hailey (Kelsey), Alyssa (Brianna), Brynn (Crystal). **Comment:** Acceptable acting is coupled with good photography.

Season 1 Episode List: *1.* A Scaly Mystery. *2.* Did I Do That? *3.* The Letter. *4.* The Siren.

Season 2 Episode List: *1.* Sweet Dreams. *2.* Reverse the Curse. *3.* Taken. *4.* Another Dimension.

339 *Scales. youtube.com.* 2013 (Children).

Intrigued by a nearby island that has been closed off to the public for unknown reasons, two curious young girls (Chloe and Brooke) decide to swim to it to see why. While exploring the island, they find strange necklaces hanging from a tree and take them. Later, when they return home and come in contact with water, they are magically transferred into Mermaids. With a secret they now share the program charts their efforts to remain the same girls they were before the transformation.

Cast as Credited: Kyla (Chloe), Angelina (Brooke), Kendra (Phoebe). **Comment:** The premise is good, the girls are pretty but the sound and photography are poor.

Episode List: *1.* Believe It. *2.* The Fight. *3.* Powers. *4.* There's Two. *5.* New Findings. *6.* Torn Pages. *7.* Lazy Days.

340 *Scales and Tails. youtube.com.* 2015 (Fantasy).

It is summer time and a young girl (Tessa) decides to relieve her boredom by going to the beach. There, she stumbles upon a secret pier that leads to a pond. As she enters the pond she finds a sea shell and takes it home with her. When she removes it from her pocket and sees that it is still wet and water has gotten on her hand, she magically transforms into a Mermaid. Although mystified as to why, Tessa must now learn to live life as a Mermaid, control her developing powers and pretend to be an ordinary school girl.

Cast (as credited): Laura (Tessa). **Comment:** Nicely presented program with good photography and acting.

Episode List: *1.* I'm a Mermaid. *2.* Power Hour. *3.* Mermaid at Mom's. *4.* Secret Notes, Secret World. *5.* Further Power Discovery. *6.* Moon Struck Tails.

341 *Scales—Down Under.* 2014 (Fantasy).

Although she believed her vacation on a cruise ship would be more exciting than it turned out to be, a young girl (Elizabeth) passes the time by making a wish to become a Mermaid. A short time later, when Elizabeth comes in contact with water, she transforms into a Mermaid. As the cruise winds down and Elizabeth returns to her normal life, a day at the beach brings an unexpected encounter when she meets a girl (Alice) who knows she is a Mermaid and claims to be the daughter of Poseidon. Alice has come to land to help Elizabeth become a Mermaid and stories follow the two girls as they look out for each other while experiencing all the pitfalls that could expose them for who they really are.

Cast (as credited): Julia Martin (Elizabeth Crosse), Savannah Spelrem (Alice Gene), Nicole Frankel (Caroline Erne), Addie (Claire). **Comment:** Although the picture is a bit blurry and reading the cast credits is near impossible in the first few episodes (improves later) the overall production is acceptable with good acting and an interesting story line. The program has since been taken offline.

Episode List: 9 untitled episodes, labeled "Episode 1" through "Episode 9" have been produced.

342 *Sea, Fins and Flippers.* 2014 (Fantasy).

The program begins with the third episode making it a bit unclear how two girls (Emma and May) became Mermaids. It appears a magic potion transformed the girls into Mermaids but how they acquired it is unknown. While the program does focus on Emma and May as they adapt to their Mermaid abilities, it also ends in the middle of nowhere with a Christmas episode.

Cast (as credited): Cheyenn (Emma), Lois (May), Riley (Amber), Cheyenne (Linda), Khanur (Ace). **Comment:** There is no explanation given as to why episodes 1, 2 and 5 are missing. It is difficult to follow the story and with very poor camerawork, staying with the program is not easy and will disappoint anyone expecting an acceptable Mermaid series. The program has since been taken offline.

Episode List: *1 and 2.* Unknown. *3.* What the… *4.* We're Mermaids. *5.* Unknown. *6.* The Kidnapping.

343 *Sea Sisters. youtube.com.* 2014 (Fantasy).

While enjoying a walk through a forest two young girls (Alaina and Ginger) stumble upon a magical cove where they find two sea shells on a large plant leaf. While they do wonder how sea shells came to be in a forest, they just shrug it off and take the sea shells home with them. That night, as the girls sleep, unknown forces transform the shells into necklaces and emit a strange wave that encompasses their bedrooms. The following morning, the girls examine the necklaces and shortly after, when they first come in contact with water, they become Mermaids—but only for as long as their skin remains wet; when the water evaporates, their tails return to their human legs. Alaina and Ginger are not alone however, as their friend Blaire had experienced the same metamorphosis a short time earlier. Three girls, a shared secret and their efforts to not only live ordinary lives but battle evil Sirens who seek to destroy them.

Cast (as credited): Ava (Aliana), Corinne (Ginger), Kenzie (Blaire), Abbey (Lexi and Luna). **Comment:** Although the sound quality is a bit poor at times (very low), the acting, photography, story and even limited special effects are good.

Episode List: 1. Changing Waters. 2. Magic Business. 3. A Strange Holiday. 4. Lexi the Wizard. 5. The Box. 6. Waves of Wonder. 7. The Sirens. 8. The Water Spirit.

344 Sea Stars. *youtube.com.* 2011 (Fantasy).

It is a warm summer day and two best friends, Marina and Macy, decide to go to the pier for a swim in a lake in preparation for an upcoming swimming meet. As the girls practice their moves, time slips by until they realize it is getting late and they need to return home. But before they can do so, a storm approaches and forces the girls to take refuge in a cave they spot. Shortly after entering the cave, the lake water begins to bubble at the same time a full moon appears in the sky. As the storm lets up Marina and Macy return home. The following day, when Marina and Macy come in contact with water each is transformed into a Mermaid; they theorize that it was their experience in the cave that caused the metamorphosis. Although they accept what has happened to them they must now learn how to control their developing powers and conceal who they really are from the rest of the world.

Cast (as credited): Marina Wells (Marina), Macy Stevens (Macy), Skyler (Skyler). **Comment:** The picture color varies from normal to a yellowish look but other than that the photography and acting are very good.

Episode List: 1. Tales of Scales. 2. Friends with Fins. 3. Water to the Rescue. 4. Double Trouble. 5. The Hike. 6. Mermaid Sitter. 7. The Moon Spell. 8. A New Neighbor. 9. The Fight.

345 Sea Tails. *youtube.com.* 2014 (Fantasy).

Friends Ashley and Kathrine are walking along a sidewalk when they find an old book that contains a map. As they look over the map they decide to follow it. It leads them to a pool where the water seems to entice them to go swimming. At the bottom of the pool they each find a necklace. The time seems to fly by and Ashley and Kathrine realize that it is getting dark and they should head for home. It is also the night of a full moon and before the girls exit the pool, the water begins to bubble. Suddenly, Ashley and Kathrine find themselves back home without a clue as to how they got there. Later, when they come in contact with water, each is transformed into a Mermaid. But that is not their only problem. Their friend Natalie has become suspicious of them (as she says, "Something's Fishy") and has set her goal to find out exactly what Ashley and Kathrine are hiding. The program follows Ashley and Kathrine as they struggle to adjust to their Mermaid powers while at the same time concealing what they have become from Natalie. Also known as *Sea Girls.*

Cast (as credited): Ella (Ashley), Grace (Kathrine), Shira (Natalie). **Comment:** The video quality is poor in the first episode but improves greatly from the second episode on. The girls are pretty and the overall production is well done.

Episode List: 1. Calling of the Sea. 2. Powers of the Deep. 3. Siren's Song. 4. Lost at Sea. 5. Sirens and Selfies. 6. Weather and Water. 7. Seas of Change. 8. The Moon Typhoon.

346 Search + Destroy. *youtube.com.* 2011 (Dolls).

Kyla Benton is a 16-year-old girl who lives in a parallel world to Earth. It is here that a president is elected every 18 years and cannot be dismissed from office. A problem arises when the president, Reginald Rebel, assumes the role of a dictator and takes over the United States and Canada. With his powerful two nations army there has been little resistance until a group of brave men set out on goal to overthrow him. A revolution develops and many lives are lost in a battle that appears to have no end. Life is no longer like it was and people caught in the middle of the conflict have retreated to the forests to live their lives in small, self-constructed homes and find whatever work they can to survive.

Three young sisters (Kayla, Vivienne and Shala) are the heart of the story. Their father has been killed in the war; their mother is unable to fully comprehend what has happened; and their brother has volunteered to join with the resistance fighters. The sisters believe that they have a plan to end the revolution: kill the President and return America and Canada to a time before the conflict. With their friend, Portland Bell, by their side the program charts what happens as four brave girls set out on a mission that could ultimately cost them their lives.

Cast (as credited): Asia Asher, Quin Hayes, Kate Kittredge, Jessica McConnell, Lynlee Holland, Peyton Black, Mason Lauren, Scarlett Frost. **Comment:** The program does read like a live action series, but it is totally acted by dolls. It is very intriguing and fast-moving with very good doll manipulation and excellent voices by a girl who prefers to remain anonymous. The stop motion opening theme is also very well done.

Episode List: 10 untitled episodes, labeled "Episode 1" through "Episode 10" Have been produced.

347 Secret Life of a Mermaid. *youtube.com.* 2009 (Fantasy).

While swimming in the ocean, a young pre-teen girl (Amy) finds that she has ventured too far offshore and, as a thunderstorm approaches, seeks shelter in a cave that she spies on shore. Although the cave is half filled with water, Amy feels safe until she is suddenly engulfed in a mysterious water fall that douses her with its mystical drops of water. As the storm lets up, Amy thinks nothing about what just happened and returns home. The following morning she accidentally spills water on herself and is magically transformed into a Mermaid with a dark blue tail (when the water dries, her Mermaid tail vanishes and her legs return to normal). Although she is a bit shocked at first, she accepts what has happened (she later discovers that her friends Brenna and Kelsey are Mermaids, also having been engulfed by that mysterious water fall in the cave). Blaire, a young girl who later befriends Amy offers an explanation as to what has happened to them. Although Blaire is not a Mermaid (at first), her mother and grandmother are. She explains that certain females are descended from Mermaids and inherit a special gene that not only grants them power but the ability to transform from humans to Mermaids through contact with water. Each girl that transforms must protect her secret and use her abilities to protect the oceans from evil. For Blaire, it began before her birth when her mother (Terra) became fascinated by the ocean and would constantly spend time in the water. One day while swimming she met a human fisherman and fell in love. They married, had a child (Blaire) and when Blaire turned 2, Terra returned to the sea to live her life as a Mermaid. Blaire has been raised by her father since (the past 10 years). Now, with magical abilities and power to control water, Amy, Kelsey and Brenna, with the assist of Blaire, struggle to keep their true nature a secret while attempting to live as normal pre-teen girls.

Amy Samuels, ten-years-old, is the first of three girls to magically transform into a Mermaid (with a dark blue tail). She has brown eyes and brown hair and her powers include the ability to manipulate water and create rain.

Blaire Harris has blonde hair, blue eyes, a multi-colored tail and the ability to breathe under water; she later develops telepathic powers. She is the only child of a fisherman (with whom she lived until she decided to fully encompass her powers and join her mother, Terra, a Mermaid, in the ocean world).

Kelsey Cork, with her brown hair and green eyes, has a green tail. She has the ability to freeze wind, rain and snow but is not as comfortable as Amy and Blaire being a Mermaid.

Brenna Edwards has green eyes, strawberry blonde hair and a yellow tail. She was the second girl to become a Mermaid and has the ability to heat water and create fire and lightning. Her powers can also place her in a trance-like state and turn her abilities into destructive forces.

Tess Samuels, Amy's older sister, has blue eyes and blonde hair. While not a Mermaid, she suspects Amy and her friends are Mermaids and has set her goal to expose their true nature.

Cast (as credited): Christine (Amy Samuels), Claire (Brenna Edwards), Emma (Kelsey Cork), Bridget (Tess Samuels), Tessa (Blaire). Christine has the on-screen credit of Teenie989. Comment: Nicely acted and produced Mermaid tale. The child actors handle their roles well and the underwater photography is quite good for a low budget production.

Season 1 Episode List:
1. Flip Flop.
2. Heat Wave.
3. Freezer Burn.
4. Tidal Wave.
5. Breathless.
6. Fishy Trouble.
7. Sea Sick.
8. Double Trouble.
9. Fish Out of Water.
10. Tail or Treat.
11. Whirl Pool.
12. Blue Moon.
13. Wet Christmas.
14. Power Hour.
15. High Tide.
16–17. The Scrapbook.
18–20. Germany Journey.
21. New Waters.
22. Practice Makes Perfect.
23. Splash of Knowledge.
24. Birthday Splash.
25. Scarce Scales.
26. Answers Found.
27. Wild Fire.
28–29. Season 1 Finale.
Season 2 Episode List:
30. Hooked.
31. Briny Dilemma.
32. Cabin Fever.
33. In Deep Water.
34. Fire & Ice.
35. In the Wake.
36. The Siren's Song.
37–38. Season 2 Finale.
Season 3 Episode List:
39. Landslide.
40. Splashin' Around the Christmas Tree.
41. Man Overboard.
42. The Lonely Islander.
43. Red Tide.
44. Changing Currents.

348 The Secret Life of a Teenage Mermaid.
youtube.com. 2012 (Fantasy).

A teenage girl is taking a shower when she mysteriously transforms into a Mermaid. She has no idea how it happened and when her sister discovers her secret, she too is perplexed as to how it occurred (as she fears she could be next). The program ends there with no text or video information as to what will transpire in future episodes. The program appears to have been abandoned although the one produced episode can still be watched.

Comment: The girls portraying the sisters are not credited (they do not even have names in the program). It is a very amateurish production (with jumpy images and bad panning from girl to girl as they speak).

Episode List: *1.* Season 1, Episode 1.

349 The Secret Life of the American Mermaids. *youtube.com.* 2012 (Fantasy).

Two young girls, Avalon and Erica, are by a pool when Avalon decides to go swimming while Erika, afraid of water, elects to relax by the side of the pool. As Avalon swims she notices a crystal on the pool floor and brings it to the surface. Avalon and Erica examine the crystal but nothing happens. Later, when Avalon and Erika are at Avalon's home, Avalon changes into a bathing suit and brings the crystal with her to her backyard pool. As Erika watches, Avalon pulls her into the water. The water begins to bubble and the girls are transformed into Mermaids. The program relates their efforts to conceal what has happened and pretend to be ordinary girls as they fear exposure could render them as scientific experiments.

Cast (as credited): Avalon, Erica and Edward (Themselves). **Comment:** The acting and photography are acceptable. The program is unusual in that between scenes either Avalon or Erika appear in very brief fashion statement segments.

Episode List: 2 untitled episodes, labeled "Episode 1" and "Episode 2" have been produced.

350 Secret Life of the 2 Mermaids. *youtube. com.* 2013 (Fantasy).

Rikki and Emma are strangers to each other until they meet at school and become instant friends. Each has a secret (they are a Mermaid) but they are not sure how they became one (both Emma and Rikki recall swimming in the ocean and entering a mysterious cave beneath the sea. The water engulfed them [at different times] and when they touched water they were transformed into a Mermaid). Shortly after befriending, the girls reveal their secret to each other—and must now safeguard their Mermaid existence while still living life as ordinary school girls.

Cast (as credited): Nicole (Rikki), McKenzie (Emma), Savannah (Melanie). **Comment:** Pretty girls, good underwater photography but poor sound hampers the production.

Episode List: *1.* The Beginning of the Tails. *2.* A Fishy Sleepover. *3.* The Magic Necklace. *4.* Full Moon Madness. *5.* Power Storm. *6.* Tail Stories Told. *7.* Halloween Mermaids. *8.* Shell Crazy.

351 Secret Mermaids. *youtube.com.* 2013 (Fantasy).

Claire and Hunter are friends, enjoying themselves at the beach when a mystical force transports them to a magic island. As the hour grows late and Claire and Hunter find they have no way to get off the island, they take shelter under a pier for the night. It is here that each finds a strange rock that when held burns the palms of their hands. It is the following morning when Claire and Hunter decide to make an S.O.S. distress signal out of stones and hope an airplane will spot them. Sometime later a helicopter is heard hovering over the island and, while not shown, the girls are rescued and returned to their homes. While only a pilot episode has been made, it shows that when Claire and Hunter come in contact with water they transform into Mermaids (as a result of the rocks they found) and it will relate their adventures as they struggle to keep their secret while pretending to be ordinary girls.

Cast (as credited): Emma (Claire), Georgia (Hunter). **Comment:** The project, which appears to be abandoned, has acceptable acting and photography.

Episode List: *1.* Magic Island.

352 Secret of the Scales. *youtube.com.* 2012 (Fantasy).

A young girl (Angela) returning home from school finds a mysterious ring in her bathroom. Not knowing where it came from but becoming fascinated by it, she places it on her finger. Later, when she takes a drink of water, she is transformed into a Mermaid (with the power of teleportation) and must now learn to accept what she has become and conceal her secret from others.

Cast (as credited): Raphael Charles (Angela), Maeve (Alex). **Comment:** The action centers around two girls and is interesting, but poor sound and sometimes equally poor photography (jumpy picture and blurry images) hampers the production.

Episode List: *1.* The Ring. *2.* Powers and More. *3.* More Powers and Teleportation. *4.* Slumber Party Antics. *5.* Sleepover Switch.

353 Secret of the Sea. *youtube.com.* 2014 (Fantasy).

Paige, Summer and Blair Doris are sisters but Blair, the eldest, is extraordinary: she is secretly a mermaid. For Blair, life changed when she found a box mixed in with her summer clothes. Although the box had a written warning telling her not to open it, curiosity got the best of Blair and she looked inside. The sea shell that she found appeared to be normal but it had a strange affect on her: it transformed her into a Mermaid when she touched water. It appears that the sea shell is mystical but is actually a curse and only those girls descended from the original Doris family can be affected if the shell is touched. Eventually Paige and Summer come to find the shell, touch it and also become Mermaids. Three young girls and their efforts to help each other adjust to what they have become while attempting to live as ordinary girls.

Cast: Blair, Summer and Paige Doris as Themselves. **Comment:** Very pretty girls in a well photographed and nicely thought out story that flows smoothly from episode to episode.

Episode List: 8 untitled episodes, labeled "Episode1" through "Episode 8" have been produced.

354 *Secret Scales. youtube.com.* 2014 (Fantasy).

It is the evening of a blood red moon and two girls (Trinity and Brooke) are on a camping trip with their families (who are not seen) when they find two necklaces in the sand on the lake shore. After placing the jewelry around their necks they decide to go swimming. The lake waters, reflecting the rays from the moon, begin to bubble and transform them into Mermaids. Now, with amazing powers, Trinity and Brooke must learn how to control them while keeping secret the fact that they are Mermaids.

Cast: Ava Ward (Trinity McKinley), Molly Gosling (Brooke Turner). **Comment:** Although the sound is poor at times, the girls are pretty and the photography good.

Episode List: *1.* Blood Moon Magic. *2.* Summer Songs.

355 *Secret Scales Forever. youtube.com.* 2014 (Fantasy).

A young girl (Amanda) finds a note attached to a glass of an ice-tea like liquid that reads "Drink me for a surprise, an exciting adventure. Mother Ocean." Not sure of what to make of it, Amanda calls her best friend Serena to come over and see what she found. Now, united with Serena, the girls decide to taste the liquid in the glass. Although the taste was not pleasant, the girls appear to be unaffected. Shortly after, when they come in contact with water they are transformed into Mermaids. Now with a secret to share, Amanda and Serena (as well as their friend Heather, who is also a Mermaid) struggle to keep secret what has happened while trying to live their lives as ordinary girls.

Cast (as credited): Kayleigh (Amanda), Carolyn (Serena), Payton (Heather). **Comment:** Very unflattering pictures of the three leads are seen in the opening theme (why???). The framing is also bad at times as the girls' heads are cut off in scenes and staging is also off at times (here one character blocks another character's actions). Overall, the program is just slightly below a standard Internet Mermaid series.

Episode List: *1.* The Drink. *2.* I've Got the Power. *3.* Playing with Magic. *4.* Friend or Foe? *5.* Cordelia's Necklace. *6.* The Scratch of Lies. *7.* The Full Moon.

356 *Secret Sea Life.* 2012 (Fantasy).

While on vacation in Hawaii, two young girls, Brooke and Destiny, enjoyed swimming in the ocean but, unknown to them at the time, the salt water had activated a recessed Mermaid gene in their bodies. Shortly after, when returning home (to another state), they discover they are Mermaids when contact with water causes their legs to became tails. When drying off they return to normal and the program charts their adventures as they try to also live life as ordinary girls.

Cast (as credited): Michelle (Brooke), Julie (Destiny), Natascha (Lauren). **Comment:** The girls are pretty but the program has very poor sound and is difficult to understand; it has since been taken offline.

Episode List: *1.* WTF?!!? *2.* You're a What? *3.* Pretty Little Mermaid. *4.* Once upon a Mermaid. *5.* Hurricane Mermaid. *6.* Tail Twister. *7.* Loss of Magic. *8.* A Change in the Past. *9.* Changes. *10.* Can You Keep a Secret? *11.* No Way Back!

357 *The Secret Sea Sister. youtube.com.* 2013 (Fantasy).

While admiring the fish in her aquarium, Oceana and her friend Aquamarine find two dolphin bracelets near the side of the tank. After examining the bracelets the girls place them on their wrists and are suddenly amazed when they are transformed into Mermaids. The girls must now help each other understand and use their powers and pretend to be ordinary school girls to safeguard their secret.

Cast (as credited): Molly (Oceana), Lily (Aquamarine). **Comment:** Very nice photography but the program is slow moving especially when several minutes are used just to show the girls searching for Mermaid information on the Internet. The program also appears to have been abandoned.

Episode List: *1.* Season 1 Episode 1 (Pilot).

358 *Secret Story of Mermaids. youtube.com.* 2012 (Fantasy).

A young girl (Jackie) is in her backyard when a book magically appears on the ground. Curious, Jackie picks up the book, opens it and finds herself on a page about Mermaids. Seemingly not interested, she tosses the book aside and goes into her home. As she enters her bedroom she spies the book she abandoned and opens the page on Mermaids. As she reads about them she also recites a spell that instantly transforms her into a Mermaid. Without really thinking first, Jackie calls her best friend (Natasha) and invites her over to see what has happened. Natasha is a bit startled at first but after learning how Jackie became a Mermaid, reads the same passage from the book. She too is transformed and the program follows Jackie and Natasha as they attempt navigate lives as Mermaids and ordinary young girls.

Cast (as credited): Christina Jones (Jackie), Jessica (Natasha), Millie Anne (Jessie), Katie Lynn (Natalia). **Comment:** Like most Mermaid series, the girls adjust much too quickly to what has happened to them. The acting and overall production, however, is good.

Season 1 Episode List: *1.* The Tails. *2.* Tails Go Wrong. *3.* Time to Show. *4.* The Help. *5.* Sleepy Tails. *6.* Outsiders. *7.* Missing Things. *8.* 1920s Mishap. *9.* Finale.

Season 2 Episode List: *1.* Spell Search.

359 *The Secret Tails (Series 1). youtube. com.* 2013 (Fantasy).

Anxious to find adventure, two girls, Sirena and Lyla, decide to go boating (on a boat called *The Stripper*). After an unspecified amount of time, the boat's motor fails and strands the girls in what appears to be the middle of the ocean. With no choice but to attempt a very long swim to a distant island, the girls, clad only in their bikinis, do manage to reach the island but now must find a way to escape. As they begin to explore the island, they come across a strange pool of water and figure it can lead them back home. The girls dive into the pool at the same time the rays from a full moon illuminates the pool. Suddenly, the girls find themselves back home with no reasonable explanation as to how it occurred (and in different clothes). Although unnerved, the girls accept what has happened and are just grateful to be home. Shortly after, however, when the girls come in contact with water, they magically transform into Mermaids and later discover they have magical abilities. The program chronicles their adventures as they attempt to control their new abilities while leading ordinary lives as young girls.

Cast: Sarah Cunningham (Sirena), Lauren Dicktel (Lyla). **Comment:** The program did make an effort to film on location and that can be seen in the ocean sequences. The sound, however, is quite bad for the location scenes and there is a serious continuity problem here. When first seen as their boat becomes disabled, the girls are wearing bikinis. On the island, when they are seen in the cave, they are wearing T-shirts over their swim wear. When they decide to dive into the pool they are seen in different colored bikinis and when magically propelled home, different clothes are again seen. The story, however, is interesting and the leads do a good job handling their roles.

Episode List: 4 untitled episodes, labeled "Episode 1" through "Episode 4" have been produced.

360 *The Secret Tails (Series 2).* 2013 (Fantasy).

More than 100 years ago a young Mermaid hid two magical necklaces inside a box and buried it in the sand of a beach. It is the year 2013 when a young girl (Kylie) finds that box and opens it to discover the necklaces but is unaware of the magic they contain. At home Kylie, now wearing one of the necklaces, comes in contact with water and is transformed into a Mermaid. Kylie must now keep her Mermaid life a secret while attempting to adjust to her developing powers.

Cast (as credited): Kendell (Kylie Summers). **Comment:** The program, which suffers from poor sound at times, has since been taken offline.

Season 1 Episode List: *1.* The Necklaces. *2.* New Discoveries. *3.* Where the Cave Leads. *4.* Paradise. *5.* Lost in the Waves.

Season 2 Episode List: *1.* New Waves.

361 *Secret Waters (2012).* 2012 (Fantasy).

After a shopping trip, friends Amber and Taylor decide to relax by taking a swim in Taylor's backyard pool. Shortly after entering the water, the girls spot two strange-looking necklaces at the bottom of the pool. Intrigued, they retrieve them and place them around their necks. Later, when the girls are at home and come in contact with water they transform into Mermaids. The program follows their efforts to adjust to their Mermaid life while pretending to be ordinary young girls.

Cast (as credited): Marta (Amber), Emily (Taylor), Karen (Olivia). **Comment:** The girls are pretty, the photography acceptable but the sound is poor at times. The program has since been taken offline.

Season 1 Episode List:
1. What the…
2. The Bad Drink.
3. Full Moon Madness.
4. Research.
5. Finale.

Season 2 Episode List:
1. Bad Karma.
2. Untitled.
3. We're Back.
4. The One Phone Call That Will Change Everything.

Season 3 Episode List:
1. The Note.
2. The Fight.
3. Exposed.
4. The Price of Being Popular.
5. The Book.
6. Pool Party.
7. The Fight.

Season 4 Episode List:
1. Remembering.
2. Where's My Brother?
3. Science Sucks!
4. The Plan.
5. What, You're a Girly Girl?
6. Just another Rainy Day.
7. Episode 7.
8. Ugh, Chores Again!
9. Season Finale.

Season 5 Episode List:
1. The Siren's Song.

2. The Watcher.
3. Who's the Watcher?
4. Amber's Missing.
5. Faith.

362 The Secret Waters (2013). 2013 (Fantasy).

During a slumber party, a dare is made by three girl friends (Prestion, Charlotte and Pathane) to visit a strange island that holds a forbidding past. The dare is taken and while on the island, the girls come in contact with its mystical waters. The water presents the experience as a dream when they return home but later, when they come in contact with water they transform into mermaids. The program charts their experiences as they attempt to adjust to their Mermaid abilities while pretending to be ordinary girls. **Cast (as credited):** PinkSnowAngel13 (Prestion), PSA12 (Charlotte), Treacky (Pathane). **Comment:** Standard Mermaid series with pretty girls and acceptable photography. The program has since been taken offline.
Episode List: *1.* The Pilot. *2–6.* Untitled.

363 The Secret Wizards. youtube.com. 2012 (Fantasy).

A young girl (Audrey) finds a box containing various items including a diary (from this point on it is rather confusing to figure out what happens). The diary apparently contains the writings of a wizard and anyone who reads the passages becomes a wizard (as Audrey is seen rhyming words to perform magic). But Audrey is not the only wizard. She discovers that her friend Jessica is also a wizard (from powers she inherited from her grandmother). The program relates their efforts to keep their abilities a secret and figure out why they were chosen to become wizards. **Cast (as credited):** Nia (Audrey), Crystal (Jessica), Amari (Arianna), Kaylin (Vanessa). **Comment:** The idea is different when it comes to series about young girls and the production has acceptable acting and photography.
Episode List: 4 untitled episodes, labeled "Episode 1" through "Episode 4" have been produced.

364 Secretly Tailed. youtube.com. 2013 (Fantasy).

Friends Jaylie and Amber are walking along the edge of a lagoon when they come across two strange-looking necklaces. The girls take the necklaces home and discover, that when worn and they come in contact with water, they transform into Mermaids. Now, with a secret they must keep, they struggle to encompass what they have become while continuing their lives as ordinary girls. **Cast (as credited):** Jolie (Jaylie), Lily (Amber), Ginny B. (Julia). **Comment:** Nicely photographed

but like others of its type, the production suffers from poor sound.
Episode List: *1.* A Fishy Secret. *2.* Party Problems. *3.* The North Star. *4.* Just a Little Walk. *5.* Splashy Secret.

365 Secrets (2013). youtube.com. 2013–2015 (Dolls).

Ava Johnson is a teenage girl with a secret: she is a Mermaid. She has just begun classes at a new school and is always fearful that someone will discover what she really is. She also possesses amazing powers and must learn to never touch water in public and be weary of nights when the moon is full (as both can cause an unexpected transformation). The program follows Ava as she interacts with people while all the time pretending to be an ordinary girl. **Cast (as credited):** Claire Russell, Alessa Mancini, Ava Moore, Lacie Rowland. **Comment:** The program has very good photography, voices and doll manipulation. It was created by a girl identified only as Ms. Flanclan and she took the concept one step further to create a live action version of the program (see the following title).
Episode List: 7 untitled episodes comprise Season 1; Season 2 consists of 8 untitled episodes and the concluding Season 3 produced 6 untitled episodes.

366 Secrets (2015). 2015 (Fantasy).

The program is actually Season 4 of the prior title but has switched from using dolls to incorporating live actors. Although only a very pretty teenage girl is seen in the produced episodes, it is revealed that she (Ava) is a Mermaid but barely establishes anything other than the fact that Ava has been successfully keeping her secret but seeking to discover who she really is and where her ancestry lies. **Cast:** Although a cast is not listed, a girl, who calls herself Ms. Flanclan plays the role of Ava. **Comment:** The program is very well done and very intriguing but it appears it will not continue as the star has produced a video explaining that she may stop making videos and is apologetic to her YouTube fans for being so loyal over the years. The program has since been taken offline.
Episode List: 2 untitled episodes, labeled "Episode 1" and "Episode 2" have been produced.

367 Secrets, Lies and Truths. youtube.com. 2011 (Dolls).

Carlie is a young girl who is jealous of her older sister Harper. She believes Harper is superior and her misconceptions have driven her into a world were she lives an inferior existence. Carlie records events as she perceives them to be in her diary with the program exposing how those secrets and misconceptions come to light to show Carlie what life is really about and how she should live it, not how she believes she should live it.

Cast (as credited): Cici Moore (Carlie Banks), Ally Freeman (Harper Banks), Emily Dott (Miley Rose), Ginger Akanor (Hailey Cook), Kanani Akiva (Savannah Chris), Julie Albright (Massie Adams), Ivy Ling (Alex Ray), Kit Kittredge (Anna Rose).
Comment: A well done series with good doll manipulation and voices. The theme uses stop motion photography, which is very well done.
Episode List: 3 untitled episodes, labeled "Episode 1," "Episode 2" and "Episode 3" have been produced.

368 *Seven Awesome Kids: Alexis. youtube. com.* 2014–2016 (Variety).

Alexis, Anya, Georgie, Holly, Katie (1), Katie (2), Klare, Lilly and Lolita are young girls who host their own programs under a parentally controlled and moderated YouTube channel. Each girl is simply herself and presents wholesome entertainment for children through skits. Programs, which contain no credits, are well produced and very entertaining. See each individual girl for episode information.

Alexis Episode List:
1. Introducing Alexis.
2. Grandma's Unlucky Day.
3. Where's Alexis' Family?
4. The Bad Babysitter.
5. The Mischievous Makeover.
6. The Cat in the Hat.
7. The Day I Became a Princess.
8. Alexis through the Decades.
9. The Crazy Dog Lady.
10. The Legend of the Chain Letter.
11. Expectations vs. Reality: Exercising.
12. The Strange Math Teacher.
13. Alexis' Summer Morning Routine.
14. The Good Voodoo Doll.
15. The Treasure Is Buried Where?
16. What Should Alexis Wear?
17. The Old Letter to the Tooth Fairy.
18. Alexis' Embarrassing Dance Moves.
19. The Day Alexis Became an Actress.
20. Alexis' First Date Disaster.
21. Alexis Is the Earth Hero.
22. Alexis' Secret Guide to Being Good.
23. The Jealous Babysitter.
24. How to Catch a Mermaid.
25. It's Halloween! Get Ready with Alexis.
26. Mission Impossible: Getting My Sister to Eat a Vegetable.
27. Alexis Has Three Wishes.
28. Alexis' School Morning Routine.
29. Alexis' Dream Life.
30. The Shoe Fairy.
31. Bean Boozled Challenge.
32. If Only I Could Get My Own Room.
33. Alexis' Christmas Haul 2015.
34. Santa Brought Me BAD Gifts.
35. Alexis Is So Jealous of Her Older Sister Georgie.
36. Alexis's Life as a Prankster.
37. Alexis Has a Texting Thumb.
38. Types of Babysitters.
39. There's Trouble in Alexis' House.
40. The Mischievous Prank.
41. Alexis Accidentally Breaks Teddie's Doll.
42. Teddie Spies on Alexis.
43. What Would a Genie Wish For?
44. A Day in the Life of a Forgetful Kid.
45. I Think My Babysitter's an Alien.

369 *Seven Awesome Kids: Anya. youtube. com.* 2011–2015 (Variety).

Alexis, Anya, Georgie, Holly, Katie (1), Katie (2), Klare, Lilly and Lolita are young girls who host their own programs under a parentally controlled and moderated YouTube channel. Each girl is simply herself and presents wholesome entertainment for children through skits. Programs, which contain no credits, are well produced and very entertaining. See each individual girl for episode information.

Anya Episode List:
1. Introducing Anya.
2. Flora Is a Cereal Killer.
3. Cheer Tryouts Gone Wrong.
4. My Pet … Easter Egg?
5. The Wisest Wizard.
6. To a Parallel Universe with the Doctor.
7. Double Trouble.
8. The Time Consuming French Essay.
9. Fan Girl's Boot Camp.
10. The Restless Nighttime.
11. Dance Battle: Scarlet vs. Storm.
12. The Crazy Obsessed Tennis Player.
13. Malfunctioning Wand.
14. Anya's New Hopes.
15. Anya's Strange Dream.
16. The Princess and the Public School.
17. Oh No, Anya's Trapped in a Fishbowl.
18. Anya's Christmas.
19. The Little Match Girl.
20. What Anya Does When She's Bored.
21. Introducing Ill Bot.
22. How to Annoy Your Teacher.
23. Fairy Dust Gone Wrong.
24. Anya's Garbage Bag Dress.
25. How Not to Fake Being Sick.
26. The Legend of the Halloweenie.
27. Oh No, Anya Has a Monster in Her Closet!
28. Three Dresses.
29. Invisible Wishes.
30. Through the Looking Glass.
31. How to Embarrass Your Twin.
32. Boating with Friends.
33. Invasion of Rosin Eating Dogs.

34. Anya's Baby Sitting Nightmare.
35. Is Anya a Unicorn?
36. Amusement Park Fun.
37. Be Careful What You Wish For.
38. Time Travel Trampoline.
39. Fan Girl Identity Crisis.
40. The Legend of the Fruit Seal.
41. Minute to Win It on the Beach.
42. Anya Draws Her life.
43. Search for Cookies.
44. Anya's Jealous Twin.
45. Dr. Wingelhardt.
46. Tomboy's Summer.
47. Scarlet's Storm.
48. Do You Really Have to Hurt a Ladybug?
49. Dinosaurs!
50. Fun with Friends on the Lake.
51. Grandma's Book.
52. Mysterious Tap on the Window.
53. Zombie Attack!
54. Linda Schlaben's Springtastic Fashion Show.
55. Revenge of the Book.
56. Being a Famous Book Writer.
57. Stabucksinator.
58. My Secret Life as a Bookworm.
59. How to Survive Solo and Ensemble Competition.
60. 5 Easy Steps to Throw a Party.
61. Magic Valentine Chocolate.
62. Toys' Wheel of Fortune.
63. Mission Impossible: Getting to a Concert.
64. What's in Anya's Backpack?
65. Did Anya Say a Lie?
66. Christmas Presents Haul.
67. A Modern Christmas Carol.
68. Winter Break Outfits.
69. Anya's Magic Tricks.
70. Anya's Halloween Costume.
71. Anya's Halloween Video.
72. Introducing TTS: Thanksgiving Termination Squad.
73. Anya's New Room Tour.
74. Anya's New Doll.
75. Morning Routine of a Camper.
76. Girl vs. Wild.
77. Anya's Halloween Costume.
78. Barbie in a Scary Movie.
79. Barbie Goes Shopping.
80. Sakkid101 Takes Over.
81. The Clone Mask Commercial.
82. 20 Random Excuses to Get You Out of Trouble.
83. Home Alone After School.
84. Anya's Minute to Win It: Back Flip.
85. Which Celebrity Are You Most Like Quiz.
86. Life in Heaven.
87. Guess Who?
88. Anya's Summer Fashion.
89. Spot the Difference.
90. Bed Maker Commercial.

91. Anya's Super Powers.
92. BC Ferry Tour.
93. Don't Close Your Eyes (Music Video).
94. Truth about Princesses.
95. Anya's Life as a Grownup.
96. Goodbye to Spring.
97. Contortionist's Performance.
98. Anya's New Bedtime Routine.
99. Anya 10 Things.
100. Anya—Chug-a-Jug.
101. Bella Swan's New Talk Show.
102. Life at the Abby Lee Dance Company.
103. Spring Fashion.
104. Quick Note.
105. One Leg Challenge.
106. A Villain's Revenge.
107. Haunted House.
108. Plastic Cup Tower.
109. The Circus Girl and the Hypnotist.
110. Valentine's Day Makeover.
111. Field Trip Vlog.
112. A Day in the Life of Amber Hawking.
113. Impossible Things to Do with Your Body.
114. A New Kid at Hogwarts?
115. The Case of the Missing Pillow.
116. Playing in the Snow on Christmas Eve.
117. Things to Do to Stay Awake on New Year's Eve.
118. 5 Things Anya Can't Live Without.
119. The Mystery Doorbell.
120. Fairyland Adventure.
121. My Life as a Super Star.
122. Wacky Hair.
123. One-Armed!
124. Horror Story of the Prom Queen.
125. How to….
126. Dress Fashion.
127. Anya's Blindfolded Taste Test.
128. Anya's Morning Routine.
129. Anya's Three Truths and One Lie.
130. Anya's Summer Recap.
131. Anya's Bedtime Routine.
132. Learn to Fly.
133. Anya Tries Her Mom's Clothes.
134. Cart Wheeling from Coast-to-Coast.
135. SAK Super Hero.
136. Two-Piece Garbage Bag Dress.
137. A True Story of a Pageant Contestant.
138. A Day in the Life of Smudge.
139. Hot Cross Buns.
140. Planking with Anya.
141. Spot the Difference.
142. Anya's Hobbies and Pastimes.
143. Anya's Room Tour.
144. Spring Clothes Collection.
145. 3 Truths 1 Lie.
146. Anya's Wonderland.
147. Gymnastics Challenge.
148. Anya's Backward Spring Break.
149. Anya's Cheerleading Routine.

150. Guess Who?
151. Naughty in the Park.
152. If Anya Ruled the World.
153. Valentine's Medicine Commercial.
154. What's in My Schoolbag?
155. Coffee (Music Video).
156. Behind the Scenes....
157. Cartwheel Challenge.
158. Awesome Gymnastics.
159. Texas Winter Fashion Show.
160. Anya's Epic Christmas Video Diary.
161. Pirate's Personality.
162. Awesome Pigs in a Blanket.
163. Anya's Impersonation for SAK.
164. Epic Skit with PJs.
165. Anya's After School Routine.
166. Burger Taste Test.
167. Anya's Healthy Cheer Routine.
168. Goodbye Anya.

370 Seven Awesome Kids: Georgie. *you tube.com.* 2011–2015 (Variety).

Alexis, Anya, Georgie, Holly, Katie (1), Katie (2), Klare, Lilly and Lolita are young girls who host their own programs under a parentally controlled and moderated YouTube channel. Each girl is simply herself and presents wholesome entertainment for children through skits. Programs, which contain no credits, are well produced and very entertaining. See each individual girl for episode information.

Georgie Episode List:
1. Grandma Can't Text.
2. The Scary Sticky Notes.
3. Babysitting a Know It All.
4. The Mischievous Phone Calls.
5. Grumpy Cat.
6. The Day Georgie Became a Troublemaker.
7. A Crime of Fashion.
8. Georgie's Smoothie Challenge.
9. Georgie's Pet Bunny.
10. The Good Witch and the Bunny.
11. Georgie Has No Internet.
12. Georgie Baby Sits a Troublemaker.
13. Georgie's After School Routine.
14. Middle School Boot Camp.
15. Georgie's Night Time Snack Fail.
16. How Georgie Gets Ready for a Dance.
17. Georgie Is Missing Her Powerful Bracelet.
18. Does Georgie Live in a Haunted House?
19. Georgie Has a Strange Fear: Nomophobia.
20. The Princess and the Sleepless Nights.
21. Georgie's Christmas Haul 2013.
22. Will Georgie Save Christmas?
23. What Georgie Does When She's Bored.
24. Georgie's Robot Dog.
25. How to Annoy Your Mom.
26. Georgie Finds Fairy Dust.
27. Garbage Bag Dresses.
28. What Georgie Does When She's Sick.
29. The Pesky Book Report.
30. Halloween Tag.
31. The Monster under Georgie's Bed.
32. Pick Georgie's Dress.
33. If Georgie Was Invisible.
34. Little Red Riding Hood.
35. Georgie Does Dares with her Crazy Twin.
36. Georgie Tries to Break World Records.
37. Cup of Water Challenge.
38. An After School Invasion of Marshmallows.
39. Georgie Loses Teddie.
40. The Day I Became Addicted to Starbucks.
41. Georgie's Summer Fun.
42. The Day I Became a Boy.
43. The Year 3000.
44. Fan vs. Super Fan.
45. The Legend of the Mascara Brush.
46. Georgie's Minute to Win It.
47. Bean Boozled Challenge with Georgie and Katie.
48. Undercover for Oreos!, Part 1
49. Undercover for Oreos!, Part 2
50. Jealous of Adults.
51. Dr. Halitosis.
52. Perks of Being A Tomboy.
53. Girly Girl vs. Tomboy.
54. Bad Luck Morning.
55. Toilet Butter?
56. What Is a True Friend?
57. The Day I Became a Ghost.
58. The Big Surprise.
59. What Happens Next?
60. Georgie's Worst Nightmare: Being Grounded.
61. Spring Fashion 2014.
62. Alarm Clock Revenge.
63. Georgie's a Hand Model.
64. The Name-Inator!
65. The Secret to Doing Your Homework Fast.
66. How to Do a Fishtail Braid.
67. How to Have An Awesome Slumber Party!
68. The Mystery Valentine.
69. The Best Friend Game Show!
70. Georgie Is a Baker!
71. The Impossible Scavenger Hunt!
72. What's in Georgie's Backpack?
73. 3 Truths and 1 Lie With Georgie!
74. Waiting for Santa.
75. Christmas Haul 2014.
76. Georgie's Winter Fashion.
77. Questions with the Magic 8 Ball.
78. Georgie's a Sour Candy Tester!
79. 25 Things Georgie's Thankful For!
80. The Living Doll.
81. The Morning of an 80s Girl!
82. The Hunt for the Perfect Present!
83. Georgie's Halloween Favorites!
84. Georgie the Exhausting Day of Super Barbie!
85. Barbie Fashion Show.
86. Georgie's Big Idea!
87. Meet Georgie's Clone!

88. My Dog Ate My Homework!
89. What to Do When You're Home Alone!
90. Minute to Win It.
91. How to Get Famous on Instagram.
92. Symmetry and the Pocket of Angels (Music Video).
93. Water Balloon Madness!
94. Who Is Georgie?
95. Georgie's Summer Fashion 2014.
96. Spot the Difference Packing for Camp.
97. Her Life Changer 5000!
98. What Super Power Would You Want?
99. Backyard Tour.
100. Georgie's Addicted … To Lip Balm!
101. Stuff Princesses Say.

371 Seven Awesome Kids: Holly. *youtube. com.* 2014. (Variety).

Alexis, Anya, Georgie, Holly, Katie (1), Katie (2), Klare, Lilly and Lolita are young girls who host their own programs under a parentally controlled and moderated YouTube channel. Each girl is simply herself and presents wholesome entertainment for children through skits. Programs, which contain no credits, are well produced and very entertaining. See each individual girl for episode information.

Holly Episode List:
1. Introducing Holly.
2. Spend Quality Time with Grandma.
3. Babysitting.
4. The Mischievous YouTuber.
5. The Cat Song.
6. Holly's an Evil Scientist?!
7. Types of Criminals.
8. Holly Does the ABC Gymnastics Challenge.
9. Holly's Magical Cat.
10. The Easter Bunny Goes Wizarding School.
11. Holly's in Candy Land??
12. Holly the Trouble Maker.
13. School Expectations vs. Reality.
14. Jail Break Boot Camp.
15. "Dance Moms" … Parody.
16. Holly's Crazy Obsession … Spicy Food?!
17. Genie's Stolen Powers.
18. Who's Haunting Holly's House?
19. The Strange and Unexpected Visitor.
20. The Princess and the Prince.
21. Positive Peyton Goes to Jail?!
22. Christmas Haul 2014!
23. Is Christmas Lost Forever?
24. Bored on Beak…?!
25. The Santabot?!
26. How to Annoy People While Doing Homework!
27. The Magical Christmas Fairydust!
28. Holly's Garbage Fashion.
29. Holly's … Sick!
30. Holly's Pesky Doggy!
31. Monster in the Closet?!

32. Pick Holly's Dress.
33. Holly's Invisible Phone?!
34. Spookilinia: The Unknown Fairytale.
35. Holly Meets Her Long Lost Crazy Twin!
36. Holly Breaks the Longest Handstand Ever?!
37. Fun with Water: Holly's Edition.
38. Invasion of the Food Stealers.
39. Holly Baby-sits Amber?!
40. What! Holly's a Chew Toy?!
41. Summer Fun with Holly!
42. Holly in the Year 3000?!
43. Holly's a Super Fan of Dora?!
44. The Legend of the Ancient Clock!
45. Holly's Minute to Win It!
46. Holly Does Wreck This Journal.
47. Holly Goes Undercover.
48. Holly's Jealous of Celebrities?!
49. Dr. Help Returns.
50. Tammy's New Hobby.
51. Gabby the Girly Girl vs. Tammy the Tomboy.
52. Holly's Bad Lucky Day!
53. Holly's Big Idea.
54. Holly and Kristen Do the Best Friend Tag.
55. Five Steps on Scaring a Ghost.
56. Holly Sleepwalks!
57. Where Are Holly's Bows?!
58. Holly's Spring Fashion 2014.

372 Seven Awesome Kids: Katie (1). *you tube.com.* 2012–2015 (Variety).

Alexis, Anya, Georgie, Holly, Katie (1), Katie (2), Klare, Lilly and Lolita are young girls who host their own programs under a parentally controlled and moderated YouTube channel. Each girl is simply herself and presents wholesome entertainment for children through skits. Programs, which contain no credits, are well produced and very entertaining. See each individual girl for episode information.

Katie (1) Episode List:
1. Grandma.
2. Katie's Scary Story.
3. Katie's Babysitting Nightmare!
4. My Mischievous Twin!
5. Katie Is a Cat!
6. The Day I Became Addicted to Shopping!
7. Katie's a Criminal!
8. Katie's Bad Luck School Day: School Struggles.
9. Katie's New Pet Puppy!
10. You're a Wizard, Katie.
11. Super Power Parallel Universe!
12. Katie's a Troublemaker.
13. Snow Boot Camp.
14. The Dance Contest.
15. One Direction Obsession!
16. Missing Lucky Powers.
17. Haunted House.
18. The Strange and Unexpected Thief!
19. The Princess and the Selfie!

20. Jail Break!
21. What I Got for Christmas 2014!
22. A Christmas Story.
23. Christmas Robots.
24. What to Do When You're Bored.
25. How to Annoy Your Parents.
26. Fairy Dust.
27. Garbage Bag Fashion!
28. How to Feel Better when You're Sick.
29. Pesky Potion.
30. DIY Halloween Fun & More!
31. Monster Makeup!–Halloween Prank.
32. Pick a Dress with Katie.
33. Katie's Invisibility Cloak.
34. Goldilocks.
35. Meet Katie's Twin.
36. Two Guinness Records.
37. Water Park Fun.
38. Invasion.
39. Baby Sitting Nightmare.
40. The Day I Became a Mermaid.
41. Summer Fun with Katie.
42. Girls vs. Boys.
43. Year 3000?
44. The Fault in Our Stars Super Fan.
45. The Legend of Buried Treasure.
46. Katie Has a Minute to Win It.
47. Katie Visits VidCon and California.
48. Katie Goes Undercover.
49. Katie's Jealous.
50. Fan Girl Doctor.
51. Girly Morning Routine.
52. Girly or Tomboy?
53. Katie Has Bad Luck.
54. Back in Time.
55. DIY Gifts for Your Friends.
56. Ghost Hunting.
57. Katie's Stuck.
58. Katie's Worst Nightmare.
59. Katie's Spring Fashion.
60. Katie Gets Revenge.
61. Katie's Dream Life.
62. Pet Translator.
63. Style Secrets.
64. 5 Cute and Awesome DIYs.
65. The Ultimate Part Machine.
66. How to Prepare for Valentine's Day.
67. Katie Can Read Your Mind.
68. Secret Agent Katie's Impossible Mission.
69. Katie's Backpack.
70. Katie Lies?
71. Christmas with Katie.
72. What Katie Got for Christmas.
73. Katie's Winter/Christmas Fashion.
74. The Magic Santa Hat.
75. Katie's Winter Favorites.
76. Katie's Crazy Job.
77. The Living Doll.
78. The Morning Routine of Secret Agent Katie.
79. A Halloween Story.

80. Katie's Exploration.
81. Katie Is a Barbie Doll.
82. Barbie Answers Questions.
83. We're in Trouble.
84. Katie Has Clones.
85. Minute to Win It with Katie and Ellie.
86. Katie's all Alone!
87–88. Touched by an Angel.
89. Stuff Famous People Say.
90. Katie's Epic Water Competition.
91. Who Is Katie?
92. Katie's Summer Fashion.
93. Katie's Beach Day.
94. Super Katie.
95. Who Has the Best Invention?
96. Katie's Travel Tour.
97. Katie's Strange Addiction.
98. Coffee (Music Video).
99. A Day in the Life of Katie—All Grown Up.

373 Seven Awesome Kids: Katie (2). *you tube.com.* 2013–2015 (Variety).

Alexis, Anya, Georgie, Holly, Katie (1), Katie (2), Klare, Lilly and Lolita are young girls who host their own programs under a parentally controlled and moderated YouTube channel. Each girl is simply herself and presents wholesome entertainment for children through skits. Programs, which contain no credits, are well produced and very entertaining. See each individual girl for episode information.

Katie (2) Episode List:
1. Introducing Katie.
2. KatieCat.
3. Katie Can Read Minds.
4. The Cookie Criminal.
5. Katie Meets Ashlynn from Seven Funtastic Girls.
6. Katie and Her Giant Pet Bunny.
7. Katie and Wanda Witch.
8. Katie Is a Dentist?!
9. Katie and the Troublemaker.
10. Bad Actress Boot Camp.
11. School vs. Home School.
12. Katie's Mother-Daughter PJ Party.
13. Katie Goes to Daddy-Daughter Dance.
14. Hannah and the Genie.
15. Katie's Unexpected Room Makeover.
16. The Princess and the Missing Crowns.
17. Katie Breaks Out.
18. Christmas Dream.
19. Katie's Christmas Haul.
20. Will Katie Die of Boredom?
21. Katie and the Chorebot 3000.
22. How to Annoy Katie.
23. Katie's Garbage Bag Dresses.
24. Fairy Dust Sneezes.
25. Katie Fakes Being Sick.
26. Katie and the Pesky Balloon.
27. Spooky Slumber Party.

28. Katie's Pet Monster.
29. Pick a Dress for Katie.
30. Katie's Invisible Pet.
31. Katie Red Riding Hood.
32. Katie Has a Crazy Twin.
33. The Day Katie Became a Unicorn.
34. Katie and the Invasion of Cookies.
35. Katie's Summer Fun.
36. Katie Becomes a Boy!
37. Katie in the Year 3000.
38. Katie is a Super Fan of One Direction!
39. Katie and the Legend of the Potato Chip Girl.
40. Katie's Minute to Win It.
41. Katie Goes to VidCon & Disneyland!
42. Agent "K" Goes Undercover.
43. Is Everyone Jealous?
44. Katie Visits Dr. Shops-A-Lot.
45. Katie's Bad Luck Curse.
46. My Alien BFF.
47. Katie and Morgan's Ultimate Sleepover.
48. Katie and the Friendly Ghost.
49. Katie Looks for the Easter Bunny.
50. Katie's Sleepover Nightmare!
51. Spring Fashion with Katie.
52. Katie and the Revenge Triangle.
53. Katie's Day Dream Life.
54. Katie Invents a Teleporter.
55. Katie Is Obsessed with Social Media.
56. How to Make Dog Treats with Katie.
57. Katie Goes to a Party.
58. Katie Has a Secret Admirer.
59. Katie and Hayley on the SAK Game Show.
60. Katie Has a Weird Dream.
61. Katie's Impossible Mission.
62. What Katie Does for Home Schooling.
63. Katie Lies?
64. Katie's Christmas Eve.
65. Katie Takes a Peek at Her Presents.
66. What Katie Got for Christmas.
67. Katie's Winter Fashion.
68. Katie's a Cat Manicurist!
69. If Dolls Ruled the World.
70. Katie's Bedtime Routine.
71. Strange Obsession.
72. Goodbye Katie.

374 Seven Awesome Kids: Klare. *youtube. com.* 2014–2015 (Variety).

Alexis, Anya, Georgie, Holly, Katie (1), Katie (2), Klare, Lilly and Lolita are young girls who host their own programs under a parentally controlled and moderated YouTube channel. Each girl is simply herself and presents wholesome entertainment for children through skits. Programs, which contain no credits, are well produced and very entertaining. See each individual girl for episode information.

Klare Episode List:
1. Introducing Klare.
2. Kit Kat the Cat.
3. You Have 3 Wishes.
4. No Wi-Fi?
5. The Trouble-Making Twin.
6. The Worst Sub Ever.
7. Girly Boot Camp.
8. Klare's Nightly Routine for School.
9. Dryer Lint Obsession.
10. Klare's Missing Powers.
11. Prankster or a Ghost?
12. The Princess and the Pea.
13. Klare Escaped Jail.
14. How Klare Saved Christmas.
15. Winter Break Boredom.
16. How to Annoy Anybody.
17. The Fairy Dust Law.
18. You Got Me Sick.
19. The Pesky Cousin.
20. Klare's Pick a Dress.
21. Perks of Being Invisible.
22. Guinea Pig Tells a Fairy Tale.
23. Klare's Crazy Twin.
24. Klare Tries to Break a World Record.
25. Klare's Fun with Water.
26. Invasion of the Pillows.
27. Klare's Baby Sitting Nightmare!
28. Klare Is a Dog.
29. Klare's Summer.
30. Dared to Be a Boy.
31. Is It Really 3000?
32. Divergent Fan.
33. Legend of the Pink Binder Curse.
34. Minute to Win It.
35. Back in Time.
36. Undone Chores.
37. Jealous and Why.
38. Dr. What!
39. Ali's Wardrobe Malfunction.
40. Sandy vs. Ally.
41. Good Luck to Bad Luck.
42. Future iPad.
43. What Friends Do at Sleepovers.
44. Necklace of Doom.
45. April Nightmares Bring May…?
46. Spring Fashion.
47. Klare vs. Kayla.
48. That's a Scary Dream?
49. Time Machine or Transporter.
50. Life Secrets.
51. How To: Evil Minion Nails.
52. Party in a Box.
53. Valentine's Day Crisis.
54. So You Think You Can Answer?
55. Just a Weird Dream.
56. What's in Klare's School Bag?
57. Klare's 3 Truths and 1 Lie.
58. What Klare Got for Christmas.
59. An Elf's Journey.
60. Winter Fashion.
61. Klare Tries a Few Magic Tricks.
62. Crazy, Crazy Jobs.

63. Quick and Easy Holiday Treats.
64. Klare's a Doll for a Day.
65. A Day in the Life of a Director.
66. Explorer Klare.
67. Happy Halloween.
68. What Should I Do?
69. Klare's Barbie Fashion Show.
70. Let's Catch the Criminal.
71. Evil Clone.
72. Home Alone.
73. Minute to Win It.
74. Ups and Downs of Being Famous.
75. Klare Meets an Angel.
76. Fun with Water.
77. Who's Klare?
78. Klare's Summer Fashion.
79. Softball: Spot the Difference.
80. Klare's Invention Doesn't Work.
81. Klare Has Super Powers?
82. Room Tour.
83. My Strange Addiction.
84. A Day at the Bakery.
85. I Will Not Let You Down (Music Video).
86. Can Klare Be in the Circus?
87. Klare's Nightly Routine.
88. What You Don't Know about Klare.
89. What Do Animals Think?
90. How to Be a Vampire Hunter.
91. Spring Fashion Show.
92. The Missing Necklace.
93. How Much Popcorn Can You Catch?
94. 5 Easy Ways to Be a Villain.
95. The Haunted House.
96. Klare Goes Back in Time.
97. Klare Gets Hypnotized.
98. Valentine's Day Fashion Show.
99. Fun in the Snow.
100. A Nerd's Morning Routine.
101. Klare Is Cleaning Her Impossible to Clean Room.
102. What it's Like to Be a Wizard.
103. The Case of the Missing Homework.
104. Klare's Christmas Eve.
105. Klare's Christmas.
106. 5 Things Klare Can't Live Without.
107. Agent Klare.
108. Goodbye Klare.

375 *Seven Awesome Kids: Lilly.* youtube. com. 2012–2015 (Variety).

Alexis, Anya, Georgie, Holly, Katie (1), Katie (2), Klare, Lilly and Lolita are young girls who host their own programs under a parentally controlled and moderated YouTube channel. Each girl is simply herself and presents wholesome entertainment for children through skits. Programs, which contain no credits, are well produced and very entertaining. See each individual girl for episode information.

Lilly Episode List:

1. Introducing Lilly.
2. Barbie's Hobbies.
3. Barbie Fashion.
4. Let's Kick Her Off.
5. Trouble.
6. Home Alone.
7. Lilly's Minute to Win It Challenge.
8. Lilly's the Cheerlebrity!
9. The Guardian Angel.
10. Lilly's Fun with Water.
11. Guess Who Lilly Is!
12. Lilly's Summer Fashion.
13. Lilly's Beachy Spot the Difference.
14. Lilly's Invention.
15. Lilly's Super Powers.
16. The Clone Craze.
17. Lilly's Tour of Clearwater Marine Aquarium.
18. Lilly's Strange Addiction.
19. A Day in the Life of a Princess.
20. Lilly's Life as a Grownup.
21. Fast Food Fantasy Music Video.
22. Lilly's Contortionist Audition.
23. Level 7 Gymnastics Floor Routine.
24. Q&A with Lilly and More.
25. Vampire Makeup for Kids.
26. "Dance Moms" Parody.
27. Lilly's Spring Fashion Show.
28. Lilly's Wonderland.
29. Arch Villain Stop Motion.
30. DIY Ghost Costume.
31. Build a…!
32. Hypnosis … Wait, Whaaat?!!!
33. How to Make Pretzel M&Hugz.
34. 60 Second Back Tuck Challenge.
35. From Chic … To Geek?!
36. Mission Impossible Sister Showdown.
37. Wizards and What Not.
38. Case of the Missing Carson.
39. Christmas Haul and More.
40. An Elf on the Shelf Christmas Story.
41. 5 Things Lilly Can't Live Without.
42. Gymnastics Disaster.
43. Gymnastics: What Happens Next?
44. Lilly is Grounded?!
45. Fairy Mary.
46. Goodbye Lilly.
47. Lilly Returns.
48. Lilly's Fun Summer Recap.
49. Lilly's Bedtime Routine.
50. Coffee.
51. Lilly Models Some of Her Mom's Clothes.
52. Summer Fun.
53. Super Powers.
54. Cup of Water Challenge.
55. Lilly Divas and Dolls.
56. A Day in the Life of a Shop-aholic.
57. Water Olympics.
58. Chick Chick Chick Chicken.
59. Planking.
60. Cupcake Catastrophe.

61. Spot the Difference.
62. Lilly's Favorite Hobbies.
63. Room Tour.
64. Lilly's Spring Fashion.
65. The Clone Craze.

376 Seven Awesome Kids: Lolita. *youtube. com.* 2012–2015 (Variety).

Alexis, Anya, Georgie, Holly, Katie (1), Katie (2), Klare, Lilly and Lolita are young girls who host their own programs under a parentally controlled and moderated YouTube channel. Each girl is simply herself and presents wholesome entertainment for children through skits. Programs, which contain no credits, are well produced and very entertaining. See each individual girl for episode information.

Lolita Episode List:
1. Introducing Lolita.
2. A Tribute to Lolita.
3. Chelsea the Climber's Nighttime Routine.
4. Break Dance War.
5. Missing Power.
6. Haunted House.
7. Meow.
8. The Princess and the Frozen Peas.
9. Locked Up Abroad—World Headquarters.
10. Christmas Haul.
11. Sledding in the Winter Snow.
12. What to Do When You're Bored.
13. Robot 101.
14. How to Annoy Your Parents.
15. Garbage Bag Outfit.
16. Sick of Doing Homework.
17. Queen of Spook.
18. The Monster in the Closet.
19. Lolita the Inviso Girl!
20. One Wish.
21. My Crazy Crazy Twin.
22. Beating World Records.
23. Fun with Water in the Summer.
24. LPS Invasion.
25. The Day I Became a Cat.
26. The Day I Became a Boy.
27. New Year's Day Year 3000.
28. Minecraft Super Fan Nerdcore Rap.
29. The Legend of the Lulk.
30. Minute to Win It.
31. America's Most Danciest: The Queen of Mean.
32. Under Cover Fun.
33. Jealous Much?
34. Dr. Hollywood.
35. Clug a Jug with Sam.
36. Identical Cousins.
37. The Unluckiest Day.
38. Save the World!
39. 3 Things to Do with Friends.
40. Ghost Friend.
41. Hiking.
42. Night of the Living Peeps.
43. Spring Fashion.
44. Revenge of the Queen of Mean.
45. Dream Life.
46. Food-inator 2000.
47. Secret Brigadeiro Recipe.
48. Party Invitations.
49. Valentine's Mousse.
50. The Blindfold Game Show.
51. My Weird Random Dream.
52. Impossible Missions Starring Loli 07 Super Spy.
53. My Backpack Stuff.
54. 3 Truths & 1 Lie.
55. 'Twas the Night before Christmas.
56. Holiday Haul.
57. Winter Fashion.
58. Loli Copperfield.
59. My New Crazy Job.
60. Vegetarian Thanksgiving.
61. Questions and Answers.
62. Cat Morning Routine.
63. Dragon Hunter.
64. Halloween Maniac.
65. Barbie with a Twist.
66. Big Mistake.
67. Me & Me.
68. Lolita's Secret Friends.
69. Minute to Win It.
70. (Un) True Hollywood Story.
71. How to Make Angel Food Cake.
72. Fun at the Lake.
73. Summer Fashion Paper Style.
74. Spot the Difference: Stalker Stuffed Disease Style.
75. Crazy Inventions.
76. Super Duper Powers.
77. Vanity Tour.
78. My Strange Addiction.
79. Princess Leia Hair Tutorial.
80. Fail!!!
81. Waiting Takes Time (Music Video).
82. SAK Circus.
83. Morning Routine.
84. 10 Things.
85. Backwards in Honor of 1 Year.
86. All about Artie.
87. "Dance Moms" Parody.
88. The Wonders of Wonderful Wonderland.
89. SAK Filmmaker Challenge.
90. The End of Seven Awesome Kids?
91. Ghostie Potion.
92. Build a Leaf Model.
93. Hypnosis for Evil Villains.
94. Valentine's Love Potions.
95. Fun-ness with the Cousins.
96. Nerd!
97. Impossible … Nope!
98–99. Shorts!!
100. The Case of the Missing Camera.
101. A Trip to the Mall.

102. What I Got for Christmas.
103. 5 Things I Can't Live Without.
104. The Queen of Mean Takes Over.
105. Grounded.
106. Kitty Superstar.
107. One Armed for a Day.
108. Halloween.
109. Oreo Pops.
110. Dresses.
111. Blind Taste Test.
112. Morning Routine.
113. Dares and Challenges.
114. 3 Truths & 1 Lie.
115. Summer Recap.
116. Bedtime Routine.
117. Coffee!
118. Mom's Fashion.
119. Summer Fun.
120. Super Stacker.
121. Cup of Water Challenge.
122. Garbage Bag Fashion.
123. "Toddlers and Tiaras" Spoof.
124. A Day in the Life of a Tree.
125. Fun with Water.
126. Harriet and the Matches.
127. Eating Blindfolded.
128. Planking.
129. Spot the Difference.
130. My Hobbies.
131. Room Tour.
132. Fashion Show.
133. Reverse World.
134. Farewell Lolita.

377 Seven Cool Tweens: Alexis. *youtube. com.* 2013–2014 (Variety).

Alexis, Anna, Anya, Contessa, Emily, Irena, Jana, Jessica, Katie, Luella, Madison, Nicole, Penny, Rebecca and Tamara are young girls who host their own programs under a parentally controlled and moderated YouTube channel. Each girl is simply herself and invites viewers to share certain aspects of her life. Programs, which contain no credits, are well produced and very entertaining. See each individual girl for episode information.

Alexis Episode List:
1. Introducing Alexis.
2. A Million Miles Away.
3. Super Villain Boot Camp.
4. The Secret Life of a Mom.
5. Mission Impossible: Getting Ungrounded.
6. A Day in the Life of a Germaphobe.
7. Alexis' Pet Rock.
8. The Revenge Brew.
9. The Mysterious Smell.
10. The Princess and the Messy Room.
11. The Pizza Challenge.
12. The Power of the Lucky Socks.
13. Dance! Dance! Dance!
14. The Girl Who Cried … Spider!
15. How to Train Your Robot.
16. The Friendly Bet.
17. Alexis' Strange Day in a Musical.
18. Alexis' Christmas Haul 2013.
19. Alexis Loves the Holidays.
20. Alexis' Invisible Friend.
21. Alexis' Garbage Bag Dress.
22. Expired Fairy Dust.
23. Things Alexis Does in Class When She's Bored.
24. The Pesky Telemarketer.
25. Alexis 3000 Opens a Time Capsule.
26. Ways to Maximize Your Halloween Candy.
27. The Princess and the Pea.
28. Dr. Advice.
29. Alexis' Crazy Twin Is a Clown.
30. Alexis Wins the Lottery.
31. The Monster under Alexis' Bed.
32. Who's Voice Has Invaded Alexis?
33. The Day Alexis Became a Super Hero.
34. Alexis' Baby Sitting Nightmare.
35. Alexis Goes Undercover.
36. Signs a Boy Likes You.
37. The Legend of the Coke.
38. The Magic Jelly beans.
39. Alexis' Summer Fun.
40. Alexis Is a Super Fan of Minecraft.
41. Alexis the Troublemaker.
42. Fearful Frannie's Fears.
43. Stuff Cheerleaders Say.
44. Alexis' Adventures at a Trampoline Park.
45. The New World of Summer!
46. Minute to Win It.
47. Who's Haunting Alexis?
48. Alexis Is Jealous of Her Dog.
49. Alexis Baby Sits … a Zombie!
50. Alexis Gets Revenge.
51. Alexis' Spring Fashion.
52. The Girl without Instagram.
53. Alexis Tries to Get Rid of a Ghost.
54. The Hypnotizing Tops.
55. Alexis' Bad Luck Day.
56. Alexis' Dream Life as a Pop Star.
57. The Perfect 5 Minute Sand Timer.
58. ABC Gymnastics Challenge.
59. Alexis' Magic Show.
60. Keeping Your Secrets Safe.
61. Interview with Alexis Twinkle Toes.
62. Alexis Is Trapped in a Scary Movie.
63. Sweet Valentine's Treats.
64. How to Annoy People While You're Eating.
65. Alexis Draws Her Life.
66. How to Deal with an Annoying Younger Sibling.
67. New Year's Resolutions.
68. Christmas Haul 2014.
69. The Fortune Cookie Writer.
70. Night of the Living Doll.
71. Goodbye Alexis.

378 Seven Cool Tweens: Anna. *youtube. com.* 2014 (Variety).

Alexis, Anna, Anya, Contessa, Emily, Irena, Jana, Jessica, Katie, Luella, Madison, Nicole, Penny, Rebecca and Tamara are young girls who host their own programs under a parentally controlled and moderated YouTube channel. Each girl is simply herself and invites viewers to share certain aspects of her life. Programs, which contain no credits, are well produced and very entertaining. See each individual girl for episode information.

Anna Episode List: *1.* Introducing Anna. *2.* The Invisible Christmas Presents. *3.* Garbage Bag Dress Fail. *4.* The Mysterious Fairy Dust. *5.* How to Throw a Surprise Party. *6.* Anna's Horrible School Morning. *7.* Pesky Halloween Candy. *8.* The Year 3000. *9.* Sarah Spooks. *10.* Anna's Fairy Tale World. *11.* Dr. Horbin Shmorbin. *12.* Anna Hannah's Crazy Twin. *13.* Anna Wins a Huge Shopping Spree. *14.* There Are Monsters Under My Bed. *15.* The Invasion of the American Girl Dolls. *16.* The Day I Became a .... *17.* Anna's Baby Sitting Nightmare. *18.* Anna Goes Undercover. *19.* The Day Anna Became a Boy! *20.* The Mysterious Red Drink. *21.* Anna's Royal Academy. *22.* Goodbye Anna.

379 Seven Cool Tweens: Anya. *youtube.com.* 2014 (Variety).

Alexis, Anna, Anya, Contessa, Emily, Irena, Jana, Jessica, Katie, Luella, Madison, Nicole, Penny, Rebecca and Tamara are young girls who host their own programs under a parentally controlled and moderated YouTube channel. Each girl is simply herself and invites viewers to share certain aspects of her life. Programs, which contain no credits, are well produced and very entertaining. See each individual girl for episode information.

Anya Episode List: *1.* Introducing Anya. *2.* Anya's Morning Routine. *3.* Isa Baby Sits Anya?!? *4.* Doctor Mischief. *5.* The Cursed Video Camera. *6.* The Legend of the Bad Luck Soccer Ball. *7.* Wait, Wait?! Anya Is a Cat?!?! *8.* Anya's Morning Routine. *9.* Anya Has ... Super Powers! *10.* Are You My Grandma? *11.* Mom, Did We Just Switch Bodies? *12.* Anya's Room Tour. *13.* Expectations vs. Reality: Back to School. *14.* Kayla Is Crazy About Bands. *15.* Blast from the Past: Arcade Museum. *16.* Anya's Embarrassing First Day of School. *17.* The Bad Luck Treasure Box. *18.* Goodbye Anya.

380 Seven Cool Tweens: Contessa. *youtube. com.* 2015 (Variety).

Alexis, Anna, Anya, Contessa, Emily, Irena, Jana, Jessica, Katie, Luella, Madison, Nicole, Penny, Rebecca and Tamara are young girls who host their own programs under a parentally controlled and moderated YouTube channel. Each girl is simply herself and invites viewers to share certain aspects of her life. Programs, which contain no credits, are well produced and very entertaining. See each individual girl for episode information.

Contessa Episode List: *1.* Introducing Contessa. *2.* Contessa's Morning Routine. *3.* The Giant ... Contessa? *4.* How to Be a Master of Pranks. *5.* Contessa's Amazing Day. *6.* If Only I Could Be an Adult. *7.* The Mischievous PrankBot. *8.* Contessa's Christmas 2015. *9.* Is Tilly Jealous of Contessa? *10.* The Fashion Game. *11.* Contessa Does the What's in My Mouth Challenge. *12.* How to Be a Witch. *13.* Contessa Carves SCT Pumpkins. *14.* Contessa's Secret Time Machine. *15.* A Day with Super Star Girl. *16.* The Evil Skeleton. *17.* Contessa's Summer Fun. *18.* Money from the Old Letter. *19.* The Princess's Treasure. *20.* Contessa's Embarrassing First Day of School. *21.* Contessa Tries Some Crazy Jobs. *22.* Contessa's Living Doll. *23.* Summer Break Expectations vs. Reality. *24.* Who Stole Contessa's Stuff? *25.* Contessa's Room Tour. *26.* The Day Contessa Turned Invisible. *27.* If Contessa Were a Grandma.

381 Seven Cool Tweens: Emily. *youtube. com.* 2013–2014 (Variety).

Alexis, Anna, Anya, Contessa, Emily, Irena, Jana, Jessica, Katie, Luella, Madison, Nicole, Penny, Rebecca and Tamara are young girls who host their own programs under a parentally controlled and moderated YouTube channel. Each girl is simply herself and invites viewers to share certain aspects of her life. Programs, which contain no credits, are well produced and very entertaining. See each individual girl for episode information.

Emily Episode List: *1.* Introducing Emily. *2.* The Lady in the Picture. *3.* Emily Is Hypnotized. *4.* Emily's Bad Luck Day. *5.* Emily's Dream Life vs. Emily's Normal Life. *6.* Emily's New Invention. *7.* Emily Is Backwards. *8.* Emily's New Magic Power. *9.* Emily's Secret Mission. *10.* Emily and the Living Doll. *11.* Emily and the Trapped Genie. *12.* Emily Makes Valentine's Day Truffles. *13.* How to Annoy Your Teacher. *14.* Fairy Tale Mashup. *15.* Emily Draws Her Life. *16.* How to Pamper Your Pooch. *17.* What Emily Got for Christmas 2013. *18.* Christmas Magic. *19.* Emily the Elf. *20.* The 2014 Winter Olympics Game Show. *21.* Emily's Winter Fashion. *22.* My Strange Addiction. *23.* Goodbye Emily.

382 Seven Cool Tweens: Irena. *youtube. com.* 2012–2013 (Variety).

Alexis, Anna, Anya, Contessa, Emily, Irena, Jana, Jessica, Katie, Luella, Madison, Nicole, Penny, Rebecca and Tamara are young girls who host their own programs under a parentally controlled and moderated YouTube channel. Each girl is simply herself and invites viewers to share certain aspects of her life. Programs, which contain no credits, are well produced and very entertaining. See each individual girl for episode information.

Irena Episode List:
1. Introducing Irena.
2. The Chocolate Lover.
3. Lola Scares Irena.
4. Irena Gets Hypnotized.
5. Irena Has a Bad Luck Day.
6. Irena's Dream Life.
7. Irena Creates the Oranginator!
8. Irena Shows You what's on Her iPad.
9. Irena's Magic Tricks.
10. The Unicorn.
11. How to Annoy Your Dog.
12. Irena Draws Her Life.
13. How to Clean Your Room Fast.
14. Christmas 2012 with Irena.
15. Irena's a Page Counter.
16. Irena's Doll Teases Her.
17. Irena's Winter Fashion.
18. Irena's Arizona Tea Addiction.
19. Brittany Can't Dance.
20. Irena's Garbage Bag Dress.
21. Irena's a Magician.
22. Irena Gets Threatened by Lola.
23. How to Avoid Dangerous Situations When You're Home Alone.
24. Irena Invents a Not-So-Ordinary Object.
25. Irena's Chairs Try to Get Rid of Her.
26. Princess Bella Shows You Her Style.
27. Irena's in Trouble.
28. "X Factor" Finals 2023.
29. Irena Has a Minute to Win It.
30. Irena's Back to School Fashion Show.
31. Rebecca's Guide on How to Stay Busy When You're Home Alone.
32. Irena's Home Alone.
33. Lola Becomes a Genie.
34. Irena Shows You What's in Her Locker.
35. Irena Has Fun with Water.
36. Iris the Fashion Ninja.
37. Irena Has Fun in the Sun.
38. Jill Does the Arizona Tea Challenge.
39. Fashionista Jill vs. Gamer Girl Lia.
40. Irena Finds a Ghost.
41. Irena's Summer Fashion.
42. 3 Truths 1 Lie.
43. Irena Goes Planking.
44. What Happens if You Procrastinate?
45. Irena Switches the Time Back.
46. 10 Facts That You Don't Know About Irena.
47. Super Irena.
48. Irena Buys a New Product.
49. Irena's After School Routine.
50. Irena's Spring Fashion Show.
51. A World without Colors.
52. Irena's Backwards Video.
53. No Mirror Makeup Challenge.
54. Tomboy vs. Girly Girl.
55. Shot Down (Music Video).
56. The Ruler Criminal.
57. Pajama Madness in the Snow.
58. How to Heart Crayons.
59. 3 Truths 1 Lie with Irena.
60. The Cartwheel Challenge.
61. The Missing Keys.
62. Irena Visits the Wishing Fairy.
63. Irena's 2013 Christmas Haul.
64. Lola Has a Party.
65. Irena Gets Ready for the Party.
66. Gymnastics in the Snow.
67. Irena Can't See Anything?
68. Goodbye Irena.

383 *Seven Cool Tweens: Jana.* youtube.com. 2014–2015 (Variety).

Alexis, Anna, Anya, Contessa, Emily, Irena, Jana, Jessica, Katie, Luella, Madison, Nicole, Penny, Rebecca and Tamara are young girls who host their own programs under a parentally controlled and moderated YouTube channel. Each girl is simply herself and invites viewers to share certain aspects of her life. Programs, which contain no credits, are well produced and very entertaining. See each individual girl for episode information.

Jana Episode List:
1. Introducing Jana.
2. The Candy Rapper.
3. The Mission Impossible Challenge.
4. Theme Park Cures Jana's Spring Fever.
5. Jana Had a Little Lamb.
6. The Dream Catcher.
7. Mystery at the Mall.
8. Princess Siri and the iPhone.
9. The Backwards Universe.
10. Jana Banana's Clinic for Lost Powers.
11. The Monkey Dance.
12. The Incredible Granni Jani.
13. Jana Bot.
14. The Magic Mirror Fairy.
15. The Skittles Overdose.
16. Jana's Q&A, Behind the Scenes and Bloopers.
17. The Sad Elf on the Shelf.
18. The Invisible Starbucks Machine.
19. Girl vs. Boy Fashion Show.
20. The Substitute Fairy.
21. The Mountain Dew Surprise.
22. Nerdy Jana Defeats Her Science Teacher.
23. The Little Sister Mischief Kit by Tween-O.
24. The Very Hungry Games.
25. Bratty Jenna vs. the Zombie.
26. The American Girl Doll Fairy.
27. Fashion Doctor Starring Dr. Jana.
28. The Clone Catastrophe.
29. Jana Wins a Trivia Game to Save Her Dog.
30. Jana Finds a Monster Energy Drink Under Her Bed.
31. Invasion of the Really Stupid Aliens.
32. The Day Jenna Became Invisible.

33. Jana Baby Sitting Bratty Jenna.
34. Jana Undercover.
35. The Tween Dating Game.
36. Legend of the Swamp Ape.
37. Jana's Princess Spell.
38. Goodbye Jana.

384 *Seven Cool Tweens: Jessica. youtube.com*. 2014–2015 (Variety).

Alexis, Anna, Anya, Contessa, Emily, Irena, Jana, Jessica, Katie, Luella, Madison, Nicole, Penny, Rebecca and Tamara are young girls who host their own programs under a parentally controlled and moderated YouTube channel. Each girl is simply herself and invites viewers to share certain aspects of her life. Programs, which contain no credits, are well produced and very entertaining. See each individual girl for episode information.

Jessica Episode List:
1. Introducing Jessica.
2. Legend of the Treasure Box.
3. A Day in the Life of Kobe & Stella.
4. 1 Million to Win It.
5. Fashion Boot Camp.
6. Secret Life of a Clean Freak.
7. Jessica Gets the Dance Fever.
8. My Pet Competition.
9. Wizard….
10. The Mystery of the Snack Thief.
11. Princess and the Pea.
12. Starbucks, Super Powers, Camera + More Q&A.
13. Powers.
14. The Lying Disease.
15. Robot.
16. The Overly Friendly Friend.
17. Strange Things Girls Do When Home Alone.
18. 'Twas the Night Before Christmas.
19. Christmas Haul.
20. Jessica Goes Invisible.
21. Garbage Bag Dresses.
22. 3 Christmas Wishes.
23. Jessica Surprises Her Friends.
24. Test!!!
25. Pesky Prankster.
26. What Does the Future Hold?
27. In the Spooky Forest.
28. The Fairy Tale of the Witch.
29. Dr. Frankenfart.
30. Jessica Has a Crazy Twin!
31. Jessica Wins a Lifetime Supply of…!!
32. Tickle Monster.
33. Invasion of the M&M's.
34. The Day I Became a YouTuber.
35. Babysitting Nightmare.
36. Jessica Goes Undercover.
37. Boy Transformation.
38. Legend of the Red Crème Oreo.
39. How to Do Magic Tricks.
40. Jessica's Summer Fun.
41. Super Fan of Bethany Mota.
42. Trouble Maker.
43. Jessica's Biggest Fears.
44. Cheer Tryouts.
45. Jessica's Camping Adventure.
46. Secret World Goes Wrong.
47. Minute to Win It.
48. Is Jessica's House Haunted?
49. Jealousy War.
50. Jealousy War.

385 *Seven Cool Tweens: Katie. youtube.com*. 2012–2013 (Variety).

Alexis, Anna, Anya, Contessa, Emily, Irena, Jana, Jessica, Katie, Luella, Madison, Nicole, Penny, Rebecca and Tamara are young girls who host their own programs under a parentally controlled and moderated YouTube channel. Each girl is simply herself and invites viewers to share certain aspects of her life. Programs, which contain no credits, are well produced and very entertaining. See each individual girl for episode information.

Katie Episode List:
1. Introducing Katie.
2. Katie's Garbage Bag Dresses.
3. Safety Girl's Safety Tips.
4. Katie Finds a Not-So-Ordinary Brush.
5. Katie Takes Lola on a Walk.
6. The Story of Katierella.
7. Katie's Pets Get Her in Trouble.
8. What's on Katie's iPhone.
9. Katie Has 1 Minute to Win It.
10. Katie's Back 2 School Fashion.
11. Home Alone.
12. Katie Is a Cereal Killer.
13. Genie Katie's Morning Routine.
14. Katie's School Supplies.
15. Katie and Hayley Have Fun with Water.
16. Katie Goes to Ninja Camp.
17. Fun in the Sun with Katie.
18. Hipster Hannah.
19. Katie, Katie, KATIE!
20. Katie Hipster Hannah vs. Mainstream Mandy.
21. Is There Ghost in Katie's House?
22. Help Katie Find an Outfit.
23. 10 Facts about Katie.
24. Dares and Challenges with Katie and Morgan.
25. Water Park Sleepover.
26. Katie Meets a Witch.
27. Katie's Night Time Routine.
28. 3 Ways to Get Super Powers.
29. A Day in the Life of Katie's Cats.
30. Katie's Morning Routine.
31. Katie's Spring Fashion.
32. Katie Is Driving!?!?
33. Katie Has to Find a Peanut.
34. Katie Stuck in a Backwards World.
35. Let's Go Shopping.
36. Girly Girl vs. Tomboy Olympics.

37. Katie's Music Video.
38. Annabelle Is a Criminal.
39. How to Make a Breakfast Smoothie … NOT!
40. Liar, Liar, Pants on Fire.
41. Katie's 60 Seconds Cartwheel Challenge.
42–43. Cliff Hanger.
44. Tomboy Fairy or Girly Girl Fairy.
45. Katie's Christmas Haul.
46. Snow Day.
47. Katie's a Super Model.
48. Gymnastics.
49. Katie's Backwards Video.
50. Goodbye Katie.

386 *Seven Cool Tweens: Luella.* youtube. com. 2015 (Variety).

Alexis, Anna, Anya, Contessa, Emily, Irena, Jana, Jessica, Katie, Luella, Madison, Nicole, Penny, Rebecca and Tamara are young girls who host their own programs under a parentally controlled and moderated YouTube channel. Each girl is simply herself and invites viewers to share certain aspects of her life. Programs, which contain no credits, are well produced and very entertaining. See each individual girl for episode information.

Luella Episode List: *1.* Introducing Luella. *2.* My School Morning Routine. *3.* The Mischievous Garden Gnome. *4.* Luella's Scary Sleepover Story. *5.* The Legend of the Cursed Mirror. *6.* Luella Becomes … a Cat! *7.* Luella's Super Powers to Control. *8.* Luella Has Grandma Got Fashion. *9.* The Day Luella Became a Celebrity Chef. *10.* Luella's 2015 Room Tour. *11.* The Lipstick Super Villain. *12.* Random Expectations vs. Reality. *13.* Luella Turns into a Living Doll. *14.* Luella's Crazy Dates. *15.* Luella Says Goodbye.

387 *Seven Cool Tweens: Madison.* youtube. com. 2014–2015 (Variety).

Alexis, Anna, Anya, Contessa, Emily, Irena, Jana, Jessica, Katie, Luella, Madison, Nicole, Penny, Rebecca and Tamara are young girls who host their own programs under a parentally controlled and moderated YouTube channel. Each girl is simply herself and invites viewers to share certain aspects of her life. Programs, which contain no credits, are well produced and very entertaining. See each individual girl for episode information.

Madison Episode List:
1. Introducing Madison.
2. Madison's Morning Routine.
3. How to Be a Babysitter.
4. The Mischievous Maid.
5. The Scary Sleepover.
6. The Legend of the Voodoo Doll.
7. Kitty Kitty Cat Nap.
8. One Million Aliens on Mars.
9. Burglar Boot Camp.
10. My Secret Life as A….

11. Mission Impossible: Finding the Easter Bunny.
12. Madison Is Love Sick?!
13. Who Stole My Cereal?
14. The Princess and the Kissing Booth?!
15. A Fun Day with Madz.
16. The Rewind Remote.
17. The Instructor Teaches Madison How to….
18. Madison Lies About….
19. Oh No, Madison Turns Into A ….
20. The Friendly Games.
21. The Very Strange Chain Mail.
22. What Madison Got for Christmas.
23. Madison Is Home Alone Again!
24. Invisible Margaret Strikes Again.
25. Party Dress Made of Plastic.
26. Madison's Nightmare Turns into Sweet Dreams.
27. School Expectation vs. Reality.
28. My Pesky Brother.
29. Spirits of the Graveyard.
30. A Fairy Perfect Wish.
31. Dr. Beeg and All His Patients.
32. Madz Has a Crazy Twin or Is Madz the Crazy One?
33. A Win Win Situation.
34. There's a Monster under Who's Bed?
35. Stop Invading My Privacy.
36. Madz Baby Sits … a 14-Year-Old?!
37. Madz Goes Undercover.
38. Who Will Win the Boy?
39. The Legend of the Demon Call.
40. The Royal Unicorn.
41. Summer Fun with Madz.
42. Super Fan of Frankie Grande.
43. Trying to Be a Trouble Maker.
44. The Fear of the Fortune.
45. The Cheerleader Tryouts.
46. Madz. vs. Wild.
47. The New World of the Crazy Carnival.
48. Minute to Win It with Madz.
49. Ghost to Win.
50. Never Ending Game of UNO.

388 *Seven Cool Tweens: Nicole.* youtube. com. 2012 (Variety).

Alexis, Anna, Anya, Contessa, Emily, Irena, Jana, Jessica, Katie, Luella, Madison, Nicole, Penny, Rebecca and Tamara are young girls who host their own programs under a parentally controlled and moderated YouTube channel. Each girl is simply herself and invites viewers to share certain aspects of her life. Programs, which contain no credits, are well produced and very entertaining. See each individual girl for episode information.

Nicole Episode List: *1.* Introducing Nicole. *2.* Nicole's Garbage Bag Dress. *3.* Nicole's Accents. *4.* Nicole Is a Barbie. *5.* Barbie Pajama Party. *6.* Nicole's Emergency. *7.* The Homework Bot. *8.* Nicole' s Clean Roominator. *9.* Circus, Circus. *10.* Nicole's Gymnastics Skill. *11.* Nicole Goes Planking.

389 Seven Cool Tweens: Penny. *youtube. com.* 2015. (Variety).

Alexis, Anna, Anya, Contessa, Emily, Irena, Jana, Jessica, Katie, Luella, Madison, Nicole, Penny, Rebecca and Tamara are young girls who host their own programs under a parentally controlled and moderated YouTube channel. Each girl is simply herself and invites viewers to share certain aspects of her life. Programs, which contain no credits, are well produced and very entertaining. See each individual girl for episode information.

Penny Episode List:

1. Introducing Penny.
2. Super Powers.
3. Penny's Morning Routine.
4. Penny's Baby Sitting Nightmare.
5. The Mischievous Kitty.
6. The Legend of ... Minecraft.
7. The Makeup Accident.
8. The Scary Zombies.
9. Super Powers!
10. The Grandma Dance-Off.
11. Penny's New Room Tour 2015.
12. Expectation vs. Reality with Penny.
13. The Legend of the Living Doll.
14. Crazy Baking Wars.
15. Blast from the Past.
16. Saige Is Back.
17. OMG! Penny Is So Embarrassed.
18. Play for a Prize.
19. Dear My Great, Great Grandma.
20. Penny's Summer Fun
21. The Day Penny Became ... Famous!
22. The 2015 Evil Games.
23. Penny's a Fashion Hero for a Day.
24. What! Penny Becomes a Wizard!
25. Halloween DIYS with Penny.
26. Impossible Mission: Penny's Party Dilemma.
27. The PinkaPatch ... Penny's Mythical Creature.
28. Blindfolded Makeup Challenge.
29. Three Wishes ... Gone Wrong.
30. 25 Things Penny Can't Live Without.
31. The Jealous Drama Queen.
32. Penny's Christmas 2015.
33. Santa ... the Present Stealer.
34. Penny's Weird Illness.
35. The Alien Stalker.
36. Penny and the Very Unlucky Day.
37. Penny the Amazing Dessert.
38. How to Be a Vampire's Friend.
39. The Prankster.
40. The Giant Surprise.

390 Seven Cool Tweens: Rebecca. *youtube. com.* 2012–2015 (Variety).

Alexis, Anna, Anya, Contessa, Emily, Irena, Jana, Jessica, Katie, Luella, Madison, Nicole, Penny, Rebecca and Tamara are young girls who host their own programs under a parentally controlled and moderated YouTube channel. Each girl is simply herself and invites viewers to share certain aspects of her life. Programs, which contain no credits, are well produced and very entertaining. See each individual girl for episode information.

Rebecca Episode List:

1. Hello Rebecca.
2. Rebecca's School Morning Routine.
3. Baby Sitting a Brat.
4. The Mischievous Sister Taylor.
5. The Girl with No Name.
6. The Legend of the Stalker Doll.
7. Day in the Life of Rigo.
8. 1 Million Chores.
9. Rebecca Joins Athletic Boot Camp.
10. Rebecca's a Celebrity.
11. Weird Illnesses.
12. My Pet Rock Rocky.
13. Rebecca Meets a Wizard.
14. The Messy Room with a Twist.
15. The Princess and the....
16. Rebecca and Georgia Try New Clothes.
17. Rebecca Loses Her Time Travel Powers.
18. Dance.
19. Rebecca Tells Lies.
20. The Bird Robot?!
21. My Imaginary Friend.
22. Strange and Unexpected Freaky Friday.
23. Christmas with Rebecca.
24. Ginger the Elf.
25. Rebecca Turns Invisible.
26. Rebecca's Bubble Dress.
27. The Magical Fairy Dust.
28. Surprise Snow Day.
29. Empty School.
30. The Pesky Cold.
31. Rebecca's Spooky Dream.
32. Fairy God Mother.
33. Doctor Stress.
34. Crazy Twin.
35. The SAKS Game Show.
36. The Creepy Monster with a Twist.
37. Invasion of the Candy Snatcher.
38. The Day I Became a Bow Queen.
39. Bedtime Routine.
40. Undercover for ... Sister.
41. What if Rebecca Was a Boy?
42. The Legend of the Magic Couch.
43. Ball Disaster.
44. Magic Starbucks Machine.
45. Fun with Rebecca.
46. Super Fan of Katy Perry.
47. Rebecca Turns into a Trouble Maker.
48. Rebecca's Biggest Fear.
49. Rebecca Goes to Cheer.
50. Trampoline Adventure.
51. Rebecca's New World.
52. Rebecca and Georgia's Minute to Win It.
53. The Haunted House.

54. Rebecca Is Jealous.
55. The Stalker Zombie.
56. Rebecca Gets Revenge.
57. Spring Fashion with Rebecca.
58. Abandon.
59. The Haunting Ghost.
60. Rebecca Gets Hypnotized.
61. Rebecca's Dream Life.
62. Rebecca Invents Raena the Robot.
63. Smoothie Challenge.
64. Rebecca Goes to Magic School.
65. Rebecca Tells Her Big Secret.
66. Olympics.
67. Trapped in a Movie.
68. DIY Valentine Gift.
69. How to Annoy Your Parents.
70. How to Make a Slushy.
71. What I Got for Christmas.
72. Rebecca's Parents Go Missing.
73. Rebecca's Crazy Job.
74. Brooklyn the Living Doll.
75. Winter Fashion.
76. Strange Addiction: Loom Bracelets.
77. Dance Mom.
78. Garbage Bag Dress.
79. Secret Life of Rebecca.
80. Zombie Apocalypse.
81. Danger!
82. Time Machine.
83. Flipped.
84. A Day in the Life of Princess Rebecca.
85. Rebecca Gets in Big Trouble.
86. Rebecca and Georgia Make Cookies.
87. Rebecca's Minute to Win It.
88. School Fashion with Rebecca.
89. Rebecca's Genie R Returns.
90. Rebecca's Back to School Shopping.
91. Rebecca Has Fun with Water.
92. Nina the Ninja's Everyday Routine.
93. Fun in the Sun with Rebecca.
94. Genie R Goes on a Scavenger Hunt.
95. Genie vs. Leprechaun.
96. The Ghost with Three Wishes.
97. Facts about Rebecca.
98. Dares and Challenges.
99. What Happens When Rebecca Does Her Homework?
100. Rebecca Is a Witch.
101. How to Make Homemade Ice Cream.
102. Rebecca Gets Super Powers.
103. Rebecca Switches Lives with Her Cat.
104. An Afternoon with Rebecca.
105. Spring Fashion with Rebecca.
106. Teens Fail at Makeup.
107. Rebecca's Fantasy World.
108. Random Backwardness.
109. A Day in the Life of Viviana.
110. Danny vs. Viviana.
111. Let It In (Music Video).
112. The Evil Criminal.

113. Randomness in Pajamas.
114. Rebecca Tells a Lie.
115. Rebecca Does the Cartwheel Challenge … in the Snow!
116. The Case of the Missing Makeup, Part 2.
117. What Happens Next?
118. A Day in the Life of Elizabeth.
119. Rebecca's Winter Fashion.
120. Some Gymnastics Moves from Rebecca.
121. Rebecca Is Blind for a Day.
122. Rebecca Has Chain Mail.
123. Rebecca Has One Arm.
124. Rebecca's Behind the Scenes.
125. Rebecca's Make-Over.
126. Rebecca's Favorite Dresses.
127. After School Routine.
128. Rebecca's School Fashion.
129. Rebecca's Dares and Challenges.
130. How to Survive Monday.
131. Rebecca's Blind Taste Test.
132. Rebecca Switches Lives with Her Mom.
133. Rebecca's Life as an Alien.
134. Moms Fashion Show by Rebecca.
135. Summer Fun.
136. Learn to Fly Music Video by Rebecca.
137. Zoey the Pageant Star (Played by Rebecca).
138. Rebecca Does the Blindfolded Cup of Water Challenge.
139. Rebecca's Summer Morning Routine.
140. Rebecca's Water Olympics.
141. Rebecca's Weekend Vlog.
142. Rebecca's Summer Fashion.

391 *Seven Cool Tweens: Tamara. youtube. com.* 2013–2014 (Variety).

Alexis, Anna, Anya, Contessa, Emily, Irena, Jana, Jessica, Katie, Luella, Madison, Nicole, Penny, Rebecca and Tamara are young girls who host their own programs under a parentally controlled and moderated YouTube channel. Each girl is simply herself and invites viewers to share certain aspects of her life. Programs, which contain no credits, are well produced and very entertaining. See each individual girl for episode information.

Tamara Episode List: *1.* Introducing Tamara. *2.* Tamara's Spring Fashion. *3.* Bullied to the Extent. *4.* A Ghost from the Dead. *5.* Hypnotizing Revenge. *6.* Five Unlucky Things That Could Happen to You. *7.* The Experience in Tamara's Dream. *8.* Tamara's Recreatenator 1000000. *9.* Tamara Plays the "What Is It" Challenge. *10.* Tamara's Magic Tricks. *11.* Tamara's Book of Secrets Is Gone. *12.* The Olympian's Morning Routine. *13.* Tamara's Valentine Hair Outfit and Makeup Ideas. *14.* How to Annoy Your Brother or Sister. *15.* The Story of Tamarella. *16.* Draw My Life By Tamara. *17.* Tamara's Christmas Haul. *18.* Tamara Does Crazy Tasks to Win an iPhone. *19.* Tamara's Doll Gets Revenge. *20.* My Strange Addiction: Tamara's Lotion. *21.* Goodbye Tamara.

**392 *Seven Epic Dancers: Alex.* *youtube.com.*
2015 (Variety).**

Alex, Cherinee, Katelyn and Lindsey are young
girls skilled in dance who share, in addition to their
dancing skills, various aspects of their lives with viewers. Each girl hosts her own show under a parentally
controlled and moderated YouTube channel. Programs, which contain no credits, are well produced
and very entertaining. See each individual girl for
episode information.

Alex Episode List:
1. Introducing Alex.
2. How Not to Do Your Makeup.
3. What's in My Dance Bag?
4. How to Be More Flexible.
5. The Mime (Updated).
6. Mysterious Contemporary Dance.
7. Costume Showcase.
8. Outdoor Dancing.
9. Dance Expectation vs. Reality.
10. Alex, Spring Is Almost Here.
11. Pirouette Tutorial.
12. Turns Montage.
13. Alex's Valentine Dance.
14. The Dancer Tag.
15. Alex's Ballet Dance.
16. Talk to Me—Jazz Dance.
17. Alex's Costume Dance.
18. Alex's Bloopers Montage.
19. Alex the Wannabe Elf.
20. Alex's Lyrical Dance.
21. 60 Second Pirouette Challenge.
22. Over Split Stretches for Better Leaps.
23. Alex Struts It.
24. End of the World.
25. The Heist.
26. Creepy Halloween Dance.
27. Insomnia Contemporary Dance.
28. Minute to Spin It Challenge.
29. Alex's Acro.
30. Beginner Dance Routine.
31. Chicken Nugget a La Seconde Challenge Video.
32. Mall Dancing.
33. Dancing in the Pines.
34. Alphabet Dance Challenge Video.
35. Together Throwback Thursday.
36. Helpful Tools to Improve Your Dancing.
37. Feeling the Love Dance.
38. Moments Contemporary Dance.
39. Tappin' in the Summer.
40. What's in My Dance Bag (Updated)?
41. Alex's Makeup, Hair and Costume.
42. Contemporary Dance.
43. Paparazzi Hip Hop Dance.
44. The Nature Sprite.
45–46. The Prisoners Dance.
47. Perspectives Dance.
48. Warm Up Routine.
49. A La Seconde Turns Tutorial.
50. Alex's Flexibility.
51. Favorite Dance Costume.
52. Alex's Dance Skills.
53. Alex's Contemporary Dance.
54. Wishing Spring Was Here.

**393 *Seven Epic Dancers: Cherinee.* *youtube.
com.* 2015 (Variety).**

Alex, Cherinee, Katelyn and Lindsey are young
girls skilled in dance who share, in addition to their
dancing skills, various aspects of their lives with viewers. Each girl hosts her own show under a parentally
controlled and moderated YouTube channel. Programs, which contain no credits, are well produced
and very entertaining. See each individual girl for
episode information.

Cherinee Episode List:
1. Cherinee's Your Wednesday Host.
2. Does Cherinee Have a Life Outside of Dance?
3. Cherinee's Contemporary Dance.
4. Dance Competition Makeup.
5. What's in Cherinee's Dance Bag?
6. Cherinee's Jazz Dance.
7. Get Over Splits Quick.
8. Cherinee's Spanish Dance.
9. Guess Which Was Cherinee's Winning Dance
Outfit?
10. Which Costume Should Cherinee Wear?
11. Cherinee's Contemporary Dance.
12. How to Do a Tilt Jump.
13. Dance to "On Brevity."
14. Favorite Dance Move Tutorial.
15. Jazz Dance.
16. Cherinee's Dance.
17. Cherinee's Valentine's Dance.
18. Cherinee's Pointe Dance.
19. Cherinee's Contemporary Improv.
20. Jazz Improv.
21. Cherinee's Jazz Dance.
22. You Are Crazy Glue.
23. Cherinee's Christmas Dance.
24. Who's in My Dance Bag?
25. 60 Seconds Pirouette Challenge.
26. Get Your Splits Easy.
27. Cherinee's Jazz Dance 2.
28. Sassy Hip Hop Dance.
29. Cherinee's a Secret Agent.
30. Creepy Halloween Doll.
31. Lyrical Dance Improv.
32. How Many Grand Jetes Can Cherinee Do?
33. How to Do a Knee Drop.
34. Country Dance.
35. Basic Lyrical Combo.
36. 60 Second a La Seconde Challenge.
37. Dancing in Public Places.
38. Fun Jazz Dance.
39. ABC Dance Challenge.
40. Sneaky Snazzy Robbery.
41. Cherinee's Lyrical to "Together."

42. The Dancer Tag.
43. Dreaming of Dance.
44. Cherinee's Lyrical Dance.
45. Dancing in the Sun.
46. What's in Cherinee's Dance Bag 2.
47. Jazz Costume, Hair and Makeup.
48. Cherinee's Fairy Dance.
49. Contemporary with Cherinee.
50. Cherinee's Mixed Contemporary Dance.
51. Cherinee's Lyrical Dance 2.
52. Cherinee's Warm up Routine.
53. Cherinee's Bed Time Routine ... Dance Edition.
54. Stretches for Your Hamstrings.
55. Cherinee's Dance.
56. Cherinee's Dance Skills.
57. Cherinee's Lyrical Dance 3.
58. Cherinee's Spring Dance.
59. Cherinee's Jazz Dance 3.
60. Dance to "Are You Having Fun."
61. Tilt Jump Challenge.
62. Cherinee's Fierce Jazz Dance.
63. Cherinee's Jazz Dance 4.
64. Pick Your Favorite Style.
65. Dance Tutorial: Floats.
66. Cherinee's Improv.
67. Cherinee's Improvement.
68. Celebrate Christmas with Cherinee.
69. Christmas Dance.
70. Dance Leaps and Jumps.
71. Contemporary Dance.
72. Cherinee's Performance Hair and Makeup.
73. Cherinee's Garbage Bag Costume.
74. Cherinee's Jazz Dance 5.
75. Pick Cherinee's Dance Wear.
76. Cinderella Story Told Through Dance.
77. Quick and Easy Dance Hair Tutorial.
78. Masquerade Dance.
79. Fun 80s Dance Party.
80. Dark Halloween Dance.
81. Cherinee's Hip Hop Improv.
82. Cherinee's Contemporary Dance.
83. Cherinee's Sunshine Dance.
84. Cherinee's Crazy before Dance Routine.
85. Cherinee's Dance.
86. Funky Jazz Dance.
87. Cherinee's Summer Dance.
88. Dance Dream Disaster.
89. Dedication to Dance Taliajoy18.
90. Cherinee's Zebra Dance.
91. Improve Your Back Flexibility.
92. 60 Second Pirouette Challenge.
93. Cherinee's Leaps and Turns.
94. Cherinee's Best Dance Moves.
95. No Armed Dancing??
96. ABC Dance Challenge 2.
97. Dances in the Wind.
98. Cherinee Dances!
99. Cherinee Changes.
100. Cherinee Attempts Changements.

101. Stuff Dancers Don't Say.
102. Cherinee Won't Go Back Again.
103. Valentine's Dance.
104. Cherinee Gets Emotional.
105. It's Time to Guess.
106. A Christmas Day with Cherinee.
107. Christmas Dance with Cherinee.
108. A La Seconde (Alisocone) Turns!
109. Cherinee's Floor Dance.
110. Dramatic Cherinee.
111. Life of a Dance.

394 Seven Epic Dancers: Katelyn. *youtube. com.* 2015 (Variety).

Alex, Cherinee, Katelyn and Lindsey are young girls skilled in dance who share, in addition to their dancing skills, various aspects of their lives with viewers. Each girl hosts her own show under a parentally controlled and moderated YouTube channel. Programs, which contain no credits, are well produced and very entertaining. See each individual girl for episode information.

Katelyn Episode List:
1. Introducing Katelyn.
2. Katelyn Does Contemporary Dance.
3. Dance Clothes Collection.
4. Katelyn's Performance Makeup.
5. What's in Katelyn's Dance Bag?
6. Katelyn's Jazz.
7. Katelyn's Favorite Stretches.
8. A Capella Tap Dance.
9. Help Katelyn Choose a Costume.
10. She Dreams in Blue.
11. How to Do a Single and Double Time Step.
12. Bloopers.
13. Katelyn's Spring Dance.
14. Toe Rise Dance Tutorial.
15. Katelyn's Jazz Dance.
16. Beautiful, Inspirational and Sensational Lyrical Dance.
17. Katelyn's Valentine's Day Dance.
18. Katelyn's Ballet.
19. Contemporary Dance.
20. Katelyn Taps.
21. Ready, Aim, Fire!
22. Katelyn's Christmas.
23. Katelyn's Christmas Dance.
24. Promises to Keep.
25. Katelyn Does the Pirouette Challenge.
26. Middle Split Stretches.
27. Katelyn's Jazz Dance.
28. Katelyn's Hip Hop.
29. The End of the World.
30. Secret Agent Training.
31. Katelyn's Broken Doll Dance.
32. Katelyn's Jazz Dance 2.
33. Katelyn's 60 Second Illusion Challenge.
34. Katelyn's Acro Tricks.
35. Katelyn Starburst Tutorial.

36. Katelyn's Favorite Dance Costumes.
37. Beginner Tap Dance.
38. Katelyn's a La Seconde Challenge.
39. Katelyn Dances Through Target.
40. Tap Challenge.
41. Katelyn's ABC Dance Challenge.
42. It Only It Wasn't Her Imagination.
43. Acro Lyrical Dance.
44. What's in Katelyn's Dance Bag?
45. Katelyn's a Spy!
46. Katelyn's Ballet Dance.
47. Katelyn's Dark Contemporary Dance.
48. Katelyn's Jazz/Acro Summer Dance.
49. Beach Tricks.
50. Katelyn's Jazz Costume, Hair and Makeup.
51. Katelyn's Hip Hop Dance.
52. If Katelyn Was a Fairy.
53. Katelyn's Epic Jazz Dance.
54. Katelyn Dances to Young Heroes.
55. Katelyn's Hip Hop Dance 2.
56. Dancer Tag.
57. Katelyn's Dancing Bed Time Routine.
58. Katelyn's Flexibility Tips.
59. Katelyn's Favorite Dance Costume.
60. Katelyn's Skill Montage.
61. Katelyn's Spring Dance.
62. Katelyn's Jazz Dance.
63. Katelyn Dances.
64. A Cinderella Dance.

395 Seven Epic Dancers: Lindsey. *youtube. com.* 2015 (Variety).

Alex, Cherinee, Katelyn and Lindsey are young girls skilled in dance who share, in addition to their dancing skills, various aspects of their lives with viewers. Each girl hosts her own show under a parentally controlled and moderated YouTube channel. Programs, which contain no credits, are well produced and very entertaining. See each individual girl for episode information.

Lindsey Episode List:

1. Introducing Lindsay.
2. Lindsey Dances Contemporary.
3. Stage Makeup with Lindsey.
4. Which Dance Costume?
5. Tips for Dance Performances.
6. Over Splits Tutorial with Lindsey.
7. Lindsey Turns.
8. It's Spring Time.
9. Calypso Tutorial.
10. Valentine's Day.
11. Things Dancers Say.
12. Lindsey's Ballet Dance.
13. Contemporary Dance.
14. Talk to Me.
15. Lindsey Dances a Mysterious Lyrical Dance.
16. Dancer Tag.
17. Lindsey's Christmas Dance.
18. 60 Second Turn Challenge.

19. Stretches to Help Improve Middle Splits.
20. Lindsey Struts It.
21. Lindsey's Hip Hop.
22. End of the World.
23. The Spy Helper.
24. The Graveyard Curse.
25. 60 Second Aerial Challenge.
26. Gymnastics/Acro!
27. How to Do a Scorpion.
28. My Neighbor Does My Makeup.
29. Beginner Contemporary Dance.
30. Lindsey Does the a La Seconde Challenge.
31. Dancing at the Mall of America.
32. ABC Dance Challenge.
33. The Lost Dog.
34. Lindsey's "Together" Dance.
35. Lindsey's Lyrical Dance.
36. The Dancing Golfer.
37. Feeling the Love (Dance).
38. Lindsey's Jazz.
39. Dancing at the Beach.
40. Lindsey's Hip Hop.
41. Fairy Dancer.
42. Park Dancing.
43. A Dancer's Dream.
44. Lindsey's Contemporary Dance.
45. Lindsey's Warm up Routine.
46. Lindsey's Bed Time Routine (Dance Version).
47. Lindsey's Stretch Routine.
48. Lindsey's Tricks Montage.
49. So Far So Close Lyrical Dance.
50. Spring.
51. Lindsey, Why I've been Gone.
52. Goodbye Lindsey.

396 Seven Fabulous Teens: Ashlynn. *you tube.com.* 2013–2015 (Variety).

Ashlynn, Irena, Jayda, Katie, Natalie, Sofie and Tamara are girls, just becoming teenagers who entertain children with skits, talk and glimpses (sometimes fictionalized) of their lives with friends and family. Programs, which contain no credits, are well produced and very entertaining. See each individual girl for episode information.

Ashlynn Episode List:

1. Introducing Ashlynn on Set.
2. Goodbye Friend! Sock Monkey's Revenge.
3. She Is Crazy!
4. Most Popular Pizza Challenge with Ashlynn.
5. Ashlynn's Babysitting Nightmare.
6. My Vampire Diaries: The Day I Became a Vampire!
7. Baby Sitting a Drama Queen.
8. I Have No Friends, the Lonely Princess.
9. Doctor, Doctor, Help! Ashlynn Is Sick!
10. Crazy Robot Gone Wild!
11. The Hunt to Save Easter.
12. Jail Break … I'm Innocent!
13. The Hidden Door … to a Bizarre Universe.

14. Ashlynn Goes to Clown Boot Camp.
15. The Wizard School of Sorcery.
16. The Leprechaun's Lost Powers.
17. Monster under My Bed.
18. Living Doll. My Crazy Obsession.
19. We're Going to Need Some Help!
20. Shake It Off
21. Girl Power! You Can Do It!
22. A Mom's Crazy Life.
23. Morning Routine.
24. What I Got for Christmas 2014.
25. Top Christmas Story.
26. The Naughty Elf on the Shelf.
27. A Princess in Training.
28. The Crazy Fortune Teller.
29. Cinderella.
30. Ashlynn's Dares and Challenges.
31. Pixie Land the Pink Wand.
32. The Day I Became a Millionaire!
33. Halloween Revenge.
34. The Pesky Grandma.
35. My Invisible Imaginary Friend.
36. Dorothy and the Invasion of the Scarecrows.
37. Ashlynn's Garbage Bag Dresses.
38. She's a Naughty Girl!
39. Legend Has It….
40. Back to School! Routine and What's in My Back Pack?
41. Year 3000.
42. Secret Ninja.
43. Ashlynn's Summer Fun.
44. The Princess and the Frog.
45. Haunted House on Manor Hill.
46. Enemy or Friend?
47. Winner, Winner Chicken Dinner.
48. Country Girl vs. City Girl.
49. Jealous of Her!
50. E.T. World.
51. Big Fears and Phobias.
52. Minute to Win It. Summer Style.
53. Opposite Day.
54. Crazy Twin Gone Wild.
55. Spring Fashion Looks.
56. I Got My Eyes on You!
57. The Most Fabulous Villain.
58. Goldilocks Is Home Alone!
59. Breaking Bad Luck.
60. Bad Girl Gets Grounded.
61. "Doctor Who" to the Rescue.
62. Hunting for the Rarest Butterfly.
63. Crazy and Odd Jobs with Ashlynn.
64. Super Styling Spray Commercial.
65–66. Creepy Noises.
67. Goodbye Adventure.
68. Crazy Challenge Competition.
69. Who Is the Real Winner?
70. DIY Valentine Sweets and Treats! Lip Gloss and Cupcakes.
71. Super Bored.
72. Fabulous Friends.

73. Back in Time.
74. Pretty Little Liar.
75. The Forgotten Land.
76. Christmas Haul with Ashlynn.
77. A Merry Mouse.
78. Fashion with Ashlynn.
79. Top Secret.
80. There's Only 1 Winner! 60 Second Makeup Challenge.
81. Exploring Home Alone.
82. Barbie Runway.

397 Seven Fabulous Teens: Irena. *youtube. com.* 2014–2015 (Variety).

Ashlynn, Irena, Jayda, Katie, Natalie, Sofie and Tamara are girls, just becoming teenagers who entertain children with skits, talk and glimpses (sometimes fictionalized) of their lives with friends and family. Programs, which contain no credits, are well produced and very entertaining. See each individual girl for episode information.

Irena Episode List:
1. Introducing Irena.
2. Summer Morning Routine.
3. Help! I'm Stuck in Your Pen!
4. Good Luck, Irena.
5. The Pizza Challenge.
6. The Baby Sitting Disaster.
7. Autograph, Please! The Day I Became a Successful Writer.
8. Hurry Up! Drama Queen Elections!
9. I'll Be Your Friend, Monster!
10. It's Not 1995 Grandma!
11. Robot, You Cheater!
12. Let's Go Find the 8-Year-Old Time Capsule.
13. Help! I'm Stuck in the Forest.
14. Irena's House … Is Upside Down!
15. Irena Goes to … Birthday Party Boot Camp.
16. Irena's Dog … Helps a Wizard!
17. Irena Teleports … to Sofie's House.
18. Not All Monsters Are Evil.
19. There's Someone in Our House.
20. Irena Becomes Sleep Obsessed.
21. Irena Is … a Famous Dancer!
22. Girls Are Equal to Boys!
23. Irena Baby Sits … Herself!
24. The Lost Friendship Bracelet.
25. Lola Crashes the Party.
26. No … Christmas Tree.
27. The Strange Phone Calls.
28. I Love Pink!
29. The French Artist … Fail!
30. Helping … Fairy Tale.
31. Helping Fairy Tale Characters.
32. Irena Does Your Dares and Challenges.
33. Everything's Making Strange Noises!
34. Becoming a … Witch!
35. Trick or Treating Double Trouble.
36. Pesky Revenge.

37. The Doorbell Prank.
38. There's Popcorn ... Everywhere!
39. The Stolen Garbage Bag Dress.
40. Irena Escapes a Baby Sitting Nightmare.
41. The Legend of the Unicorns.
42. Irena's School Bedtime Routine.
43. Me, the Spray Bottle and the Future.
44. Secrets to Being a Ninja.
45. Irena Has Summer Fun.
46. Princess in the 21st Century.
47. Irena's House Is Haunted.
48. Irena Helps Lola Make Friends.
49. Phone Freak Faith's Phone Runs out of Battery.
50. Irena Is Jealous of Her Twin.
51. The Earth Is Square.
52. Irena Has Monsters Under Her Bed.
53. Irena Has a Minute to Win It.
54. Irena Becomes a Boy!
55. Irena Gets a Twin?!
56. Irena's Spring Fashion.
57. Irena Has a Nightmare from Cheese.
58. Irena's Dog Is a Villain.
59. Irena's Home Alone.
60. Irena Gets Bad Luck.

398 *Seven Fabulous Teens: Jayda.* youtube. com. 2014–2015 (Variety).

Ashlynn, Irena, Jayda, Katie, Natalie, Sofie and Tamara are girls, just becoming teenagers who entertain children with skits, talk and glimpses (sometimes fictionalized) of their lives with friends and family. Programs, which contain no credits, are well produced and very entertaining. See each individual girl for episode information.

    Jayda Episode List:
1. Introducing Jayda.
2. The Mischievous Witch Is Back.
3. Jayda Has a Twin.
4. Jayda's Pizza Challenge.
5. Baby Sitting Fail.
6. I'm a Soccer Fan.
7. The World's Biggest Drama Queen.
8. Friends Do Have Differences.
9. The Worst Illness Ever.
10. Robots Are Taking Over!
11. The Easter Bunny Is Real!
12. Jayda's Breaking Free.
13. Colors Are Gone ... Or Are They?
14. Super Hero Boot Camp.
15. Hats 'n' Potions.
16. My Powers Are Gone.
17. There's a Monster Under My Bed!
18. The Truth Comes Out.
19. Obsessed with Spoons.
20. Mean Mandy vs. Jayda Dance Battle.
21. Girl Power!
22. In Mum's Shoes.
23. Bean Boozeled Challenge.
24. Jadya's Christmas Gifts.
25. The Naughty Elf.
26. Everything's Black and White.
27. Teenaged Princess.
28. Bad Luck Prom Day.
29. Fairy Tale Dome Tree.
30. Dares and Challenges with Jayda.
31. Twisted Tales!
32. The Day I Became a....
33. Jayda's Spooky Halloween.
34. Day of the Pesky Friend.
35. Invisible Touch.
36. Invasion of Cats!
37. Garbage Bag Wedding.
38. Pooey Nightmare.
39. The Legend of the Crystal Rock.
40. Back to School Dislikes.
41. Saving the Year 3000!
42. Ninja's Morning Routine.
43. Summer Fun in the My Winter!
44. Royal Winner.
45. The Haunted Attic.
46. Fun Friendship.
47. Super JJ Stops A Thief.
48. Super JJ vs. Mandy.
49. Jealous of a Dog.

399 *Seven Fabulous Teens: Katie.* youtube. com. 2015 (Variety).

Ashlynn, Irena, Jayda, Katie, Natalie, Sofie and Tamara are girls, just becoming teenagers who entertain children with skits, talk and glimpses (sometimes fictionalized) of their lives with friends and family. Programs, which contain no credits, are well produced and very entertaining. See each individual girl for episode information.

    Katie Episode List: *1.* Introducing Katie. *2.* Katie's Crazy Morning. *3.* Pizza Challenge. *4.* Bad Baby Katie. *5.* The Nifty 50s. *6.* The Creepy Cookies. *7.* School Mornings vs. Summer Mornings. *8.* Katie Gets her Braces. *9.* Katie Says Goodbye.

400 *Seven Fabulous Teens: Natalie.* you tube.com. 2013–2015 (Variety).

Ashlynn, Irena, Jayda, Katie, Natalie, Sofie and Tamara are girls, just becoming teenagers who entertain children with skits, talk and glimpses (sometimes fictionalized) of their lives with friends and family. Programs, which contain no credits, are well produced and very entertaining. See each individual girl for episode information.

    Natalie Episode List:
1. Introducing Natalie.
2. Natalie Is Stuck in the Witch's Creepy Forest.
3. The Evil Queen's Powers Are Lost.
4. There's a Monster Somewhere ... But Where?
5. Let's Put This Plan in Action!
6. I Eat ... Bugs! EW! My Crazy Obsession!

7. Dance Classes with Abby the Prankster.
8. Cookies, Valentine's Day and ... Girl Power!
9. What's It Like Being a Mother?
10. Natalie Encounters ... Flying Pancakes!
11. What Natalie Got for Christmas 2014.
12. Psycho Elf ... Return from the North Pole!
13. The Strangest Talking Frog?!
14. Roses from Prince Charming.
15. Holiday Shopping with the Christmas Fairy.
16. Dancing with the Gingerbread Man.
17. Natalie's Fabulous Dares and Challenges.
18. Snow Days, Noises and You.
19. I'm Alice in Wonderland! Pocahontas! Cinderella!
20. Happy Halloween! Costume Edition.
21. The Pesky Pumpkin.
22. Oh No! Prankster Abby Is ... Invisible!
23. Clones Are Everywhere ... It's an Invasion!
24. A Fabulous Dress Made Out of Garbage Bags!
25. Natalie's Worst Baby Sitting Nightmare!
26. Ouija Board Nightmare?!
27. Natalie's School Morning Routine 2014.
28. Let's Travel Into the Future!
29. Everything Pink Is ... Gone?!
30. Natalie Has a Blast in the Sun.
31. I Want That Tiara!
32. Trapped in a Haunted Castle.
33. The Ultimate Surprise Party—Ruined?!
34. The Angel Quits?!
35. Angel vs. Devil.
36. Is Prankster Abby Jealous?
37. A New World, a New Person and Me.
38. Oh No! They're All Terrifying.
39. Minute to Win It—Crazy Forfeit Version.
40. Opposite Day Disaster.
41. Natalie's Crazy Twin.
42. Spring Fashion.
43. Nightmares.
44. The Creepy Clown Villain.
45. Natalie Is Home Alone! Or ... Is She?!
46. Natalie Gets Bad Luck.
47. How to Survive Being Grounded.
48. Natalie Pretends to Be Sick.
49. Draw My Life with Natalie.
50. Natalie's Wacky Job as a Magician.
51. Sweet Revenge (Commercial).
52–53. What Happens Next.
54. Natalie's Adventure.
55. Red Riding Hood vs. Tinker Bell.
56. Natalie Wins a Lifetime Supply of What?!
57. A Terrifying Valentine's Day.
58. Crazy Things to Do When You're Bored.
59. Friendship Dares.
60. My Strange Invention.
61. Natalie Is a Big Liar!
62. Donut Paradise.
63. Natalie's Christmas Gifts.
64. Return of the Psycho Elf!
65. Winter Fashion with Natalie.
66. Natalie Hunts for a Secret.
67. Natalie Is a Pro Makeup Artist.
68. Christmas Elves Come Alive!
69. Barbie!
70. Barbie Horror Story.
71. Natalie Auditions for "Dance Moms."
72. Natalie's Halloween Scare!
73. Experiment Gone Wrong: Cats Style.
74. Natalie's Got Ghosts!
75. The Not So Super Hero.
76. Guess Who?
77. Minute to Win It: Natalie Edition.
78. Prankster Abby's in Trouble!
79. Natalie's Crazy Twin.
80. Cupcake Wars.
81. Goodbye Natalie.

401 Seven Fabulous Teens: Sofie. *youtube.com.* 2014–2015 (Variety).

Ashlynn, Irena, Jayda, Katie, Natalie, Sofie and Tamara are girls, just becoming teenagers who entertain children with skits, talk and glimpses (sometimes fictionalized) of their lives with friends and family. Programs, which contain no credits, are well produced and very entertaining. See each individual girl for episode information.

Sofie Episode List:

1. Guess Your New Wednesday (Host)?
2. That Is One Crazy Fan.
3. Sofie and the Mischievous Fan.
4. Sofie Fails the Pizza Challenge.
5. EW Grandma! You Are Disgusting!
6. Sofie the Sneaky Snitch.
7. Drama Queen in a Box.
8. My Stuffed Friend Daisy.
9. There's Ants Everywhere—My Weird Illness.
10. Where Did My Robot Go?
11. Sofie Wins It All!
12. Locked in and Grounded.
13. Door to the Parallel Universe.
14. Sofie Goes to Boot Camp ... Kind Of.
15. My Broom Is Alive.
16. I Think I Can Read Your Mind.
17. Mom! There's a Monster Inside My Suitcase!
18. Time to Investigate....
19. Obsessed Over a ... Bouncy Ball!
20. Sofie Gets Danced Pranked.
21. Sofie's Got Girl Power!
22. Being a Mom Is Hard Work.
23. Sofie Fast Forwards to 2015!
24. Santa Wants My Help!
25. What a Strange Pen.
26. The Mischievous Crown.
27. Sofie's Bratty Disaster.
28. Penelope, the Trapped Fairy.
29. Sofie Does Dares and Challenges.
30. Cursed By the Music Box.
31. Becky Becomes Girly.
32. The Spooky Hand.
33. Sofie's ... Invisible!

34. Math Equation Invasion.
35. Sofie's Fabulous Garbage Bag Dress.
36. Baby Sitting the Devil Clone.
37. Legend of the Picture Frame.
38. Late for School! Morning Routine 2014.
39. Year 3000 Chaos.
40. Crime of the Cookies.
41. Summer Fun in the Sun.
42. The Princess and the Fairy.
43. He's Watching You!
44. What a Disaster.
45. Wish Granted.
46. It's a War.
47. Jealousy Attack.
48. Stickman Crazy!
49. Scaredy Cat!
50. Only 1 Minute to Win It.
51. Don't Be Mean.
52. My Crazy Fan Girl Twin.
53. Sofie's Spring Outfits.
54. Just a Nightmare.
55. Down in the Dumps.
56. Home Alone Clone.
57. Ouch, That's Bad Luck!
58. Time to Sneak Out.
59. Doctor, Doctor, Sofie's Sick!
60. April Fools!
61. The Craziest of Jobs.
62. The All New 3D You.
63-64. The Scare.
65. Adventure of the Missing Voice.
66. Endless Possibilities.
67. SAK's Game Show.
68. The Valentine's Heart Break.

402 Seven Fabulous Teens: Tamara. *you tube.com.* 2014–2015 (Variety).

Ashlynn, Irena, Jayda, Katie, Natalie, Sofie and Tamara are girls, just becoming teenagers who entertain children with skits, talk and glimpses (sometimes fictionalized) of their lives with friends and family. Programs, which contain no credits, are well produced and very entertaining. See each individual girl for episode information.

Tamara Episode List:
1. Introducing Tamara.
2. The Mischievous Secret Admirer.
3. My Crazy Doctor.
4. Family Pizza Challenge.
5. I Have to Baby Sit a Nerd! Why Me?
6. Tamara Becomes a Horrible Makeup Artist.
7. 3-2-1 Action! Drama Queen Actress!
8. Tamara Has the Evil Eye.
9. Irena, Stop! The Color of My Nose Is Changing!
10. The Robot Toy ... Is Alive!
11. The Scavenger Hunt Cheater ... Easter Edition.
12. Please Don't Ground Me ... It's a Reverse Jail Break.

13. Blue and Black, No. White and Gold!
14. Enough! Time for Bad Manners Boot Camp!
15. The Grumpy Wizard.
16. Cupid Lost the Power of Love.
17. The Monster Under My Bed Is a Girly Girl Thief.
18. Lola Be Gone!
19. My Crazy Obsession ... with Myself!
20. Tamara Learns Hip Hop from a Dancer.
21. Tamara Auditions to be a Guy!
22. Tamara Is Baby Sitting Bratty Sophia Again!
23. Tamara Breaks Guinness World Records.
24. Tamara Is Home Alone at Christmas.
25. Tamara's Christmas Haul 2014.
26. Strange ... Everything Is Reversed.
27. Tamara Princess vs. Evil Queen.
28. Help! There's a Magical Creature!
29. Little Red Riding Hood ... Grandma's Lying!
30. Tamara's Crazy Dares and Challenges.
31. Bedtime Stories Come to Life.
32. Tamara Becomes Addicted to Candy.
33. Trick or Treating ... Alone! Not a Good Idea.
34. Everyone Is ... Sooo Annoying!
35. Tamara's Invisible ... Evil Takes Over.
36. The Oreo Invasion.
37. Tamara Wears a Garbage Bag Dress.
38. Tamara Is Babysitting ... A Complete Nightmare.
39. The Legend of the ... Nerds.
40. Tamara's Back to School Morning Routine
41. Back from the ... Future!
42. Summer Fun with Tamara.
43. If Tamara Was Royal....
44. Haunted Hotel Room?!
45. Friendship Challenge: Water Edition.
46. Rebellious Dares.
47. Cheery vs. Gloomy.
48. Chef Jealousy on Set.
49. The New World of ... School.
50. Tamara Fears Chocolate.
51. Minute to Win It Tamara Style.
52. What Would You Rather?
53. Crazy Twins Prank War.
54. Spring Shopping with Tamara.
55. Tamara's Clown Nightmare.

403 Seven Funtastic Girls: Anna Jane. *you tube.com.* 2013–2015 (Variety).

Anna Jane, Ellie, Faye, Katherine, Klare, Jazz, Lauren, Madison, Natalie, Rowan, Sadie, and Sofia are young girls just being themselves. They welcome viewers to share certain aspects of their real lives through skits and other entertainment geared to pre-teen and teenage girls. Programs, which contain no credits, are well produced and very entertaining. See each individual girl for episode information.

Anna Jane Episodes:
1. Introducing Anna Jane.
2. The Legend of the Vanishing Girl.

3. The Day Anna Jane Became a Mermaid.
4. Anna Jane's Super Scary Day.
5. Anna Jane's Night Routine.
6. Anna Jane Is a Robber!
7. Anna Jane's Morning Routine.
8. How to Look Like a Troll!
9. A Wizard's School Morning Routine.
10. Anna Jane Enters a Parallel Universe!
11. Being Home Schooled Is Awesome!
12. Singing Boot Camp.
13. The Epic Mystery of the Ring.
14. Tour Anna Jane's Room.
15. What Should Anna Jane Wear to the Dance?
16. Anna Jane's Crazy Obsession: Starbucks!
17. Anan Jane's Missing Power.
18. My Secret Admirer.
19. Anna Jane's Crazy Mixed up Birthday!
20. Unexpected! Anna Jane's Vlog!
21. The Princess and the Normal Girl.
22. The Doll That Lives.
23. The Friendly Cookie Maker.
24. Christmas Story Gone Wrong!
25. What Did Anna Jane Get for Christmas?
26. Where Are Anna Jane's Keys?
27. Biggest Fear!!
28. Strangest Day Ever!
29. Day of the Pesky Anna Jane.
30. Anna Jane's Game Show.
31. Funtastic Girl Saves the Day!
32. Anna Jane's Best Day Ever.
33. Anna Jane's Spooky Halloween.
34. The Day Anna Jane Became a Model!
35. Tomboy Invasion!
36. Anna Jane's World.
37. Anna Jane's Cotton Ball Challenge.
38. Anna Jane's Original Song "Eye of a Tiger."
39. What Will Happen in Year 3000?
40. Anna Jane's Room Tour.
41. The Legend of the Prom Dress Mannequin.
42. Anna Jane, Jenna and Oceane's Summer Fun!
43. Anna Jane Has a Crazy Twin.
44. Monster Maddy!
45. Worst Day Ever!
46. Anna Jane Can't Find Her Dogs.
47. Cup of Water Challenge.
48. Anna Jane's Minute to Win It!
49. Anna Jane Is in the Fairy Tale World!
50. Anna Jane Has a Super Fan.
51. Kayla Teaches Anna Jane How to Be a Cheerleader.
52. Biggest Fear!
53. The Skirt That Makes You a Millionaire!
54. Anna Jane Does the Furry Friend Tag!
55. Anna Jane Is a Troublemaker!
56. Beauty Pageant Answer Fails.
57. The Difference Between Girls and Boys!
58. Anna Jane Goes Haunted House Hunting!
59. Chug a Jug!
60. Anna Jane Goes Under Cover!
61. Home Alone … Gone Wrong.

62. Anna Jane's Spring Fashion.
63. Dream Life!
64. Can You Spot the Difference?
65. Doctor Chaos.
66. How to Escape from Doing Homework.
67. Why I Love You!
68. Valentine's Hypnosis!
69. The Smackinator 3000!
70. Say Goodbye.
71. 10 Ways to Annoy People.
72. Anna Jane's Faves!
73. Anna Jane's Winter Fashion.
74. No Presents?!
75. Anna Jane's Christmas Presents.
76. Anna Jane Finds a Secret Door.
77. Anna Jane Is a Princess.
78. Anna Jane's 3 Lies and 1 Truth.
79. Anna Jane and Jenna Do the Best Friend Tag.
80. Help! I'm a Dog!
81. Anna Jane Is a Living Doll!
82. Anna Jane's Awesome Room Tour.
83. How to Be a Cat.
84. Anna Jane Goes to the Pumpkin Patch.
85. How to Not Be a Drama Queen!
86. Anna Jane's Secret Life of a Super Star!
87. Anna Jane Gets in Trouble.
88. Whipped Cream Madness!
89. Anna Jane Answers Your Questions.
90. Anna Jane's Strange Addiction.
91. The Curse of Anna Jane's Hair.
92. The Princess and the Dog.
93. Anna Jane's Fun with Water Video.
94. Anna Jane Has a Clone.
95. Girly Gabby Redecorates Her Room.
96. Anna Jane's Summer Fashion.
97. Tomboy vs. Girly Girl.
98. Anna Jane Invents a Tele-porter.
99. Anna Jane's Model Competition.
100. Anna Jane's Circus Clown Audition Fail!
101. Summer Fun with Anna Jane and Jenna.

404 *Seven Funtastic Girls: Ellie.* *youtube. com.* 2014–2015 (Variety).

Anna Jane, Ellie, Faye, Katherine, Klare, Jazz, Lauren, Madison, Natalie, Rowan, Sadie, and Sofia are young girls just being themselves. They welcome viewers to share certain aspects of their real lives through skits and other entertainment geared to preteen and teenage girls. Programs, which contain no credits, are well produced and very entertaining. See each individual girl for episode information.

Ellie Episode List:
1. Introducing Ellie.
2. The Legend of the Invisibility Cloak.
3. The Day Ellie Became a Bad Beautician!
4. Ellie's Creepy Doll.
5. Ellie's Night Time Routine.
6. Ellie's Sneaky Food Thief.
7. Ellie's Morning Routine.

8. Ellie's New Friend ... the Ogre?!
9. Ellie's Quest to Find the Magic Wand.
10. The Edible Universe.
11. Ellie's Day in the Life of a Teacher.
12. Ellie's Circus Boot Camp.
13. Ellie's Reverse Mystery.
14. Room Tour.
15. Ellie's Dance Music Video.
16. The Crazy YouTube Obsession.
17. Ellie's Missing Mermaid Powers.
18. How to Make Your Crush Be Your Valentine.
19. Ellie's Crazy Stalker ... Miranda Sings!
20. Ellie Has a Twin?!
21. The Princess and the Selfie.
22. Pageant Princess Is a Living Doll.
23. Tiffany's Back ... but Friendly?
24. Ellie's Magical Christmas Eve.
25. Ellie's Missing Presents!
26. Ellie's Christmas Gift Haul.
27. I'm a YouTuber ... Get Me Out of Here!
28. Strange Day.
29. The Very Pesky Day.
30. Bat Girl Ellie!
31. Ellie's Spooky Movie Trailer.
32. The Day Ellie Became a Gymnast.
33. The Disco Ninja Invasion.
34. Ellie's New World.

405 Seven Funtastic Girls: Faye. *youtube. com.* 2013–2015 (Variety).

Anna Jane, Ellie, Faye, Katherine, Klare, Jazz, Lauren, Madison, Natalie, Rowan, Sadie, and Sofia are young girls just being themselves. They welcome viewers to share certain aspects of their real lives through skits and other entertainment geared to preteen and teenage girls. Programs, which contain no credits, are well produced and very entertaining. See each individual girl for episode information.

Faye Episode List:
1. Introducing Faye.
2. Things Kids Say to Baby Sitters.
3. The Bad Genie.
4. Things Teenagers Do.
5. The End of Seven Funtastic Girls?
6. Faye's After School Routine.
7. Faye's Morning Routine for Filming.
8. An Ogre's Morning Routine.
9. Harry Potter: Faye Style!
10. Parallel Universe Gone Wrong.
11. How to Prank Your School Teachers.
12. Fairy Boot Camp.
13. "Monster High" Doll Defeats Evil Tracy.
14. Faye's Awesome Room Tour.
15. Faye Makes a Hugh Dance Mistake!
16. Faye's Way Too Obsessed.
17. Faye Frees the Fairy!
18. Faye Does the Valentine Tag with her Valentine.
19. What Is in That Box?
20. The Princess and the Ball ... Football!
21. The Evil "Monster High" Doll.
22. The Friendly Ghost.
23. Faye's Christmas Haul 2014.
24. Faye's Christmas Presents ... Are Gone!
25. Best Homework Excuses.
26. Faye's Food Fears.
27. Faye's Invisible? What a Strange Day!
28. The Pesky Day in the Life of Faye.
29. How Well Do You Know Me?
30. Faye's Best Day Ever?
31. The Day Faye Became a Super Hero.
32. Faye Gets Pranked! But By Who?
33. Faye's World without Seven Funtastic Girls.
34. Faye's Blindfolded Taste Test.
35. What Faye Got for Her 14th Birthday.
36. Faye's Updated Room Tour.
37. The Legend of the Gift Mirror.
38. Summer Fun.
39. Faye's Crazy Twin.
40. Close Encounter with the Monster Kind!
41. Faye Tests Bad Luck Superstitions.
42. Faye's Baby Sitting Nightmare.
43. Summer Splash-Tacular.
44. Minute to Win It: Toilet Roll Special.
45. Faye Interviews Fairy Tale Characters.
46. Faye's a Fan of....
47. Cheer Leading Trials.
48. Faye's Biggest Fears (Skit).
49. The Things Advertisers Say.
50. Faye's PJ Fashion.
51. Pageant Queen.
52. Finding a New Dance Partner.
53. Haunted House!
54. Faye Chugs-a-Jug.
55. The Detective's Disguises.
56. How to Enjoy Being Home Alone.
57. Faye's Spring Fashion.
58. Faye's Dream Career.
59. Can You Spot Faye's Differences?
60. The Doctor Jokes!
61. 5 Ways to Escape from Doing Chores.
62. Sweet Revenge.
63. Time Challenges.
64. The Valentine's Grinch.
65. Hypo-therapy for Dummies!
66. Invention or In-veg-tion.
67. The Biggest News Ever.
68. How to Annoy Everybody.
69. Faye's Five Favorites!
70. Winter Outfits for All Occasions.
71. 4 Easy Things to Make and Do.
72. Riddles, Riddles, Riddles.
73. Modern Fairy Tales.
74. Liar, Liar Pants on Fire.
75. Katniss Everdeen's Morning Routine.
76. Switching Lives with Molly.
77. Buy Your Living Doll Today (Skit).
78. Dance Moms.
79. Cats Rule the World!

80. How to Make a Halloween Card.
81. How Drama Queens Act.
82. Meow!
83. A Day in the Life of a Caveman.
84. Room Nag Finds a Shoe!
85. Faye's Favorite Gifts.
86. Annabelle's Strange Addiction.
87. The Curse of Seven Funtastic Girls.
88. Princess Penelope and Her Butler Barrington.
89. Summer Splash-Tacular!
90. Cinderella with a Twist.
91. Olivia's Indoor Shock!
92. Summer Fashion.
93. A Day in the Life of a Model.
94. Circus.
95. A Bully's Interview.
96. How to Relax.
97. The Colorful Ninja.
98. Faye's Room Tour.

406 Seven Funtastic Girls: Jazz. *youtube. com.* 2015 (Variety).

Anna Jane, Ellie, Faye, Katherine, Klare, Jazz, Lauren, Madison, Natalie, Rowan, Sadie, and Sofia are young girls just being themselves. They welcome viewers to share certain aspects of their real lives through skits and other entertainment geared to preteen and teenage girls. Programs, which contain no credits, are well produced and very entertaining. See each individual girl for episode information.

Jazz Episode List:
1. Introducing Jazz.
2. Legend of the Playground Ghost.
3. The Day I Became Homeless.
4. Bloody Mary.
5. The Basketball Thief.
6. Weekend Morning Routine.
7. There's a Troll in My House!
8. Siamese Twins?!
9. How to Escape Your Homework.
10. Fitness Boot Camp.
11. The Epic Mystery of the Necklace.
12. Jazz's Room Tour 2015.
13. "Dance Moms" Parody.
14. My Money Obsession.
15. Valentine's Day Snack.
16. The Crazy Sister!
17. Strange Happenings!
18. The Princess and the Geek.
19. The Creepy Living Doll.
20. Scary Goth Halloween Look.
21. Beanboozled Challenge.
22. Three Wishes Gone Wrong.
23. Mission Impossible.
24. The Forgetful Model.
25. Alien Visit.
26. Buried Treasure Hunt.
27. A Mermaid Tail.
28. The Old Letter.
29. Summer Expectations vs. Reality.
30. My Embarrassing Cousin.
31. Crazy Upside Down World.
32. The Donut Burglar.
33. Grandma Syndrome.
34. The Mischievous Ghost.
35. Dog Sitting Disaster.
36. Legend of the Playground Ghost.
37. Bloody Mary.
38. The Basketball Thief.
39. Goodbye Jazz.

407 Seven Funtastic Girls: Katherine. *you tube.com.* 2011 (Variety).

Anna Jane, Ellie, Faye, Katherine, Klare, Jazz, Lauren, Madison, Natalie, Rowan, Sadie, and Sofia are young girls just being themselves. They welcome viewers to share certain aspects of their real lives through skits and other entertainment geared to pre-teen and teenage girls. Programs, which contain no credits, are well produced and very entertaining. See each individual girl for episode information.

Katherine Episode List: *1.* Introducing Katherine. *2.* Looking Good with Katherine. *3.* Katherine's Dance Moves. *4.* Home Alone Can Be a Real Scary Story! *5.* Agent Katherine and the Impossible Mission. *6.* Katherine's Gymnastics Skills. *7.* Coffee (Music Video). *8.* Behind the Scenes with Katherine. *9.* Katherine's Morning Routine. *10.* Katherine's Chug-a-Jug Fail.

408 Seven Funtastic Girls: Klare. *youtube. com.* 2015 (Variety).

Anna Jane, Ellie, Faye, Katherine, Klare, Jazz, Lauren, Madison, Natalie, Rowan, Sadie, and Sofia are young girls just being themselves. They welcome viewers to share certain aspects of their real lives through skits and other entertainment geared to pre-teen and teenage girls. Programs, which contain no credits, are well produced and very entertaining. See each individual girl for episode information.

Klare Episode List: *1.* Introducing Klare. *2.* Lazy Baby Sitter. *3.* The Legend of the Emojis. *4.* The Day I Became Addicted to Slushies. *5.* What Happened to Delilah? *6.* The Mischievous Villain. *7.* Klare's Morning Routine. *8.* Lazy Babysitter. *9.* How to Be Mischievous. *10.* When I Was Your Age. *11.* There's No Cookies. *12.* You Get a Time Out. *13.* Crazy Tuesday. *14.* Expectation vs. Reality: Being a You Tuber. *15.* Klare's Exciting Summer. *16.* The Scary Doll. *17.* The Hidden Treasure Letter. *18.* It's So Fluffy. *19.* The Day I Became a Wizard. *20.* The Alien Visit. *21.* The Forgetful Tuesday. *22.* Impossible Tasks. *23.* Klare's 3 Wishes. *24.* Halloween Costume Inspiration.

409 Seven Funtastic Girls: Lauren. *you tube.com.* 2014–2015 (Variety).

Anna Jane, Ellie, Faye, Katherine, Klare, Jazz, Lauren, Madison, Natalie, Rowan, Sadie, and Sofia are young girls just being themselves. They welcome viewers to share certain aspects of their real lives through skits and other entertainment geared to preteen and teenage girls. Programs, which contain no credits, are well produced and very entertaining. See each individual girl for episode information.

Lauren Episode List:

1. Introducing Lauren.
2. Lauren's Baby Sitting Nightmare: Fattest Kid Ever.
3. The Legend of Cleopatra.
4. The Day Lauren Became a Boy.
5. Lauren's Scary Kidnapping Story.
6. Lauren's Bedtime Routine in Asia.
7. Lauren's a "Cereal" Killer.
8. Lauren's Morning Routine.
9. OMG! Lauren's in Trouble!
10. Love Spell.
11. Lauren Is a Mom!
12. Morning Routine for School.
13. Gymnastics Boot Camp.
14. You'll Never Believe What Lauren Found in Her Room.
15. Lauren's Room Tour 2014.
16. "Dance Moms" Parody.
17. Lauren's Crazy Obsession.
18. The Naughty Invisible Tooth Fairy.
19. Lauren's DIY Valentine's Day Treats.
20. Lauren's Crazy Dream.
21. I'm an Internet Sensation.
22. Princess and the Celebrity.
23. Lauren's Creepy Doll.
24. Lauren's New Friend.
25. Afraid of Christmas
26. Christmas Expectation vs. Reality.
27. Lauren's Christmas Gift Haul.
28. The Lost Identity.
29. The Talking Cat.
30. The Pesky Princess.
31. Minute to Win It Game Show.
32. Super Not Super Hero.
33. I Got My Braces Off.
34. Return of the Spooky Doll.
35. The Day Lauren Became a Cat!
36. Invasion of the Reese's Peanuts Butter Cups.
37. In a World with No Parents!
38. Lauren Has No Hands!
39. Lauren's Mystery of the....
40. The Year 3000.
41. Lauren's Room Tour 2015.
42. The Legend of Katniss Everdeen.
43. Lauren's Summer Fun.
44. Return of the Crazy Twins.
45. Monster in Lauren's Closet?
46. Lauren's Bad Luck Day.
47. Lauren's Baby Sitting Nightmare.
48. Lauren's Fun with Water.
49. Minute to Win It with Lauren.

410 Seven Funtastic Girls: Madison. *you tube.com.* 2011–2015 (Variety).

Anna Jane, Ellie, Faye, Katherine, Klare, Jazz, Lauren, Madison, Natalie, Rowan, Sadie, and Sofia are young girls just being themselves. They welcome viewers to share certain aspects of their real lives through skits and other entertainment geared to preteen and teenage girls. Programs, which contain no credits, are well produced and very entertaining. See each individual girl for episode information.

Madison Episode List:

1. Introducing Madison.
2. The Kardashian Legend.
3. The Day I Became a Ghost!
4. My Sister Is Possessed!
5. Madison's Bedtime Routine.
6. Spider-Man Goes Bad!
7. Madison's Summer Morning Routine.
8. Finding a Baby Ogre!
9. Magic Makes Her Pretty!
10. Gender Swap!
11. Model Boot Camp.
12. Madison Fashion Detective!
13. Madison's Room Tour.
14. Dance Warm Ups + Montage.
15. Obsessed with Electronics!
16. Genie Is Stuck in Her Lamp!
17. Valentine's Day Outfit Ideas.
18. My Crazy Hair.
19. The Strange Makeup.
20. The Princess and the Hipsters.
21. My Living Doll Escaped!
22. The Over Friendly Cat.
23. DIY Holiday Drinks.
24. Can't Escape the Elf on the Shelf.
25. Where's My Camera?
26. Afraid of Shopping.
27. It's Not Christmas!
28. The Pesky Little Sister!
29. Deal or No Deal?
30. Finding a Treasure.
31. It's Spooky out Here!
32. The Day I Became a YouTube Superstar!
33. Invasion of the Populars.
34. Madison's Perfect World.
35. Phone Booth Challenge.
36. Game Addict.
37. Nerds of the Future.
38. Tour Madison's Bathroom.
39. The Legend of the Walls.
40. Better than Revenge.
41. Madison's Summer Trip.
42. Who's the Crazy Twin?
43. Madison Has a Monster Under Her Bed!
44. Bad Luck Bella.
45. Double Trouble.
46. Water Balloon Fight.
47. Madison's Minute to Win It.
48. The Princess and the Dog.

49. Justin Bieber vs. Miley Cyrus.
50. The Anti-Cheerleader.
51. Madison's Biggest Fears.
52. Instant Mermaid Tail.
53. Madison's Morning Routine.
54. Trouble Maker with a Water Gun.
55. How to Win a Beauty Pageant.
56. Boys vs. Girls.
57. Madison's House Is Haunted!
58. A Painful Chug-a-Jug.
59. Don't Tell Your Secret Identity.
60. A Super Hero, Home Alone.
61. Madison's Spring Fashion.
62. Madison's Dream Life.
63. Spot Madison's Differences!
64. Escape from the Bathroom.
65. Teddy Bear Revenge.
66. Extreme Sledding Competition.
67. Valentine's Day Gift Ideas.
68. The Hypnotizing Glasses.
69. The Sister Bot.
70. Madison's Favorite Things.
71. Madison's Winter Fashion.
72. What I Got for Christmas.
73. What to Do During the Holidays.
74. Winter Wonderland.
75. A Cinderella Twist.
76. 3 Lies 1 Truth.
77. Effie Trinket Makeup Tutorial.
78. Time Traveling Switch!
79. The Doll Is Alive!
80. How to Make a Mermaid Tail.
81. Crazy Cat Lady.
82. The Haunted Hat!
83. Literal Drama Queen.
84. Secret Life of a Secret Agent.
85. Madison Travels Back in Time!
86. Alien Discoveries.
87. Awkward Callie's Adventure.
88. One Direction Obsession.
89. The Gymnastics Curse.
90. Morning Routine of a Princess.
91. Fun with Water.
92. How to Clone Yourself.
93. A Day in the Life of a Sim.
94. Minecraft vs. Sims.
95. Madison's Summer Fashion.
96. Model Meltdown.
97. Circus Adventure.
98. It Gets Better.
99. The Shrink Ray.
100. How to Be a Hipster.
101. Real Ninjas of New Jersey.
102. Messy Room Tour.
103. Madison's Challenges.
104. Talking with Toddlers.
105. Madison: My Tennis Routine.
106. 10 Facts You Probably Don't Know.
107. Madison's Garbage Bag Dress.
108. A Day without Thumbs.

109. Spring Fashion.
110. Madison in Wonderland.
111. Dangerous Weather.
112. Geeks Unite.
113. The Biggest Drama Queen.
114. Madison's Makeup Routine.
115. Wreck This Journal.
116. What to Do on a Snow Day.
117. 3 Truths 1 Lie.
118. The Strange Girl.
119. Zombies: A Deep Documentary.
120. Welcome to 2013.
121. The Christmas Elf!
122–123. What Happened?
124. Where Am I?
125. The Transformation.
126. Chug a Jug!
127. Madison's Competition.
128. One Armed for a Day.
129. How to Dress Up Like Harry Styles.
130. My Favorite Dresses.
131. Barbie for President.
132. I'm a Barbie Girl!
133. Madison the Fairy.
134. Madison's Dares.
135. Insta-Fortune.
136. The Alphabet Game.
137. How to Survive Blonde Stereotypes.
138. Madison's Bedtime Routine (Skit).
139. Out of Body Experience.
140. The 52nd Hunger Games.
141. Barbie's Dream House.
142. Mommy's Clothes Fashion Show.
143. Madison's Gymnastics Moves.
144. Flutter by Butterfly (Music Video).
145. Rock Star Makeover.
146. Water Olympics Training.
147. My Evil Sister!
148. Sleepover Gone Wrong!
149. No YouTube in the Future!
150. How to Get Active.
151. Opposite Day.
152. Attack of the Dead School Girl.
153. Case of the Missing Girl.
154. The Amazing Model Ever.
155. Madison's Morning Routine.
156. Pick a Dress.
157. I Dream of Dance.
158. Valentine's Day Makeup Tutorial.
159. Madison Doesn't Get Invited.
160. School Uniforms.
161. Madison's Back Bend Challenge.
162. A World Full of Color.
163. The Future Is Aliens.
164. Girl Wanted Justin Bieber for Christmas.
165. 12 Days of Christmas Outfits.
166. Messed Up Hypnosis.
167. An Orphan's Chores.
168. After School Vlog.
169. Epic Push Ups.

170. How Madison Gets Fit.
171. World's Grossest Bug Collection!
172. Madison Carves a Pumpkin!
173. Remembering My Death.
174. PJ's with a Mind of Their Own.
175. Madison Cheers for Seven Funtastic Girls.
176. How to Make an Imaginary Friend.
177. Tiffany Plays Volleyball.
178. Tiffany vs. Ali ... I Mean Al.
179. I Am Not a Brat!
180. OMG Dresses.
181. Wacky Hair Music Video.
182. Will That Make Me Barf?
183. Robots Do Have Feelings!
184. Madison's Gymnast Story.
185. Banana Bread!
186. Water Fight with Myself.
187. Madison's Totally True Bedtime Routine.
188. The Tornado That Destroyed the World.
189. Double Best Friend How-To.
190. Dizzy Cartwheel Challenge.
191. The Amazing Outfit in a Can!
192. Sick Survivor.
193. Garbage Is Beautiful.
194. Chugging with Madison.

411 Seven Funtastic Girls: Natalie. *you tube.com.* 2014–2015 (Variety).

Anna Jane, Ellie, Faye, Katherine, Klare, Jazz, Lauren, Madison, Natalie, Rowan, Sadie, and Sofia are young girls just being themselves. They welcome viewers to share certain aspects of their real lives through skits and other entertainment geared to pre-teen and teenage girls. Programs, which contain no credits, are well produced and very entertaining. See each individual girl for episode information.

Natalie Episode List:
1. Introducing Natalie.
2. My Crazy House Tour.
3. The Princess and the Perfect Dress.
4. Stalked by the Living Doll.
5. The Friendly Monster under the Bed.
6. Natalie's Christmas Presents.
7. The Christmas Potion.
8. How to Find a Lost Object!
9. Fear of the Outdoors.
10. Natalie Is a Bunny!
11. The Pesky Salesperson.
12. Random Questions Game Show.
13. The Homework Hero.
14. Millionaire Shopping Spree! Natalie's Best Day Ever!
15. A Not So Normal Halloween!
16. The Day I Became a Ninja.
17. Invasion of the Cereal Killer.
18. New World or Abandoned World?
19. 60 Seconds Clothes Challenge.
20. Addicted to My iPhone!?
21. Time Traveling to the 3000s.

22. Natalie's Dresser Tour.
23. The Legend of the Hidden Treasure.
24. Natalie's Summer 2014.
25. Crazy Twins Birthday Party.
26. Monster Madness! A Monster in Natalie's Closet!
27. Natalie's Bad Luck Curse.
28. Bratty Brittany: Natalie's Baby Sitting Nightmare!
29. Natalie Has Fun with Water.
30. Natalie's Minute to Win It.
31. Natalie the Princess and the Duck.
32. The World's Biggest Hunger Games Fan.
33. Seven Funtastic Girls Cheer Tryouts.
34. Natalie's Biggest Fears.
35. Cool Shades Commercial.
36. Natalie's New Room Tour.
37. Natalie Gets Into Trouble.
38. Beauty Pageant Makeover.
39. Attempting to Do Things Boys Do!
40. The Haunted Graveyard.
41. Chug-a-Jug with Natalie.
42. Natalie Goes Undercover—Literally!
43. Home Alone Girl Returns!
44. Natalie's Spring Tops.
45. Natalie's Dream Life.
46. Spot the Difference with Natalie.
47. Dr. Electron the Electron Doctor!
48. Escaping from a Phone Addiction!
49. Natalie Gets Sweet Revenge!
50. Goodbye Natalie.

412 Seven Funtastic Girls: Rowan. *youtube. com.* 2011–2013 (Variety).

Anna Jane, Ellie, Faye, Katherine, Klare, Jazz, Lauren, Madison, Natalie, Rowan, Sadie, and Sofia are young girls just being themselves. They welcome viewers to share certain aspects of their real lives through skits and other entertainment geared to pre-teen and teenage girls. Programs, which contain no credits, are well produced and very entertaining. See each individual girl for episode information.

Rowan Episode List:
1. Introducing Rowan.
2. The Dressy Adventure.
3. Macy or J?
4. J's Challenge!
5. How to Make the OMG Cookie.
6. Macy Takes Over.
7. The Dumb Blonde Challenge.
8. The Hello Kitty Sock Party.
9. Lampy Is Kidnapped!
10. Mallory's Scary Obsession.
11. Ninja for Dummies.
12. How to Look Absolutely Amazing.
13. Get Fit!
14. Rowan's Push up Challenge.
15. If Rowan Had an After School Routine....
16. Build-a-Bear Hypnosis.

17. Rowan's Christmas Fashion.
18. Rowan's Christmas Vlog.
19. The Time Traveling Pug.
20. Your Own World Quiz.
21. Rowan's Gymnastics Challenge.
22. What Am I Gonna Wear?
23. Rowan's 3 Truths 1 Lie.
24. Rowan's Room Tour.
25. Wanna Be My Valentine?
26. Rowan Busts a Move.
27. Rowan's Pick-a-Dress.
28. More about Rowan.
29. How to Do the Cotton-Eyed Joe.
30. Poking Fun at the Sims.
31. The Super Model's Associates.
32. The Case of the Missing Chocolate Bunny.
33. The Prank Caller's Revenge.
34. Rowan's Backwards Clips.
35. Makeup and Hair for Chorus.
36. Planking Contest.
37. Be Yourself.
38. Time Traveling Pug, Part 2.
39. The Hunger Games Distopia.
40. The Nicki Minaj Quoter
41. The Cup of Water Challenge.
42. Zero to Phantom: Josh Woodward (Music Video).
43. Seven Funtastic Girls Tribute.
44. Hipster Zombies.
45. Rowan's Mom's Clothing.
46. Rowan's Virtual Birthday Party.
47. Deep Thoughts with Katniss Everdeen.
48. Switching Lives.
49. Trapped.
50. Survival Guide to Being Blonde.
51. Pieces of Your Fortune.
52. Backyard Fairy.
53. Barbie Takes Over.
54. What, Do You Wanna Play Barbie?
55. Dress Talk.
56. Halloween Is Cancelled.
57. Rowan's One-Armed Day.
58. Rowan's Competition.
59. Help Alice Get Out of Wonderland!
60. I Hate Warm Winters.
61. What Happens Next?
62. Molly's Christmas Eve Stakeout.
63. The Cup Song Tutorial.
64. A Tribute to Rowan.
65. Hipster Zombies.

413 Seven Funtastic Girls: Sadie. youtube. com. 2012 (Variety).

Anna Jane, Ellie, Faye, Katherine, Klare, Jazz, Lauren, Madison, Natalie, Rowan, Sadie, and Sofia are young girls just being themselves. They welcome viewers to share certain aspects of their real lives through skits and other entertainment geared to preteen and teenage girls. Programs, which contain no credits, are well produced and very entertaining. See each individual girl for episode information.

Sadie Episode List:

Most of Sadie's episodes have been taken offline and labeled "Private Video." The following episodes remain on line. 1. Introducing Sadie. 2. Dresses. 3. Competition. 4. What Should Barbie Wear? 5. Spooky Halloween Movie. 6. Barbie Lost Her Shoe. 7. Cliff Hanger. 8. Sadie Meets the Christmas Fairy. 9. Sadie Gets Ready for the Holidays.

414 Seven Funtastic Girls: Sofia. youtube. com. 2011–2014 (Variety).

Anna Jane, Ellie, Faye, Katherine, Klare, Jazz, Lauren, Madison, Natalie, Rowan, Sadie, and Sofia are young girls just being themselves. They welcome viewers to share certain aspects of their real lives through skits and other entertainment geared to preteen and teenage girls. Programs, which contain no credits, are well produced and very entertaining. See each individual girl for episode information.

Sofia Episode List:

1. Introducing Sofia.
2. Gifts from the Year 3000.
3. A Change of Themes.
4. Attack of the Annoying Mom.
5. Guess the Favorite.
6. Sophie's Winter Fashion.
7. The Secret Christmas Ninja.
8. Christmas Wonderland ... Or Is It?
9. The Rotten Lazy Queen.
10. Guess the Truth.
11. Minute to Win It.
12. Switched to a Fairytale.
13. Doll-saster.
14. 60 Second Makeup Challenge.
15. Stuck in a Cat's Body.
16. Haunted Doll Halloween Tutorial.
17. Fan Girl Drama.
18. The Secret Life of a ....
19. Back in Time Catastrophe!
20. The Not So Normal Bow.
21. Back to School Tag.
22. The Sleep Addict.
23. Princess Gone Bad.
24. Splash!
25. Sofia's Cloned!
26. Fan Girl Sophie.
27. Self Obsessed vs. Fan Girl.
28. Summer Outfits.
29. What Models Do.
30. Clown Transformation.
31. Behind the Scenes.
32. DIY Sea Salt Spray.
33. How to Waterfall Braid.
34. Pajama Ninja.
35. Bedroom Tour.
36. Cotton Ball Challenge.
37. Crazy Coffee Girl.

38. Pack with Me.
39. 10 Facts about Me.
40. Weekend Morning Routine.
41. Spring Fashion Show.
42. Magic Never Lasts Forever.
43. Valentine's Orphan.
44. When I Grow Up….
45. The Gymnast Failure.
46. It's My Own Little World.
47. Time Traveling Ring.
48. Sofia's Christmas Gifts.
48. Hypnotizing Friend.
49. Jobs and Chores.
50. After School.
51. Greatest Push up Fail.
52. Keeping Fit.
53. Gross Prank.
54. Ninja Skills.
55. The Halloween Curse.
56. Isabel Was … Kidnapped!
57. Isabel Told a Lie!
58. Sofia's Cheer.
59. How to Dance.
60. The Sleeping Beauty.
61. Girly Girl vs. Tomboy.
62. Hamster Cuteness.
63. Pick-a-Dress.
64. Blind Taste Test Turns into Fishy Ketchup.
65. Robot Dancer.
66. In the Kitchen with Hamsters.
67. Sofia Has Fun with a Baby Pool.
68. Sofia's Bedtime Bloopers.
69. Goodbye Sofia.

415 Seven Gymnastics Girls: Caitlin. *you tube.com.* 2011–2015 (Variety).

Caitlin, Colette, Hayley and Katie, Jazmyn, Mary, Megan and Ciera, Rachel and Zoe are young girls, talented in gymnastics, who share their skills with viewers as well as relate incidents in their lives.

Programs, which contain no credits, are well produced and very entertaining. See each individual girl for episode information.

Caitlin Episode List:
1. Introducing Your New Tuesday (Host).
2. Not Gymnastics Video.
3. Teaching My Sister Gymnastics.
4. Gymnastics Conditioning Challenge.
5. Gymnastics Fun!
6. Front Walk-Over Challenge.
7. Front Limber Tutorial.
7. How to Get Better Flexibility.
8. Gymnastics Back Handspring Challenge.
9. Back Handspring Tutorial.
10. Gymnastics in Public.
11. How to Do a Back Walk-Over.
12. Good Leg vs. Bad Leg Gymnastics.
13. Gymnastics Kip Challenge.
14. How to Do a Back Limber.

15. Beam Dismount Challenge.
16. Gymnastics Walking Handstand Challenge.
17. Gymnastics Level 6 Bar Routine.
18. Caitlin Shows You How to Do a Back Extension Roll.
19. How to Do a Press Handstand.
20. Christmas Haul.
21. Handstand Crazy.
22. Caitlin's Stick It Challenge.
23. Caitlin's Contortion and Flexibility Skills.
24. Caitlin Takes the Back Hip Circle Challenge.
25. Caitlin's Artsy Gymnastics Montage.
26. Caitlin Takes the Front Handspring Challenge.
27. Gymnastics Bars Tutorial Kips with Caitlin.
28. Zombie Takes Over Seven Gymnastics Girls!
29. Caitlin Takes the Tick Tock Challenge.
30. Caitlin's Spot the Difference Challenge.
31. Caitlin's Room Tour + Ideas for Fall.
32. Lower Body Conditioning with Caitlin.
33. Hair and Makeup for Gymnastic Meets with Caitlin.
34. Caitlin's Conditioning While She Heals.
35. Caitlin's Tips and Tricks for Splits.
36. Back Handspring Combinations + Arm Update.
37. Where Is Caitlin's Video?
38. Reverse Gymnastics with Caitlin.
39. Caitlin's 60 Second Front Walk-Over Challenge.
40. Caitlin Takes the Beam Cartwheel Challenge.
41. Caitlin's Extreme Tumbling.
42. Caitlin Takes the Aerial Challenge.
43. Summer Gymnastics Fun.
44. Caitlin Takes the ABC's Challenge.
45. How to Do a Front Tuck.
46. Airborne Splits.
47. Front Handspring Tutorial.
48. Caitlin Takes the Back Handspring Challenge.
49. Caitlin Takes the Giants Challenge.
50. How to Do an Aerial!
51. Caitlin Takes the Handstand Push up Challenge.
52. Round Off Tutorial.
53. One-Handed Gymnastics Challenge.
54. Gymnastics Tutorial Bow and Arrow.
55. Caitlin Takes the Switch Leap Challenge.
56. How to Hold a Longer Handstand.
57. Strengthening and Conditioning.
58. Caitlin's One-Handed Cartwheel Challenge.
59. Backbend Kick Over Tutorial.
60. Caitlin Takes the Back Extension Roll Challenge.
61. 60 Second Aerial Challenge.
62. Gymnastics Injuries.
63. Caitlin's Beam Routine.
64. Caitlin's Most Impressive Gymnastics Skills.
65. Straddle Jump Half Turn Tutorial.
66. Round Off Back Handspring Tutorial.
67. Round Off Back Handspring Tutorial.

68. Candlestick Bridge Kick Over.
69. Caitlin's Christmas Picture.
70. Level 1 Gymnastics: Forward Roll.
71. Bar Routine.
72. Caitlin's Handstands.
73. Back Extension Tutorial Roll.
74. Candlestick Challenge.
75. Double Back Handspring Tutorial.
76. Gymnastics Level 4 Skills.
77. Good Leg vs. Bad Leg.
78. Blindfolded Skills Challenge.
79. Caitlin's Favorite Clips.
80. Straddle Hold Challenge.
81. Gymnastics Montage.
82. Splits Tutorial.
83. Caitlin's Split Variations.
84. Caitlin's Beam Skills.
85. Gymnastic Poses and Positions.
86. Caitlin's Room Tour.
87. Back Walk-Over Tutorial.
88. Caitlin's Bar Skills.
89. Caitlin Takes the Tick Tock Challenge 2.
90. Caitlin's Extreme Tumbling Video.
91. New USAG Level 3 Skills.
92. Caitlin's Chest Stand Challenge.
93. Caitlin's Connected Round Offs.
94. Caitlin's 4th of July.
95. Caitlin Gets Ready for the Gym.
96. Straddle Jump Challenge.
97. Caitlin's Leaps and Jumps.
98. Caitlin's Forward Moving Skills.
99. Caitlin's Mini Gymnastics Routines.
100. Handstand Tutorial.
101. Caitlin's Stretching Routine.
102. Common Gymnastics Mistakes.
103. Caitlin's Blindfolded Taste Test.
104. Gymnastics Charades.
105. A to Z Gymnastics Challenge.
106. Caitlin's Splits.
107. Caitlin's Flexibility.
108. Back-Tuck Tutorial.
109. One-Handed Cartwheel.
110. Airborne Splits.
111. Uneven Bar Skills.
112. Caitlin's Gymnastics Standing Skills.
113. Caitlin's Freestyle Gymnastics Video.
114. Caitlin Takes the 60 Second Press Hand-stand Challenge.
115. Caitlin's Back Extension Roll Tutorial.
116. 10 Things about Caitlin.
117. Caitlin Takes the Back Extension Roll Challenge.
118. Caitlin's Level 3 Gymnastics Skills.
119. Caitlin's Level 4 Beam Routine.
120. Caitlin Plays Her Instrument.
121. Caitlin's Gymnastic Montage.
122. Back Handspring Tutorial.
123. Caitlin's Front Walk-Over Tutorial.
124. Caitlin's Top 5 Gymnastics Skills.
125. Caitlin's Not So Backwards Skills.

126. What's in My Gym Bag?
127. Pull Ups, Sit Ups and Push Ups.
128. Various Types of Cartwheels.
129. Caitlin's Contortions.
130. Caitlin's Gymnastics Grading.
131. Caitlin's 60 Second Gymnastics Challenge.
132. Caitlin's Straddle Hold Challenge.
133. Caitlin's Round-Off Back Handspring Tutorial.
134. Caitlin's Level 4 Floor Routine.
135. Caitlin's Spot the Difference.
136. Caitlin's A–Z Gymnastics Video.
137. One-Handed Gymnastics Skills.
138. Help Caitlin Do an Aerial.
139. Caitlin Takes the Back Walk-Over Challenge.
140. How to Do a One-Handed Front Walk-Over.
141. Hand Stand Tutorial.
142. Tramp-lining with Caitlin.
143. Stretching and Flexibility Exercises for Gymnastics.
144. Caitlin's High Fashion Mini-Routine.
145. Caitlin's Crazy Fashion Show.
146. Gymnastics Strengthening.
147. Chest Stand Challenge.
148. Caitlin's Adventures at the Strawberry Farm.
149. Tick Tock Challenge 3.
150. Floor Event Warm-Up.
151. Gymnastics Level 1 Skills.
152. 3 Truths and 1 Lie.
153. Caitlin's Freestyle Gymnastics.
154. Bad Leg Challenge.
155. What I Want to Be When I Grow Up.
156. Backbend Stand Ups.
157. Chin-Ups and Cruiser Boards.
158. How to Do a Back Limber.
159. Caitlin Returns to Seven Gymnastics Girls.
160. Caitlin Goes Cartwheel Crazy.
161. Caitlin's Top Tricks.
162. Caitlin through the Years on Seven Gymnastics Girls.
163. Caitlin Saves Seven Gymnastics Girls.
164. Caitlin's Chin Ups in 60 seconds.

416 Seven Gymnastics Girls: Colette. *you tube.com.* 2014–2015 (Variety).

Caitlin, Colette, Hayley and Katie, Jazmyn, Mary, Megan and Ciera, Rachel and Zoe are young girls, talented in gymnastics, who share their skills with viewers as well as relate incidents in their lives.

Programs, which contain no credits, are well produced and very entertaining. See each individual girl for episode information.

Colette Episode List:
1. Introducing Colette.
2. How to Do a Double Back Handspring Step Out.
3. Summer Fun.
4. Front Walk-Over Tutorial.
5. One Minute V up Challenge.

6. Fun at Gymnastics.

7. Gymnastics Front Walk-Over Challenge.

8. How to Get Your Front Limber.

9. Flexibility and Conditioning Exercises for Gymnasts.

10. Back Handspring Minute Challenge.

11. Ultimate Gymnastics Montage.

12. How to Do a Back Handspring.

13. Gymnastics While Rock Climbing.

14. Trampoline Tumbling.

15. How to Do a Back Walk-Over.

16. Good Leg vs. Bad Leg Gymnastics Challenge.

17. Gymnastics Bars Pull Over Challenge.

18. How to Do a Back Limber.

19. Beam Dismount Stick It Challenge.

20. Gymnastics Handstand Walking Challenge.

21. Mini Gymnastics Bar Routine.

22. How to Do a Back Extension Roll.

23. Gymnastics Back Walk-Over Challenge.

24. How to Do a One-Handed Cartwheel.

25. Christmas Haul 2014.

26. Handstand Crazy Montage.

27. How to Do a Round Off Back Handspring Back Tuck.

28. Gymnastics Flexibility.

29. Gymnastics Back Hip Circle Challenge.

30. Colette's Front Handspring Challenge.

31. How to Do a Gymnastic Pull Over on Bars.

32. Handstand Walking Montage.

33. Family and Friends Gymnastics.

34. Gymnastics Tick Tock Challenge.

35. How to Do a Bow and Arrow.

36. Tips and Tricks for a Chest Stand.

37. How to Do a Back Handspring.

38. Slow Motion Gymnastics.

39. Gymnastics Back Extension Roll Challenge.

40. Stretches to Quickly Get All Your Splits.

41. Gymnastics Back Handsprings.

42. Tumbling Combination Challenge.

43. Reverse Gymnastics.

44. Gymnastics Front Walk-Over Challenge.

45. Cartwheel on Beam Challenge.

46. Extreme Tumbling.

47. Aerial Challenge.

48. Summer Gymnastics.

49. Alphabet Gymnastics Challenge.

50. Round Off Back Handspring Tutorial.

51. Airborne Splits.

52. Front Handspring Tutorial.

53. Back Handspring Challenge.

54. Gymnastic Bar Challenge.

55. Front Walk-Over Tutorial.

56. Front Aerial Tutorial.

57. Handstand Pushup Challenge.

58. Back Handspring Tutorial.

59. One Handed Gymnastics Challenge.

60. How to Do a Heel Stretch.

61. 60 Second Switch Leap Challenge.

417 *Seven Gymnastics Girls: Hayley and Katie.* *youtube.com.* 2012–2015 (Variety).

Caitlin, Colette, Hayley and Katie, Jazmyn, Mary, Megan and Ciera, Rachel and Zoe are young girls, talented in gymnastics, who share their skills with viewers as well as relate incidents in their lives.

Programs, which contain no credits, are well produced and very entertaining. See each individual girl for episode information.

Hayley and Katie Episode List:

1. Introducing Hayley.

2. 10 Things Hayley and Katie Enjoy.

3. How to Do a Cartwheel Correctly.

4. 60 Second V-Up Challenge.

5. Fun Gymnastics Skills.

6. Front Walk-Over Gymnastics Challenge.

7. How to Do a Front Limber.

8. Simple Stretches to Improve Flexibility.

9. 60 Second Handspring Challenge.

10. Slow Motion Gymnastics.

11. How to Do a Back Handspring.

12. Gymnastics in Public.

13. Hayley vs. Katie Handstand Contest.

14. How to Do a Back Walk-Over.

15. Good Leg vs. Bad Leg Gymnastics.

16. 60 Second Kip Challenge.

17. How to Do a Back Limber.

18. Beam Dismounts: Stick It Challenge.

19. Walking on Hands Gymnastics.

20. Gymnastics Bar Routines.

21. How to Do a Back Extension Roll.

22. Back Walk-Over Challenge.

23. Back Bend Stand Up Tutorial.

24. Christmas Haul.

25. Handstand Crazy.

26. New Gymnastics Skills.

27. Flexibility Skills.

28. Back Kip Circle Gymnastics Challenge.

29. Artistic Gymnastics Montage.

30. 60 Second Front Handspring Challenge.

31. How to Do a Kip.

32. Numbers Gymnastics Challenge.

33. Halloween Gymnastics.

34. 60 Second Tick Tock Challenge.

35. How to Do a Pop Cartwheel.

36. How to Do a Tinsica.

37. Synchronized Cartwheels.

38. Backward Roll Push Up Tutorial.

39. Gymnastics Vault Skills.

40. Simple Stretches for Split.

41. Back Handsprings, Layouts and Layout Step Outs.

42. Tumbling Combination Challenge.

43. Reverse Gymnastics.

44. Front Walk-Over Gymnastics Challenge.

45. Cartwheels on Beam Challenge.

46. Extreme Gymnastics Tumbling.

47. 60 Second Aerial Challenge.

48. Summer Gymnastics.

49. Alphabet Gymnastics Challenge.
50. Standing Back Tuck: Gymnastics Tutorial.
51. Airborne Splits.
52. How to Do a Front Handspring.
53. 60 Second Back Handspring Challenge.
54. Gymnastics Giant Challenge.
55. Front Walk-Over Tutorial.
56. How to Do an Aerial.
57. Handstand Push-Up Challenge.
58. How to Do a Back Handspring.
59. One-Handed Gymnastics Challenge.
60. Flexibility Tutorial: Heel Stretch.
61. 60 Second Switch Leap Challenge.
62. How to Do a Handstand.
63. 60 Second Back Walk-Over Challenge.
64. Gymnastics Competition.
65. Gymnastics Strengthening Exercises.
66. One-Handed Cartwheel Challenge.
67. Backbend, Bridge, Kick Over Gymnastics Tutorial.
68. Back Extension Roll Challenge.
69. Alphabet Gymnastics Challenge.
70. Gymnastics Injuries.
71. Gymnastics Beam Routine.
72. Impressive Gymnastics.
73. Back Walk-Over Gymnastics Tutorial.
74. Handstand Forward Roll Gymnastics Tutorial.
75. How to Do a Backward Roll.
76. Christmas Haul.
77. Gymnastics Forward Roll Tutorial.
78. Gymnastics Bar Skills.
79. Forward Gymnastics vs. Backward Gymnastics.
80. Gymnastics Back Tuck Tutorial.
81. Gymnastics Candlestick Challenge.
82. Back Extension Roll Tutorial.
83. Level 6 Gymnastics Floor Skills.
84. Good Leg vs. Bad Leg Gymnastics.
85. Blindfolded Gymnastics.
86. Gymnastics Bloopers.
87. Straddle Hold Challenge.
88. Gymnastics Skill Challenge.
89. Front Walk-Over Tutorial.
90. Splits Variations.
91. Pull Ups and Chin Ups.
92. Gymnastics Poses and Positions.
93. Gymnastics Everywhere.
94. Round Off Tuck Back Tutorial.
95. Hayley's Best Bar Skills.
96. 60 Second Tick Tock Challenge.
97. New Level 2 and 3 Compulsory Skills.
98. Tumbling.
99. Chest Stand Challenge.
100. Connected Round Offs.
101. Gymnastics Grading.
102. Getting Ready for Gymnastics.
103. 60 Second Straddle Jump Challenge.
104. Leaps and Jumps.
105. Forward Gymnastics Skills.
106. Balance Beam Routines.
107. Handstand Tutorial.
108. How Long Can We Hold a Handstand?
109. Gymnastics Warm Up Routine.
110. Hayley Round Off Back Handspring Mistakes.
111. Trampoline Tricks.
112. 60 Second Back Bend Stand Up Challenge.
113. Gymnastics Charades.
114. Alphabet Gymnastics Challenge.
115. Hayley's Splits.
116. Flexibility.
117. One-Handed Gymnastics Challenge.
118. Airborne Splits.
119. How to Do a Pull Over.
120. Hayley's Standing Gymnastics Skills.
121. Gymnastics Challenge.
122. Handstand Challenge.
123. Back Extension Roll Tutorial.
124. Hayley's Christmas.
125. 1 Minute Back Extension Challenge.
126. Level 3 Gymnastics.
127. Beam Routine.
128. Gymnastics Grading 2.
129. Hayley's Gymnastics Montage.
130. How to D a Standing Back Tuck.
131. Hayley's Top 5 Skills.
132. Backwards Moves.
133. Splits!
134. How to Do a Scorpion.
135. What Is Inside Katie and Hayley's Gymnastics Bags?
136. Sit-Ups, Push-Ups and Pull-Ups.
137. Cartwheels!
138. Gymnastics Grading 3.
139. Hayley Does the 60 Second Move Challenge.
140. Straddle Hood.
141. Hayley's Gymnastics Routine.
142. Freestyle Gymnastics.
143. Spot the Difference.
144. Alphabet Gymnastics.

418 Seven Gymnastics Girls: Jazmyn. *you tube.com.* 2015 (Variety).

Caitlin, Colette, Hayley and Katie, Jazmyn, Mary, Megan and Ciera, Rachel and Zoe are young girls, talented in gymnastics, who share their skills with viewers as well as relate incidents in their lives.

Programs, which contain no credits, are well produced and very entertaining. See each individual girl for episode information.

Jazmyn Episode List:
1. Introducing Jazmyn.
2. Jazmyn's 5 Favorite Things to Do.
3. How to Do a Cast Handstand.
4. The 60 Second V-Up Challenge.
5. Fun with Gymnastics.
6. The Front Walk-Over Challenge.

7. How to Do a Front Limber.

8. Flexibility and Conditioning Training.

9. The Connected Back Handsprings Challenge with Jazmyn.

10. One Arm Gymnastics Challenge.

11. Ho to Do a Back Handspring.

12. Gymnastics at Target.

13. Gymnastics with My Sister.

14. How to Do a Back Walk-Over.

15. Good Leg vs. Bad Leg Gymnastics Challenge.

16. How to Do a Front Limber.

17. The Front Walk-Over Challenge.

18. Fun with Gymnastic.

19. The 60 Second V-Up Challenge.

20. How to Do a Cast Handstand.

21. Jazmyn's Five Favorite Things to Do.

22. How to Do a Back Handspring Step Out.

23. How to Do a Switch Leap.

24. The 60 Second Full Turn on a Beam Challenge.

25. The 60 Second Aerial Challenge.

26. One Handed Front Walk-Over Tutorial.

27. Helpful Gymnastics Balance Beam Drill.

28. The ABC Gymnastics Challenge.

29. Elbow Stand Challenge.

30. How to Master a Front Aerial.

31. Starting Gymnastics: What to Expect.

32. The 60 Second Pull Up Challenge.

33. How to Do a Back Limber.

34. The Gymnast Tag.

35. Jazmyn's 60 Second Skills Challenge.

36. The Alphabet Gymnastics Challenge on a Beam.

37. Trick or Treat Stick It Challenge.

38. The One Minute Kip Challenge.

39. The Tumbling Connection Challenge.

40. How to Do a Side Aerial.

41. Gymnastics Strengthening and Conditioning.

42. The 60 Second Split Leap Challenge.

43. Two Person Acro Stunts.

44. My Mom Tries Gymnastics.

45. Gymnastics Obstacle Course.

46. The Blindfolded Gymnastics Challenge.

47. Jazmyn's Gym Tour.

48. The Bad Leg ABC Gymnastics Challenge.

49. The Dizzy Gymnastics Challenge.

50. Back Handspring Connections Fun.

51. Cool Acro Trick Tutorial: Front Handspring to Knees.

52. Gymnastics Level 1: Requirements on Bars.

53. Artistic Gymnast Tries Rhythmic Gymnastics.

419 *Seven Gymnastics Girls: Mary.* you *tube.com.* 2015 (Variety).

Caitlin, Colette, Hayley and Katie, Jazmyn, Mary, Megan and Ciera, Rachel and Zoe are young girls, talented in gymnastics, who share their skills with viewers as well as relate incidents in their lives.

Programs, which contain no credits, are well produced and very entertaining. See each individual girl for episode information.

Mary Episode List:

1. Introducing Mary.

2. How to Get Your Splits.

3. My Favorite Things Besides Gymnastics.

4. Handstand Challenge.

5. 60 Second V-Up Challenge.

6. Fun Gymnastics.

7. 60 Second Front Walk-Over Challenge.

8. How to Do a Front Limber.

9. Flexibility Stretches and Tips.

10. Connected Back Handspring Challenge.

11. Gymnastics Expectations vs. Reality.

12. Back Hand Spring Tutorial and Tips.

13. Gymnastics in Public.

14. Back Walk-Over Tutorial.

15. Creative Gymnastics Beam Dismounts.

16. Gymnastics with My Coach.

17. Gymnastic Levels 1–5: Requirements on the Floor.

18. How to Quickly Get Your Round Off Back Handspring.

19. Fun Gymnastics Back Handspring Connections.

20. Gymnastics in Jeans Challenge.

21. The Dizzy Gymnastics Challenge.

22. ABC Gymnastics Challenge with My Bad Leg.

23. Ultimate Gymnastics Truth or Dare.

24. Mary's Home Gym Equipment.

25. Blindfolded Gymnastics Challenge.

26. Mary Tries Gymnastics in the Snow.

27. Mary's Gymnastics and Tumbling in the Gym.

28. Teaching My Cousins Gymnastics.

29. Split Leap Challenge.

30. Teaching My Mom Gymnastics.

31. Tumbling Combination Challenge.

32. Gymnastics in Different Halloween Costumes.

33. Mary's Gymnastic Challenge: 60 Second Kip Challenge.

34. ABC Gymnastics Challenge on a Beam.

35. 60 Second Gymnastics Skills Challenge.

36. Starting Gymnastics: My Mini Floor Routine.

37. Kip Challenge.

38. Gymnastics Truth or Dare.

39. How to Hold Longer Handstands.

40. Beam Drills.

420 *Seven Gymnastics Girls: Megan and Ciera.* youtube.com. 2011–2013 (Variety).

Caitlin, Colette, Hayley and Katie, Jazmyn, Mary, Megan and Ciera, Rachel and Zoe are young girls, talented in gymnastics, who share their skills with viewers as well as relate incidents in their lives.

Programs, which contain no credits, are well produced and very entertaining. See each individual girl for episode information.

Megan and Ciera Episode List:
1. Introducing Megan and Ciera.
2. Gymnastics Grading.
3. Beam Routine.
4. Level 3 Gymnastics.
5. Back Extension Roll Challenge.
6. One-Handed Cartwheel (Tutorial).
7. Back Extension Roll Tutorial.
8. Handstand Challenge.
9. Level 6 Gymnastics.
10. Synchronized Standing Skills.
11. How to Do a Stride Circle (Bars).
12. Airborne Splits.
13. One-Handed Gymnastics Challenge.
14. Gymnastics Montage.
15. Megan and Ciera's Flexibility.
16. Megan and Ciera's Splits.
17. Alphabet Gymnastics Challenge.
18. Megan and Ciera's Gymnastics Charades.
19. Gymnastics Level 1 and 2 Demonstration.
20. Perfect Balance.
21. Common Gymnastics Mistakes.
22. Gymnastics Warm Up Routine.
23. How to Do a Handstand.
24. How Long Can We Hold a Handstand?
25. Gymnastics Mini Routines.
26. Forward Gymnastics.
27. Leaps and Jumps.
28. Straddle Jump Challenge.
29. How We Get Ready for Gymnastics.
30. Connected Round Offs.
31. Our Longest Chest Stand.
32. New USAG Compulsory Gymnastics Levels 4 & 5.
33. Extreme Tumbling.
34. 60 Second Tick Tock Challenge.
35. Uneven Bar Skills.
36. How to Do an Aerial Cartwheel.
37. Graceful Gymnastics vs. Powerful Gymnastics.
38. Gymnastics Poses and Positions.
39. Gymnastics Beam Skills.
40. Pull Up Challenge.
41. Split Variations.
42. How to Do a Back Handspring.
43. Top Gymnastics Skills in a Row.
44. Straddle Hold Challenge.
45. Blindfolded Gymnastics.
46. Good Leg vs. Bad Leg Gymnastics.
47. Level 6 Gymnastics Floor Skills.
48. The Candlestick Challenge.
49. How to Improve Flexibility.
50. Tumbling Freestyle.
51. Level 7 Bar Routines.
52. How to Do a Cartwheel.
53. Christmas Haul.
54. How to Do a Front Handspring.

421 Seven Gymnastics Girls: Rachel. you tube.com. 2011–2015 (Variety).

Caitlin, Colette, Hayley and Katie, Jazmyn, Mary, Megan and Ciera, Rachel and Zoe are young girls, talented in gymnastics, who share their skills with viewers as well as relate incidents in their lives.

Programs, which contain no credits, are well produced and very entertaining. See each individual girl for episode information.

Rachel Episode List:
1. Introducing Your New Saturday (Host).
2. A Day in the Life of Rachel.
3. How to Do a Standing Back Tuck.
4. Gymnastics V-Up Challenge.
5. Gymnastics at Home.
6. Gymnastics Front Walk-Over Challenge.
7. How to Do a Front Limber.
8. Gymnastics Stretching and Flexibility Exercises.
9. Gymnastics Back Handspring Challenge.
10. Family Gymnastics Challenge.
11. How to Do a Back Handspring.
12. Gymnastics in Public Places.
13. Rachael's Aerial Acrobatics.
14. How to Do a Back Walk-Over.
15. Bad Leg vs. Good Leg Gymnastics.
16. Gymnastics Hip Challenge.
17. How to Do a Back Limber.
18. Gymnastics Bean Dismount Challenge.
19. Handstand Walking Gymnastics Challenge.
20. Gymnastics Back Walk-Over Challenge.
21. How to Do a Valdez.
22. Rachel's Gymnastics Montage.
23. Gymnastics Handstand Montage.
24. Mexican Handstand Tutorial.
25. Extreme Flexibility.
26. Gymnastics Back Hip Circle Challenge.
27. Artistic Gymnastics.
28. Gymnastics Front Handspring Challenge.
29. Kip Tutorial.
30. Back Tuck Tutorial.
31. Rachel's Halloween Routine.
32. Gymnastics Tick Tock Challenge.
33. How to Walk in a Handstand.
34. Gymnastics Dive Roll Tutorial.
35. Gymnastics Handstand Montage.
36. Press Handstand Challenge.
37. Chest Roll Tutorial.
38. Tips and Tricks for Better Splits.
39. Gymnastics Back Handsprings and Layouts.
40. Tumbling Combination Challenge.
41. Rachel's Reverse Gymnastics.
42. Gymnastics Front Walk-Over Challenge.
43. Gymnastics Tumbling.
44. Gymnastics Aerial Challenge.
45. Gymnastics in Public.
46. Rachel's ABC Gymnastics.
47. Chest Stand Tutorial.
48. Gymnastics Airborne Splits.
49. Front Handspring Tutorial.
50. Rachel's Gymnastics Back Handspring Challenge.

51. Gymnastics Giants Challenge.
52. Gymnastics Front Walk-Over Tutorial.
53. Gymnastics Front Aerial Tutorial.
54. Gymnastics Handstand Pushup Challenge.
55. Gymnastics Back Handspring Tutorial.
56. One Handed Gymnastics Challenge.
57. Gymnastics Scorpion Tutorial.
58. Gymnastics Switch Lap Challenge.
59. Scorpion/Arched Handstand Tutorial.
60. Gymnastics Back Walk-Over Challenge.
61. How to Improve Back Flexibility.
62. Gymnastics Strengthening and Conditioning.
63. Gymnastics One-Handed Cartwheel Challenge.
64. Gymnastics Backbend Kick Over Tutorial.
65. Gymnastics Back Extension Roll Challenge.
66. Gymnastics Handstand Challenge.
67. Caring for Gymnastic Rips.
68. Rachel's Gymnastics Beam Routine.
69. Impressive Gymnastics Skills.
70. Gymnastics Front Handspring.
71. Beginner Gymnastics: Splits Tutorial.
72. Beginner Gymnastics: Kick Over Tutorial.
73. Rachel Attempts Men's Gymnastics.
74. Beginner Gymnastics: Handstand Tutorial.
75. Gymnastics Flexibility.
76. How to Do a Press Handstand.
77. The Candlestick Challenge.
78. Gymnastics Aerial Tutorial.
79. Level 6/7 Gymnastics.
80. Bad Leg vs. Good Leg Gymnastics.
81. Rachel's Blindfolded Gymnastics.
82. Rachel's Gymnastics Bloopers.
83. Gymnastics Skill Challenge.
84. Back Handspring Step Out Tutorial.
85. Rachel's Gymnastics Splits.
86. Rachel's Chin-Up Challenge.
87. Rachel's Gymnastics Beam Skills.
88. Artistic Gymnastics Poses.
89. Rachel's Gymnastics Everywhere.
90. Front Aerial Gymnastics Tutorial.
91. Gymnastic Bar Skills.
92. Rachel's Tick Tock Gymnastics Challenge.
93. Freestyle Tumbling.
94. Level 6 Gymnastics Skills.
95. Rachel's Tumbling Skills.
96. Rachel's Handstand Montage.
97. Getting Ready with Rachel.
98. Straddle Jump Challenge.
99. Rachel's Leaps and Jumps.
100. Rachel's Forward Gymnastics.
101. Rachel's Gymnastics Floor Routine.
102. Mexican (Arched) Handstand Tutorial.
103. Rachel's Longest Handstand.
104. Rachel's Warm Up Routine.
105. Gymnastics Handstand Mistakes.
106. Rachel's Gymnastics in Cancun.
107. Rachel's Gymnastics Leaps.
108. Rachel's Gymnastics Charades.
109. Rachel's ABC Gymnastics.
110. Rachel's Perfect Splits.
111. Rachel's Flexibility Skills.
112. Rachel's Gymnastics at the Gym.
113. 60 Second V-Sit Challenge.
114. One-Handed Back Handspring Challenge.
115. Rachel's Gymnastics Bar Skills.
116. Rachel's Best Gymnastics.
117. Rachel's Handstand Challenges.
118. Back Extension Roll Tutorial.
119. Rachel's Circus Training.
120. Back Extension Roll Challenge.
121. Level 3 Gymnastics Demonstration.
122. Rachel's Beam Routine.
123. Gymnastics Grading.
124. Gymnastics Montage.
125. Back Tuck Tutorial.
126. Front Walk-Over Tutorial.
127. Rachel's Top Gymnastics.
128. Backwards Gymnastics.
129. Gymnastics Splits Tutorial.
130. How to Do a Scorpion/Needle.
131. What's in Rachel's Gymnastics Bag?
132. Gymnastics Conditioning Challenge.
133. Cartwheels and Aerials.
134. Rachel's Contortion Skills.
135. Rachel's Gymnastics Skills.
136. Rachel's 60 Second Gymnastics Challenge.
137. Rachel Straddle Holds.
138. Handstand Forward Roll Tutorial.
139. Rachel's Gymnastics Floor Routine.
140. Ellen's Dance Dare.
141. Spot Rachel's Differences.
142. Alphabet Gymnastics Challenge.
143. One-Hand Gymnastics.
144. Acrobatic Gymnastics.
145. Back Walk-Over Challenge.
146. Gymnastics Around the World.
147. Handstand Tutorial.
148. Rachel's Bloopers 2.
149. Chest Stand Tutorial.
150. Rachel's Outfits.
151. Home Conditioning for Gymnastics.
152. Level 2 Gymnastics.
153. Chug-a-Jug Gymnastics.
154. Tick-Tock Challenge 2.
155. Level 1 Gymnastics Challenge.
156. The Truth About Rachel.
157. Gymnastics Freestyle.
158. Rachel's Bad Leg Gymnastics.
159. When Rachel Grows Up.
160. Rachel's 60 Second Bridge Challenge.
161. How to Make Brownies.
162. How to Do a Back Limber.
163. The Epic Push Up Challenge.
164. Back Walk-Over Tutorial.
165. Rachel's Handstand Competition.
166. Gymnastics Competition Hair.
167. Rachel's Beam Practice.
168. How Long Can You Hold Your Bridge?

169. Rachel's World Is Backwards.
170. Pick Rachel's Outfit.
171. 3 Truths and 1 Lie with Rachel.
172. Rachel's Top Tricks.

422 Seven Gymnastics Girls: Zoe. *youtube. com.* 2014–2015 (Variety).

Caitlin, Colette, Hayley and Katie, Jazmyn, Mary, Megan and Ciera, Rachel and Zoe are young girls, talented in gymnastics, who share their skills with viewers as well as relate incidents in their lives.

Programs, which contain no credits, are well produced and very entertaining. See each individual girl for episode information.

Zoe Episode List:
1. Introducing Zoe.
2. High Arabesque: Gymnastics Tutorial with Zoe.
3. Gymnastics Not! 10 Facts about Zoe.
4. Gymnastics Leo Designs for Seven Gymnastics Girls.
5. V-Ups Gymnastics Conditioning Challenge.
6. Gymnastics Hairstyle: French Braid Variation.
7. Gymnastics—Ouch!
8. How to Do a Front Limber: Gymnastics Tutorial with Zoe.
9. Gymnastics Flexibility, Conditioning Plus Strength Training.
10. Back Handsprings in a Row: Gymnastics Challenge.
11. Gymnastic Hairstyles: How to Style Your Hair for a Gymnastic Meet.
12. How to Do a Back Handspring: Gymnastic Tips.
13. Hand Stand Crazy in Mexico.
14. The Gymnast Tag with Zoe.
15. How to Do a Back Walk-Over: Gymnastics Tutorial with Zoe.
16. Good Leg vs. Bad Leg Gymnastic Skills.
17. Hip Crazy: Gymnastics Bars Challenge with Zoe.
18. Back Limber Gymnastic Tutorial with Zoe.
19. Dismounts on Beam: Stick-It Gymnastics Challenge.
20. Walking on Your Hands Gymnastics Challenge.
21. Gymnastics Level 4 Bar Routine.
22. Easy Tips to Help Get Your Back Extension Roll Gymnastic Tutorial.
23. 60 Second Back Walk-Over Gymnastic Challenge.
24. How to Do a Cartwheel Tutorial with Zoe.
25. Zoe and Caitlin Have Fun: Holiday Sleep Over.
26. Handstand Crazy: Gymnastics Skills.
27. Getting Ready for Gymnastic Practice.
28. Gymnastics Flexibility Contortion Skills.
29. Back Hip Circle Bars Challenge with Zoe.
30. Gymnastics Montage with Zoe.
31. Flipping Front Handspring Challenge with Zoe.
32. Hip Tips Tutorial.
33. Zoe Coaches Her Brother on Basic Gymnastic Skills.
34. Spooky Halloween Gymnastics Puzzle.
35. Tick Tock Gymnastic Challenge.
36. Handstand Forward Roll: Gymnastic Floor Skills.
37. Pop Dive Cartwheel: Gymnastics Tutorial with Zoe.
38. Backwards Roll to Push Up: Gymnastics Tutorial.
39. Forward Roll 60 Second Gymnastics Challenge.
40. Zoe's Level 4 Vault Skills.
41. How to Get Your Split and Middle Split.
42. Back Handspring Flipping Crazy.
43. Tumbling Combinations: Gymnastics Challenge with Zoe.
44. Reversed Gymnastics with Zoe.
45. Front Walk-Over Gymnastics Challenge with Zoe.
46. Cartwheels on the High Beam: Level 4 Gymnastics.
47. Extreme Tumbling with Zoe.
48. Zoe Takes on the One-Handed Cartwheel Challenge.
49. Gymnastics in Public: Summer Fun with Zoe.
50. Alphabet Gymnastics ABC Challenge with Zoe.
51. Elbow Stands with Zoe: Gymnastics Tutorial.
52. Gymnastic Splits and Leaps in the Air with Zoe.
53. Front Handspring Gymnastic Tutorial with Zoe.
54. Gymnastic Back Handspring Challenge.
55. Gymnastics Pull Over Challenge.
56. Gymnastics Front Walk-Over Tutorial.
57. How to Master an Awesome Aerial with Zoe.
58. Handstand Push-Up Challenge.
59. Back Handspring Tutorial.
60. One-Handed Gymnastic Challenge.
61. Gymnastics Scorpion with Zoe.
62. Switch Leap Challenge.
63. How to Walk on Your Hands.
64. 60 Second Back Walk-Over Challenge.
65. Handstand Crazy in Mexico.
66. Gymnastics Strengthening Exercises.
67. Zoe's One-Handed Cartwheel Challenge.
68. Backbend, Bridge, Kick Over Tutorial.

423 Seven Perfect Angels: Anna and Avery. *youtube.com.* 2014–2015 (Variety).

Anna and Avery, Emily, Heather, Jaidyn, Jana, Kaelyn, Laura, Lia and Mimi are young girls who entertain children with skits, talk and glimpses of their lives with friends and family. Programs, which contain no credits, are well produced and very entertaining. See each individual girl for episode information.

Anna and Avery Episode List:
1. Introducing Anna.
2. *Pretty Little Liars* Parody.
3. The Day We Became Vampires.
4. A Cat's Morning Routine.
5. Crazy Experiments with Coke and Mentos Finale.
6. Black Gloved Villain.
7. Pizza Challenge.
8. 1 Million Outfits.
9. Mission Impossible: Baby Sitting Edition.
10. Girls Play Football!
11. Magic Spells to Cure Boredom.
12. *Dance Moms* Parody.
13. Epic Dance Lessons.
14. Crazy Nutella Obsession.
15. Anna Is Stuck in the TV.
16. Anna's Super Hero Powers Go Missing.
17. Fashion Boot Camp.
18. The Princess and the Basketball Player.
19. Anna Discovers Princess Land.
20. Q&A with Anna and Avery.
21. American Girl Doll Jail Break.
22. Anna and the Fairy Dust.
23. The Strange and Unexpected Scavenger Hunt.
24. Anna's Morning Routine.
25. Anna's Christmas Haul.
26. Princess Cinderbella and the Ball Disaster.
27. Things All Vampires Do.
28. Shambo and Shampo the Troublemakers.
29. Mission Impossible: Babysitting Crazy Kids.
30. Avery Accidentally Ruins Anna's Birthday.
31. My Boyfriend Is an Alien.
32. Avery's Amazing Pranks.
33. If Only I Could Have Anything I Want.
34. The Mermaid Sisters.
35. The Princess and the Genie.
36. The Forgetful Frappuccino: Avery Loses Her Memory.
37. What We Got for Christmas 2015.
38. Buddy the Elf Gets Revenge.
39. Anna Has the Christmas Pox.
40. Bratty Brittany Gets Ready for Christmas.
41. Our Dream Life: Living on an Island.
42. My Secret Life As Miranda Sings.
43. The Day We Became Vampires.
44. A Visit from the Christmas Fairy.
45. The Baby Food Challenge with Baby Avery and Baby Anna.
46. Eat It or Wear It with Avery and Anna.
47. Halloween Expectation vs. Reality.
48. Secret Brownie Recipe.
49. Summer Fun with Avery and Anna.

424 Seven Perfect Angels: Emily. *youtube. com.* 2014 (Variety).

Anna and Avery, Emily, Heather, Jaidyn, Jana, Kae-lyn, Laura, Lia and Mimi are young girls who entertain children with skits, talk and glimpses of their lives with friends and family. Programs, which contain no credits, are well produced and very entertaining. See each individual girl for episode information.

Emily Episode List: *1.* Introducing Your New Super Saturday (Host)! *2.* Emily's Spring Fashion. *3.* Home Alone. *4.* The Bad Luck Games. *5.* Emily Gets Revenge. *6.* Emily Win Win Situation. *7.* Emily Makes Cheerleader Pom Poms. *8.* Emily's Biggest Fear. *9.* Emily Makes Summer Lemonade. *10.* Emily Turns into a Boy?!? *11.* Emily and the Legend of the Fairies. *12.* Emily's Crazy Twin. *13.* Goodbye Emily.

425 Seven Perfect Angels: Heather. *youtube. com.* 2013–2015 (Variety).

Anna and Avery, Emily, Heather, Jaidyn, Jana, Kae-lyn, Laura, Lia and Mimi are young girls who entertain children with skits, talk and glimpses of their lives with friends and family. Programs, which contain no credits, are well produced and very entertaining. See each individual girl for episode information.

Heather Episode List:
1. Introducing Heather.
2. Heather Becomes a Cell Phone.
3. Cool Cat's Unlucky Day.
4. Heather's Crazy Prom Date.
5. No More You Tube?!
6. Heather's Ultimate Pizza Challenge.
7. Heather's Homework Hotline: 1 Million Homework Excuses.
8. Mission Impossible: Creating a Perfect Audition.
9. Girls Can Do Anything!
10. Switch Witch's Makeup Madness.
11–12. A *Dance Moms* Parody
13. Sabrina the Obsessive Selfie Sender.
14. Heather Lives Her Life … Backwards.
15. Heather's Missing Prankster Powers.
16. Girly Girl Gabbie and the Phone Free Boot Camp.
17. The Princess and the Fairy Wish.
18. Heather Discovers a Frozen World Under Her Stairs!
19. The Valentine's Day Mix Up.
20. Sneaky Stella and Chompin' Charlie Break Free!
21. Gabbie and Tori Need Fairy Dust.
22. The Strange and Unexpected Return of Mrs. Fairlady!
23. Heather Swims with Dolphins in the Caribbean.
24. Christmas with Heather.
25. Heather's Christmas Gifts + Holiday Adventures.
26. Heather's Holiday Shopping Adventure.
27. Uh Oh! Pesky Pop-Up Peter Visits Heather!
28. Heather Has the Best Day Ever!
29. Heather's Awesome Room Tour.

30. Heather's Robot Disaster.
31. Heather Tries the Smoothie Challenge.
32. Is Heather ... Invisible?
33. Heather's Spooky Follower.
34. Heather's Stylish Garbage Bag Dresses.
35. Beauty Walk of ... Fame?!
36. Girly Girl Gabbie Calls a Rematch ... and the Winner Is?!
37. Is Heather ... Jealous?!
38. Heather! The Troublemaker!
39. Heather's Monster Madness.
40. Heather Gets Invaded By ... School Supplies!
41. Heather and the Blueberry Fairy.
42. Oh No! Heather Looks Like a Nightmare!
43. The Day Heather Walked the Runway.
44. Pushed in the Pool?! Heather's Baby Sitting Nightmare!
45. Summer Fun Cottage Edition.
46 Heather's Crazy Twin.
47. The Legend of the Mermaid.
48. If Heather Was a Boy?!
49. Heather's After School Routine.
50. Heather's Biggest Fear.
51. A Day in the Life of a Cheerleader.
52. Heather and the Win Win Game.
53. Heather Gets Revenge.
54. Heather Goes Back in Time.
55. Heather's Unlucky Day.
56. Heather Is Home Alone!
57. Heather's Spring Fashion.
58. Heather's Crazy Commercial.
59. Minute to Win It.
60. The Royal Ball.
61. Heather Trapped in the Caribbean Sea!
62. A Fairytale with a Twist.
63. Heather's Crazy Jobs.
64. How to Have the Perfect Sleep Over!
65. Heather Discovers a Crazy Forest.
66. 3 Truths and 1 Lie with Heather.
67. Help Heather Pick a Graduation Dress.
68. How to Spice Up Your Room.
69. Countdown to Christmas.
70. What I Got for Christmas and Holiday Travels.
71. Heather's Magical Moments.
72. Most Useful Inventions with Heather.
73. Goodbye Heather.

426 Seven Perfect Angels: Jaidyn. *youtube. com.* 2015 (Variety).

Anna and Avery, Emily, Heather, Jaidyn, Jana, Kaelyn, Laura, Lia and Mimi are young girls who entertain children with skits, talk and glimpses of their lives with friends and family. Programs, which contain no credits, are well produced and very entertaining. See each individual girl for episode information.
Jaidyn Episode List:
1. Introducing Jaidyn.
2. Caterpillar Jaidyn Becomes a Beautiful Butterfly.

3. Awesome April Teaches JoJo to Dance.
4. My Crazy Pet Giraffe.
5. Who Stole the Cookie from the Cookie Jar?
6. Jaidyn and Lyla's Epic Pizza Challenge.
7. 1 Million Views Challenge.
8. Mission Impossible.
9. Gun Range Girl Power with Jaidyn.
10. Hermione Granger ... Prime Suspect!?!
11. Eggcellent Eggstravaganza Obstacle Course.
12. The Craziest Cat Lady.
13. An Alternate Universe ... in Reverse?
14. Missing Powers.
15. Emergency YouTube Boot Camp.
16. The Princess and the YouTuber ... Miranda Sings!
17. Jaidyn Makes a Crazy Discovery ... Braces.
18. Family Oreo Challenge with Jaidyn.
19. The iPhone Jailbreak.
20. The Clumsy Fairy.
21. Strange Prank or Unexpected Admirer?
22. Jaidyn and Lyla Take the Smoothie Challenge.
23. Jaidyn's 2014 Christmas Haul.
24. Jaidyn's Christmas Spirit Story.
25. The Pesky Actress.
26. Best Day Ever.
27. Room Tour.
28. Rosa the Robot.
29. Family Yoga Challenge.
30. The Invisible Cereal Incident.

427 Seven Perfect Angels: Jana. *youtube. com.* 2015 (Variety).

Anna and Avery, Emily, Heather, Jaidyn, Jana, Kaelyn, Laura, Lia and Mimi are young girls who entertain children with skits, talk and glimpses of their lives with friends and family. Programs, which contain no credits, are well produced and very entertaining. See each individual girl for episode information.
Jana Episode List:
1. Introducing Jana.
2. Jana Is Home Alone.
3. Tabitha the Teenage Witch.
4. Jana Adopts a Kitten.
5. My Crazy Aunt Moonbeam.
6. Princess Siri and the Crown Thief.
7. The Nasty Pizza.
8. A Million YouTube Views.
9. Jana's Guardian Angel.
10. The Mermaid Kiss.
11. My Prom Date Bites.
12. The Mean Girls of Middle School.
13. My 13th Birthday: Ruined By Troublemakers.
14. A Boyfriend for a Brat.
15. Princess Siri and the Magic Surprise Egg.
16. Redneck vs. Alien.
17. The Amazing Princess from the Frozen North.
18. Mermaids and Fairies and Brats, Oh My!
19. Jeannie the Teen Genie Wants to Be Human.
20. A Forgetful Fairy Tale.

21. What if Miranda Sings Went Trick or Treating?
22. Goober Girl to the Rescue.
23. The Cookie Challenge.
24. Two Secret First Dates for Jana.
25. Goober Girl to the Rescue.
26. Frozen Fairy.
27. The Rescue of a Little Mermaid.
28. Jana Is in … a Cartoon!
29. Jana's First Day with Braces.
30. Brat-in-a-Box.

428 *Seven Perfect Angels: Kaelyn.* youtube. com. 2011 (Variety).

Anna and Avery, Emily, Heather, Jaidyn, Jana, Kaelyn, Laura, Lia and Mimi are young girls who entertain children with skits, talk and glimpses of their lives with friends and family. Programs, which contain no credits, are well produced and very entertaining. See each individual girl for episode information.

Kaelyn Episode List: 1. Introducing Kaelyn. 2. Kaelyn's Awesome Coke Machine. 3–4. Wacky Hair Color. 5. Pajama Madness!!! 6. Kaelyn's Mad Ninja Skills. 7. Kaelyn's Interesting Morning Routine. 8. Kaelyn's Epic Cupcakes. 9. Kaelyn Says … Toodles!

429 *Seven Perfect Angels: Laura.* youtube. com. 2013–2015 (Variety).

Anna and Avery, Emily, Heather, Jaidyn, Jana, Kaelyn, Laura, Lia and Mimi are young girls who entertain children with skits, talk and glimpses of their lives with friends and family. Programs, which contain no credits, are well produced and very entertaining. See each individual girl for episode information.

Laura Episode List:
1. Introducing Laura.
2. I'm a Cat???
3. Bean Boozled Challenge.
4. My Crazy Morning!
5. My Sister Is a Super Villain.
6. Pizza Challenge!! Gross Pizza.
7. A Million Prom Dresses!!
8. This Mission Is Impossible!
9. Girl Power Rules!
10. I'm a Witch! Do You Believe Me?
11. JJ Pranks Laura.
12. Will Aubrey Get the Solo?
13. Gwen's Obsessed with Her Phone.
14. Laura and Emma Switch Bodies?!?
15. Why Can't I Fly?
16. Gymnastics Boot Camp.
17. The Princess and the 3 Wishes.
18. Goodwill Trip to Cuba.
19. How the Witch Wizard Lost Her Powers.
20. How to Break Out of School.
21. The Eye Lash Fairies.
22. Laura's Unexpected Snow Day.
23. Is Laura a Princess?

24. Christmas Haul 2013.
25–26. Crazy Christmas Lights.
27. Upside Down World.
28. Elf on the Shelf Madness.
29. Laura's Room Tour.
30. What to Do When You're Bored.
31. Laura, the New iRobot!!!
32. Something New.
33. Laura Becomes Invisible!?!
34. Spooky Skit.
35. 3 Truths 1 Lie.
36. Garbage Bag Dresses.
37. Fairy Dust.
38. Tomboy Tries to Be a Girly Girl.
39. Girly Girl vs. Tomboy Madness.
40. Laura Is Jealous.
41. Trouble Maker.
42. The Back to School Monster.
43. The Crazy Costume Invasion.
44. The Magical Swing.
45. Nightmare.
46. The Day I Became a….
47. Baby Sitting Nightmare.
48. Crazy Twin.
49. Laura's Boy Outfits.
50. Hacked (Skit).
51. Laura's Biggest Fear.
52. How to Do a Scorpion.
53. Laura's Revenge.
54. Laura Becomes a Mom.
55. Bad Luck.
56. Home Alone.
57. Spring Fashion.
58. Lip Maniac 5000.
59. Minute to Win It.
60. The Show Goes On.
61. Laura Needs a Doctor.
62. Laura Is Trapped.
63. Fairy Tale.
64. Winter Olympics.
65. Crazy Jobs.
66. 17 Things to Do with Friends.
67. Laura Discovers….
68. 3 Truths and 1 Lie with a Twist.
69. Pick a Dress with Laura.
70. How to Have the Perfect Bedtime Routine.
71. A Christmas Story.
72. Christmas Haul 2014.
73. Magic Wand.
74. Invention.
75. Dream Life.
76. The Life of a Doll.
77. The Evil Sock Monkey.
78. Commercials (Skit).
79. Halloween Decorating.
80. Pranks.
81. How to Convince Your Parents to Get You a Dog.
82. Drama Queen.
83. Secret Life.

84. Worst Nightmare.
85. Back to School Clothes Haul.
86. Laura Back in Time.
87. My Strange Addiction.
88. Super Models.
89. Laura, the Curse of....
90. Laura Makes an Invention.
91. Laura's in Reverse.
92. A Day in the Life of a Super Star.
93. Behind the Scenes with Laura.
94. Questions and Answers with Laura.
95. Laura's At the Beach.
96. Gymnastics.
97. The Case of the Missing Socks.
98. The Note Maker.
99. Laura's Home Alone.
100. How to Do a Back Handspring.
101. Laura's a Hypnotist.
102. Happy Holidays.
103. Grounded.
104. The End of the World.
105. Christmas with Laura.
106. Villain!
107. DIY Valentines with Laura.
108. My Bedtime Routine.
109. My Trip to Mexico.
110. How to Make a Delicious Smoothie.
111. 60 Second Gymnastics Challenge.
112. Blind Taste Test.
113. Laura's Morning Routine.
114. Laura's Room Tour.
115. The Summer Fashion Pageant.
116. Laura Princess.
117. Angel.
118. How to Escape from a Vampire.
119. Spot the Differences.
120. My After School Routine.
121. Undercover Food Thief.
122. Laura Says Goodbye.

430 Seven Perfect Angels: Lia. *youtube.com.* 2013–2014 (Variety).

Anna and Avery, Emily, Heather, Jaidyn, Jana, Kaelyn, Laura, Lia and Mimi are young girls who entertain children with skits, talk and glimpses of their lives with friends and family. Programs, which contain no credits, are well produced and very entertaining. See each individual girl for episode information.

Lia Episode List:
1. Introducing Lia.
2. Is the Zombie Apocalypse Real?
3. Lia Becomes a Mermaid!
4. Lia's Dark Side.
5. Lia's Crazy Baby Sitter.
6. The Photo Bomber.
7. Extreme Pizza Challenge with Lia and Gabby.
8. Lia's 1 Millionth Customer ... Not!
9. OMG: A Disgusting Mess! ... Mission Impossible.
10. Girl Power Official Music Video.
11. The Wicked Smoothie.
12. Truth or Dare.
13. *Dance Moms* Parody.
14. Goodbye Lia ... Chad Is Over You!!
15. Lia's Freaky Adventure.
16. Lia's School Picture ... Epic Fail.
17. Cupcake War!! Crazy Boot Camp Training.
18. Minecraft: The Princess and the Creeper.
19. Lia Has a Starbucks Under Her New Bedroom.
20. Lia's Bedtime Routine.
21. Chad's Magical Make Over.
22. Strange Addictions with Dr. Mulberry.
23. Interviewing Boys.
24–25. Lia's Christmas Gift.
26. Lia Goes Christmas Shopping.
27. Lia's Magical Christmas Bear.
28. Lia's Disney Cruise Adventure.
29. Lia's Pesky Neighbor Chad.
30. Lia's New Room Tour.
31. Lia's Robot Goes Crazy.
32. Lia Gets Braces?!
33. Lia Has Disappeared!!!
34. Lia's Spooky Halloween Adventure.
35. My Life as Catwoman.
36. *Project Runway*: Garbage Bag Edition.
37. The Curse of the Beauty Pageant.
38. The Bean Boozled Challenge with...?
39. Gilry Girl vs. Tomboy.
40. OMG!!! Lia Is So Jealous!
41. Lia's a Troublemaker at School.
42. The Monster under My Bed.
43. Invasion of the Pig Virus.
44. Oh No, Fairytale Trouble.
45. Fun with Water, Lia and Friends.
46. Lia's Bed Bug Nightmare.
47. The Day Lia Became a Barbie.
48. Lia's Baby Sitting Nightmare.
49. Summer Fun with Lia.
50. Lia's Crazy Twin Is a Mermaid.
51. Legend of the Talking Dog.
52. Lia Has a Boyfriend.
53. Lia's Room Tour.
54. Lia's Biggest Fears.
55. Awkward Times to Cheer.
56. Lia Wins a Million Dollars.
57. Out of Control Revenge.
58. Lia and the Wizard of Socks.
59. Lia's Bad Luck Bracelet.
60. Lia Shops for Hot Spring Fashions.
61. Lia's Makeup Commercial.
62. Lia Spies on Her School Teachers.
63. Minute to Win It.
64. Prince Charming.
65. The Strange Addiction Specialist.
66. Lia Traps a Leprechaun.
67. Super BFF to the Rescue!
68. Two Princesses and a Frog.

69. The Winter Olympics with a Twist.
70. Lia's Crazy Job.
71. Lia's Odd New Friend.
72. Lia Discovers a Weird City in Her Closet.
73. 3 Truths and 1 Lie.
74. The Lazy Fairy Won't Pick a Dress.
75. Lia's Unique Valentine Card.
76. Lia's Christmas Gifts and New Year's Party.
77. The Story of the Mischievous Elf.
78. Lia's Magical Adventure.
79. Lia Invents the Yes-Inator.
80. What Lia Does When She Is Bored.
81. Goodbye Lia.

431 *Seven Perfect Angels: Mimi. youtube. com.* 2014–2015 (Variety).

Anna and Avery, Emily, Heather, Jaidyn, Jana, Kaelyn, Laura, Lia and Mimi are young girls who entertain children with skits, talk and glimpses of their lives with friends and family. Programs, which contain no credits, are well produced and very entertaining. See each individual girl for episode information.
   Mimi Episode List:
1. Introducing Mimi.
2. The Day Mimi Became a Dream Keeper.
3. Mimi's Addicted to a Song.
4. Mimi's Crazy Summer Camp.
5. The Spoiler Super Villain.
6. Mimi's Gross Pizza Challenge.
7. 1 Million Ways to Break a World Record.
8. Mission Impossible: Last Minute Math Test.
9. The Boys vs. the Girls Game Show.
10. Mimi's Bad Luck Curse.
11. Mimi's Sweet Job.
12. Mimi and Muriel Do the Dancer Tag.
13. Mimi's Crazy Cookie Obsession.
14. No Way! Mimi's President?!
15. Mimi Loses her Ninja Powers.
16. The Crazy Sister Boot Camp.
17. The Sister and the Pranks.
18. Mimi Discovers She's an Apple Whisperer!
19. Mimi Des the Bean Boozled Challenge.
20. Uh-Oh! Mimi's Trapped in a Movie.
21 Faith, Fluffy and the Fairy Dust.
22. Mimi's Strange Cousin Muriel.
23. What Mimi Got for Christmas 2014.
24. Mimi's Story of Sunny the Elf.
25. Mimi's Elf Adventure.
26. Mimi's Pesky Math Teacher.
27. Candy for Breakfast? Mimi's Best Day Ever!
28. Mimi's Room Tour.
29. Robotana, the Sassiest Robot!
30. Mimi's Awesome Cake.
31. Invisoblind!
32. Mimi's Halloween Candy Wrap.
33. Mimi's Minute to Win It.
34. Toddlers and Trash Bags.
35. Mimi's Pageant Mistake.
36. Tiffany Takes You Shopping.
37. Tiffany vs. Chris.
38. Sibling Jealousy.
39. Annabelle Is Back.
40. Mimi's Monster Sleep Over.
41. Mimi's Marshmallow Madness Invasion.
42. Fairy Tale Auditions.
43. Mimi's Crazy Hair Nightmare.
44. The Day I Became an Alien!
45. Mimi's Baby Sitting Nightmare.
46. Mimi's Summer Fun.

432 *The Seven Seas. youtube.com.* 2010 (Fantasy).

Two girls (Avery and Nikki) possess magic rings that enable them to transform into Mermaids when they come in contact with water. How they acquired the rings is not stated and it has to be assumed from the only episode that was produced that the program would follow their efforts to keep secret what they are while adjusting to their Mermaid powers.
   Cast (as credited): Avery and Nikki as Themselves. **Comment:** The program appears to have been abandoned. The girls are pretty but the picture is not very clear and has rather jerky movement.
   Episode List: 1. Shark in the Water.

433 *Seven Super Girls: CJ. youtube.com.* 2012–2015 (Variety).

Caitlin (better known as CJ), Emily, Jazzy, Jenna, Kaelyn, Katherine and Rachael (sisters), Kayla, Nicole and Oceane are young girls who host their own programs under a parentally controlled and moderated YouTube channel. Programs, which contain no credits, are well produced and very entertaining. See each individual girl for episode information.
   CJ Episode List:
1. CJ Is Your New Tuesday (Host).
2. Hidden Talents.
3. CJ's Cat Dream.
4. CJ's Planking.
5. Garbage Bag Dresses.
6. CJ's Fantasy World.
7. CJ's Interactive Challenge.
8. CJ's Gymnastics.
9. How to Be a Model with CJ.
10. CJ's Model Fashion Show.
11. How Well Do You Know CJ?
12. A Day in the Life of Lady Kaka.
13. Ellen's Dance Dare.
14. Missing Socks.
15. Dancing CJ.
16. CJ Models Her Mum's Clothes.
17. Interactive Scary Story.
18. One Armed for a Day CJ.
19. CJ's Q&A.
20. You're Going to School with CJ.
21. Stalker Doll.
22. Spam Mail.

23. You Pick CJ's Dress.
24. CJ Is the Devil.
25. CJ Is a Unicorn.
26. How to Survive a Breakup.
27. A Day in the Life of a Nerd.
28. The Magic Money Box.
29. Girly vs. Boyish.
30. You're New Tuesday, Olivia.
31. Christmas in Australia.
32. CJ vs. Her Brother at Gymnastics.
33. Mission Impossible.
34. Reality Show Disaster. CJ Is the Mess Villain.
35. Australia Day with CJ.
36. Valentine's Day from a Single Point of View.
37. How to Annoy Your Mum.
38. Safe or Dangerous?
39. The Truth Behind Lady Kaka.
40. A Dance Moms Dance Off.
41. Spring Fashion with CJ.
42. Escaping from the Paparazzi.
43. The Lady Kaka Commercial.
44. How Well Do You Know CJ?
45. Mermaid vs. Vampire.
46. The New Face of Seven Super Girls???
47. Coffee Music Video.
48. Fairy Tale Trouble.
49. My Strange Addiction: Pewdiepie.
50. If You Had One Wish.
51. Lost.
52. 5 Fairy Tales, I Video.
53. CJ Gets Revenge on Her Sister.
54. Summer Fashion CJ Style!
55. I'm an Angel.
56. 25 Facts about CJ.
57. A Surprising Visitor.
58. Minute to Win It with CJ.
59. Cat-Napped By Kaka.
60. How to Make Polka Dot Cake.
61. 15 Random Things You Do When You're Bored.
62. Best Invention Ever.
63. An Unbearably Scary Story.
64. Ever After High Music Video.
65. Dare the CJ!
66. CJ vs. Evil Witch.
67. CJ Is a Living Doll.
68. CJ's Secret Life as Lady Rara.
69. Getting Ready for a Secret Ninja Mission.
70. Blindfolded Make Over.
71. Fortune Cookie Writer.
72. A Christmas Story.
73. My Crazy Christmas.
74. Lady Kaka vs. Marina Mermaid.
75. My Super Candy Power.
76. A Very Strange Dream.
77. How to Get Your Splits Quickly.
78. 25 Things I Can't Live Without!
79. Valentine's Day from a Single Point of View.
80. How Well Do You Know SSG?
81. Set in Stone.

82. Boy Logic.
83. A Day in the Life of a She-Devil.
84. Goodbye CJ.

434 Seven Super Girls: Emily. *youtube.com.* **2014–2015 (Variety).**

Caitlin (better known as CJ), Emily, Jazzy, Jenna, Kaelyn, Katherine and Rachael (sisters), Kayla, Nicole and Oceane are young girls who host their own programs under a parentally controlled and moderated YouTube channel. Programs, which contain no credits, are well produced and very entertaining. See each individual girl for episode information.

Emily Episode List:
1. Introducing Emily.
2. Emily's Blast from the Past.
3. Grandma Comes to Visit.
4. Emily and Ruby Make AmiGamis.
5. Egg Roulette Challenge.
6. The Scariest Day.
7. The Mischievous Kitten.
8. The Day I Became an Invisible Prankster.
9. Emily's Pizza Challenge.
10. The Legend of the Russian Doll.
11. Emily's Parallel Universe.
12. The Kids' Choice Awards Game Show.
13. Behind the Scenes with Emily.
14. Emily's Animal Magic.
15. Get Set Bake.
16. Emily and the Witch's Spell.
17. Emily's Teenage Boot Camp.
18. Valentine's Day Treats.
19. The Cupcake Mystery.
20. Emily and Lola's Special Power.
21. Emily's SSG Dance.
22. Emily Can Do It.
23. Princess Isabella and the Fortune Teller.
24. What Emily Got for Christmas 2014.
25. Emily's Christmas Story.
26. Bean Boozled Challenge.
27. What a Strange Day.
28. Who Believes in Father Christmas?
29. Emily's Impossible Mission.
30. Emily Meets a Fairy.
31. Emily's Dares and Challenges.
32. Emily and the Secret Door.
33. Emily's Spooky Day.
34. The Strangest Thing Ever.
35. Emily and Her Pesky Sister.
36. Emily Does the Furry Friend Tag.
37. Emily and the Tooth Fairy.
38. Emily's Invisible Powers.
39. Emily's Blind Taste Test.
40. Emily Loses Lola.
41. Emily's Back to School Morning Routine.
42. Emily Time Travels.
43. Emily's Weird Illness.
44. Emily and the Monster Mystery.

45. Emily and Princess Lilly.
46. Emily's Worst Nightmare.

435 Seven Super Girls: Jazzy. *youtube.com.* 2014–2015 (Variety).

Caitlin (better known as CJ), Emily, Jazzy, Jenna, Kaelyn, Katherine and Rachael (sisters), Kayla, Nicole and Oceane are young girls who host their own programs under a parentally controlled and moderated YouTube channel. Programs, which contain no credits, are well produced and very entertaining. See each individual girl for episode information.

Jazzy Episode List:
1. Introducing Your Totally New Terrific Tuesday.
2. Jazzy's Video Flashback.
3. Classes with Jazzy and Grandma.
4. Jazzy's New DIY Delicious Drinks.
5. A Totally Terrific Day with Jazzy.
6. Five Nights at Jazzy's.
7. Jazzy's Failed Filming Routine.
8. Something's Fishy with Jazzy.
9. The 3 J's Pizza Challenge.
10. The Legend of April Pranks Day.
11. Jazzy's in a Game World.
12. Jazzy's Crazy Camp Experience.
13. Jazzy Gets ... Braces.
14. Jazzy's Animal Magic Spray.
15. Jazzy Sees Another Perspective ... Gasp!
16. Jazzy Joins Wizarding School.
17. Boot Camp ... Literally.
18. Jazzy's Bean Boozled Challenge.
19. Jazzy's Epic Fuzz Mystery.
20. Jazzy's Missing Magic Powers.
21. Jazzy's 15 New Dance Moves.
22. Jazzy's Breaking Boards Karate.
23. Mission Impossible: Christmas Decorating
24. What Jazzy Got for Christmas 2014.
25. Jazzy's Elf Christmas Story.
26. Jazzy's DIY Gifts.
27. Bad Jazzy Becomes a Mermaid.
28. Jazzy's Princess Test ... Fail.
29. Jazzy's Black Friday ... Fail.
30. Jazzy's Pixie Dust Commercial.
31. Dares and Challenges with Jazzy.
32. Jazzy's After Midnight Routine.
33. Jazzy's Super Spooky Halloween.
34. Jazzy's Strange Dream.
35. Jazzy's Pesky Morning.
36. Jazzy's Power Shopping Trip.
37. Jazzy's Water Fun ... During Fall!
38. Jazzy's Fairy Make Over.
39. Jazzy's Invisible Wishes.
40. Jazzy Follows Her own Destiny.
41. DIY School Supplies with Jazzy.
42. Jazzy Travels Through Time.
43. Jazzy's Allergic To...
44. The Monster in Jazzy's Closet.
45. Jazzy's Princess 101 Class.

46. Jazzy and the Donut Portal.
47. Jazzy's Peanut Butter Curse.
48. Jazzy's Sleepover War.
49. 10 Things About Jazzy.
50. It's a Jazzy and Jazzunel Sleep Over.
51. Jazzy Baby Sits Bad Joshua.
52. The Day Jazzy Became a Hipster.
53. Jazzy's Laundry Invasion.
54. Jazzy's Saturday Routine.
55. The Legend of the Unknown Super Girl.
56. Spring Fashion with Jazzy.
57. Jazzy Gets Revenge on Her Brother.
58. Jazzy's House Tour.
59. How to Be a Clown.
60. How to Be a Clown.
61. Jazzy's House Is Haunted.
62. Jazzy's an Undercover Donut Spy.
63. Jazzy's Lost Unicorn.

436 Seven Super Girls: Jenna. *youtube.com.* 2011–2015 (Variety).

Caitlin (better known as CJ), Emily, Jazzy, Jenna, Kaelyn, Katherine and Rachael (sisters), Kayla, Nicole and Oceane are young girls who host their own programs under a parentally controlled and moderated YouTube channel. Programs, which contain no credits, are well produced and very entertaining. See each individual girl for episode information.

Jenna Episode List:
1. Introducing Jenna.
2. Girl Power.
3. Blast from the Past.
4. A Trip to Grandma's.
5. Jenna Tries Something New.
6. Jenna's Updated Morning Routine.
7. Jenna's Scary Story.
8. Jenna and the Mischievous Mouse.
9. The Day I Became a Mind Reader.
10. The Pizza Challenge with Jenna.
11. Jenna and the Legend of the Lake Monster.
12. Jenna's Parallel World.
13. Jenna's Kids' Choice Awards Trivia with a Twist.
14. Jenna's Christmas 2011.
15. Jenna and the Magic Peacock.
16. Jenna and the Strange Letter.
17. Jenna and the Wish Wizard.
18. Super Model Boot Camp.
19. Jenna's Charming Prince AmiGami.
20. Jenna and the Mystery of the Missing Chapstick.
21. Jenna and the Missing Power.
22. So Jenna Thinks She Can Dance.
23. Jenna Does It Bella Style.
24. The Princess and the Mixed Up Narrator.
25. Christmas Haul with Jenna and Friends.
26. A Jenna Christmas Story.
27. Jenna Studies for Finals.
28. Jenna's Strange Day.

151. Jenna's 3 Favorite Things.
152. Haunted.
153. Jenna's Crazy Adventure.
154. Jenna Answers Your Questions.
155. Jenna Impersonates ... Who?
156. In the Kitchen ... Pizza.
157. Jenna Is a Mermaid.
158. Jenna's Winter Fashion.
159. The Making of a Dead School Girl.
160. Jenna's Auditions (Closed).
161. Emo.
162. Jenna's Pushup Challenge.
163. Halloween.
164. Gross!!!
165. Werewolf.
166. Makeup Tutorial.
167. When Jenna Grows Up.
168. Jenna's Dance Moves.
169. Jenna's Cheerleading Routine.
170. Jenna Goes Freestyle.
171. Jenna's Pick a Dress.
172. Jenna's Wacky Adventure.
173. Wacky Hair.

437 Seven Super Girls: Kaelyn. *youtube. com.* 2012–2015 (Variety).

Caitlin (better known as CJ), Emily, Jazzy, Jenna, Kaelyn, Katherine and Rachael (sisters), Kayla, Nicole and Oceane are young girls who host their own programs under a parentally controlled and moderated YouTube channel. Programs, which contain no credits, are well produced and very entertaining. See each individual girl for episode information.

In addition to playing herself, Kaelyn also plays Mimi, the adorable Mermaid (who yearns to experience life as a human girl) and Lucy, her pretty but bratty, tantrum-throwing younger sister (in other words, a drama queen). Kaelyn's episodes are the most popular with over 93 million hits for a single episode and over four-and-one-half billion views for her entire series.

Kaelyn Episode List:
1. Meet Kaelyn.
2. The Day Kaelyn Became a Zombie!?
3. The Pizza Challenge with Kaelyn!
4. The Legend of the Kiss.
5. A Parallel World of Lucy.
6. The Ultimate Obstacle Course.
7. At Your Request: Kaelyn's Morning Routine.
8. Warning: Giant Animal Like Peep on the Loose!
9. This Isn't Kaelyn's Life ... Is It!
10. A Day in the Life of WizLocke the Wizard.
11. Boot Camp Gone Wrong!
12. The Curse.
13. An Unexplained Mystery!
14. Missing Powers: Kaelyn Saves the Day.
15. Lucy vs. Kaelyn: Dance Wars.
16. Kaelyn Takes on the Challenge.
17. Princess Tatiana & the Book of Crowns.
18. Kaelyn's Christmas Special & Ham.
19. Mr. Smiley: A Strange Christmas Story.
20. A Day Out with Kaelyn.
21. Holidays Schmolidays.
22. Secret Notes.
23. Mission Impossible: Up All Night.
24. Fairy Dust Disaster!
25. Dares & Challenges with Kaelyn and Lucy.
26. The Tail of Mimi the Mermaid.
27. Kaelyn's Halloween Extravaganza.
28. Kaelyn's Past Characters Pester Her!
29. Kaelyn's DIY Halloween Goodies!
30. A Day with Lucy.
31. Fairies at War.
32. Is Kaelyn Really Invisible?
33. Lost Forever? The Princess Crown.
34. Back to School Kaelyn Style.
35. Kaelyn's Time Travel Disaster.
36. Kaelyn Comes Down with a Weird Illness.
37. Monsters in Kaelyn's Room.
38. The Missing Princess Crown.
39. Public School? Kaelyn Is Trapped in a Nightmare.
40. Has a Crime Occurred at Kaelyn's House?
41. Minute to Win It Showdown!
42. Kaelyn's Guide to a Perfect Sleep Over.
43. Kaelyn and Bailey Go on a Shopping Adventure.
44. The Return of Mimi the Mermaid.
45. What a Nightmare: Kaelyn Baby Sits Lucy.
46. The Day I Became Dr. Higglebottom.
47. Invaded by Minecraft.
48. The Truth Spell.
49. The Legend of the Love Necklace.
50. Kaelyn's Spring Fashion.
51. Kaelyn Gets Revenge!
52. Kaelyn's House Tour.
53. The Singing Clown.
54. Is Kaelyn's House Haunted?
55. Undercover: Desperate for Brownies.
56. Kaelyn's Draw My Life.
57. Kaelyn and the Bad Luck Penny.
58. Kaelyn's Bathroom Tour.
59. What ... Kaelyn Becomes a Boy?
60. The Crazy Game Show.
61. The Mysterious Diary.
62. 25 Things Kaelyn Can't Live Without.
63. Kaelyn's New Room Tour.
64. What a Weird Dream.
65. Reading Minds: Kaelyn's Crazy Power.
66. Lucy's Morning Routine.
67. Kaelyn's Christmas 2013.
68. A Christmas Story ... with a Twist.
69. Kaelyn's Crazy Jobs.
70. Natural or Made Up? You Decide!
71. Help Kaelyn Shop for Her New Room.
72. Ninja Kaelyn's Training Missions.
73. Garbage Bag Fashionista.
74. My Secret Life As ...

75. Life Through the Eyes of a Doll.
76. Kaelyn Needs Help!
77. Kaelyn Does Your Dares & Challenges.
78. Ever After High Music Video.
79. 10 Random Things You Don't Know About Kaelyn.
80. Kaelyn's Not So Scary Story.
81. Invention ... Gone Wrong!
82. What Kaelyn Does When She Is Bored.
83. How to Fake Being Sick! (Fail).
84. The Dog Snatcher.
85. Lucy's Return.
86. Kaelyn's Birthday Gifts!
87. Kaelyn's Summer Fashion!
88. Sweet Revenge.
89. The Curse of the Dance Shoes.
90. Kaelyn's Things are Lost!
91. The Annoying Genie.
92. My Strange Addiction ... Eating Soap!
93. A Message from Kaelyn.
94. Kaelyn Is Red Riding Hood?
95. Suzie Gets a Make Over!
96. Shy Suzie vs. Glamorous Gretchen.
97. How to Be Like Kaelyn.
98. My Home School Routine.
99. More Questions, More Answers.
100. My Escape from the Reality of ... Life!
101. Spring Fashion Kaelyn Style.
102. The World of Princess Lucy.
103. The Dangerous ... Doll.
104. Kaelyn's Tips on Surviving Your Parents.
105. Where Did Kaelyn's Thumbs Go?
106. Seven Super Girls: Kaelyn.
107. Is Lucy a Drama Queen?
108. Kaelyn's Valentine Favorites.
109. Help Kaelyn Shop.
110. Symptoms of Pajama Madness.
111. The Criminal Hypnotist.
112. Kaelyn's on TV.
113. Kaelyn's Impossible Mission.
114. Kaelyn Shows You What She Got for Christmas.
115. It's Christmas Time with Kaelyn.
116. Gianna Needs Your Help.
117. Girly Girl Gianna or Tomboy Alice.
118. Kaelyn Receives a Surprise.
119. What Happens Next?
120. If Kaelyn Was a Nerd...
121. Which Witch Would You Pick?
122. No Electronics! How Will Kaelyn Survive?
123. Elfiona the Elf.
124. Dresses, Dresses, Dresses!
125. Chain Mail.
126. Kaelyn's American Girls.
127. The Unlucky One.
128. Kaelyn's After School Routine.
129. Kaelyn's School Bedtime Routine.
130. Kaelyn Shows You Her Mom's Clothes.
131. Don't Close Your Eyes (Music Video).
132. Where Do Missing Socks Go?

133. A Day in the Life of Kaelyn.
134. It's Summer Fashion Time.
135. Pageant Princess Lucy?
136. Dance Styles.
137. Kaelyn's Morning Routine.
138. SSG Dance Contest.
139–140. Mall Madness.
141. My Fantasy World.
142. The Alien Abduction.
143–144. Barbie: Curse of the Missing Dress.
145. Kaelyn Goes Planking.
146. Toodles Needs a Home.
147. 3 Truths and 1 Lie.
148. Kaelyn's Epic Room Tour.
149. Kaelyn's a Barbie Girl!
150. Kaelyn Does ... Sit Ups?
151. Kaelyn Goes Backwards.
152. My Life as a Super Model.
153. The Mystery Valentine.
154. Can You Spot the Differences?
155. Kaelyn Can't Live Without...

438 Seven Super Girls: Katherine and Rachael. *youtube.com.* 2011–2015 (Variety).

Caitlin (better known as CJ), Emily, Jazzy, Jenna, Kaelyn, Katherine and Rachael (sisters), Kayla, Nicole and Oceane are young girls who host their own programs under a parentally controlled and moderated YouTube channel. Programs, which contain no credits, are well produced and very entertaining. See each individual girl for episode information.

Katherine and Rachael Episode List:
1. The Granny Olympics.
2. Katherine and Rachael Go Thrift Shopping.
3. Katherine and Rachael Go to the Aquarium.
4. The Scariest of Stories.
5. The Mischievous Leprechaun.
6. The Day Rachael Became President.
7. Katherine and Rachael's Pizza Challenge.
8. The Legend of the Gnome.
9. Parallel Universes.
10. Katherine and Rachael's KCA Competitions.
11. Katherine and Rachael Taste New Food.
12. Magically Swapped.
13. Who's Got Your Back?
14. Which Witch Will Win This Witch Pageant?
15. Super Hero Boot Camp.
16. Katherine and Rachael React to Old Videos.
17. An Epic Annie Mystery.
18. The Power of the Pickle.
19. The Dance.
20. Katherine and Rachael Play Football.
21. The Princess and the Popper.
22. Katherine and Rachael's Christmas Gifts.
23. A Dogalicious Christmas.
24. Another Cinderella Story.
25. Strange and Unexpected.
26. Santa's Watching.
27. Mission Impossible.

146. Katherine and Rachael's Garbage Bag Dresses.
147–148. Katherine and Rachael's Planking.
149. Crazy Cat People.
150. Makeup Review.
151. Room Tours.
152. Katherine Is a Barbie.
153. The Sit-Up Challenge with the Eiffel Tower.
154. Our Backwards World.
155. Our Lives as Super Models.
156. Extreme Tub Make Over.
157–158. Love Potion.
159. The Truth Behind Katherine and Rachael's Videos.
160. Spot the Difference Melting Crayons.
161. 3 Things We Could Not Live Without.
162. Haunted House.
163. Katherine and Rachael's Christmas.
164. Impersonations with Katherine and Rachael.
165. Delicious Oreo Balls.
166. A Mixed-Up Fairy Tale.
167. Winter Fashion Show.
168. Return of the School Girl.
169. Auditions for Katherine and Rachael (Closed).
170. Emo Girls.
171. The Push Up Challenge.
172. Halloween with Katherine and Rachael.
173. Rachael and Katherine's Super Powers.
174. Gross Smoothie.
175. The Signs of Being a Werewolf.
176. Rachael and Katherine Are Pop Stars.
177. When Katherine and Rachael Grow Up.
178. Dance!
179. Rachael and Katherine's Cheer.
180. Rachael's Blind Taste Test.
181. Katherine and Rachael's Dresses.
182. Wacky Hairstyles.
183. Rachael and Katherine's Morning Routine.
184. Girl Power Spray.
185. Rachael's Weird Dream.
186. The Year 3011.
187. Making Waffles with Rachael and Katherine.
188. Katherine and Rachael Then and Now.

439 Seven Super Girls: Kayla. *youtube.com.* 2011–2015 (Variety).

Caitlin (better known as CJ), Emily, Jazzy, Jenna, Kaelyn, Katherine and Rachael (sisters), Kayla, Nicole and Oceane are young girls who host their own programs under a parentally controlled and moderated YouTube channel. Programs, which contain no credits, are well produced and very entertaining. See each individual girl for episode information.
Kayla Episode List:
1. What's Going On? Everything Is New.
2. Kayla's Homework Trick.
3. Kayla and the Ghost Lady.
4. The Mischievous Fairy.
5. The Day I Became a Ghost.
6. Kayla Takes on the Pizza Challenge!

7. The Legend of the Granola Bar.
8. If This Were a Parallel World.
9. So You Wanna Be a Princess?
10. Spring Break Surprise.
11. The Necklace That Makes Dreams Come True.
12. Are You Ready for Wizard School.
13. Babysitting Boot Camp.
14. Kayla Goes to Play List Live.
15. Kayla Scares Herself.
16. Use It … Wisely.
17. New Dance Craze.
18. Girls Can Too Do It.
19. Princess Chloe Lost her Crown.
20. Christmas with Kayla.
21. How Kayla Saved Christmas.
22. The Unlucky Lucky Socks!
23. Unexpected Wish Come True.
24. Let's Go on an Adventure.
25. Kayla's Time Traveling Mission.
26. Descended From Fairies.
27. Return of the Ghost.
28. Kayla's Ghost Friend.
29. Super Kayla's Strange Day.
30. Kayla's Pesky Clone.
31. Alice the Nerd.
32. Kate vs. the Evil Lady.
33. Invisible Kayla.
34. Kayla's Solo Cheer Competition.
35. Kayla's Phone … Lost or Stolen?
36. Kayla's School Morning Routine.
37. Kayla's Time Traveling Adventure.
38. Kayla's Weird Illness.
39. There's a Monster in Kayla's Closet.
40. Princess Kaylarella.
41. Kayla's Worst Nightmare.
42. Audition to Be a Magical Creature.
43. Kayla Plays Minute to Win It.
44. A Sleepover Disaster.
45. Kayla's Updated Gymnastics.
46. Kate's Magical Fairy Tale.
47. How Not to Have a Babysitting Nightmare.
48. The Day Kayla Became a Cheerleader.
49. The Invasion of the Shoes.
50. The Furry Friend Tag Featuring Misty.
51. The Legend of the Missing Homework.
52. Spring Fashion 2013 with Kayla.
53. Revenge of the Kitten Cat.
54. Kayla's House Tour.
55. Kayla Visits a Haunted Hotel.
56. Kayla and Her Cousin Go Undercover.
57. Kayla Draws Her life.
58. Kayla's Bad Luck.
59. Kayla Answers Your Questions.
60. Kayla Is a Boy!
61. The Awesome Kayla Show.
62. Gymnastics with Kayla.
63. 25 Things Kayla Can't Live Without.
64. Rewrite Your Destiny.
65. Kayla's Weird Dream.
66. Kayla's Weird Super Power.

67. Kayla Stole Lauren's Cat.
68. Kayla's Awesome Christmas Haul.
69. Kayla's Christmas Catastrophe.
70. Kayla's Crazy Job.
71. What's in Kayla's Cheer Bag?
72. Kayla's Blindfolded Taste Test.
73. Kayla's Secret Ninja Mission.
74. Kayla's Garbage Bag Dress.
75. The Secret Life of Kayla the Chapstick Fanatic.
76. Kayla's a Real Doll.
77. Kayla the Mummy.
78. Kayla's Dares and Challenges.
79. "Ever After High" Music Video.
80. Kayla's "Scary" Story.
81. Kayla's New Invention.
82. 3 Things Kayla Does When She's Bored.
83. How to Study (Fail).
84. Where Is My Blanket?
85. Kayla's Minute to Win It.
86. Lauren's Back.
87. Brother Does My Makeup Challenge.
88. Kayla Attempts to Be an Angel.
89. Summer Fashion with Kayla.
90. Kayla Gets Revenge on Anna Jane.
91. Airhead Abbey Fairy Tale Adventure.
92. Kayla Shouldn't Be a Genie.
93. My Strange Addiction.
94. We're in Trouble.
95. Airhead Abbey Gets Ready for a Dance.
96. Are You Kayla or Lauren?
97. Kayla's Weekend Morning Routine.
98. Escape a Bad Hair Day.
99. Kayla's Spring Fashion 2014.
100. "Dance Mom's" Trailer (Parody).
101. Kayla vs. Lauren.
102. Gymnastics at the Beach.
103. Dangerous Bucket List.
104. How to Convince Your Parents.
105. The Girl with No Thumbs.
106. Drama Queen Tips.
107. Cupid's Valentine Help.
108. Relatable Things.
109. Kayla's Pajama Revenge.
110. Bring It On.
111. Save the World ... Gymnastics Style.
112. Gymnastics Grading Level 1–6.
113. It's Christmas Time with Kayla.
114. A Day in the Life of Tiffany.
115. The Sweet Revenge.
116. How Will It End?
117. Kayla's Do's and Don'ts for Being a Nerd.
118. Kayla's Top 5 Gymnastics Skills.
119. Mythical Makeup Kayla.
120. Halloween Experiments.
121. Dresses by Kayla.
122. Kayla Gets Chain Mail.
123. Kayla's Throwback Tag.
124. Strangers.
125. My School Schedule.
126. Kayla Answers Some Questions from You Guys.
127. Kayla's One-Armed for the Day.
128. Kayla Goes to a Bat Mitzvah.
129. My Mom's Clothed Fashion Show.
130. Dance!
131. The Girl Who Was Obsessed with Socks.
132. A Day in the Life of the Birthday Girl.
133. Kayla's Freestylin' Firecracker & Fireworks.
134. Kayla's Summer Fashion.
135. Kayla Is a Glitz Beauty Queen.
136. How to Do Double Braided Pigtails.
137. Gymnastics with a Twist.
138. Kayla's Dream.
139. Ellen's Dance Dare.
140. Kayla's Fantasy World.
141. Alien Makeover.
142. My Life as a Cheerleader.
143. Planking with Kayla.
144. Kitty Hair Styles.
145. Kayla's Bedroom Tour.
146. Barbie: I Can Be Anything I Want to Be.
147. Sit Up Challenge with Kayla.
148. Awesome Backwards Contest.
149. A Day in the Life of Kayla the Super Model.
150. Kayla's Valentine's Day.
151. Kayla's Melted Crayon Fail.
152. Kayla's Spot the Difference.
153. Kayla's 3 Things.
154. Kayla's Fun with Fire and Marshmallows.
155. Kayla's Christmas.
156. Christmas Cookies with Kayla.
157. Kayla's Collaboration.
158. Kayla's Winter Fashion and Hair Styling.
159. Kayla's Auditions.
160. Audition Results.
161. Kayla's Sunset Timelaps.
162. Kayla's Pushup Challenge.
163. Ugly Pumpkin Contest.
164. Super Powers.
165. Gross!
166. Attack of the ...
167. Kayla's Crazy Cartwheels.
168. Justin Bieber vs. Dustin Vieber.
169. Kayla Grows Up.
170. Random Dancing with Kayla.
171. Kayla's New Bedroom Tour.
172. Kayla's Favorite Dresses Fashion Show.
173. Kayla's Strange Adventure.
174. Bye Bye Kayla.
175. Kayla's Time Travel.
176. Kayla's Blind Taste Test Challenge.
177. Kayla's Perfect Cartwheel Challenge.
178. Randomness with Kayla.
179. Kayla's Blind Tasks.
180. Bedtime Kayla.
181. Gymnastics Through the Years with Kayla.
182. Kayla's Dance Contest.
183. Kayla's Stop Motion Fashion Show.
184. After School with Kayla.

185. Are You a Vampire?
186. Hypnotics are Crazy.
187. Kayla's Harry Potter Experience.
188. Kayla's Impossible Mission.
189. Kayla Shows You How to Draw a Lightening Storm.
190. Kayla's Bedroom Tour.
191. Kayla Needs Coffee (Music Video).

440 *Seven Super Girls: Nicole.* youtube.com. 2012–2015 (Variety).

Caitlin (better known as CJ), Emily, Jazzy, Jenna, Kaelyn, Katherine and Rachael (sisters), Kayla, Nicole and Oceane are young girls who host their own programs under a parentally controlled and moderated YouTube channel. Programs, which contain no credits, are well produced and very entertaining. See each individual girl for episode information.

Nicole Episode List:
1. Meet Nicole.
2. A Grandma's Morning Routine.
3. Nicole's New Pet.
4. Home Alone.
5. The Mischievous Mystery.
6. The Day I Saw Your Future.
7. Nicole's Pizza Challenge.
8. Legend of the Flower Necklace.
9. A World without WIFI!
10. Nicole Gets Ready for the Kids' Choice Awards.
11. Nicole's After School Routine.
12. Nicole Has CAT Powers ... What!?
13. Nikki's Fashion Sneak Peek.
14. Nicole Is a Wizard.
15. Girly Girl 101 Boot Camp.
16. Nicole's Valentine Cookie Disaster.
17. The Mystery of the Missing Backpack.
18. Missing Mom Powers.
19. Seven Super Dance Moves.
20. Extreme Home Makeover Girl Edition.
21. The Princess and the Tea.
22. Nicole Goes Christmas Shopping
23. Nicole's Christmas Haul.
24. A Very Mermaid Christmas.
25. Unexpected Christmas Gifts.
26. Nicole's Worst Day Ever.
27. Nicole's Mission Impossible.
28. Nicole's Magical Pixie Dust.
29. Nicole's Dares and Challenges.
30. The Day I Became an Actress.
31. Vampires Bedtime Routine.
32. Nicole's Strange Addiction: Chapstick.
33. The Pesky ... I Don't Know.
34. Nicole's Blind for a Day.
35. Gilry Girl Wars.
36. The Fairy Book ... Gone Wrong.
37. Nicole's Day of Being Invisible.
38. The Yoga Challenge.
39. Nicole's Lost Money.
40. Nicole's After School Routine.
41. Nicole Time Travels.
42. Nicole's Crazy Illness: Turning into a Pig!
43. Girly Girl Monster Makeover.
44. A Day in the Life of Sassy Princess Nikki.
45. Nicole's Biggest Nightmare ... No More Hair Flowers.
46. The Missing Money.
47. Nicole's Summer Fun.
48. Nicole's Minute to Win It Games.
49. How to Have a Fabulous Sleepover.
50. Nicole's Summer Morning Routine.
51. Lost in a Backwards World.
52. Babysitting Disaster! Watching Bratty Nikki.
53. The Day I Became Taylor Swift.
54. Online Shopping Invasion.
55. Things to Do on a Rainy Day.
56. The Legend of the Nerd.
57. Nicole's Spring Fashion.
58. Nicole's Oreo Revenge.
59. Nicole's Dream Job: A Clown.
60. Nicole's Haunted Basement.
61. How to Hunt for Ghosts.
62. Draw My Life.
63. Nicole's Bad Luck Day.
64. Cheesy Pickup Lines.
65. Seven Super Girls Game Show.
66. True Hearts Day.
67. 25 Things Nicole Can't Live Without.
68. Nicole's Nerdy Twin.
69. Nicole's Weird Dream.
70. Nicole Can Teleport.
71. The Stuff Girly Girls Say.
72. What Nicole Got for Christmas.
73. Girly Girl Christmas Disaster.
74. Super Crazy Jobs.
75. What's in My Backpack?
76. Get Anything You Want.
77. How to Be a Ninja.
78. Nicole's Garbage Bag Dress.
79. My Secret Life as a Nerd.
80. Nicole Meets a Living Doll.
81. Will the Curse Be Lifted?
82. Nicole's Dares and Challenges.
83. Blindfold Taste Test.
84. Home Alone.
85. Nicole's New Invention.
86. What to Do When You're Bored.
87. Nicole's Minute to Win It.
88. Who Did It?
89. Nerd's Bedtime Routine.
90. Angel or Demon?
91. Summer Fashion 2013.
92. Nicole Gets Revenge.
93. Trapped By a Troll (Fairy Tale).
94. How to Find Lost Items.
95. Genie Wishes.
96. My Strange Addiction: Hair Flowers.
97. Nicole vs. Evil Dragon.
98. Nicole's Improved Style.

99. Nicole Is a Tomboy.
100. Goodbye Girly Girl Skirts.
101. How to Be Like Nicole.
102. Nicole's Bedtime Routine.
103. Nicole's Room Tour.
104. How to Escape Going to School.
105. Spring Fashion.
106. "Dance Moms"—Maddie Forgets Her Solo (Parody).
107. Wonderless Wonderland.
108. After School Routine with Nicole.
109. Dangers of Being a Girly Girl.
110. How to Survive Your Parents.
111. Drama Queen.
112. What to Do on Valentine's Day.
113. Blind Folded Taste Test.
114. The Girly Girl Stealer.
115. Reality Show Takedown.
116. Girly Girl Bedtime Routine.
117. Christmas Haul 2012.
118. Nicky's Morning Routine.
119. Nick or Nicky?
120. Nicole's Scavenger Hunt.
121–122. Scavenger Hunt.
123. A Nerd's Morning Routine.
124. Nicole's Bedtime Routine.
125. How to Survive Being Grounded.
126. Dresses.
127. Chain Mail.
128. 3 Truths and 1 Lie.
129. Home Alone.
130. School Fashion.
131. Nicole Answers Your Questions.
132. One Arm for a Day.
133. Nicole's Morning Routine.
134. My Mom's Clothes.
135. Zero to Phantom Music Video.
136. What Happens to Socks?
137. A Day in the Life of an Orphan.
138. Nicole Is Blind.
139. Nicole's Summer Fashion.
140. Nicole Gets a Make Over.
141. Pick a Dress.
142. Nicole Time Travels.
143. Who Stole the Cookies from the Cookie Jar?
144. Smoothie Challenge.
145. Goodbye Georgie/Hello Nicole.
146. "Ever After High" Music Video.
147. Nicole Recreates Her Past Videos.

441 Seven Super Girls: Oceane. *youtube. com.* 2012–2014 (Variety).

Caitlin (better known as CJ), Emily, Jazzy, Jenna, Kaelyn, Katherine and Rachael (sisters), Kayla, Nicole and Oceane are young girls who host their own programs under a parentally controlled and moderated YouTube channel. Programs, which contain no credits, are well produced and very entertaining. See each individual girl for episode information.

Oceane Episode List:
1. Introducing Oceane.
2. A Tribute to Oceane.
3. 5 Ways to Have an Awesome Date.
4. The Easiest Way to Get Famous on the Internet.
5. Quick Fall Makeup.
6. Weird Adventures in the Tub.
7. Free Tour of the Backwards Island.
8. Fake Sit Up Challenge.
9. Barbie's Death!
10. Room Tour: Fort Narina.
11. The Kitty Swap Movie Trailer.
12. Planking, Seizuring, Falling, Oceaning.
13. The Scary House of the Dead School Girl.
14. The Girl Who Loved Green.
15. The Secret Fantasy World in Oceane's House.
16. Oceane's Bedtime Routine.
17. The Interactive SSG Quiz.
18. Angry Birds Is So Violent!
19. Glitz, Glam, Drama.
20. Summer Fashion with Oceane.
21. A Day in the Life of a Tissue.
22. Truth or Dare with Oceane and Celia.
23. The Sock's Revenge.
24. Snooter Don't Care.
25. Oceane Tries Her Mom's Clothes.
26. Back to School: Expectations vs. Reality.
27. Oceane Has One Arm?!
28. Oceane Gets Interviewed ... By You!
29. My Dream School.
30. The Killer Basement.
31. Minute to Lose It.
32. How to Have a Sleepover with Yourself.
33. The Noodle Challenge.
34. How to Get Rid of a Witch.
35. Baby Sitting Myself.
36. The Day I Became a Seven Super Girls Member!
37. Invaded By Problems.
38. Stuck in TV Shows.
39. The Legend of Seven Super Girls.
40. Oceane's 2013 Spring Fashion.
41. Easter's Revenge.
42. Oceane's House Tour.
43. Spot the Clown.
44. Deep Thoughts about Dresses.
45. How to Scare Your Parents.
46. Oceane's Secret Identity.
47. Draw My Life.
48. Does Oceane Have Bad Luck?
49. Oceane's After School Routine.
50. How to Get a Boy to Notice You.
51. Internet Addict Games.
52. 25 Things I Can't Live Without.
53. The Same Faces.
54. Oceane's Secret Power!
55. Christmas Room Tour.
56. The Mysterious Christmas Gift.
57. The 5 Coolest Jobs.

58. 3 Things to Try.
59. Where Is the Chocolate Bar?
60. Oceane Is a Total Fashion Designer!
61. What's It's Like to Be YouTube Famous.
62. Dares with Oceane.
63. Rewrite Your Destiny.
64. The Girl in the Mirror.
65. Making Useless Objects Useful.
66. What Girls Do When They're Bored.
67. Minute to Win It with Oceane.
68. Oceane's Biggest Fan.
69. Oceane's Fabulous Room Tour.
70. Are You an Angel or a Demon?
71. Pick Oceane's Summer Outfit.
72. Revenge, Greatest New Object.
73. The Nutella Princess.
74. Why Do Hair Ties Disappear?
75. Never Mess with Starbucks.
76. The Cup Song Addiction.
77. SSG is Trapped.
78. SSG's Beauty Pageant.
79. You Could Be Oceane's Best Friend!
80. Oceane Tries Gymnastics.
81. How to Escape from the Zombie Apocalypse.
82. Dress Oceane for Spring.
83. Oceane Spoofs *Dance Moms*.
84. What Really Happened to the Missing School Girl?
85. Extreme Twister.
86. Dangerous Objects to Avoid.
87. What Not to Do When You're Angry at Your Parents.
88. Oceane Cuts off Her Thumb!
89. How to Annoy a Drama Queen.
90. Valentines for Singles.
91. Pajama Party!
92. Seven Super Girls Reality Show.
93. Nutella Problems.
94. Oceane's Biggest Secret.
95. 3 Things to Do Before 2013.
96. Christmas Gifts for People You Don't Like.
97. Help Rrrrh Find Her Nail Polish.
98. Girly or Tomboy.
99. How to Make Your Own Nutella.
100. Finish Oceane's Video!
101. Oceane's a Nerd Wannabe!
102. Oceane's Interactive Dress Up Game.
103. How to Not Die in Math Class.
104. Help Oceane Go to Unicorn Land.
105. Oceane's Ultimate Halloween Quiz.
106. Goodbye Oceane.

442 Seven Twinkling Tweens: Contessa. *youtube.com.* 2014–2015 (Variety).

Contessa, Ellie, Emily, Holly, Jaidyn, Jazz, Jessica, Kaelyn, Lauren, Luella, Madison, Penny and Tamara are young girls who entertain children via skits (including creating their own characters) while also re-lating facts about themselves and how they deal with life at school, at home and with friends. See each individual girl's name for episode information.

Contessa Episode List:
1. Introducing Contessa.
2. Finding the Secret Box.
3. Contessa's Party Fail.
4. Vikki the Villain's Morning Routine.
5. Is Contessa a Drama Queen? You Decide!
6. 5 Things I Do When I'm Bored in Class.
7. Tilly Goes to Princess Boot Camp.
8. The Life of Contessa's Pet Unicorn.
9. Contessa's Impossible Mission.
10. Beautifying Spray Commercial.
11. Is Contessa's New House Haunted?
12. The Princess and the Potions.
13. The Day Contessa Became a Boy!
14. Invasion of the Marshmallows.
15. If Contessa Were Invisible.
16. Contessa's 2014 Christmas Haul.
17. The Tale of Ella and Jasmine the Elves.
18. Five of Contessa's Biggest Fears.
19. Morning Routine.
20. Belle's Interview.
21. Contessa's Dares and Challenges.
22. The Year 3000.
23. The Day I Became a Monster.
24–25. Tillie's Return.
26. Contessa's Gymnastics Tricks.
27. Opposite Day.
28. Contessa's Bedtime Routine.
29. The "Monster" in Contessa's Closet.
30. Contessa Baby Sits Tilly.
31. Contessa's Crazy Twin.
32. The Legend of Elsa's Tiara.
33. Summer Fun with Contessa.
34. Goodbye Contessa.

443 Seven Twinkling Tweens: Ellie. *you tube.com.* 2014 (Variety).

Contessa, Ellie, Emily, Holly, Jaidyn, Jazz, Jessica, Kaelyn, Lauren, Luella, Madison, Penny and Contessa, Ellie, Emily, Holly, Jaidyn, Jazz, Jessica, Kaelyn, Lauren, Luella, Madison, Penny and Tamara are young girls who entertain children via skits (including creating their own characters) while also relating facts about themselves and how they deal with life at school, at home and with friends. See each individual girl's name for episode information.

Ellie Episode List: *1.* Introducing Ellie. *2.* Ellie's Baby Sitting Nightmare. *3.* The Opposite Universe. *4.* Ellie's Gymnastics. *5.* The Nerdy Troublemaker. *6.* The Monster Showdown. *7.* Ellie's Night Time Routine. *8.* Goodbye Ellie.

444 Seven Twinkling Tweens: Emily. *you tube.com.* 2013 (Variety).

Contessa, Ellie, Emily, Holly, Jaidyn, Jazz, Jessica,

Kaelyn, Lauren, Luella, Madison, Penny and Tamara are young girls who entertain children via skits (including creating their own characters) while also relating facts about themselves and how they deal with life at school, at home and with friends. See each individual girl's name for episode information.

Emily Episode List: *1.* Introducing Emily. *2.* Emily Answers Your Questions. *3.* Lola's Journey Official Trailer. *4.* Emily Makes Halloween Treats. *5.* Sleepover Spot the Difference. *6.* Another Boring Sunday. *7.* Extraordinary Surprise! *8.* Angel in Disguise. *9.* Emily Does Wreck This Journal! *10.* Emily Has Super Powers. *11.* Minute to Win It. *12.* Emily's Delicious Talent. *13.* A Day in the Life of a Parent. *14.* Emily's Summer Fashion. *15.* Ella's Energizing Smoothies. *16.* Energetic Ella vs. Couch Potato Chloe. *17.* Water Time Challenge. *18.* Emily Does Gymnastics. *19.* Fun with Water. *20.* Emily's Room Tour. *21.* Emily Saves the Day! *22.* Hats—My Strange Addiction. *23.* Emily vs. Princess Lily. *24.* Emily's Magical Journey. *25.* Emily Says Goodbye.

445 Seven Twinkling Tweens: Holly. *youtube.com.* 2014 (Variety).

Contessa, Ellie, Emily, Holly, Jaidyn, Jazz, Jessica, Kaelyn, Lauren, Luella, Madison, Penny and Tamara are young girls who entertain children via skits (including creating their own characters) while also relating facts about themselves and how they deal with life at school, at home and with friends. See each individual girl's name for episode information.

Holly Episode List: *1.* Holly Introducing Holly! *2.* Deedee the Drama Queen. *3.* The Magic Key. *4.* Payton Gets Grounded. *5.* Positive Payton vs. Negative Nelly. *6.* The Sassy Angel. *7.* Dr. Help. *8.* Holly's Morning Routine. *9.* Addicted to Bethany Mota. *10.* Kid Gets Stuck in Snow Bank for 2 Whole Months?!?? *11.* Hug-a-fume! Gone Wrong. *12.* Holly's 2014 Room Tour. *13.* Did Holly Lie?! *14.* Holly's Christmas Gifts. *15.* Rosebud's Christmas Dream. *16.* Nerdy Holly's Favorite Things. *17.* Holly Says Goodbye.

446 Seven Twinkling Tweens: Jaidyn. *youtube.com.* 2014 (Variety).

Contessa, Ellie, Emily, Holly, Jaidyn, Jazz, Jessica, Kaelyn, Lauren, Luella, Madison, Penny and Tamara are young girls who entertain children via skits (including creating their own characters) while also relating facts about themselves and how they deal with life at school, at home and with friends. See each individual girl's name for episode information.

Jaidyn Episode List: *1.* Introducing Jaidyn. *2.* Trash Bag Dresses of Hollywood Icons. *3.* Advice from the Year 3000 Saves the World. *4.* The Day I Became a Super Hero. *5.* A World Without Color. *6.* Jaidyn as Troublemaker Ruby. *7.* Jaidyn's Glow-in-the-Dark Gymnastics. *8.* Jaidyn's Ideas for Opposite Day. *9.* Jaidyn's School Bedtime Routine. *10.* The Monster Spray. *11.* Baby Sitting Nightmare. *12.* Sister Tag with Jaidyn and Her Crazy Twin. *13.* Legend of the Secret Code. *14.* Summer Fun with Jaidyn. *15.* Goodbye Jaidyn.

447 Seven Twinkling Tweens: Jazz. *youtube.com.* 2012–2013 (Variety).

Contessa, Ellie, Emily, Holly, Jaidyn, Jazz, Jessica, Kaelyn, Lauren, Luella, Madison, Penny and Tamara are young girls who entertain children via skits (including creating their own characters) while also relating facts about themselves and how they deal with life at school, at home and with friends. See each individual girl's name for episode information.

Jazz Episode List:
  1. Introducing Jazz.
  2. Are You Afraid of Zombies?
  3. A Christmas Story.
  4. Fairy Dust War.
  5. Jazz Is Invisible.
  6. Jazz's Morning Routine.
  7. The Day of the Pesky Siblings!
  8. The Lazy Princess.
  9. Dares and Challenges.
  10. How to Make a Garbage Dress!
  11. In the Year 3000!
  12. The Day I Became a Hipster.
  13. A Word without Ice Cream!
  14. How to Be a Troublemaker.
  15. Jazz Goes Reverse.
  16. Jazz's Bedtime Routine.
  17. A Baby Sitting Nightmare.
  18. Jazz's Crazy Twin.
  19. Legend of the Werewolf.
  20. Jazz's Diving Contest.
  21. Princess Makeover.
  22. Jazz's Cheerleading Training.
  23. Sims 3 Real Life.
  24. Jazz Goes Planking.
  25. The Potato Chip Adventure.
  26. Minute to Win It.
  27. Undercover as Boys.
  28. Professor Hypnosis.
  29. Jazz's Nightmare.
  30. Spring Fashion Parody.
  31. The Curse of Bad Luck Brian.
  32. Not-So-Secret Life as a Stalker.
  33. Jazz's After School Routine.
  34. Jazz's Dream Life.
  35. Don't Be a Drama Queen.
  36. Jazz's Disappearing Act.
  37. Bertha's Big Adventure.
  38. Nerd vs. Popular.
  39. Angels or Demons.
  40. My Strange Addiction to Plastic Friends.
  41. Hobo in My House.
  42. The Man Purse.
  43. Jazz's Room Tour.
  44. Jazz's 3 Truths and a Lie.
  45. Jazz's Christmas.

46. No Presents.
47. Jazz's Favorite Things.
48. Jazz Says Goodbye.

448 Seven Twinkling Tweens: Jessica. *you tube.com.* 2013–2014 (Variety).

Contessa, Ellie, Emily, Holly, Jaidyn, Jazz, Jessica, Kaelyn, Lauren, Luella, Madison, Penny and Tamara are young girls who entertain children via skits (including creating their own characters) while also relating facts about themselves and how they deal with life at school, at home and with friends. See each individual girl's name for episode information.

Jessica Episode List: *1.* Introducing Jessica. *2.* Spring Fashion. *3.* Bad Luck. *4.* Trapped in a Scary Movie. *5.* The Secret Snatcher. *6.* Jessica's After School Routine. *7.* Jessica's Awesome Dream Life. *8.* A Day in the Life of a Drama Queen. *9.* The Audition for the Magic Show. *10.* Girly Girl Gabriela Gets Ready for Her Party. *11.* Gabriela vs. Brooke. *12.* Angel Goes on Assignments. *13.* The Dr. Who Saved Flappy Bird. *14.* How to Make a Valentine's Themed Cake in a Jar. *15.* Jessica's Fabulous Rocking Funtastic Magic Styler. *16.* Jessica's Room Tour. *17.* 3 Truths 1 Lie with Jessica. *18.* What I Got for Christmas. *19.* Elf's First Christmas. *20.* Jessica's Favorite Things. *21.* Jessica Says Goodbye.

449 Seven Twinkling Tweens: Kaelyn. *you tube.com.* 2011–2012 (Variety).

Contessa, Ellie, Emily, Holly, Jaidyn, Jazz, Jessica, Kaelyn, Lauren, Luella, Madison, Penny and Tamara are young girls who entertain children via skits (including creating their own characters) while also relating facts about themselves and how they deal with life at school, at home and with friends. See each individual girl's name for episode information.

Kaelyn Episode List: *1.* Introducing Kaelyn. *2.* The Epic Dance. *3.* Kaelyn's Not a Morning Person. *4.* Kaelyn's Blind Taste Test. *5.* Grow-So-Mo! Commercial. *6.* Kaelyn's Magical Magic Show. *7.* Behind-the-Scenes with Kaelyn. *8.* Kaelyn and the Cup of Water. *9.* What to Wear, What to Wear? *10.* After School Routine. *11.* Kitchen Krazy with Kaelyn. *12.* Brrr! It's Winter Fashion Time! *13.* Christmas with Kaelyn. *14.* Goodbye Kaelyn.

450 Seven Twinkling Tweens: Lauren. *you tube.com.* 2012 (Variety).

Contessa, Ellie, Emily, Holly, Jaidyn, Jazz, Jessica, Kaelyn, Lauren, Luella, Madison, Penny and Tamara are young girls who entertain children via skits (including creating their own characters) while also relating facts about themselves and how they deal with life at school, at home and with friends. See each individual girl's name for episode information.

Lauren Episode List: *1.* Introducing Lauren. *2.* No More Toaster Waffles. *3.* Lauren's Spring Fashion.

4. Bad Luck Day. *5.* Trapped! *6.* Lauren's Secret Shhhhh! *7.* My After School Routine. Dream Life of a Movie Star. *8.* The Drama Queen. *9.* The Magic Potion Fail. *10.* Tallia's Worst Nightmare ... Chores! *11.* Techno Tilly vs. Selfie Sage. *12.* Angels and Demons. *13.* The Wacko Doctor Shubugan. *14.* My Strange Addiction: Screaming. *15.* It's Raining French Fries and Frosties! *16.* Lauren's Awesome Room Tour. *17.* Lauren's a Liar!? *18.* How to Make Hidden Surprise Holiday Cookies. *19.* Santa Crime! *20.* My Christmas Favorites. *21.* Lauren Says Goodbye.

451 Seven Twinkling Tweens: Luella. *you tube.com.* 2014–2015 (Variety).

Contessa, Ellie, Emily, Holly, Jaidyn, Jazz, Jessica, Kaelyn, Lauren, Luella, Madison, Penny and Tamara are young girls who entertain children via skits (including creating their own characters) while also relating facts about themselves and how they deal with life at school, at home and with friends. See each individual girl's name for episode information.

Luella Episode List:
1. Introducing Luella.
2. Teacher Trouble.
3. Madame JoJo's Hairstyling Boot Camp.
4. My Pet ... Alien.
5. Can Luella Complete Mission Impossible?
6. The Witches Date Night.
7. The Super Heroes Have a Day Off!!
8. Luella's Life in a Parallel Universe.
9. Luella's Tales of the Strange and Unexpected.
10. Don't Go Into the Haunted Shed!
11. 3 Easy Ways to Get Revenge!
12. The Princess and the Tramp.
13. Invasion of ... the Teenagers.
14. Invisible Me.
15. Luella's Christmas Day.
16. Santa's Fairy Helper.
17. Luella's Biggest Fear.
18. My Fairytale Adventure.
19. My Fabulous Morning Routine by Luella.
20. Day of the Pesky Fitness Instructor.
21. Luella Dares & Wins Almost!
22. My Spooky Friend.
23. How to Look Good in a Garbage Bag!
24. The Year 3000.
25. The Day I Became a Rock Star.
26. Teleport to a New World.
27. Luella the Troublemaker.
28. Luella's Gymnastics Competition.
29. Opposite Day.
30. Bedtime Routine.
31. Luella's Monster in Her Closet.
32. Luella's Baby Sitting Nightmare.
33. Luella's Crazy Twin.
34. The Legend of the Magical Ring.
35. Luella's Summer Fun.
36. Goodbye Luella.

452 *Seven Twinkling Tweens: Madison.* *youtube.com.* 2014–2015 (Variety).

Contessa, Ellie, Emily, Holly, Jaidyn, Jazz, Jessica, Kaelyn, Lauren, Luella, Madison, Penny and Tamara are young girls who entertain children via skits (including creating their own characters) while also relating facts about themselves and how they deal with life at school, at home and with friends. See each individual girl's name for episode information.

Madison Episode List:
1. Introducing Madison.
2. Jolie's Secret Surprise Birthday.
3. The Report.
4. A Day in the Life of a Super Villain.
5. Mission Impossible.
6. A Parallel Universe!?
7. Dance.
8. Is Madison's House Haunted?
9. Revenge!
10. Minecraft Invasion.
11. Madison's Christmas.
12. Madison's Biggest Fear.
13. Flora's Fairy Dust.
14. Dance Mums.
15. The Day of the Pesky Tooth Fairy.
16. Interview with a Fairy Tale Character.
17. Madison's Dances and Challenges.
18. Garbage Bag Dress.
19. The Year 3000!
20. The Day Nancy Became a Nerd.
21. The New World with No Candy!
22. Opposite Day.
23. Bedtime Routine.
24. The Ghost Monster?!
25. Madison's Baby Sitting Nightmare.
26. 7 Years of Bad Luck.
27. Madison Gets Trapped on Her Roof.
28. The Secret Place.
29. Madison's Home School Routine.
30. My Dream Life as a Model.
31. The Life of Being a Drama Queen.
32. Madison's Majestic Magic.
33. The Winner Is….
34. Wild Willy vs. Frieda Fresca.
35. The Demon Call.
36. No More Monkeys Jumping on My Bed!
37. Operation Fruit Cup.
38. I'm Addicted to Bob.
39. Cereal Killer on the Loose.
40. Chipmunk Juice.
41. Madison's Room Tour.
42. 3 Truths 1 Lie.
43. Madison's Christmas Treats.
44. Madison Is Home Alone!
45. Madison's Favorite Things.
46. Goodbye Madison.

453 *Seven Twinkling Tweens: Penny.* *you tube.com* 2013–2015 (Variety).

Contessa, Ellie, Emily, Holly, Jaidyn, Jazz, Jessica, Kaelyn, Lauren, Luella, Madison, Penny and Tamara are young girls who entertain children via skits (including creating their own characters) while also relating facts about themselves and how they deal with life at school, at home and with friends. See each individual girl's name for episode information.

Penny Episode List:
1. Introducing Penny.
2. The Super Villain Story.
3. Meet Leah … the Drama Queen!
4. Nerd vs. Popular … School Edition.
5. Clean Freak Boot Camp.
6. My Pet … Unicorn!
7. Impossible Mission … Penny Is a Mum!
8. How to Be an Evil Witch.
9. A Day in the Life of Maddie Ziegler.
10. The Best Universe Ever.
11. Dancing at the Beach.
12. The Haunted House.
13. Time for Revenge.
14. A Princess's Crazy Adventure.
15. A Complete Boy Makeover!
16. The Invasion of the Juice Box.
17. The Day When Everything Went Invisible.
18. What Penny Got for Christmas 2014.
19. The Elf's Need Help.
20. Ahhhh!! Biggest Fears.
21. Fairy Dust Fail.
22. Penny's Awesome Morning Routine.
23. The Day of the Pesky … What!!
24. It's a Fairytale in the 21st Century.
25. 1 Challenge and 1 Dare with Penny!
26. A Spooky Story with Penny.
27. Penny's Garbage Bag Dresses.
28. A Day in the Year 3000.
29. The Day Penny Became a Shop-a-holic!
30. The World with No WiFi!
31. Introducing … the Troublemaker!
32. Penny the Gymnast.
33. Opposite Leg Gymnastics Challenge.
34. Penny's Sleepover Bedtime Routine with Annabelle.
35. Monster Under Your Bed Makeup Look! Dun Dun Dun!
36. Sage the Nightmare.
37. Penny What! Penny Has a Crazy Twin!
38. The Legend of the Secret Book.
39. Penny's Summer Fun in the Winter Time!
40. Penny in Royal Training.
41. Some of Penny's Cheerleading Skills.
42. Memory Photos.
43. Crazy Planking.
44. Epic Minute to Win It.
45. The Curse of the Juice Box.
46. Undercover to Find a Unicorn.
47. A Not Seen Crime.
48. This Is What Happened!
49. Spring Fashion.
50. Bad Luck Day.

51. What! Penny Trapped in a Nerd Box!
52. Penny's After School Routine.
53. Penny's Awesome Dream Life.
54. A Day of 2 Drama Queens.
55. The Magic Show.
56. Hyper Lexi vs. Lazy Crista.
57. Angel vs. Demon.
58. Penny's a Unicorn Doctor.
59. One Direction Is Coming to Town.
60. You Can Do Gymnastics Backwards!
61. Penny's Room Tour.
62. Penny Tells a Lie!
63. Christmas Is Just Around the Corner.
64. Penny's Christmas Gifts.
65. Penny's 5 Favorite Things.
66. Penny Says Goodbye.

454 Seven Twinkling Tweens: Tamara. *you tube.com.* 2012–2014 (Variety).

Contessa, Ellie, Emily, Holly, Jaidyn, Jazz, Jessica, Kaelyn, Lauren, Luella, Madison, Penny and Tamara are young girls who entertain children via skits (including creating their own characters) while also relating facts about themselves and how they deal with life at school, at home and with friends. See each individual girl's name for episode information.

Tamara Episode List:
1. Introducing Tamara.
2. Tamara's Top Ten.
3. The Dancer with a Dream.
4. Cinnamon Banana Fall Smoothie (Spot the Difference).
5. The 10 Boredom Busters!
6. Cinnamon Toast Crunch Disaster.
7. An Angel Saves a Kid's Life.
8. How to Make a Burger Cake with Tamara.
9. Tamara's Heroes … One Direction.
10. Tamara Has a Minute to Win It.
11. Tamara Finds Her Hidden Talent.
12. A Day in the Life of Tamara the Perfectionist.
13. Tamara's Summer Outfit Ideas.
14. Paige Teaches Livia a Lesson.
15. Athlete vs. Shop-a-holic.
16. Tamara's Three Tweens Water Competition.
17. A Tribute to Tamara.
18. Don't Close Your Eyes (Music Video).
19. Tamara's an Adult?!
20. Tamara's Italy Hotel Room Tour.
21. Famous Tamara.
22. Rebecca's Light Bulb Addiction.
23. Behind the Scenes with Tamara.
24. Tamara Is a Princess.
25. Where Is Stitch?
26. Spot the Difference with Tamara.
27. Nancy's Mission to Become Cool.
28. Tamara's Awesome Dares and Challenges.
29. Chug-a-Jug Gymnastics with Tamara.
30. Tamara's Spring Fashion.
31. What Would It Be Like if Tamara Was Blind?

32. The Scary Fortune.
33. People Are Wrong About Danger.
34. Tamara's Sleepy Morning Routine.
35. Tamara's Room Tour.
36. Pick a Dress with Tamara.
37. Tamara Has No Thumbs for a Day.
38. Alex is a Girly Girl for a Day.
39. Girly Girl Mackenzie vs. Tomboy Alex.
40. Drama Queen Interviews.
41. 3 Truths and 1 Lie with Tamara.
42. Tamara's Life as a Ninja.
43. Lost Parents (Official Trailer).
44. Tamara Doesn't Believe Dr. Wimpy….
45. Tamara's Christmas.
46. Packing Disaster.
47. Favorite Things.
48. DIY Halloween Costume: Jelly Bean.
49. Goodbye Tamara.

455 Sez Me. *sezme.com.* 2013 (Reality).

"There's so many ways to be, there's so many you's and me's, sez me" is the motto of a program that attempts to acquaint children with and help them understand the LGBTQ community. Ultra Charmin, a drag queen, is the host and the program encompasses colorful animation, sound effects and an unscripted segment between a child and an adult as its teaching tool. A child, chosen by the producer from a diverse family (e.g., gay, lesbian or single parent) interviews an adult who represents a non-traditional gender (e.g., drag queens, feminine men, masculine women) in an effort for children to learn by asking questions about their subjects.

Cast: Jeff Marras (Charmin Ultra), Michelle Matlock (Parker Pumernickle), Audrey London (Herself). **Credits:** *Producer-Director:* Mor Erlich. **Comment:** A beautiful pixie (*Pixanne*), a mouse (*The Mickey Mouse Club*), a slapstick comedian (*The Soupy Sales Show*), a scruffy Old West coot (*The Gabby Hayes Show*) and even a Muppet frog named Kermit (*The Muppet Show*) have hosted television series for children in fantasy-like presentations. *Sez Me* surpasses those programs and tries to be as real as possible in its aim to create a dialogue about those who may appear different to children. The presentation is well done and the children chosen as interviewers are knowledgeable about the LGBTQ community and their insights could help other children acquire a better understanding as to why some people are different.

Episode List: *1.* Sez Charmin and Duy. *2.* The Weivretni (the title refers to Interview spelled backwards). *3.* Charmin's Angels—Sez Cypress and Eve.

456 Shells and Scales. *youtube.com.* 2014 (Fantasy).

Skylar is a young girl who has secretly lived most of her life as a Mermaid. She inherited the ability from her mother, a Mermaid, when she was very young. As careful as Skylar tried to be keeping her secret, an accidental encounter with spilled water reveals her true being to her friend Alex when she transforms in front of her. Alex is astonished at what she sees and immediately tells Skylar that she too wants to become a Mermaid. Skylar believes there is a means by which Alex can become a Mermaid (through a special potion left to her by her late mother) but the series ends unresolved only detailing how Alex promises to keep Skylar's secret and help her adjust to her developing powers.

Cast: Amber Moore (Skylar), Emma Carter (Alex), Dennis Walsh (Det. Lewis), Jolie (Wizard), Anna (Sea Nymph). **Credits:** *Producer-Director*: Dennis Walsh. **Comment:** The program is filmed in Dublin, Ireland, and only the first three episodes remain on line. The program has acceptable acting and photography and episode three has muted sound (due to music copyright infringement).

Episode List: *1.* She's a Mermaid. *2.* Power Outrage. *3.* Mer Lesson. *4.* Stranger Danger. *5.* Fishy Class. *6.* Mer-Quest. *7.* Day Moon.

457 Shimmer Tails. *youtube.com.* 2014 (Fantasy).

Kaeyln and Lexi are walking trough the woods when they stumble across a small box and open it. Inside they find two necklaces and an attached note: "Wear these necklaces and become one of us." The scene immediately switches to a swimming pool and shows Kaelyn and Lexi transforming into Mermaids. As the first episode ends Kaelyn and Lexi are discussing what has happened and the series itself relates their efforts to adjust to and keep secret what has happened to them.

Cast (as credited): Kaelyn Walsh (Kaelyn), Alex (Lexi). **Comment:** Good acing and photography highlight the program.

Episode List: *1.* The Necklaces. *2.* Help Needed. *3.* More Secrets Revealed. *4.* The Party. *5.* Stupid Rain. *6.* The New Friend. *7.* Never Trust a Human. *8.* Running for Our Lives. *9.* We Always Knew Alex (Lexi) Was the One.

458 Shorts 'n' Scales: A Mermaid Tail. *youtube.com.* 2012 (Fantasy).

Three friends (Nikki, Izzy and Becca) are enjoying swimming in a pool when a mysterious force causes the water surrounding them to bubble. The girls appear to be unaffected—at first. The following day, however, when the girls return to the pool for a swim, the water transforms them into Mermaids. Three girls, one secret, and their efforts to adjust to their developing powers while pretending to be ordinary girls.

Cast (as credited): Tara (Nikki), Rachel (Izzy), Jillian (Becca). **Comment:** Pretty girls, a good story line and acceptable acting and photography.

Episode List: *1.* Into the Water. *2.* We Need Answers. *3.* Power It Up. *4.* Power It Up Again. *5.* Party It Up. *6.* Rain, Rain Go Away. *7.* Test It Out. *8.* Magic Moon and Madness. *9.* Power Outage. *10.* Finale.

459 The Silver Shell. *youtube.com.* 2014 (Fantasy).

While in the backyard of her home, a teenage girl (Lina Ferson) finds a strange looking rock that changes color from yellow to red. Lisa picks up the rock, goes into her house and begins washing it under running water. The colors fade and what remains is a silver sea shell. Lina suddenly acquires a headache and blacks out. As she awakens, she sees four color orbs (yellow, blue, red and white) floating above her. Each orb (Aqua, Windy, Gaia and Fraya) has the ability to talk and through them Lina learns they are the Spirits of the Sea and came to life when she touched the shell. Lina also learns that she is a Mermaid (will change when she comes in contact with water) and that the Spirits of the Sea have been sent to teach her how to control the elements of earth, wind, fire and water and use those abilities to defeat evil. As the series progressed it is learned that the Spirits of the Sea were once alive (and possessors of the shell) and their essence is now held by the silver shell. They have no memories of whom or what they were and only seek to escape from the shell. This can only be accomplished by a current host (like Lina)—if she will destroy the shell and release them.

Cast: Anita Macpherson as Lina Ferson, Aqua, Fraya, Gaia, Monica Ross and Anna Lee Clark. **Comment:** Considering the fact that a teenage girl, with more on her plate than just making videos, not only appears as all the characters but is also the creative force behind the series, it is a remarkable achievement. Special effects are used and are for the most part quite well done (they do improve as the series progresses). Attempting to incorporate several characters in the same scene (when only one girl plays them) is difficult with non-professional equipment and this is quite noticeable in the first few episodes (the characters appear in jerky movements and the dividing lines for splicing scenes are also visible).

Season 1 Episode List: *1.* Pilot. *2.* Lesson: Water. *3.* Flames. *4.* Earth. *5.* Previous Wind. *6.* Monica Ross. *7.* Dates Back. *8.* Who is AC (Anna Lee Clark). *9.* Christmas Special. *10.* The Secret Behind the Spirits.

Season 2 Episode List: *1.* Fresh Start. *2.* The Changeling. *3.* Orb of Hope. *4.* Crista and Monica.

460 Simon's Cat. *youtube.com.* 2008–2015 (Cartoon).

An unnamed cat, owned by a man named Simon, struggles to live a life more complex than ordinary house cats as he is continually hungry but rarely gets fed and must rely on his instincts and ingenious schemes to survive. Other characters are Simon's Sister's Dog; The Bird (first seen "alive" then as a squeaky toy); The Garden Gnome (since Simon's Cat loves fish, birds and mice, and the gnome holds a fishing rod, Simon's Cat recruits his help in acquiring food); the Bunny, the Frog, the Kitten, the Squirrel, the Mouse and the Female Cat (who becomes Simon's Cat's love interest).

Voices: Simon Tofield. **Credits:** *Writer-Director:* Simon Tofield. **Comment:** Although somewhat crudely drawn, the short episodes are quite amusing and are reminiscent of the Garfield cartoon cat that is somewhat in the same situation as he constantly seeks food. Although the principal character has no name, the series creator, Simon Tofield, based him on his own cat, Hugh.

Episodes 1–22: *1.* Cat Man Do. *2.* Let Me In. *3.* TV Dinner. *4.* Fed Up. *5.* Fly Guy. *6.* Hot Spot. *7.* Show Business. *8.* The Box. *9.* Cat Chat. *10.* Lunch Break. *11.* Santa Claws. *12.* Sticky Tape. *13.* Hop It. *14.* Hidden Treasure. *15.* Cat & Mouse. *16.* Double Trouble. *17.* Cat Nap. *18.* Fowl Play. *19.* Shelf Life. *20.* Tongue Tied. *21.* Window Pain. *22.* Ready, Steady, Slow.

Episodes 23–47: *23.* Springtime. *24.* Fetch. *25.* Nut Again. *26.* Icecapade. *27.* Feed Me. *28.* Screen Grab. *29.* Flower Bed. *30.* Suitcase. *31.* Mirror, Mirror. *32.* Scary Legs. *33–34.* Christmas Presence. *35–36.* Smitten. *37.* Pawtrait. *38.* Hot Water. *39.* Washed Up. *40.* Scaredy Cat. *41.* Let Me Out. *42.* Catnip. *43.* Butterflies. *44.* April Showers. *45.* Pizza Cat. *46.* Box Clever. *47.* Pug Life.

461 Sink or Swim. *youtube.com.* 2012 (Fantasy).

It is the morning of her twelfth birthday and as Marissa wakes up and first comes in contact with water she receives a present she never expected—transforming into a Mermaid. Marissa learns, after doing some research on her family, that she is descended from the Guardian of Atlantis and a Rose Quartz Mermaid. It is now her time to take her place in the world as a Mermaid and stories relate Marissa's efforts to keep secret what happened (especially from her snooping brother Garrett), adjust to her developing powers and pretend to be an ordinary girl.

Cast (as credited): Robyn (Marissa), Jake (Garrett). **Comment:** A slow-moving program with acceptable acting but poor camera work and sometimes dark scenes.

Episode List: *1.* Something New. *2.* Revealed. *3.* Boiling Point. *4.* Potion in Motion.

463 The Siren's Tale. 2013 (Fantasy).

Katherine is a mischievous Mermaid (born in the sea) whose antics (causing ships to sink) have come to the attention of her kingdom's rulers. As punishment, Katherine is stripped of her Mermaid abilities, transformed into a Siren and banished to live on land in the human world. The program follows Katherine as she attempts to adjust to her new life and somehow learn that her mischievous ways are the cause of all her problems. (Although Katherine is a Siren, a mythical evil Mermaid, she has not adapted those ways and has retained the goodness of a Mermaid.)

Cast (as credited): Sophie Kordzakhia (Katherine), Anunka (Ashely). **Comment:** Interesting concept with a twist on normal Mermaid series. The girls are pretty but the overall production suffers at times from an unsteady picture; it has since been taken offline.

Season 1 Episode List: *1.* Pilot. *2.* Fitting In. *3.* A Long Awaited Cousin. *4.* Answers. *5.* Untitled. *6.* Unexpected. *7.* New Mermaid. *8.* Sleepless Nights. *9.* Power of the Four. *10.* Finale.

Season 2 Episode List: *1.* New Tail. *2.* Broken. *3.* Spirits. *4.* Unexpected Powers. *5.* Losing Control.

463 Sirena por Casualidad (Mermaid by Chance). 2013–2015

Spanish produced series (filmed in Madrid, Spain) about a sister (Claudia) and her brother (Alberto) who find magic bracelets that transform them into Merfolk when they come in contact with water. While Claudia and Alberto struggle to maintain their secret they must also use their abilities to battle killer plants and avoid capture by the mysterious Senor E.

Cast (as credited): Lucia Fernandez Ruiz (Claudia), Alberto, Luis Julian, Lorena, Ana Julia, Lucas, Ivan, Natalia, Diego, Rosetta, Juan, Jorge, Miguel, Carlos. **Comment:** The program sports a large cast, pretty girls but is difficult to follow as there are no English subtitles; it has since been taken offline.

Season 1 Episode List:
1. Even the Strangest Things Happen.
2. The Cave Has Powers.
3. The Sweeper Lurks and the Powers of a Mermaid.
4. Tortura in Almería.
5. More Powers.
6. Igualitus.

Season 2 Episode List:
1. Venom by Accident.
2. A Bath after a Long Time and a Strange Itch.
3. Strange Phenomena in the House of Lorraine.
4. Becoming Strong.
5. The Letter and the Evil Spirit.

Season 3 Episode List:
1. The New Tail of Alberto.
2. Tasks and Tasks.
3. The History of the Tribes.
4. The Answer to the Letter.
5. The Book of Magic.
6. Codes of the Mermaids.

Season 4 Episode List:
1. The Cold is the Worst.
2. Weird Stuff.

3. The Replica.
4. Nightmares.
5. Memories of the Past.
6. The Ring.
7. The Movie.

Season 5 Episode List:
1. Footprints.
2. Nanny Natalia.
3. Zeroes and Tens on the Test.
4. The Killer Plants.
5. The Conch of the Mermaids.
6. Poisoned Potion.

Season 6 Episode List:
1. The Dream and the Encounter.
2. The Story and the Mother's Message.
3. The Meeting with Mom and Free Time.
4. The Mysterious Dream.
5. The Anti-De-Mermaid-Tail Potion.
6. Metamorphosis.
7. Tension.

Season 7 Episode List:
1. Vacations.
2. Treasure Hunt.
3. Changing Tails.
4. Swimming in the Sea and Fear.
5. My Sister Julia.
6. Mr. E.

Season 8 Episode List:
1. Julian's Quirk.
2. Advances.
3. The Curse of Neptune.
4. Days in the Village.
5. The Nosy Neighbor.
6. The Shooting.
7. The Crime.

Season 9 Episode List:
1. And Julian's Powers?
2. The Pearls of the Mermaids.
3. The Bottle and the Potion.
4. The Mother's Crown Lost in the Snow.
5. The Editors.
6. The Vengeance of Neptune.
7. The Kidnapping.

Season 10 Episode List:
1. Mermaid Fever.
2. Secret Powers in the World.
3. Julian's Powers.
4. The Birthmark and the Pendant.
5. Goodfellas and the Mystery of the Tail.
6. The Memory of Julian.

Season 11 Episode List:
1. Problems Around the Corner.
2. Señor E Returns to the Fray!
3. Fear and Disloyalty.
4. Weird Stuff.
5. Man Overboard.
6. Finale.

464 *The Sister Scales*. *youtube.com.* 2011 (Fantasy).

On the morning of her 16th birthday, a recessed Mermaid gene becomes activated and prevalent when a girl named Ella goes for a swim and transforms into a Mermaid. Later that day, a girl (Serenity) arrives at Ella's home claiming to be her long-lost sister and immediately tells her that she is, like her, a Mermaid (although Serenity does not possess the normal tail, only scales on her feet). Serenity goes on to explain that their father was human and their mother was a Mermaid. Each accepts the other and, while not explained how much time passes, the next scene shows that Serenity has enrolled in college and Emma has begun a mission to find a locater shell that will reveal the truth about who they really are. A third episode, to continue the story, is announced but highly unlikely after five years have passed.

Cast (as credited): Ithica (Ella), Tiffani (Serenity). **Comment:** A good story line is coupled with acceptable acting and photography.

Episode List: 2 untitled episodes, labeled "Episode 1" and "Episode 2" have been produced.

465 *Sisters in Black*. *youtube.com.* 2014 (Dolls).

A *Charmed*-liked TV series about three teenage girls who are actually witches. It begins when Tori, Jessie and Kenna, using a Ouija Board, are led to a book containing spells. They read one but nothing happens—at first. The following day, while at school, Tori, Jessie and Kenna are being bullied by a group of girls when they hold each other's hand and realize they are different; they can will the bullying to stop. The girls realize that the spell has made them witches and they must now not only keep secret what has happened, but learn to control and harness their powers for good and not self gain.

Cast (as credited): Fiona Lancaster (Jessie Reid), Asia Asper (Tori Harlowe), Noelle Rey (Kenna O'Connor), Kate Kittredge (Ophelia Ravensdale). **Comment:** Very well done program with excellent doll manipulation, voice characterizations and photography.

Episode List: 13 untitled episodes, labeled "Episode 1" Through "Episode 13" have been produced.

466 *Solar Sirens*. *youtube.com..com.* 2014 (Fantasy).

After taking in the mail, a young girl (Lola) finds a letter addressed to her that contains a message: "The Local Pond. All the Magic and Fun You Need. Come and Explore It at 2:00 p.m." Intrigued, Lola decides to check it out. When she arrives at the pond it appears to be vacant but she does find a bottle on a tree limb and takes it home with her. The bottle contains a gem wrapped in a piece of paper that contains a message: "Potion of Destiny. Signed The Ocean." The paper also contains a recipe that Lola makes and tries. She immediately suffers a headache and falls asleep on the couch in her living room. After an unspecified amount of time she awakens and when she first comes in contact with water she transforms into a Mermaid. The program follows Lola as she attempts to adjust to what has happened while pretending to be an ordinary girl to conceal the fact that she is a real Mermaid.

Cast (as credited): Mei (Lola), B. (Luna). **Comment:** More episodes were apparently planned (as a very pretty girl listed as only "B." is seen in the opening theme but not in the episode) but at the time of publication this has not occurred. The overall production is well-done with good acting and photography.

Episode List: *1.* A New Beginning.

467 Something About the Tide. *youtube. com.* 2014 (Fantasy).

Ellie and Lacy are young girls and best friends who, while near the shore of a beach, each find a crystal on a rock. The girls pick up the crystals and while looking at them, place them together. A spark occurs and magically transports them (and changes their dresses into bikinis) to a pool in a secret world where they are situated in bubbling water that is releasing electrical charges. The scene immediately switches to "The Next Day." Ellie and Lacy appear to be fine until each comes in contact with water and is transformed into a Mermaid. The girls quickly accept what happens and must now keep a secret, learn how to cope with their developing powers and pretend to be ordinary school girls.

Cast (as credited): Nikki (Ellie and Alexia), Erika (Lacy), Nicole (Taylor). **Comment:** The girls are pretty and the overall production is acceptable.

Episode List: *1.* How It All Happened. *2.* Popping Tails. *3.* Run from Her. *4.* Taylor Came to Town. *5.* Standing Frozen. *6.* Thawing Out. *7.* Flame Power. *Lacy Is Missing. 9.* Lost Is Found. *10.* Season Finale.

468 Something Fishy. *youtube.com.* 2011 (Fantasy).

While studying (hoping to get better grades in Social Studies) a young girl (Alyssa) decides to take a break and goes to the kitchen for a drink. She removes what appears to be an ordinary pitcher of liquid but, upon drinking it, she transforms into a Mermaid. She is also perplexed—as to what happened (it is not explained what the liquid is or how it got into the refrigerator) but she soon exclaims "Totally Awesome!" Awesome or not, Alyssa must now learn to lead two lives—Mermaid and ordinary girl.

Cast: Ale Maria (Alyssa). **Comment:** Ale Maria is pretty but the scenes are not well lit and her dog's barking overpowers some of her dialogue. It can also be heard that someone (possibly her mother) is giving Ale verbal cues as what to do during certain scenes. Had any additional episodes been produced they would have no doubt explained the liquid Alyssa drank and how it turned her into a Mermaid.

Episode List: *1.* Something Fishy Pilot.

469 Spell Bound Tails. *youtube.com.* 2012 (Fantasy).

Hoping to discover more about her late mother, a young girl (Phoebe) finds a box that contains a false bottom. In it is a piece of paper (actually a spell) that, when Phoebe reads, transforms her into a Mermaid when she comes in contact with water. The program follows Phoebe as she navigates life as both a girl and a Mermaid. She shares her experiences with Alisandra, a girl she later discovers is also a Mermaid.

Cast (as credited): Raegan (Phoebe Wavly), Kaylyn (Alisandra Harris), Marlena (Violet Wavly). **Comment:** Good underwater photography but poor sound quality hampers the production.

Episode List: 6 untitled episodes, labeled "Episode 1" through "Episode 6" have been produced.

470 Spellbound. *youtube.com.* 2014 (Dolls).

It is a time when witches fear the Red Beast, a demon that tracks down and destroys witches to absorb their powers. Charlotte is a woman who fears that the life of her one-year-old daughter, Scarlet, is in jeopardy and in an attempt to hide her from the Red Beast, places her in the custody of her sister (a non-witch) named Delilah. Charlotte, however, like her husband a year earlier, is killed by the Red Beast. Scarlet is raised in secret by Delilah and remains unharmed. It is the day of Scarlet's 16th birthday when Delilah feels it is time for Scarlet to become a part of society and begin school. She also feels the time is right for Scarlet to know who she really is: a Red Witch. Scarlet's mother was a White Witch (good) but her father was a Black Warlock (evil, although he never used his power for that purpose). Scarlet, born of a White and Dark witch has become a Red Witch, the only one known to exist. Such a witch is very powerful and her abilities, if used for evil, could wreck havoc on the earth. Charlotte believes, like other witches, that the Red Beast no longer exists and thus releasing Scarlet to the outside world is best for her. Scarlet leaves home with a warning from her Aunt Delilah "not to trust anyone" and the program follows Scarlet as she begins life as an ordinary school girl unaware that forces beyond her control are seeking to capture her and encompass her powers.

Voices (as credited): Lex. **Comment:** Although the story reads like a horror film, its presentation through dolls is anything but. The voices, photography and doll manipulation are very good.

Episode List: *1.* Red Witch. *2.* Cursed and Controlled. *3.* Lost and Found. *4.* Welcome to Merlin High.

471 Spells. 2012 (Fantasy).

Kortny and her friend Julia are enjoying themselves at a picnic when it appears a book just magically falls from the sky. Kortny thinks the book may be magical while Julia feels it is just best to ignore it. Kortny takes the book home and opens it. As Kortny finds a passage that Julia is trying to prevent her from reading, a mystical force lingers over them. Shortly after, when each comes in contact with water they transform into Mermaids. Having regained their human legs by drying off their Mermaid tails, Kortny and Julia are visited by a strange girl who will???? (The program ends at this point with no text or video information explaining what will happen next or what the series is actually about).

Cast (as credited): Emma (Kortny), Veronica (Julia), Gabreilla (Halley), Ally (Madlene). **Comment:** It is apparent that the program has been abandoned. The sound is very confusing as there are two different tracks playing at the same time. One appears to be in an unidentified foreign language and one in English (but both playing at the same time just makes it impossible to understand). The program has since been taken offline.

Episode List: *1.* The Book and the Strange Girl.

472 *Spider-Woman: Agent of S.W.O.R.D.* *youtube.com.* 2009 (Cartoon).

S.W.O.R.D. (The Scientific World Observation and Response Department) is an organization that responds to alien threats, especially those of a race called the Skrull. Prior to their current round-up by S.W.O.R.D., the Skrull secretly invaded Earth with a diabolical plan to use their shape-shifting abilities to overtake the bodies of America's greatest super heroes and use their powers for their own means. One super hero, Spider-Woman (alias Jessica Drew) was one such victim whose life was ruined before her shape shifter, the Queen of the Skrull, could be caught. Jessica, angered by what happened, leaves The Avengers (America's super hero fighting team) and, at the urging of Abigail Brand, the director of S.W.O.R.D., joins her organization to get her life back and bring an end to the Skrull invasion. Stories follow Jessica as she begins her quest to capture the Skrull imposers who are still posing a threat. Also hindering Jessica's efforts is HYDRA, a diabolical organization headed by the evil Lady Hydra. Jessica is an Avenger with super strength, endurance, reflexes and capable of producing bioelectric venom blasts (as a result of her transformation when her father used an experimental spider venom to save her life after she was bitten by a poisonous spider).

Voice Cast: Nicolette Reed (Jessica Drew/Lady Hydra), Stephanie K. Thomas (Abigail Brand), Andy MacKenzie (Det. Chong). **Credits:** *Director:* Joe Quesada. *Writer:* Brian Bendis, Sal Buscema, Archie Goodwin, Jim Mooney. **Comment:** In 1949 a TV series called *The Telecomics* used panel drawings to tell stories. *Spider-Woman* incorporates that same concept but in a much more sophisticated manner. Although the presentation will seem a bit odd at first, it will soon become an intriguing series to watch. There is limited action animation and the story is told mostly through the narration of Jessica over expertly executed panel drawings of what happens. It is like watching a comic book come to life and it does capture the viewer's attention.

Episode List: Five untitled episodes, labeled "Episode 1" Through "Episode 5" have been produced.

473 *Splash (2011).* 2011 (Fantasy).

After a day of anticipation, Annabeth, Crystal and Skye gather for a sleepover. All is progressing well until Skye discovers candy that she does not recall bringing with her. Thinking nothing of it, the girls each take some and soon realize it was magical when their first contact with water transforms them into Mermaids. The girls must now learn to accept what has happened to them, adjust to their developing powers and pretend to be ordinary young girls.

Cast (as credited): Skye, Crystal, Annabeth. **Comment:** The girls are pretty but poor sound hampers the production; it has since been taken offline.

Episode List: *1.* Splash of Difference. *2.* Secrets Revealed. *3.* Spooks.

474 *Splash (2012).* 2012 (Fantasy).

While hiking in the woods three young girls (Summer, April and May) stumble upon a cave that seems to have magically appeared before them. As they enter the cave they discover an enticing pool that beckons them to enter. As they do, the water begins to bubble, frightening them, but apparently not harming them. Later, when the girls come in contact with water they transform into Mermaids. The program charts their efforts to adjust to their Mermaid powers while pretending to be ordinary girls.

Cast (as credited): Ellie (Summer Crystal), Katie (April Waters), Gracie (May Fin). **Comment:** The concept is a bit different than other Mermaid programs and the girls are pretty but poor sound and an unsteady picture at times hampers the production. The program has since been taken offline.

Episode List: *1.* The Change. *2.* Power Play. *3.* School Party.

475 *Splash (2013).* 2013 (Fantasy).

Dominique and her brother Aidan are playing in Dominique's room when she finds a strange necklace. Dominique places it around her neck but nothing happens until Aidan accidentally spills water on her and Dominique transforms into a Mermaid. It appears that only a pilot episode was made and judging by it, it appears the story would follow Dominique as she learns how to keep secret and conceal her developing powers.

Cast (as credited): Dominique Davis (Dominique), Aidan (Aidan). **Comment:** The Mermaid tail seen on Dominique is clearly just a blanket thrown over her legs. The actual production is quite bad with poor audio, a jumpy picture and, with Dominique looking directly into the camera, quite unrealistic (she even places her hand over the camera lens to end the episode). The program has since been taken offline.

Episode List: *1.* Pilot.

476 *Splash of a Merman. youtube.com.* 2011 (Fantasy).

Max is a young boy who dreams about Mermaids. In one such dream, he encounters one and swims along side her. That following morning, Max finds a glass-like pendant in his bathroom that when touched and he comes in contact with water turns him into a Merman. Like typical Mermaid series, Max's efforts to adjust to what has happened are chronicled.

Cast: Fahim Shafi (Max). **Comment:** Very bad photography coupled with awful sound and atrocious acting. Simply put, it is not even worth watching. It appears that the program was filmed by Fahim with a relatively inexpensive camera as the picture is not very clear. He also moves the camera by himself for each scene and when motion is involved, the scene becomes quite unsteady.

Season 1 Episode List: *1.* The Transformation. *2.* New Power. *3.* Getting the Tail Back. *4.* Good Morning Max. *5.* Isn't Easy to Be a Merman. *6.* Season Finale.

Season 2 Episode List: *1.* Moon Howling Out of Control. *2.* Crazy Day. *3.* Don't Even Think About It. *4.* Scales. *5.* Mixed Together.

477 *A Splashy Tale. youtube.com.* 2012–2014 (Fantasy).

Legend states that in the oceans of the world there exists Mermaids, creatures with the upper body of a woman and the lower portion of a fish. Fishermen and sailors on long journeys are said to be the only humans to have seen or come in contact with them. How such creatures came to be or how they have remained a mystery is one of the unsolved riddles of the sea. One such Mermaid is Summer, a once ordinary girl who, while walking along the beach, found a magic necklace and a sea shell that contained an enchanted potion (perhaps the answer to the mystery) that transformed her into a Mermaid. Summer, an apparently only child with few friends, accepted her transformation but longed for a friend who was also a Mermaid. Hoping to get her wish, Summer placed the potion in the bottom of a public swimming pool and hid the magic necklace a short distance away.

For three friends, Izzy, Razundull and Zalika, their day at that swimming pool would soon change their lives forever. While swimming, Izzy spies a strange object (the potion in a bottle) at the bottom of the

pool and retrieves it. While showing it to Razundull and Zalika, the contents spill onto Izzy's hand (she is more concerned that her hand is stained rather than what the substance could be). Izzy appears to be fine but, after her friends leave to get a snack and Izzy returns to the water, she not only finds the necklace Summer hid, but discovers that her legs have become a tail and she is a Mermaid. While not shown, Izzy exited from the pool and when the water on her tail dried, her legs reappeared.

Although Izzy had apparently intended to keep secret what happened, Zalika and Razundull's return from the snack stand changes all that. Upset that Izzy chose not to join them (to get refreshments) a confrontation ensues followed by a shoving match that knocks the three girls into the water. Razundull and Zalika are shocked to see that Izzy has become a Mermaid. Now, with a secret first known only to Zalika and Razundull (later by Zannia, a girl at school, and Summer and Aqua, Mermaids Izzy later befriends), Izzy must face the challenges of not only being a pretty teenage girl—but a teenage girl who is also a Mermaid.

The introduction of the Mermaid Aqua adds suspense and intrigue to the story and the following background information will help to understand the story: In a flashback sequence, it is shown that Aqua was walking along the beach when she noticed a girl floating in the water. "I ran into the ocean to get her. She was so cold. I turned her over.... She was dead. So I pulled the body ashore and called the police." While waiting for the police to arrive, Aqua notices that the girl didn't drown; that she was murdered. "Scared that the police would think I was the murderer, I ran." Aqua, however, was not as free as she thought when her face appeared on the news as the prime suspect. "That's the day I left home. I didn't know where to go. All I could think of was the beach" (and what happened). Now, all alone and strolling along the beach, Aqua finds a strange bottle containing a liquid. As she poured the liquid on her hand, thinking it was perfume, water from the ocean washed it off but left a stinging sensation and a transformation occurred that changed her into a Mermaid. She began her new life as a creature of the sea and one year later would befriend Izzy.

Cast: Danika Green (Izzy Sho), Kimberly Banks (Aqua Star), Cierra Hutcheson (Zalika "Zali" Collins), Dakota Hutcheson (Razundull "Razzy" Kin), Jessica (as credited; Summer), Charlee Witham (Zannia Zulie). **Credits:** *Producer:* Danika Green. *Director:* Danika Green, Charlee Witham, Cierra Hutcheson, Dakota Hutcheson, Kimberly Banks, Jessica, Jessica P. (both as credited). *Writer:* Danika Green, Charlee Witham, Cierra Hutcheson, Dakota Hutcheson, Kimberly Banks, Allison Akins, Jessica, Jessica P. (as credited). **Comment:** Although the entire production is acted, produced, written and directed by teenage girls, it is quite an accomplishment. While there are some visual and audio flaws (remember, these are not professionals) it is a well-executed and entertaining. There are numerous Mermaid-themed series and *A Splashy Tale* is, with its attractive cast and well-constructed story line, one of the more enjoyable Mermaid fables.

Episode List: *1.* Metamorphosis. *2.* The Fight. *3.* The Power in Your Hand. *4.* A Fishy Surprise. *5.* Best Friends Fade Away. *6.* Christmas Fishes. *7.* Strange Moon. *8.* Fishy Book. *9.* Mermaid Journal. *10.* Mermaid Proof. *11.* Dangerous Waters. *12.* Wish to Fish. *13.* Jealous of Fishes. *14.* Only Magic. *15.* Wings Between Us. *16–17.* Wish for a Change. *18.* Christmas Police. *19.* Fish Stuck. *20.* Fishy Troubles. *21.* Lost Magic. *22–23.* The Ocean's Calling.

478 Splish Splash. 2010 (Fantasy).

A young girl (Eve) is returning home from school when she sees an unusual ring on her front porch. Fascinated by the ring, Eve picks it up and brings it into the house with her. Anxious to show her parents what she has found she instead finds a note from them telling her that they have left for a concert and will be home later that evening. As Eve examines the ring she goes to the kitchen for a glass of water but when the water touches her skin, she transforms into a Mermaid. Eve must now keep secret what happened as she pretends to be an ordinary girl.

Cast (as credited): Eve Wave (Eve). **Comment:** While the program has acceptable acting and photography, the plot stretches the left alone aspect a bit too much as Eve is just too young to be by herself and must learn through a note why her parents are away. The program has since been taken offline.

Episode List: *1.* The Dream. *2.* Reality. *3.* Questions and Answers.

479 Spook House Dave. *facebook.com.* 2009 (Puppets).

Mount Savage is a small town in Pennsylvania that is home to Dave, a 12-year-old boy who attends the Mount Savage Middle School. He is an average student, likes video games and is starting to show an interest in girls. He is also a most unusual kid. He is called Spook House Dave because he lives in a haunted castle on top of Mount Savage and is cared for by a group of lovable but unearthly creatures (a crazy mummy, a cranky vampire, a mischievous witch and a romantic werewolf). Legend has it that as a baby Dave was left on the doorstep of the castle with a note attached saying "Please Take Care of Dave." The creepy family took him in and now Dave must actually live in two different worlds—one with a family of monsters and one in the world of ordinary humans. Dave's experiences are charted as he contends with the antics of his adopted family.

Morlock is a 700-year-old grumpy vampire that sleeps all day and complains all night about the local villagers. He "earned his fangs" in Medieval Europe and is now the owner of the haunted castle in which Dave lives. His age has slowed him down a bit (his back may go out when he transforms into a bat—but he can still drain the blood out of a young woman at a moment's notice).

Bobo is the Frankenstein-like monster created by a mad scientist in the 1800s from a mix of body parts and steam engine coils. He is literally a grown baby and very strong and kept locked in the castle's dungeon (to keep him from stomping through the village and destroying it).

Umberto, a werewolf, is the seventh son of a seventh son and was born in Argentina. Although he is a werewolf, he is treated by the others as the family's pet dog (until the full moon rises and transforms him—not only into a wolf, but sometimes, he dons a dress and calls himself Margarita).

Old Pharris is a 3,000-year-old mummy from the Pyramids of Giza in Egypt. Although he has no brain and his skull has been stuffed with sawdust, he enjoys life although he occasionally loses a limb if he is too active (his bandages need to be tightened now and then to keep all his parts together). He also has a mummified pet cat named Edgar.

Ghost is a castle resident who comes and goes as he pleases. Who or what he was is unknown (and no one seems to care) and his job appears to be giving the castle its haunted reputation.

Hagatha is a 296-year-old ugly witch (wart on nose and all) who rides a broom, cackles and delights in casting spells on unsuspecting villagers. Her potions for youth (goblin heads and roaches) keep her young at heart and she hopes that Dave will become a warlock and someday marry a witch.

Forry is Dave's pet monster, an unknown creature with large grin and razor-sharp teeth (whom Dave found living under Hagatha's cauldron).

Voices/Puppeteers: Lucky Yates, Jason von Hinesmeyer, Scott Warren. **Credits:** *Producer:* Melissa Honabach, Michael Koziol. *Director:* Deb A. Davis. *Writer:* Lucky Yates. **Comment:** Enjoyable horror-comedy mix that is well produced with characters that will appeal to both children and adults.

Episode List:

While information can be found on Facebook.com, the official website has since been taken offline. Prior to this occurrence, it was still difficult to determine how many episodes were produced. The deleted official website (spookhousedave.com) claimed eight episodes but it also had pages for 31 Halloween accented mini-episodes and several episode extras. Only four of the eight episodes were available in 2016 ("Mascot," "School Dance," "Backpack" and "Soup Night"); all the mini-Halloween episodes were also available as were the episode extras for episode four ("Soup Night"). Like the actual series episodes, the holiday-themed and extras episodes involve the characters in a brief predicament.

The episode "Mascot" finds Dave wanting to change his innocent boy persona into that of a beastly

Mount Savage Goat. Dave searches the catacombs of the castle seeking his missing backpack in the premiere episode, "Backpack." In "Soup Night," the family prepares for the scariest evening of the year—the night Hagatha makes her homemade soup. Dave seeks to find a date for the upcoming school dance in "School Dance."

The extras are "Pharris' Story" (wherein the mummy relates how the game of hide-and-go-seek was invented 3000 years ago) and "DNN Nudists" (The Dave News Network reports a startling fact: "Naked nakedness in Mount Savage").

480 Spy Girls. *youtube.com.* 2013 (Dolls).

It is summer time and two sisters, Bella and Lilly, are becoming bored with nothing to do. One day they become suspicious of their mother's actions and decide to follow her. They discover she is a spy (their father was also a spy but he mysteriously disappeared while on a mission and is presumed missing in action). Bella and Lilly also get more than they bargained for when they are captured by their mother's superior and offered a choice: have their minds wiped clean as to just what happened or (although not specifically stated) become spies. They choose the latter and the program, which appears to have been abandoned, was to follow their adventures as spies (in the only episode presented, they are sent on a mission to stop Dominique and Stephanie, women plotting a nefarious deed involving fast food hamburgers).

Comment: There is no cast information and the program just vanished after the first episode. The voice characterizations for the American Girl Dolls are good but the entire production is hampered by an unsteady camera (making scenes a bit jumpy at times).

Episode List: *1.* I Could Go for a Burger.

481 Spy High. *youtube.com.* 2013 (Dolls).

Laiyla Roberts appears to be just an ordinary high school girl. And that is what she is meant to be as she is secretly a spy for the U.S. government (sort of like the movie *Spy Kids* and the TV series *The New Adventures of Beans Baxter*). The program relates the missions Laiyla must perform to save the world—yet still find time to be herself, attend school and be with her friends.

Cast (as credited): Dawn Azora Skyrian (Laiyla Roberts), Aisa Taylor Page (Cassandra E'Claire), Sierra Megan Cameron (Gladis), Lunar Ember Lovegood (Genievera Cloake), Harry Potter (Talon Steffords), Juliet Albright (Mindy McClain). **Comment:** Overall, a very well done program with good voices, doll manipulation and photography.

Episode List: 4 untitled episodes, labeled "Episode 1" Through "Episode 4" have been produced.

482 Stan Lee's Time Jumper. *youtube.com.* 2009–2010 (Cartoon).

Terry Dixon is a 20-year-old college student who has lived under the shadow of his father, Arthur, a technological genius who created the Articulus, a time machine that has been coded to work only with the DNA of a Dixon family member. The sudden death of Arthur through mysterious circumstances brings Terry in contact with H.U.N.T. (Heroes United, Noble and True) who believe that Charity Vyle, head of C.U.L.T. (Unstoppable, Lethal Terrorists) killed Arthur in a failed plan to steal Articulus and use it to change crucial moments in history. When Terry learns that Charity may be responsible for his father's death, he joins H.U.N.T. and must now seek a way to capture Charity and destroy C.U.L.T. before they can alter history for their own diabolical goals. Created by Stan Lee and also known as *Time Jumper*.

Voice Cast: Bart Fletcher (Terry Dixon), Natasha Henstridge (Charity Vale). **Credits:** *Producer;* Stan Lee, Gill Champion. *Writer:* Stan Lee, Omar Ponce. **Comment:** Still-like animation is used with the camera performing movement. The words spoken by the characters make it appear as a comic book come to life.

Episode List: *1.* Free Ride. *2.* A Wrinkle. *3.* Secrets and Lies. *4.* Unauthorized Call. *5.* As It Was. *6.* Destination Unknown. *7.* The Dixon Legacy. *8.* The Birthright.

483 Star Quality. *youtube.com.* 2009 (Dolls).

Inspired by the Fox TV series *Glee* the program follows the lives of five very different girls and how their lives are affected when they pull a prank on a teacher and, in punishment must become members of the school's glee club (the alternative was a two-week suspension).

Cast (as credited): Marisol Luna (Bridget), Kate Kittredge (Tatian), Megan Masche (Amanda), Savannah Loues (Stephanie), Chrissa Maxwell (Valerie). **Comment:** Very well done program with good doll manipulation, voices and photography.

Episode List: 4 untitled episodes, labeled "Episode 1" through "Episode 4" have been produced.

484 The Star Tails. 2015 (Fantasy).

Ella and Amber are cleaning a bird bath in Ella's backyard when they find two star-shaped fish berets (which they place in their hair) followed by the discovery of two necklaces in a pond. The necklaces appear to be harmless until Ella and Amber wear them, touch water and transform into Mermaids. Amber and Ella believe its "cool" and "awesome" at first but soon realize they have changed and must keep it a secret while pretending to be ordinary girls.

Cast (as credited): Ella (Ella), Jill (Amber). **Comment:** An overall good production with pretty girls, acceptable acting and nice photography. The program has since been taken offline.

Episode List: *1.* We Have Taaiils!?

485 The Stinky and Dirty Show. *youtube. com.* 2015 (Cartoon).

Stinky, a brown garbage truck, and Dirty, a yellow backhoe loader, are friends who face life as humans in a world where inanimate objects are alive. The program, based on the books by Jim and Kate McMullan, looks at a world where two friends learn life lessons as they attempt to solve the problems they encounter.

Cast: Jacob Guenther (Dirty), Ethan Wacker (Stinky). **Credits:** *Producer:* Guy Toubes, Alice Wilder, Gillian Higgins. *Director:* Darragh O'Connell. *Writer:* Jim McMullan, Kate McMullan, Guy Toubes. **Comment:** Very good computer animation coupled with good stories and voice characterizations make for an entertaining program geared mostly to preschool children. It is a bit like the PBS series *Thomas and Friends* (which uses computer animated, talking trains to convey messages to children).

Episode List: 13 untitled episodes, labeled "Episode 1" through "Episode 13" have been produced.

486 Stitches. 2013 (Dolls).

The LPS (Littlest Pet Shop) dolls are incorporated in a rather adult-in-nature program (although geared to children) about an abused child (Daniel Valentine) and what happens when the abuse twists his way of thinking and he becomes, at the age of 19, a serial killer. An advisory is posted before the program begins.

Voices (as credited): K (as she says, "My name is a letter, deal with it"). K also says she loves horror movies and her programs reflect that dark image. **Comment:** Despite its premise, the YouTube comments posted by children do indicate that they like the program. It is quite different from other doll-themed series and does contain some very minor gore (blood). The voices, photography and doll manipulation are very good. The program has since been taken offline.

Episode List: *1.* Tears of Blood. *2.* Nightmare. *3.* A Little Insane. *4.* All Stitched Up.

487 Strange Hill High. *youtube.com.* 2013–2015 (Cartoon).

Strange Hill High appears to be a normal high school but is, in reality, a school where secrets and mysteries are also a part of the agenda. The experiences of three friends (Mitchell, Becky and Templeton) as they deal with all the unusual aspects of their school (from ghosts to monsters to paradoxes) are depicted.

Voice Cast: Ben Smith (Mitchell Tanner), Emma Kennedy (Becky Butters), Richard Ayoade (Temple-

ton), Marc Silk (Tyson), Matt King (Mr. Creeper), Jonathan Keeble (Principal Abercrombie), Melissa Sinden (Miss Grackle), Caroline Aherne (Stephanie/Croydonia), John Thomson (Peter Dustpan), Alison Moyet (Joy), Chris Johnson (Ken Kong). **Credits:** *Producer:* Bob Higgins, Sarah Muller, Sander Schwartz, Kat Van Henderson. *Director:* Chris Tichborne, Geoff Walker. *Writer:* Andrew Burrell, Connal Orton, James Griffiths, Mark Oswin, Stuart Kenworthy, Josh Weinstein. Bede Blake, Joel Morris, Emma Kennedy, Reid Harrison, Ben Teasdale, Kat Van Henderson. **Comment:** The program, produced in England, cleverly combines animated puppets with Japanese vinyl toys and special digital effects to create a program, although using "teenage" puppets is actually geared to younger children. The voice characterizations are good and are easy to understand (no thick British accents). It was produced for the pay service Netflix but can be viewed for free on You Tube.

Season 1 Episode List: *1.* King Mitchell. *2.* 99 Cool Things to Do with a Time Machine. *3.* The Lost and Found Boy. *4.* Snoozical. *5.* Big Mouth Strikes Again. *6.* The Most Boring Book in the World. *7.* Read All About It. *8.* Health and Safety. *9.* The Ghost Writers of Strange Hill High. *10.* Teacher's Pets. *11.* Lucky Becky. *12.* Becky vs. Bocky. *13.* End of Terminator.

Season 2 Episode List: *1.* The Curse of Were-Teacher. *2.* Invasion of the Templetons. *3.* The 10% Solution. *4.* Little School of Horrors. *5.* Big Templeton Is Watching You. *6.* Crushing Embarrassment. *7.* Mitchell Who? *8.* Innercrombie. *9.* Ken Kong. *10.* Mitchell Junior. *11.* The MCDXX Men. *12.* The Snide Piper. *13.* A Strange Hill Christmas.

488 The Strange Life of the Mermaids (Series 1). 2013 (Fantasy).

While walking, friends Harper and Spencer stumble across a mysterious pool that appears to beckon them to swim in its waters. The girls come under its spell and while enjoying the water they are suddenly engulfed by a foam-like substance that transforms them into Mermaids. Harper and Spencer must now keep secret what happened and pretend to be ordinary girls while attempting to understand and control their Mermaid powers.

Cast (as credited): Rachel (Harper), Kenzie (Spencer). **Comment:** The form is actually soap suds and over-powering music obstructs what is being said (especially when the girls are discussing what has happened to them). Other than that, the photography and acting are acceptable. The program has since been taken offline.

Episode List: 3 untitled episodes, labeled "Episode 1," "Episode 2" and "Episode 3" have been produced.

489 The Strange Life of the Mermaids (Series 2). *youtube.com.* 2013 (Fantasy).

As two friends (Raquel and Stacey) are walking they find an old map on the ground. As they examine the parchment, they decide to follow its directions and see where it leads them. They are lead to a strange land where, although it is winter time (as evidenced by the snow on the ground) they decide to go swimming in a body of water that lies before them. The water doesn't appear to be cold but it soon begins to bubble and shortly after transforms them into Mermaids. The program appears to have been abandoned and other than establishing the fact that Raquel and Stacey are Mermaids, just ends without delving further into what they will encounter or do. **Cast (as credited):** Rachel (Raquel), Abby (Stacey), Caitlin (Jane), Aidan (Michael). **Comment:** The program is a bit confusing to figure out what is happening as it was not well thought out. The picture is also a bit unsteady due to movement by the person holding the camera. **Episode List:** *1 and 2:* Walk-Talk and Swim.

490 Super Hero Chronicles. *youtube.com.* 2013 (Dolls).

Ace High is a school for super hero training and home to three best girl friends, Serina, Gwen and Jordan. Incorporating Littlest Pet Shop (LPS) animal figures, the program chronicles the mishaps the girls encounter—not only with their training with boys but other classmates. **Cast (as credited):** Carmen Jones (Serina Cortez), Chess Waston (Gwen Hunter), Jamie Ford (Jordan Kane), Tiffany Sparrow (Herself), Sage Bond (Damian Woods), Tulin Williams (Pierce Hamilton), Leo Jackson (Miguel Carson), Antonio Dixon (Shad Summers), Alexandra Drew (Avalon Hawthorne). **Comment:** Handling the tiny LPS dolls is difficult due to their size. The manipulation is good and the program voicing is well done. **Episode List:** *1.* New Girls Watch Out. *2.* Trying to Get the Girl. *3.* Loosening Up. *4.* Christine's Revenge. *5.* Disco Mayhem. *6.* Young Love Everywhere. *7.* Another New Girl, Something's Up. *8.* Secrets Revealed. *9.* Serina's Mission. *10.* Decisions, Part 1. *11.* Decisions, Part 2. *12.* Another Ordinary Day. *13.* Plans Finally in Action. *14.* Caution. *15.* The Date. *16.* New Attitudes. *17.* Saving Iris. *18.* One after the Other. *19.* Preparing for War. *20.* The War. *21.* Back to Normal.

491 Supergirl. *youtube.com.* 2011 (Fantasy).

Adaptation of the *Supergirl* legend about Kara, a survivor of the planet Krypton (the home of Superman) after it was destroyed in an explosion caused by it being drawn into its sun. Kara, a teenager, has established herself on the planet Earth and is now attending college and appears to be just an ordinary co-ed; however, when evil strikes, Kara dons a blue costume and becomes Supergirl, a hero to those who are unable to protect themselves. The program was to follow Kara as she struggles to lead two lives—college student and the mysterious Supergirl. Kara lives with her roommate Barbara, who is secretly Batgirl; however, although they share a room neither knows of the other's secret identity (even when they team to battle evil, their dual identities are not revealed). **Cast:** Tiffany Giardina (Kara/Supergirl), Kaight Zoia (Barbara/Batgirl), David Klein, Ryan McIntyre, Eric Rhodes, Jarda Beeber, Kyle Rutchland. **Credits:** *Producer-Writer-Director:* Tom Madigan. **Comment:** Only a pilot has been produced (and well at that). Tiffany Giardina is perfect as Supergirl and the special effects, though very minimal, are good. The program has no character introduction and just assumes the viewer knows who Kara is. Not so as Kara's history is not as legendary or common knowledge as Clark Kent/Superman. While Kara is dazzling as Supergirl, there is no explanation as to how she came to Earth, where she lives, how she got the costume, or what college she attends. Adding to the mystery is Barbara. While her identity (to the viewer) is unknown at first, at the program's conclusion, her Batgirl costume is seen under her bed. But is she Barbara Gordon (one of the Batgirl aliases?) or someone else? Her costume is lighter in color than prior Batgirl incarnations and not as sexy, leading to the conclusion that had more episodes been produced, the mysteries surrounding Kara and Barbara would have been explained. Despite the continuity problems, the episode is enjoyable. **Episode List:** *1.* Supergirl—The Pilot.

492 Superman: The Unofficial Web Series. *youtube.com.* 2011 (Adventure).

The Superman legend is adapted to the Internet in an under two minute introduction that begins with the planet Krypton exploding and the parents of the baby Kal-El (Jor-El and Lara) placing him in a rocket ship. The ship lands on Earth where the baby is found by a farm couple (John and Martha Kent) who raise him as Clark Kent. Clark is next seen as Superboy then in Metropolis as Superman. It is here that Clark has already established himself as a reporter for the *Daily Planet* and fellow reporter Lois Lane and editor Perry White are first seen. The program shows Clark, as Superman, preventing a robbery at the Metro Bank and concludes in a cliffhanger with an evil mastermind, the Toyman plotting to wreck havoc on Metropolis. **Cast:** Erik Baker (Superman), Talia Thelen (Lois Lane), Aaron Davies (Jimmy Olsen), Joel Habeli (Perry White), Greg Blatto (Jor-El), Briann Gagnon (Lara), Brian Deckhart (Superboy), Daniel Sentoro (John Kent), Victoria Bundoni (Martha Kent), Joe Amato (Lex Luthor), Christopher Johnson (Winslow

Schot), Trevor Zhou (Jack Numball). **Credits:** *Producer*: Erik Baker. *Director*: Steve LaMorte. *Writer*: Michael Nixon. **Comment:** The program is very fast-moving and a lot happens in the six minute and forty-three second pilot episode. It also appears, however, that the program was abandoned (even YouTube viewer comments are asking where the second episode is). Green screen technology appears to have been used for the backgrounds and is well done. The acting and photography are excellent and the series did show potential for being one of the better super hero web series.

Episode List: *1.* Convictions (Pilot).

493 Supernatural. *youtube.com.* 2012 (Dolls).

Five friends, possessing special witch-like powers and their efforts to escape the clutches of those who are seeking to capture them and harness their powers for sinister means. Leo, age 18, is the oldest member of the group. He has enhanced senses. Sam, 17 years old, has the power to levitate objects with her mind and has become the group's leader. Luna, age 17, has the ability to enter a person's dreams and control what happens; she is Sam's twin sister. Sparkie, 17 years of age, has the ability to control and generate electricity. Krystal, age 14, has the power of invisibility.

Comment: A cast is not credited. The program is well done with good voices, doll manipulation and photography.

Episode List: 7 untitled episodes, labeled "Episode 1" through "Episode 7" have been produced.

494 Surplus Waves. *youtube.com.* 2011 (Fantasy).

Lani is a very studious young girl who simply overworks herself. One day, after returning home from school, Lani complains about drinking too much soda. Feeling that she needs to still quench her thirst, she takes a bottle of water from the refrigerator, begins sipping it and transforms into a Mermaid. It does not seem to faze Lani and, after drying her tail (to regain her legs) she just goes about her normal business. Although it not explained how soda combined with water can cause a girl to become a Mermaid, Lani soon realizes that she is different and must now learn to keep secret what happened as she pretends to be an ordinary girl.

Cast (as credited): Christy McLaughlin (Lani), Paula (Lily). **Comment:** The program was abandoned after the second episode. Although Christy McLaughlin is very pretty, she alone cannot save a program that has very poor audio and video quality.

Episode List: *1.* Fish Tail. *2.* True Lies.

495 Survivor: Mermaid Secrets of the Deep. *youtube.com.* 2015 (Fantasy).

A young boy, walking along the beach spies something on the sand—a Mermaid (Raida), who beached herself when "something in the water" threatened her life. The boy (unnamed) rushes to her and finds that she is alive, but fearful of returning to the ocean. The boy tells her that he will take her home to his backyard pool where she can recover. Raida agrees but tells him she must return to the sea and her pod by morning. The boy replies with "I know." As the boy places Raida in the pool and she begins to reenergize herself, the boy jumps in and is revealed to be a Merman. The program ends here.

Comment: Unfortunately, only the pilot episode has been released at the time of publication. The cast is not identified but the program is very well done and does present an intriguing concept based on what has been released. The girl playing Raida is very pretty and is sure to make a splash if more episodes are produced.

496 Sweet Waters. 2014 (Fantasy).

As a young girl (Marlena) swims, the waters beneath her begin to bubble and seconds later she is transformed into a Mermaid. Although Marlena quickly adjusts to what has happened she must now pretend to be an ordinary girl to protect her secret Mermaid identity.

Cast (as credited): Emily (Marlena and Ashley), Mia (Molly). **Comment:** Although the program has since been taken offline, it establishes too quickly what has happened to Marlena without really going into details about her transformation. The girls are pretty but poor sound hamper the production.

Episode List: *1.* One Crazy Dream. *2.* You Aren't Who You Say You Are. *3.* Secrets Uncovered. *4.* Not What I Thought. *5.* Where Is This.... *6.* Finale.

497 Switching Scales. *youtube.com.* 2014 (Fantasy).

Best friends Cadence and Nissa are walking along the beach shore when Cadence finds a rock covered in moss. She picks it up, makes a wish then throws it into the water. Seconds later Cadence and Nissa see what appears to be a girl floating in the water. As they go to help her, they discover she is a Mermaid (Riley) and has been injured by the rock Cadence threw. The injury is minor (a cut on the side of her head) but Riley is grateful to Cadence and Nissa for saving her from drowning. Over powering music makes it virtually impossible to hear what is happening, but Riley gives each of the girls a bracelet. As Riley returns to the ocean Cadence and Nissa head for home. It is the following day when Cadence and Nissa come in contact with water that each discovers what Riley's present to them has caused: their transformation into Mermaids. Cadence and Nissa must now learn to navigate life as both ordinary girls and Mermaids but also find a way to keep their identities a secret while learning how to use their magical abilities.

Cast (as credited): Ella R. (Cadence), Hannah (Nessa/Solkie), Ella S. (Riley/Cerulean), Adrienne (Atargatis/Tess), Brian (Roy), Evan (Ernest). **Comment:** Although the program is well acted and an interesting story line is presented, loud background music and bad sound (wind blowing in the microphone) spoil the overall effect.

Episode List: *1.* Pilot. *2.* Nearly Paradise. *3.* Cerulean. *4.* Easy Magic. *5.* Mystery Solved. *6.* Ring of Fire. *7.* Atargatis' Daughters. *8.* Landlubbers. *8.* Uprising. *9.* They're Real.

498 Sylvia's Super Awesome Mini Maker Show. *youtube.com.* 2011–2012 (Educational).

Understanding electronics made simple—not by a college professor, but by a young girl (Sylvia) who explains and demonstrates to children the ins and outs of electronic devices.

Cast (as credited): Sylvia as Herself. **Comment:** A modern-day, kid version of the 1950s TV series *Watch Mr. Wizard.* It is truly amazing what Sylvia knows about electronics at her age and how she makes the most complicated sounding circuit boards seem so simple. Sylvia does use a soldering gun and, although not stated, parental guidance should be observed. The program is not only informative (for both kids and adults) but it is also very well acted and produced. See also *Circuit Playground.*

Episode List: *1.* Squishy Circuits. *2.* Holiday Gift Guide 2011. *3.* Super Sewable Circuitry. *3.* Cardboard Periscope. *4.* Super Simple Copper Etching. *5.* Build the Monochron Clock Kit. *6.* No Heat Lava Lamp. *7.* How to Build the LOL Shield Kit. *8.* Build the Mini POV. *9.* Super Simple Screen Printing. *10.* Mousey the Junkbot. *11.* Simple Molding and Casting for Toy Duplication. *12.* Sylvia's Super Awesome Make Holiday Gift Guide 2012. *13.* Sidewalk Chalk. *14.* Crazy Putty. *15.* Rockets. *16.* Backpack Buddy.

499 The Tail Beyond the Rock. *youtube. com.* 2011 (Fantasy).

There is a mysterious cave in Tennessee called Beyond the Rock. It is supposedly cursed and any human girl that enters it will be transformed into a Mermaid and never be able to reverse the curse. Three sisters (Lily, Aleysia and Lyrical) fall victims to the curse when they take refuge in a cave to escape an approaching storm. The girls are unaware at first that they are in the cursed cave but have a strange sensation that something is just not right. Their fears are realized when they transform into Mermaids. The program follows their efforts to keep secret what happened and now that they know where the cursed cave is, protect it from humans who may wander into it and expose their secret.

Cast (as credited): Lily, Aleysia and Lyrical as Themselves. **Comment:** The program, which has acceptable acting and photography, does present an in-

teresting twist on the "how a girl became a Mermaid" premise.

Episode List: 3 untitled episodes, labeled "Part 1," "Part 2" and "Part 3" have been produced.

500 Tail Flip. *youtube.com.* 2015 (Fantasy).

While jogging with her dog, a teenage girl (Chloe) stumbles upon a hidden book in the woods when her dog breaks lose and she chases after him. At home, Chloe begins to examine the book and finds a recipe and a pouch of ingredients. Chloe follows the recipe and creates a potion that soon turns into a necklace. She places the jewelry around her neck but when she comes in contact with water, she is transformed into a Mermaid (removing the necklace returns her to normal). Rather than keep secret what has happened, Chloe tells her friend Finn, who becomes intrigued and wants to become a creature of the sea. Chole recreates the formula and Finn, when he tries on the necklace, becomes a Merman. Chloe soon begins to realize what she has done and the program follows what happens as she begins to delve into the mysteries of the book and the magic it contains.

Cast: Renae Nickens (Chloe), Zoe Smith (Miranda), Keenan Braunberger (Finn), Nyssa Sara-Lee (Melusina), Amanda Smith (Miranda's mother), Amy White (Chloe's mother). **Comment:** Excellent underwater photography coupled with good acting and directing make for enjoyable watching.

Episode List: *1.* It Started with a Book. *2.* The Merman. *3.* The Other Friend. *4.* Apology. *5.* A Shadow in the Woods. *6.* The Shadow Appears. *7.* Miranda's Choice. *8.* Who Do You Trust? *9.* Book of Secrets. *10.* A Useless Book. *11.* The Search for Miranda. *12.* The Journey Has Just Begun.

501 Tail of a Mermaid & Merman. *youtube. com.* 2013 (Fantasy).

Jewel and Rin are a sister and brother (twins) and the Mer-children of a Mermaid. Years ago an evil Shape Shifter (Davilin) kidnapped them and brought them to his world on the earth. Jewel and Rin lost their Mer-powers and memories and began living life as ordinary humans. It is the day of their 16th birthday and Jewel is taking a bath when the water activates long-lost memories and abilities and transforms her into a Mermaid. Her screams bring Rin to her side and when he touches her tail, he too is transformed (into a Merman). As memories of their prior life slowly return they realize they are not human and must now defeat Davilin and return to their rightful world as a princess and a prince.

Cast: Nikki Crawford (Jewel Adams), Alexander Warren (Rin Adams), Heidi Fairgrive (Nixe Ocean), Nicole Katherine (Esther), L.J. Cleave (Makenna Seastar), Iona Worgan (Ruby Smith). **Comment:** Produced in Scotland and very difficult to understand (poor sound coupled with Scottish accents). It is also visually unimpressive (not very clear and a bit out of aspect ratio [has stretched images]).

Episode List: 1. A Magical Dream. 2. Powers, Crazy Aunt & Another Mermaid. 3. Demonic Possession. 4. A Very Fishy Christmas.

502 The Tail of 2 Mermaids. *youtube.com.* 2012 (Fantasy).

It is a warm summer's day and two young girls, Emma and Jackie, head to an area called Mako to cool off in its swimming pool. Everything appears to be normal until the water begins to bubble and the girls are magically transported back to Emma's house—but it doesn't seem to faze them as they go about their normal business. However, when Emma goes for a drink of water, she is transformed into a Mermaid. When Jackie attempts to dry her off, she too becomes a Mermaid when the water on Emma's tail touches her skin. Emma and Jackie quickly realize what has happened to them and must now accept the fact that contact with water will transform them into young Mermaids. The program charts their experiences, assisted by their friend Jack (an apparent expert on Mermaids) as they seek to conceal their secret and live as ordinary pre-teen girls.

Cast: Eiligh Rush (Emma), Alyssa Duncan (Jackie), Ian Rush (Jack). *Comment:* With the exception of episode 3, wherein Jackie's performance is embarrassing, the program plays well as kids (especially Jack) try to solve problems without help from adults. It is obvious that the child stars are non-professionals and do a good job of performing their roles.

Episode List: 1. Magic. 2. Revealed! 3. The Spell.

503 A Tail of Wonder. *youtube.com.* 2012 (Fantasy).

While swimming in the ocean, a young girl (Crystal) finds a magic necklace that has no effect on her at first, but when she returns home and comes in contact with water, the necklace transforms her into a Mermaid. Unable to contain her secret, Crystal tells her best friend Bella what has happened. As the pilot film ends, Bella has learned Crystal's secret and it is assumed she will either become a Mermaid herself or provide the help Crystal needs to navigate life as both a Mermaid and ordinary girl.

Cast (as credited): Hollie (Crystal), Emily (Bella). *Comment:* Only a pilot film has been produced that has noticeable editing problems coupled with poor sound but good acting by the girls.

Episode List: 1. Tails (Pilot).

504 The Tail That Should Have Never Come. *youtube.com.* 2012 (Fantasy).

After reading about Mermaids in a book, three young girls (Chloe, Katlyn and Elizabeth) enter a Jacuzzi. After enjoying a swim, the girls exit to find a glass containing a blue liquid. Believing it is safe to drink, each girl takes a sip and seconds later Chloe, Katlyn and Elizabeth are transformed into Mermaids. Vowing to keep each other's secret, the girls must now learn how to cope with their developing powers while at the same time pretend to be ordinary girls.

Cast (as credited): Emma (Chloe), Maggie (Katlyn), Madison (Elizabeth). *Comment:* The girls do a good job with their roles but the production has its faults: very bad framing (the girls heads are cut off at times), poor sound (especially in the echoing Jacuzzi room) and while the photography is nice, the picture jumps a bit on occasion.

Episode List: 1. The Mystery. 2. The Dream. 3. Episode 3.

505 Tail Us Bout It. 2012 (Fantasy).

Six episode program about two young girls (Kenya and Loala) who magically become Mermaids while at the beach and whose adventures, while attempting to adjust to their new life, are experienced by Aqua, a life-long Mermaid who is still having difficulty adjusting to life on land as a human.

Cast (as credited): Mirisa (Loala), Soleil (Kenya), Aysha (Aqua), Katelyn (Anne Thea). *Comment:* All episodes and text information have been since been taken off-line. The program (correct with the word "Bout" in the title) is filmed in the Virgin Islands and, judging by the photographs on the website, it did appear to be an interesting variation on the Mermaid genre.

Episode List: 1. Pilot. 2. A Found Book. 3. Forget-Me-Knot. 4. Who Are You? 5. The Fish Trap. 6. Try and Catch Me.

506 The Tails of a Wish. 2013 (Fantasy).

Two young girls, Livi and Tori, turned into Mermaids as the result of a wish, now struggle to navigate life as both humans and creatures of the sea.

Cast (as credited): Emily (Livi), Abi (Tori), Monique (Monique). *Comment:* Australian-produced program (where the TV series inspiration *H20: Just Add Water* was also produced) that has good underwater photography but, like American Mermaid series, suffers at times from poor sound quality. The program has since been taken offline.

Episode List: 6 untitled episodes, labeled "Episode 1" through "Episode 6" have been produced.

507 Tails of Hawaii. *youtube.com.* 2011 (Fantasy).

Hawaii provides the backdrop as two girls (Josephine and Jordan) walking by a very large tree, magically plunge into a water-filed cave beneath it. But just as magically, the girls are propelled back to the surface where they have been transformed into Mermaids. Now with a secret they must keep, Josephine and Jordan must also navigate lives as ordinary girls.

Cast (as credited): Chloe (Josephine), Victoria (Jordan), Isabelle (Gabrielle). **Comment:** Slightly above the ordinary Mermaid series with decent acting and photography.

Episode List: 3 untitled episodes, labeled "Episode 1," "Episode 2" and "Episode 3" have been produced.

508 *Tails of the High Seas. youtube.com.* 2013 (Fantasy).

In the home of the Lord of Atlantis, who has taken human form, it is learned that he met two girls, Susan and Grace at a county fair and realized they were not ordinary girls, but girls destined to become his "children" (Mermaids). He has granted them the power to transform into Mermaids and it has to be assumed their adventures would be chronicled as they attempt to keep secret what happened to them. Although Susan and Grace receive credit they do not appear as the episode focuses entirely on the Lord of Atlantis as he speaks.

Cast: Fabrisio Flayfel (Lord of Atlantis), Sarah Houston (Susan), Shanna McMillian (Grace). **Credits:** *Producer-Writer-Director:* Fabrisio Flayfel. **Comment:** Very poor presentation with nothing but the Lord of Atlantis speaking (with hesitation at times). The camera work is rather bad (also not clear) and it appears that the program has been abandoned. Fabrisio's name appears numerous times in the closing theme (not only for what is listed here—but as creator, editor, script, photography, etc.).

Episode List: *1.* A Story Is Told.

509 *Tails of the Sea (2011).* 2011 (Fantasy).

Sophie is a 12-year-old girl whose life changes forever when she enters a mystical waterfall while walking through a steam and transforms into a Mermaid. Based on what information appeared on line, it appears that Sophie will encounter problems as she struggles to adjust to her powers and keep secret what has happened to her.

Cast (as credited): Maria G. (Sophie). **Comment:** With the exception of a 78-second trailer all episodes (including titles) have been taken offline. While the trailer does present an overall view of what happens it is not really possible to evaluate an entire series based on that. The trailer has since been taken offline.

510 *Tails of the Sea (2012). youtube.com.* 2012 (Fantasy).

Lybbie and her friend Makenna are on a river paddling a canoe when they spot and cave and decide to explore it. Inside, as they walk through water, it be-

gins to bubble and engulfs them. They are able to swim out of the cave and safely return to their canoe. The following day, they decide to return to the cave and further explore it. They again encounter the bubbling water but it apparently does not affect them. Later that day the girls discover they have power over water but have not yet transformed into Mermaids. The program, which has been abandoned, just ends at that point (it is assumed they will transform into Mermaids and struggle to keep secret what has happened to them as they learn to adjust to their powers).

Cast (as credited): Olivia (Lybbie), Maddy (Makenna). **Comment:** Once viewing the only produced episode it can be seen why the series didn't continue. Although the photography is acceptable, the plot leaves a lot to be desired. The girls appear to be seven or eight years old and, for their age, do a decent job of acting. Their situations, however, are just too unbelievable. When rowing their canoe, they are photographed from the shoulders up and pretending to paddle (grass can be seen instead of water). When they are in the cave, it is obviously a backyard as a house can be seen. And when they swim, bubble effects are seen on the screen with the girls pretending to be in water.

Episode List: *1.* The Power in Our Hands.

511 *Tails, Scales and Everything. youtube.com.* 2010–2011 (Fantasy).

Ellie and her sister, Ricky, are in their backyard and using a metal detector when they find an old metal box (the Shell Box). Curious about what the box may contain, they bring it into the house and open it. Ellie and Ricky believe the box is magic and can grant wishes. They each wish to become a Mermaid. Shortly after, when they come in contact with water, they transform into Mermaids, are granted special powers and the program follows their efforts to keep a secret while pretending to be ordinary girls.

Cast (as credited): Savannah (Ellie), Ricky (Ricky). **Comment:** Overall, the production and acting is acceptable. The first episode has low sound and episode four has a number of technical problems (it was actually remade, in part, as the fifth episode).

Episode List: 5 untitled episodes, labeled "Episode 1" through "Episode 5" have been produced.

512 *The Tale of a Mermaid Tail. youtube.com.* 2015 (Fantasy).

Two young girls (Skye and Maddie) are playing hide and seek in the woods when they stumble across sea shells set in a path that leads them to a tree with a crudely made book attached ("Ancient Mermaid Spell Book"). The girls take the book and upon opening it find only one filled page, that of a handwritten spell. Curious, they recite the spell but nothing happens. They toss the book aside and decide to return home. Later, however, when they come in contact with water, they transform into Mermaids. They must now keep secret what happened, adjust to their developing powers and pretend to be ordinary young girls.

Cast (as credited): Skye (Skye), Maddie (Maddie). **Comment:** The girls are cute, the acting is acceptable and the photography pleasing and steady.

Episode List: *1.* Pilot.

513 *The Tale of a Tail.* *youtube.com.* 2012–2015 (Fantasy).

It is the first day of summer and a boy (Andy) is enjoying his swim in the ocean when a sudden storm forces him to take refuge in a sea cave that he discovers. It is also the time of a quarter moon and rays emanating from it fill the cave and cause the water to bubble. The bubbles appear harmless but play tricks on Andy's mind when he suddenly finds himself back home and theorizes that he just imagined the whole thing. The next morning, however, when he again goes swimming, he becomes a Merman and realizes that what he thought happened in the cave actually happened. Although Andy tries to conceal what he has become, his friend, Jordan, accidentally uncovers his secret and in doing so, reveals that she is a Mermaid (as she found the same cave but at a different time). Their adventures as they struggle to adjust to what they have become and keep their new beings secret are the focal point of stories.

Cast (as credited): Jake (Andy Carter), Anna (Jordan), Haley (Bella). **Comment:** One of the very few Mermaid series to feature a Merman as the leading character. The sound and acting are good but the picture is a bit unsteady at times.

Season 1 Episode List:
1. Transformation.
2. A Long Day.
3. Sunset.
4. Jordan's Back.
5. The Secret's Out.
6. Both Merpeople.
7. The Legend Has It.
8. Tail or Toes.
9. Exposed.

Season 2 Episode List:
1. Going or Staying.
2. The Move.
3–4. The Potion.
5. Wizards.
6. The Book Returns.
7. Jordan's Fortune.
8. The Necklace.
9. Revealed.

Season 3 Episode List:
1. Down the Hill.
2. It's Christmas.
3. Locked Up.
4. The Escape.
5. Stuck and Seen.

6. Forgot.
7. The Fall.
8. Secret Cave and the Secret Room.
9. Who Is the Watcher?

Season 4 Episode List:
1. Detention.
2. Too Sick to Go.
3. The Chase.
4. Gone Forever.
5. Defeated.
6. Pong Is the Trick.
7–9. The Waters Attack.

Season 5 Episode List:
1. Done with Water.
2. An Ocean Treasure.
3. Power from the Ring.
4. Moonstruck.
5. The Box of Tails and Treasures.
6. Watched.
7. Something's Fishy.
8. Stranded with Stormy Waters.
9. Trapped.

Season 6 Episode List:
1. Spotted Watched and Followed.
2. No Going Back.
3. Time to Tell.
4. Battle Power.
5. Destroying Human Fish.
6–7. Searching for Jordan.
8. Pranks a lot.
9. Wonked Up Chips.

Season 7 Episode List:
1. I'm Normal!

514 *Tales of Tails.* *youtube.com.* 2013 (Fantasy).

While boating on a lake friends Zoe and Jessica find two necklaces entangled in some lily pads. After retrieving them, they realize the bracelets are special when they come in contact with water in a swimming pool and are transformed into Mermaids. Now with special abilities derived from water, Zoe and Jessica must guard their secret while at the same time continue life as ordinary girls. Originally titled *A Mermaid Secret: The Other Side of Us.*

Cast (as credited): Mermaidgirl1999 (Zoe), Cuteocelot (Jessica), Mermaidgirl1999's cousin (Rosabelle). **Comment:** The girls are pretty, the underwater photography good but the sound can become difficult to understand at times.

Episode List: *1.* A Splash of Magic. *2.* Water + Water = Powers. *3.* Potion. *4.* Uncovered. *5.* Bye, Bye Fishies.

515 *The Teddy Post.* *youtube.com.* 2013 (Comedy).

Theodora Bayer is a talking teddy bear and the host of a television-like news program called *The*

Teddy Post. Each episode is a look at a topic covered by Theodora with comical skits portraying the expose she is conducting (like the unfair treatment of Scarecrows or the secret behind robots).

Cast: Reebie Sullivan (Voice of Theodora). **Credits:** *Producer-Writer-Director:* Reebie Sullivan, Scott Crawford. **Comment:** Theodora is always stationary and positioned on the left side of the screen. Her movement consists of her mouth and eyes and inserts on the right side of the screen are often used for the stories behind the story. The program itself is well produced and a clever way of presenting comedy skits.

Episode List: *1.* Scarecrow Hunting. *2.* When Bunnies Attack. *3.* It's Hard Out There for a Samurai. *4.* Phobias. *5.* Spy School. *6.* Hurling. *7.* Ostrich Egg. *8.* Robots. *9.* Dogs vs. Cats. Welcome to the Catsino. *10.* Alternative Careers. *11.* Man Eating Plants. *12.* Flying Pan Fandango. *13.* Sharks vs. Humans. *14.* How to Get Rid of Monsters. *15.* The Security Blanket. *16.* The Big Bad Wolf. *17.* Gnomes.

516 Teen Girl Squad. youtube.com. 2002 (Cartoon).

Cheerleader, So and So, What's Her Face and The Ugly One are four girls who call themselves The Teen Girl Squad. They attend high school and while they do not have typical names, they encounter and try to overcome situations that typical teenage girls may experience at home and at school. The characters are very crudely drawn (on purpose) on notebook paper and lack any real detail (that is, while girls, they are not especially pretty or even have figures) and the program is simply a comical look at what happens as they attempt to become part of high school life (although, being a cartoon, some not so typical situations).

Voice Cast: Mike Chapman, Matt Chapman, Missy Palmer. **Credits:** *Producer:* Matt Chapman. *Writer-Director:* Matt Chapman, Mike Chapman. **Comment:** Although the animation is crude, the program now has a cult following and is quite enjoyable for what it is: totally unique and unlike any network or cable cartoon series.

Episode List: 17 untitled episodes, labeled "Issue #1" through "Issue #17" have been produced.

517 Teenage Mermaids. youtube.com. 2011 (Fantasy).

Two sisters (Mia and Haliea) are conducting research on Mermaids via the Internet when it appears that the information they have found has affected them in ways they never thought possible. When the sisters each come in contact with water they transform into Mermaids and, although the program just ends at this point, it is assumed they will attempt to keep secret what happened as they adjust to their developing powers.

Cast (as credited): Mia and Haliea as Themselves. **Comment:** Very poorly presented program as it looks like two girls just having fun and not really devoted to making an acceptable series. The girls are pretty, but pretty in this case cannot salvage the concept (especially when other family members can be seen lingering in the background and trying to avoid being seen on camera).

Episode List: *1.* Pilot.

518 Teenage Tails. youtube.com. 2013 (Fantasy).

Friends Dani and Holly are in a public park when they find a mysterious box that was supposedly placed there by an unknown person in 1962. The girls take the box home and upon examining its contents, find a magic potion that transforms them into Mermaids. It is assumed, since all episodes have been taken offline, that the girls will struggle to keep secret what happened while pretending to be ordinary girls.

Cast (as credited): Dani and Holly as Themselves. **Comment:** Only a 63 second teaser remains on line and, while is does have nice photography and pretty girls, it is not possible to make an evaluation of the entire series based on just that.

519 Tennessee Tailz. youtube.com. 2013 (Fantasy).

It appears to be an ordinary day for a young girl (Marissa) who is enjoying herself at the beach until she takes a walk and discovers a girl (Oceana) lying on the sand. As Marissa approaches the girl she learns that, other than her name, she has no memory of who she is or where she came from. Without her parents' permission, Marissa invites Oceana to live with her until she can remember who she is and where she lives. It is soon revealed that Oceana is a Mermaid when she comes in contact with water and the program is basically a look at how Marissa helps Oceana adjust to her new circumstances and how Oceana finds numerous mishaps living as a human girl.

Cast (as credited): Vickie (Marissa), Belinda (Oceana), Megan (Melody), Zoe (Roxy), Amanda (Chloe). **Comment:** The photography and acting are acceptable but there are very limited Mermaid sequences and the introduction is kind of hard to accept as one girl just invites another girl to live with her without knowing anything about her.

Episode List: *1.* Washed Up. *2.* Secrets. *3.* Blackout. *4.* A New Girl. *5.* Oceana's Christmas. *6.* The Weirdness of It All. *7.* It's a Secret. *8.* Full Moon Party. *9.* Continental Drift. *10.* Season Finale.

520 Three Sea Tails. youtube.com. 2015 (Fantasy).

An unusual presentation wherein a young girl (Asia), situated in her bedroom, fantasies about what it would be like to become a Mermaid. Asia talks directly to the camera and uses the accessories in her bedroom to simulate a pool, its bubbling water and how her entrance into that pool transforms her into a Mermaid. She then relates the problems associated with being a creature of the sea and how she must live two different lives. **Cast:** Asia White (Asia). **Comment:** Asia controls the entire production and while it would seem unlikely that such a premise would work, it does as Asia is pretty, personable, at ease and able to relate to an audience. **Episode List:** 3 untitled episodes, labeled "Episode 1," "Episode 2" and "Episode 3" have been produced.

521 *The Three Tails.* *youtube.com.* 2013 (Fantasy).

Three young girls (Jackie, Selena and Emily) meet on a beach, become instant friends and decide to go swimming. It is the time of a half moon and, as the girls enter the water, strange sounds are heard (like whale "singing"). Suddenly, as the water becomes increasingly rough, they swim to the safety of an underwater cave. Here, Jackie spies writing on the wall and, as she reads it, she, Selena and Emily are transformed into Mermaids (with lime green tails and green bikini tops). Before the girls can even comprehend what has happened, they are magically transported to Emily's home and dressed as they were before the transformation. The situation does not seem to faze the girls until Emily accidentally spills water on herself and transforms into a Mermaid. When Jackie and Selena attempt to dry Emily's tail, they touch the water and are also transformed. When the water evaporates, the girls return to their normal selves but now must guard their secret, learn to encompass their developing Mermaid powers and try to live their lives as ordinary girls.

Season one episodes are basically an introduction to Jackie, Serena and Emily (and their nemesis, Mia) and their efforts to adjust to becoming Mermaids. The second season finds Mia attempting to adjust to the fact that she is now a Mermaid and her involvement with Jackie, Emily and Serena when Jackie finds a book once owned by a girl named Faith. Faith, an evil Siren who died 200 years ago, is awakened from her long sleep when Jackie begins reading passages from the book and finds the girls' the instruments through which to return to life—by acquiring their powers. Their effort to destroy Faith's spirit concludes the season when they concoct a potion that appears to accomplish their goal. However, Faith is a feline Mermaid and has nine lives—and to destroy her, they must literally kill her nine times (the plot of the concluding third season episodes). In season two, the Mermaid tail colors change to aqua and conclude in the third season with orange and purple colors.

Cast: Natasha Garreton (Emily Emery), Sofia Garreton (Jackie Sky), Marlena Lerner (Selena White), Julianna Goldsmith (Faith), Ruby Ray (Mia), Saga Dios (Nikki). **Comment:** A bit more complex than an ordinary Mermaid series that encompasses more than just young girls becoming Mermaids as they also have to battle an evil foe. The acting is acceptable and like most such series, the audio and video quality is poor at times.

Season 1 Episode List:
1. Waters Change.
2. The Fight.
3. Cancun's Waters.
4. Birthday Tail.
5. Charmed.
6. Halloween Horror Night.
7. Study Hazard.
8. Mia's Revenge.
9. Christmas Disaster.
10. The Attack.
11. Sea Change.
12. Pressure Tail.

Season 2 Episode List:
13. Tail Trouble.
14. School Tail.
15. Fish Can't Swim.
16. Answers or Not.
17. Power Outage.
18. Scaly Troubles.
19. Black Revenge.
20. 1871.

Season 3 Episode List:
21. It's Back.
22. Back Again.
23. Christmas Magic.
24. Is This a Trick?
25. Spells and Magic.
26. Secrets Aren't Safe.
27. Somebody Is Hiding Something.

522 *The Three Water Girls.* 2011 (Fantasy).

While enjoying themselves at the lake, three girls (Nikki, Melissa and Selena; later Kylie) find what appear to be ordinary rings and lockets in the water. The girls elect to keep the jewelry and return home. Later when the girls come in contact with water (after using a waterslide) a metamorphosis occurs and they transform into Mermaids. While the girls do develop powers and have to battle an evil Mermaid hunter, they also acquire strange side effects after watching an eclipse and must now navigate life as magical creatures of the sea.

Cast (as credited): Nikki, Melissa, Selena, Kylie. **Comment:** A good idea (incorporating a Mermaid hunter) but the program has very poor sound coupled with equally bad photography (very jumpy picture). The program has since been taken offline.

Season 1 Episode List: *1.* Something Fishy. *2.* Diving In. *3.* A Day at the Beach. *4.* Unknown Title.

5. The Rings. 6. Who Had Seen Them? 7. Season Finale.

Season 2 Episode List: 8. Kylie Arrives. 9. Heat Vision. 10. The Lockets. 11. Surprise!! 12. Missing.

523 Too Many Secrets. *youtube.com.* 2013 (Fantasy).

While enjoying a swim in a river, three girls (see cast) encounter a waterfall and swim into it. The following day the girls decide to revisit the waterfall and again swim into it. This time, however, the water begins to bubble and strange lights encircle them. The experience transforms them into Mermaids and grants them each special powers. The girls attend a boarding school (and share room 336) and now must keep secret what happened as they attempt to control their powers and pretend to be ordinary girls. The fourth episode introduces a new roommate (Lily), who also becomes a Mermaid as the story progresses.

Cast: The cast lists that follow are how they appear in certain episodes. Either the mix ups are a mistake or done on purpose (an inside joke). *Episode 1*: Lanie as Missy; Claire as Lily; Kylee as Lauran; Pailsey as Alsie. *Episodes 2 and 3*: Claire as Lily; Jess as Lauren (not spelled as before—Lauran); Lanie as Missy; Paisley (as Alcie; also not spelled as before—Alsie). *Episodes 5 and 6*: Jess as Lauren; Lilly as Claire; Lainie as Missy; Peyton as Alsie. Both Lily (now spelled as Lilly) and Lanie (now as Lainie) have changed. *Episodes 7 and 8*: Jess as Lauren; Lilly as Claire; Lainie as Missy; Peyton as Alsie.

Comment: Other than the confusing cast listing the program has good acting and photography.

Episode List: *1.* Waterfall. *2.* Powers. *3.* Boarding School. *4.* The New Girl. *5.* Mermaids. *6.* Practice Makes Failure. *7.* Mission Impossible. *8.* New Powers, New Places.

524 Traci Hines, Mermaid. *youtube.com.* 2010–2011 (Variety).

Traci Hines is a gorgeous young woman who is equally gorgeous as a Mermaid and who has come ashore to relate various aspects of the Mermaid world (and what it would be like to be one) to young girls.

Cast: Traci Hines as Herself. **Comment:** Television series quality production that is simply Traci Hines being a Mermaid to the fascination of the young girls who envision themselves as being in the same position. See also *A Day in the Life* and *Hipster Mermaid.*

Episode List: *1.* Hipster Mermaid Teaser. *2.* Part of Your World, Traci Hines. *3.* The Little Mermaid Sings "In Harmony" Featuring Traci Hines as Ariel. *4.* Sirenia Mermaid Photo Shoot. *5.* A Mermaid Tutorial with Traci Hines. *6.* Traci Hines' Fantasy—Live in Hollywood. *7.* Little Mermaid Medley, Traci Hines (at Anime LA 2011). *8.* Traci Hines Performs "Kiss the Girl" as Ariel from *The Little Mermaid. 9.* Traci

Hines as The Little Mermaid Talks about Seeing a Human for the First Time. *10.* Traci Hines as The Little Mermaid. *11.* I'll be at MerPalooza in Orlando Next Week! *12.* Mermaids Are Real! MerPalooza in Orlando.

525 Transformers: Cyber Missions. *you tube.com.* 2010 (Cartoon).

A computer animated project in the Hasbro Transformers toy line that is a supplement to the live action film series that takes place between *Transformers: Revenge of the Fallen* and *Transformers: Ark of the Moon.* Like the films, it continues to depict the Autobots (robots capable of transforming themselves into vehicle-like weapons) battle against the evil Decepticons. Optimus Prime is the leader of the Autobots (which include Bumblebee, Ironhide, Ratchet and Sideswipe), while Megatron leads The Decepticons (Starscream, Soundwave, Bludgeon, Lockown, Mindwipe, Barricae and Frenzy).

Voice Cast: Eric Edwards (Optimus Prime), Tom Anderson (Bumblebee), Tony Gialluca (Megatron, Smolder, Chopster, Barricade, Bludgeon, Frenzy, Ironhide), Bronco D. Jackson (Bludgeon, Frenzy, Lockdown, Mindwipe, Ratchet, Sideswipe, Soundwave). **Credits:** *Producer:* Aaron Archer, Erin Hillman, Michael Verrecchia. *Writer:* Scott Beatty. **Comment:** The animation matches the style of the movie and TV versions but it is really directed at fans of the franchise as having prior knowledge of what the characters are helps greatly to understand what is going on.

Episode List: 13 episodes, titled "Cyber Missions 1" through "Cyber Missions 13" have been produced.

526 Trapped in a Fairy Tale Book. *youtube. com.* 2013 (Comedy).

An extension series adapted from *Seven Super Girls* (see entry). Here Kaelyn, C.J., Nicole, Jenna, Katherine, Rachel and Grace are in the spotlight (and appear together as opposed to individual segments on *Seven Super Girls*). When Nicole finishes reading a book of fairy tales and wishes that she and her friends could visit a fairy tale world, her wish is granted and now she, Kaelyn, C.J., Jenna, Katherine, Rachel and Grace are not only transformed into fairy tale characters but must find a way to return to their own world when they discover that Nicole's wish has also trapped them in Fairy Tale World.

Cast (as credited): Kaelyn (Red Riding Hood), Jenna (Goldilocks), Nicole (Evil Dragon), Grace (Cinderella), Katherine and Rachel (Evil Stepsisters), C.J. (Princess). **Comment:** The acting and production is very good but there are no elaborate backgrounds (as would be seen in a fairy tale). It is charming and will appeal to children who adore the stars of the parent series.

Episode List: *1.* SSG (Seven Super Girls) Trapped.

2. Fairy Tale Trouble. 3. Kaelyn is Red Riding Hood. 4. Jenna or Goldilocks? 5. SGG Turns Evil? 6. We're in Trouble. 7. Nicole is Evil Dragon?

527 Trapped Mermaid: Barbie Mini Doll Series. *youtube.com*. 2014–2015 (Dolls).

A program that encompasses the Mattel line of Barbie doll Mermaids: Ashley and Alex (teenage Mermaids), Adora, a pre-teen Mermaid and Purple, Ashley's pet sea turtle. Ashley and Purple are enjoying a swim in the ocean when they are spotted by a human diver seeking a valuable treasure called the Sea Diamond. As Ashley and Purple try to avoid the diver, Ashley is shot by a tranquilizer dart and rendered unconscious. As the diver takes Ashley back to his boat (where he and his partner believe they can make a fortune for capturing a Mermaid), Purple summons the help of Alex and Adora. The program follows Alex, Adora and Purple's efforts to rescue Ashley before she is taken into the human world and put on display as an aquarium attraction.

Comment: A cast or credits is not given (other than the name Candy, which appears on the program's website). The girls who handle the dolls and provide the voices do an excellent job against well designed underwater scenes. The story is well thought out and the photography and presentation are excellent.

Episode List: 5 untitled episodes, labeled "Episode 1" through "Episode 5" have been produced.

528 Travel Sisters. *youtube.com*. 2012 (Comedy).

With only one episode produced, it appears that the lives of two girls, Jacqueline and Jacky, will be followed as they just go about their daily activities. The project appears to have been abandoned and there is no text information or any additional videos by which to figure out the story line.

Cast (as credited): Mia (Jacqueline), Katarina (Jacky). **Comment:** While the only produced episode is acceptable in picture quality and acting, and the girls are pretty, why it was just stopped is left a mystery.

Episode List: 1. Season 1, Episode 1.

529 The Treasure Secret. 2011 (Fantasy).

Many years ago a sailor supposedly hid a great treasure in an area called Climber's Rock. A legend grew over the years and now people have come to suspect the story is true, but the exact location of the treasure is unknown. Two sisters (Haile and Niki) intrigued by the legend, decide to search for the treasure. Using the only known clue that exists (sea shells marking the spot), the girls begin searching Climber's Rock and stumble across the sea shells and what appears to be a hollow tree stump. Haile and Niki look inside, find a box and take it home with them. Upon opening the box they find jewels, necklaces and two pouches—one red and one black. Each contains a necklace and a strange stone. The necklaces are too pretty not to wear and Niki and Haile each place them around their necks. Later, however, when they each come in contact with water, they transform into Mermaids. Although the girls have uncovered an apparent great wealth, their only concern is dealing with what happened and keeping that a secret. The program follows Niki and Haile as they adjust to their Mermaid powers and efforts to deal with all the problems that go along with them.

Cast (as credited): Haile and Niki as Themselves. **Comment:** A different approach to how girls become Mermaids with pretty girls, good acting and nice photography. The program has since been taken offline.

Episode List: 7 untitled episodes, labeled "Episode 1" through "Episode 7" have been produced.

530 True Blue. 2012 (Fantasy).

Emma and Kensley are best friends who, while walking along the beach, discover a strange willow tree that they had never seen before. Upon examining the tree they uncover two mysterious lockets that when touched endows them with the abilities of a Mermaid. While they are not affected at first, they do discover what they have become when they first touch water. The program follows their efforts to adjust to what has happened and somehow adjust to the dual lives they must now live.

Cast: Bay Patterson (Emma), Abby Evans (Kensley). **Comment:** The premise is a bit different, the girls are pretty but the sound and photography are a bit poor at times; the program has since been taken offline.

Episode List: 1. Ocean Potion. 2. Episode 2. 3. Fishy Friend. 4. Tide Rising. 5. Christmas Tail. 6. Finale.

531 Truly Fishy. 2011 (Fantasy).

Two girls (Carlee and Lauren) lost during a long walk, come across a river and decide to swim it upstream to get back home. Unknown to them, its waters are magic and has the power to make young girls Mermaids. Carlee and Lauren are unaffected at first, but once home and once they come in contact with water, their transformation begins and each becomes a Mermaid. Now, faced with living dual lives, Carlee and Lauren must keep secret their Mermaid abilities while trying to live as ordinary girls.

Cast (as credited): Brooke (Carlee Harper), Sierra (Becca Adams), Maddie (Lauren Stoll). **Comment:** The underwater photography is good, the girls seem to be enjoying themselves (acting natural) but the sound is poor and the above water scenes are somewhat shaky at times. The program has since been taken offline.

Episode List: *1.* Something Fishy. *2.* Blue Waters. *3.* Double Life. *4.* No Control. *5.* Tough Seashells. *6.* A Splash of Truth. *7.* The Last Goodbye? *8.* Too Much Sunlight. *9.* Three's a Charm. *10.* Falling in Sunset. *11.* Some Things Change.

532 *Truly H2O.* youtube.com. 2013 (Fantasy).

"We have to keep it a secret. We don't want to become science experiments or something worse" is said by a young girl named Marina when she and her two girlfriends (Dylan and Sanna) find their lives changed forever after swimming in enchanted waters and being transformed into Mermaids (it occurred when Dylan and Marina's identical necklaces locked and they were transported to a mysterious underwater cave that endowed them with the unique ability to transform). With each there to help the other, Dylan, Sanna and Marina must now keep secret what happened to them and convince the world they are ordinary girls.

Cast (as credited): Claudia (Marina), Genevieve (Dylan), Sara (Sanna). **Comment:** Good acting, pretty girls and underwater photography coupled with adequate special effects. Like most Mermaid series, the program suffers from poor sound at times.

Episode List: *1.* Changes in the Water. *2.* Miss Popularity's Pool. *3.* Frostbite. *4.* Moonstruck Mermaid. *5.* Boiling Over. *6.* Knowledge Is Power. *7.* Suspicions Rising. *8.* T Is for Trouble.

533 *Tumble Leaf.* youtube.com. 2013–2014 (Cartoon).

Fig, a blue fox, and Stick, his caterpillar friend, live on a magical island called Tumble Leaf. It is here, through the playful adventures they share with their friends (Maple, Rutabaga, Hedge, Pine and Ginkgo) that basic scientific lessons are taught to pre-school children (Fig lives in an abandoned shipwreck where the ins and outs of items found on the ship are explored).

Voice Cast: Christopher Downs (Fig/Stick), Brooke Wolloff (Maple), Jodi Downs (Rutabaga), Landon Clay (Hedge), Addie Zintel (Pine), Gary Littman (Ginkgo), Emily Downs (Butternut), Alex Franzenburg (Zucchini). **Credits:** *Producer:* Kelli Bixler, Alice Wilder, Drew Hodges. *Director:* Drew Hodges. *Writer:* Douglas Wood, Kacey Arnold, Drew Hodges, Dev Ross, Corey Powell, Villamor Cruz, Noelle Wright, Christopher Keenan. *Producer:* Kelli Bixler, Alice Wilder, Drew Hodges. **Comment:** The program airs for a fee on Netflix (its original channel) but can be viewed for free on YouTube. Each computer animated episode consists of two segments (hence the A-B listing) and while adults will find it a bit ridiculous, toddlers (its target audience) will find it quite amusing as they discover what constitutes an everyday item (like a wheel or tire).

Episode List:
1A. Shiny Coins.
1B. Fig Finds a Shadow.
2A. Fig Flies a Kite.
2B. Missing Muffin.
3A. Beat of the Drumsticks.
3B. Springy Surprise.
4A. On a Roll.
4B. Popcorn Picture Show.
5A. Fig Blends In.
5B. Twirling Top.
6A. The Swimming Hole.
6B. Bucket of Mud.
7A. Loopy Straw.
7B. Tumble Leaf Parade.
8A. Ice Igloo.
8B. The Big Dig.
9A. Woohoo Kazoo.
9B. Hide and Seek.
10A. Fig's Speedy Sled.
10B. Parachute Play.
11A. The Lost Spyglass.
11B. Fig's Breakfast Surprise.
12A. Bedtime Story.
12B. A Treasure Hunt.
13A. Merry-Gear-Round.
13B. Pushy Pulley.

534 *Turbo Fast.* youtube.com. 2013 (Cartoon).

A spin off from the computer animated feature film *Turbo* that continues the story of Turbo, a snail living in Starlight City and addicted to racing. It began when Turbo won the Indianapolis 500 and a special racing track was built for him and all snails. Now, with his brother Chet and his friends Burn, Whiplash, Skidmark, White Shadow and Smoove Move, their adventures in the world of racing are explored.

Voice Cast: Reid Scott (Turbo), Eric Bauza (Chet), Michael Bell (White Shadow), John Eric Bentley (Whiplash), Grey DeLisle-Griffin (Burn), Phil LaMarr (Smoove Move), Amir Talai (Skidmark), Ken Jeong (Kim Ly). **Credits:** *Producer:* Ben Kalina, Shannon Barrett Prynoski, Jennifer Ray. *Director:* Anthony Lioi, Phil Allora, Anthony Chun, Nate Clesowich, Juno Lee, Michael Moloney. **Comment:** Flash animation is used as opposed to the computer animation for the feature film. It resembles the kind of animation one would see on The Cartoon Network or Nickelodeon and becomes acceptable after adjusting to it. The program is available for free viewing on YouTube or for a fee on Netflix, the channel for whom the program was made. It is the first series for children produced for Netflix.

Episode List:
1. Crazy Fast.
2. Dungball Derby.
3. Ace of Race.
4. Bumperdome.

5. Broaches.
6. African Queen.
7. Mega Snails.
8. Ants Revolution.
9. Clamsquatch.
10. Turbo Stinks.
11. Snails in Jail.
12. A Tale of Two Turbos.
13. The Escargot Affair.
14. Srurf 'n' Turf.
15. Hardcase Returns.
16. Turbo Drift.
17. Ready, Set, Glow.
18. Breakneck's Back.
19. Cruise Control.
20. R/C Turbo.
21. Curse of the Cicadas.
22. Beat-a-Fajita.
23. Karmageddon.
24. Chet Gets Burned.
25. Gypsy Moth Prophecies.
26. Skidzo-Brainia.
27. No Can Do.
28. Adopt-a-Toad.
29. Buster Move.
30. Gills.
31. The Terror of Tickula.
32. Prank'd.
33. Over Shadowed.
34. Beware the Chickipede.
35. Mall Is Well.
36. Taco Tank.
37. Zoo Lander.
38. Balloonatics.
39. The Packet Racket.
40. Smack Me Down.
41. Smoovin' on Up.
42. The Great Shell Robbery.
43. Chet vs. Dr. Disorder.
44. Damselfly in Distress. Dome Sweet Dome.
45. My Pet Clamsquatch.
46. Hard Luck Hardcase.
47. To Bee or Not To Bee.
48. Tur-bros.
49. The Snail Man.
50. The Challenge.
51. Home on Our Own.
52. The Mighty Snails.
53. Silent but Deadly.
54. Agent Ace.
55. Smoove as Ice.
56. The Disappearing Act.
57. The Sting of Justice.
58. The Treasure of Sierra Madre.
59. Big Baby.
60–61. Turbodly Go.
62. Crow Pox.
63. Faking Amends.
64. Deuce Is Wild.
65. To Fire a Squire.
66. Maggotron.
67. Love Hurts.
68. Ransom of White Shadow.
69. Kicked Off.
70. The Day Mel Fell.
71. Burn's Ex-Boo.
72. Tough as Snails.
73. Conspiracy.
74. Groundhog, Stay.
75. Gone Guys Gone.

535 Twins. 2012 (Dolls).

The Mattel Barbie dolls are used to relay the story of Emily and Emma, twin sisters who share a love/hate relationship.

Cast (as credited): Sweetie and Cutie. **Comment:** The pilot presents only the series theme and nothing else. It has a fuzzy picture, low sound and the hands of the girls who manipulate the dolls can be seen. The concept is good but the presentation is flawed. The program has since been taken offline.

Episode List: *1.* Pilot.

536 Twins of the Atlantic. *youtube.com.* 2011 (Fantasy).

While walking to school two friends (Alice and Faith) find two strange-looking necklaces that each contain several unusual gems. Thinking nothing of it, the girls keep the necklaces—but when they return home and come in contact with water, each transforms into a Mermaid. As they learn to accept what has happened to them, they must also lead double lives and protect their Mermaid abilities from being discovered by others.

Cast (as credited): Paige (Alice), Savannah (Faith), Sierra (Riley). **Comment:** Poor sound quality but pretty girls coupled with good underwater photography.

Episode List: *1.* Sea Change. *2.* Fire and Ice. *3.* Party Time. *4.* Marilia. *5.* Babysitting Troubles. *6.* Ancestor Bracelet. *7.* Dance Camp.

537 The Two Mermaids (Series 1). *youtube. com.* 2014 (Fantasy).

Friends Maddy and Melissa are at the beach when they decide to explore the surrounding area. As they walk they stumble across a cave filled with colorful beads. Maddy becomes attracted to a gold one and Melissa a purple one. Walking further into the cave, they find an old chest covered with sand. Curious, they dig out the chest, open it and not only find jewels but an old piece of parchment with instructions on it (actually a spell to become a Mermaid). As the girls read the instructions they are confused by the last line which tells them the change was permanent. Soon afterward, both Maddy and Melissa experience light headedness and pass out. Each has a dream:

Maddy about something gold and scaly and swimming in water; Melissa about something purple and scaly and also swimming in the water. It is twenty minutes later when the girls awake and they figure it is best if they just head for home. A short time later, when the girls come in contact with water they are transformed into Mermaids—Maddy with a gold tail and Melissa with a purple one. Now with a secret they must keep and with powers they do not fully understand, Maddy and Melissa must navigate a new life with the program chronicling what happens as they attempt to do so. **Cast (as credited):** Hannah (Maddy), Monie (Melissa). **Comment:** The girls are very pretty and act like a comedy team with Maddy as the straight "man" and Melissa as the patsy; it truly adds fun to the presentation. Overall, the acting and production are very good. **Episode List:** *1.* A Mystery. *2.* A Scaly Surprise. *3.* A Powerful Change. *4.* Danger. *5.* The Strike. *6.* Changes. *7.* Jealousy. *8.* The Potion. *9.* The Fight. *10.* The Finale.

538 *The Two Mermaids (Series 2). youtube. com.* 2014 (Fantasy).

While walking along the beach a young girl (Shelly) finds a strange-looking rock near the opening of a cave. Curious that other such rocks may be inside the cave, Shelly enters and begins exploring it. She suddenly finds herself near a water fall and is doused by its magical waters. Shelly appears to be unharmed and returns home. The following morning, however, when Shelly comes in contact with water, she transforms into a Mermaid. As Shelly comes to terms with what has happened to her, she meets her new neighbor, Rose, a girl who discovers her secret when Shelly accidentally spills water on herself and transforms into a Mermaid. Although startled, Rose promises to keep her secret and help her adjust to her Mermaid abilities. All is progressing well until a girl (Bella) sees what she believes is a Mermaid (Shelly) swimming in the ocean and sets out on a mission to uncover just what she saw. It is later revealed that the magic waterfall was created by a Marine Biologist who, with Bella's help, is seeking to capture the elusive sea creature (Shelly) it created. Shelly and Rose's efforts to foil Bella and remain free are the focal point of stories. **Cast (as credited):** Ruby (Shelly Court), Georgia (Rose Summon), Tallulah (Bella Matthews). **Comment:** The program is produced in Australia and is a bit difficult to understand at times due to accents. Its production is typical of American Mermaid shows with acceptable acting and production values. **Season 1 Episode List:** *1.* New Girl in Town. *2.* Something Fishy. *3.* Spotted. *4.* The Secret's Out. *5.* Not So Secret. *6.* Full Moon. *7.* Finale. **Season 2 Episode List:** *1.* Spells and Potions. *2.* Forgotten.

539 *Two Scales.* 2012 (Fantasy).

Friends Emma and Bella are walking through the woods when they stumble across two necklaces hanging from a tree branch. While their curiosity is aroused as to how they got there, they remove them from the branch and place them around their necks. As they continue walking and find they need to cross a stream, the water transforms them into Mermaids. The program ends as this point with no text or video information indicating what will happen next. **Cast (as credited):** Chloe (Emma), Hannah (Bella). **Comment:** The acting is acceptable but the camera is a bit shaky at times. It has since been taken offline. **Episode List:** *1.* The Beginning.

540 *Two Secrets. youtube.com.* 2014 (Fantasy).

Taylor and Courtney are friends who are about to go swimming when they find two necklaces that, when touched, opens a magical portal that transports them to a cave. Bubbling water soon engulfs them but they are apparently unaffected by what has happened. Later, after finding their way out of the cave and returning home, Taylor and Courtney find their lives changed forever when they come in contact with water and transform into Mermaids. The girls theorize that wearing the necklaces they found triggered the metamorphosis and they must now accept what has happened to them. The program chronicles their efforts to keep their secrets while helping each other learn how to use and control their Mermaid powers. **Cast (as credited):** Elizabeth (Taylor), Krista (Courtney), Nicole (Melissa). **Comment:** The camera work is a bit jerky at times but the girls are pretty and the overall concept well handled. **Episode List:** *1.* Our Story Begins. *2.* Problems Arise. *3.* Is It the Moon? *4.* She's Not Who We Think She Is. *5.* Trouble in Target. *6* A New Friend.

541 *The Two Silver Tails. youtube.com.* 2014 (Fantasy).

While talking with her girlfriend Brooklyn, a young girl (Blaire) spots a bracelet hanging from the side of her home. After examining it, Brooklyn sees a similar bracelet just a few feet away and takes it. Each girl places her bracelet around her neck not realizing their lives are about to change forever. Later that day, when the girls touch water, they transform into Mermaids with specific powers: teleportation, shape-shifting and control over water (Blaire can heat water; Brooklyn can freeze it). The program charts their experiences as they struggle to guard their secret (especially from Blaire's stepsister, Katie) and pretend to be ordinary girls. **Cast (as credited):** Erin (Blaire), Julie (Brooklyn), Natalie (Katie). **Comment:** The acting is acceptable, the girls pretty, the underwater photography good but poor sound hampers the production. **Episode List:** *1.* Two Necklaces and One Big Secret. *2.* Power Hour. *3.* Splash from the Past. *4.* A Day at the Lake. *5.* Step Sister Trouble. *6.* Episode 6. *7.* Magical Tail Change and Bottle.

542 *The Two Tailed Mermaids. youtube. com.* 2012 (Fantasy).

Two young girls (Annie and Emma) are playing soccer in a public park when they chase a stray ball and find it has lead them to the banks of a river. Thinking nothing of it, the girls retrieve the ball from the water and return to their game. Later, however, when Annie and Emma return home and come in contact with water they transform into Mermaids. They theorize that the river water was magical and caused their metamorphous. With their lives suddenly changed, Annie and Emma must now navigate life not only as magical Mermaids, but as ordinary girls as well. **Cast (as credited):** Megan (Annie), Sam (Emma), Alyssa (Amber), Cassidy (Jamie). **Comment:** Enjoyable story that is sometimes hampered by poor sound resulting from the use of the camera microphone. **Episode List:** *1.* Just the Beginning. *2.* Power Stones. *3.* Power Hour. *4.* One More Power. *5.* Sea Sick. *6.* Night of the Full Moon. *7.* Picture Perfect. *8.* Memory Loss. *9.* Double Crossed. *10.* Mermaid Amber. *11.* Birthday Wave. *12.* Lost on Shore. *13.* Washed Away. *14.* Power Storm.

543 *The Two Tails Mermaids. youtube.com.* 2012 (Fantasy).

Two girls (Alisa and Anya) are swimming in a river when they suddenly find themselves in a mysterious cave pool. As they attempt to adjust to where they are, the water begins to bubble and as mysteriously as they found themselves in the pool they are just as mysteriously transported back to the river. They are apparently unharmed but when they again go swimming, they are transformed into Mermaids. The program, based in Russia, follows Alisa and Anya as they attempt to deal with what has happened while pretending to be ordinary girls. **Cast (as credited):** Julia (Alisa) Sofia (Anya), Nastia (Lera). **Comment:** The program is produced in Russia and has no English subtitles or captions. Thus it is difficult to follow the series after the first episode (where just the visual images establish the story line). The girls are pretty and the acting and photography very good. **Season 1 Episode List:** *1.* Waters Change. *2.* Magic of Mermaids. *3.* New Tails. *4.* Full Change of Tails.

5. Third Mermaid. *6.* Mermaids Have Fun. *7.* The Strange Magic. *8.* Lera Was Not Meant to Be a Mermaid. *9.* Lera's Revenge. *10.* Unplanned Conversation. **Season 2 Episode List:** *1.* Anya and Alisa vs. Lera. *2.* Victory of Girls. *3.* Case in the Pool. *4.* Mermaid Dreams. *5.* Updating. *6.* Treachery. *7.* Alisa's Return. *8.* Revenge. *9.* New Spell. *10.* A New Image. **Season 3 Episode List:** *1.* Return. *2.* A Serious Mistake. *3.* New Riddle. *4.* Rescue. *5.* Riddle. *6.* Julia. *7.* Attack in the Woods. *8.* Magic. *9.* Magic Force. *10–11.* The Help. *12.* Journey. *13.* Finale.

544 *Two Tails, Three Wishes. youtube.com.* 2012 (Fantasy).

April and Nidia are friends whose lives change forever when, during a sleepover, each experiences a strange dream involving monkeys. While the dream has no apparent affects (other than unnerving them) they just shrug it off until they come in contact with water and are transformed into Mermaids. How monkeys figure into such transformations is not explained and the program follows the girls as they attempt to live normal lives while concealing their true existences as Mermaids. **Cast (as credited):** Sophie (April), Anna (Nidia), Lisa (Both mothers). **Comment:** The program has very poor sound and is not in the proper aspect ratio (instead of a normal image it has a badly stretched picture that presents the girls in an unflattering "fat" image). **Episode List:** *1.* Pilot.

545 *Under Sea Secret. youtube.com.* 2012 (Fantasy).

Cassidy is a young girl who, while walking through the woods, discovers a cave she has never been before. Afraid to enter it alone, Cassidy returns home and tells her sister Mckenna about the cave and if she will help her explore it. Mckenna agrees and Cassidy takes her to the scene of her find. As they explore the cave nothing appears to happen and they simply return home after becoming bored. Later, however, when each of the girls comes in contact with water she is transformed into a Mermaid. The program follows Cassidy and Mckenna as they struggle to keep secret what has happened while also living the lives of ordinary school girls.

Cast (as credited): Katelyn (Mckenna), Sara (Cassidy). **Comment:** The program is plagued by low sound but the photography is nice and the acting acceptable. The first episode of the second season ("Winter Woahs") has no sound.

Season 1 Episode List: *1.* Cave of Wonder. *2.* Warm Water. *3.* Trampoline Trouble. *4.* Double Tail. *5.* Ghostly Happenings. *6.* Christmas Fun. *7.* Florida Mermaid. *8.* The Magic Shell.

Season 2 Episode List: *1.* Winter Woahs. *2.* Rose Carpenter. *3.* All That Jazz.

546 Under the Sea Secrets. *youtube.com.* 2013 (Fantasy).

Zanna, a young girl with fanciful dreams, decides to make a potion (from a recipe she found) that she believes will turn her into a Mermaid. She drinks the potion and when she first comes in contact with water she transforms into a Mermaid—a secret she must keep as she struggles to also live life as an ordinary school girl.

Cast (as credited): Jessie (Zanna), Tala (Scarlette). **Comment:** A twist on how a young girl becomes a Mermaid, here using a home-brewed potion. The production suffers from poor audio quality but is acceptable in other aspects (acting and photography).

Episode List: *1.* I'm a What? *2.* The Forbidden Forest. *3.* Crazy Mermaid Stuff? *4.* Dangerous Waters. *5.* No Moon. *6.* Home Alone. *7.* Season Finale.

547 Undercover Mermaids. *youtube.com.* 2014 (Fantasy).

Three young girls (Kindle, Grace and Claire) are in the backyard of Kindle's home when Claire, curious to know if there are fish in her pond, loses balance and falls in. Kindle and Grace come to her rescue and in the process find three necklaces. The girls each take one of the necklaces and are enjoying their find until they come in contact with water and transform into Mermaids. The girls now share a secret they must keep as they attempt to adjust to their developing powers while pretending to be ordinary school girls.

Cast (as credited): Parker (Kindle), Lydia (Grace), Sarah (Claire). **Comment:** With the exception of bad sound produced when wind blows into the microphone, the production is very good with good acting and nice photography.

Episode List: *1.* Diving in Deep. *2.* Bloopers. *3.* Close Call. *4.* Power Discovered.

548 Underwater Adventures. *youtube.com.* 2015 (Fantasy).

While swimming in her backyard pool, a ten-year-old girl (Emily) finds a gem stone with a note attached: "This gem is going to make me into something different." Suddenly, the water beings to bubble but Emily is apparently unharmed. That evening, when Emily comes in contact with water, she is transformed into a Mermaid. As Emily accepts what has happened the program follows her progress as she begins to develop the power to control water and somehow manage to keep her secret yet live the life of an ordinary school girl.

Cast (as credited): Tereza P. (Emily). **Comment:** Although Emily is the only character, Tereza performs her role well. The photography is good (although the picture is a bit jumpy at times) and a nice touch has been added to compensate for occasional bad sound: adding sub titles.

Episode List: *1.* The Change. *2.* The Power Discovery. *3,4,5* Untitled episodes.

549 Underwater Life: Just Add Water. *you tube.com.* 2011 (Fantasy).

Three friends (Shelby, Rachel and Amanda) are walking through a forest when they suddenly find themselves in a pool (in someone's backyard). Nothing happens and the next scene shows the girls sleeping in the same bed together (it is assumed the girls had a sleepover). That morning, when each girl comes in contact with water, she is transformed into a Mermaid. How the girls adjust to what has happened to them and learn how to control their magical abilities is the focal point of stories.

Cast (as credited): Shelby, Rachel and Amanda (Themselves). **Comment:** The girls are very pretty but the production is bad (perhaps that is why the girls' state: "We know it's fake and we're just doing it for fun"). Only one camera was used and when it is not placed on a steady surface, the girl who has the least to do in a scene handles the camera, thus making for truly annoying and terrible photography (as she has to act and shoot a scene as well, producing very unsteady images as she moves about).

Episode List: 6 untitled episodes, labeled "Episode 1" through "Episode 6" have been produced.

550 Veggie Tales in the House. *veggietaes. com.* 2014 (Cartoon).

An extension series based on *Veggie Tales* (which ran on NBC and Qubo). The program, featuring a group of talking vegetables, continues in the tradition set by the original series with incidents revealed in their everyday lives as they interact with each other.

Bob the Tomato, a greeter at Pa Grape's Corner Store, is the main character, a level headed tomato who shares a room with the not-so-bright Larry the

Cucumber (who thrives on odd jobs and drives an ice cream cart and is secretly Veggie Town's super hero protector, LarryBoy).

Petunia Rhubarb, who loves plants, works part time for Pa Grape and is good friends with Bob and Larry (and she is often the only one who can resolve their differences).

Laura Carrot is a friend of Bob and Larry and also best friends with Junior Asparagus, a young "boy" who admires Larry.

Pa Grape is the elderly but wise green apple that runs Pa Grape's Corner Store.

Jerry and Jimmy Gourd are brothers who enjoy helping others they feel are in trouble (and not always with the best results).

Archibald Asparagus is the Mayor of the town.

Voice Cast: Phil Vischer (Bob the Tomato/Pa Grape/Jimmy Gourd/Archibald Asparagus), Mike Nawrocki (Larry the Cucumber/Jerry Gourd), Tress MacNeille (Petunia Rhubarb/Laura Carrot/Junior Asparagus). **Credits:** *Producer:* Douglas TenNapel, Chris Neuhahn, Randy Dormans. *Director:* Tim Hodge, Bill Breneisen, Craig George. *Writer:* Mike Nawrocki, Phil Vischer, Ethan Nicolle, Eric Branscum. **Comment:** Captures all the charm of the original series with excellent computer animation. The program, although produced for the pay service Netflix, can be viewed for free on YouTube.

Episode List:
1. Puppies and Guppies.
2. Sorry, We're Closed Today.
3. Bob and the Awesome Frosting Mustache.
4. Bob and Larry: Getting Angry.
5. Bob's Bad Breath.
6. Trading Places.
7. Jimmy and Jerry Are Rich.
8. Feelin' Hot, Hot, Hot.
9. Laura at Bat.
10. Pie Fight.
11. Pa Grape's Son.
12. Larry's Cardboard Thumb.
13. The Gong Heard 'Round the House.
14. When Dust Bunnies Came to Town.
15. The Bucket List.
16. A Gist for Singing.
17. Lie-Monade.
18. Let's Build a Fort.
19. Bacon and Ice Cream.
20. For the Honor of Larry Boy.
21. The Birthday Thief.
22. Jimmy Gets a Pet.
23. Cool as a Cucumber.
24. The Rich Young Comic Ruler.
25. Popcorn-tastrophe.
26. Junior Jetpack.
27. Monster Manners.
28. You, Me and Tiny Pea.
29. Jenna Chive Live.
30. Captain Larry Beard.
31. The Great Ice Cream Chase.
32. The Guppy Whisperer.
33. The Silly Ray.
34. The Camp Out.
35 Monster Truck Flower Delivery.
36. Vote for Archibald.
37. Ready for Action.
38. Sick-a-beezer.
39. Plant-demonium.
40. DUO Day.
41. Mayoral Bike Lessons.
42. It.
43. Callie Flower.
44. Word of Whiners.
45. Two Birthdays.
46. Playground Tales.
47. Spacetato.
48. Starved for Attention.
49. The Imposers.
50. Place Trading.
51. Locked Out.
52. Coach Ichabeezer.

551 *Video Game High School.* *rocketjump. com.* 2012 (Comedy).

It is the near future and video gaming has become the number one sport. Gamers vie for the opportunity to become enrolled at Video Game High School (VGHS), a prestigious academy for the world's best gamers, but achieving that honor is not easy: one must play matches in which they "kill" their opponents. One gamer, Brian soon develops a reputation for defeating his opponents as "The One Shot Wonder" and becomes a member of VGHS, but incurs the wrath of "The Law," the worlds best gamer and academy member who now fears his celebrity status is at risk. Stories follow Brian as he seeks to maintain his position despite The Law's efforts to humiliate him and force him out of the school.

Cast: Josh Blaylock (Brian Doheny), Johanna Braddy (Jenny Matrix), Jimmy Wong (Ted Wong), Ellary Porterfield (Ki Swan), Brian Firenzi (The Law), Benji Dolly (Games Dean), Harley Morenstein (Dean Ernie Calhoun). **Credits:** *Producer:* Matthew Arnold, Freddie Wong, Brandon Laatsch, Reza Izad, Sam Maydew, Dan Weinstein. *Director:* Matthew Arnold, Freddie Wong, Brandon Laatach. *Writer:* Josh Blaylock, Johanna Braddy, Ellary Porterfield, Jimmy Wong. **Comment:** Excellent special effects highlight the video game sequences that are incorporated into the program. The acting and production are also excellent and the program quite entertaining—even if you are not into video games.

Season 1 Episode List: *1.* Shot Heard Round the World. *2.* Welcome to Me. *3.* When You Know the Pit… *4.* Any Game in the House. *5.* And Then … the Law. *6.* Carpe Diem. *7.* Sign Up to Sign Out. *8.* Locked in the System. *9.* It's All About the Game.

Season 2 Episode List: *1.* Welcome to Varsity. *2.* You Can't Stop a Sandwich. *3.* Double XP Weekend.

4. 30 Foot Range. 5. Some Like It Bot. 6. Three Laps, Three Rounds, Three Words.

Season 3 Episode List: *1.* OMGWTFPS!? *2.* Nobody Cool Goes to Prom. *3.* A Map to Sex Town. *4.* Video Game Home School. *5.* Being a Teen Is Hard, I Guess. *6.* The N-64.

552 *Want to Know My Secret?* youtube.com. 2013 (Fantasy).

It is the night of a pending eclipse when a 12-year-old girl (Emily) stumbles across a green pearl necklace. Fascinated by it, Emily places it around her neck at the exact moment the eclipse occurs. Instantly she is transformed into a Mermaid and must now not only navigate life as a creature of the sea, but as an ordinary school girl as well. **Cast (as credited):** Emily Sinclair (Emily), Lucy (Melissa), Alicia (Gracie). **Comment:** The program is typical of the numerous Mermaid series created and filmed by young girls. It has generally good photography and acting but low sound and an unsteady picture at times.

Season 1 Episode List: *1.* Eclipse. *2.* A Secret for Two. *3.* Mermaid Meeting. *4.* The Test. *5.* Powers? *6.* The Dark Storm Cloud. *7.* A Casual Day at the Park. *8.* The Battle.

Season 2 Episode List: *1.* Paranoia. *2.* Zapped. *3.* Watch Your Back. *4.* Evil in Disguise. *5.* Keeping Secrets. *6.* Good Gone Bad. *7.* Broken Friendships. *8.* Two against One.

553 *Wastelander Panda.* wastelanderpanda. com. 2013 (Adventure).

In an unknown time in a post-apocalyptic world, a seven-year-old girl (Rose), wanders into an area called the Wasteland after she witnesses the murder of her parents but escapes undetected. As she decides to rest for the night she is awakened from her sleep by a rustling sound in the bushes. She discovers the noise to be coming from Isaac, a rogue panda that has left his home to explore new territories. Unfortunately, before the two can become close, Isaac is killed and Rose, having previously learned that he has a brother (Arcayus), vows to find him and avenge Isaac's death. After days of searching Rose finds Arcayus but Arcayus has settled into a life of solitude and refuses at first to help her; he later heeds to Rose's pleas and agrees to assist her. The program charts their adventures in strange lands and encounters with fantasy-like creatures as Rose sets out to accomplish her goal. **Cast:** Mandahla Rose (Rose), Sunny Heartfield (Young Rose), Marcus McKenzie (Arcayus), Roger Newcombe (Voice of Arcayus), Marcel Blanch de Wilt (Isaac), Richard Magarey (Voice of Isaac), Ryan Cortazzo (Akira), Bob Ramos (Voice of Akira), Andreas Sobik (Sweet Pete), Aaron Schuppan (Leopard Jacket), Nathan Cain (Decks), Colin Gould (Slate).

Credits: *Producer:* Sophie Hyde, Rebecca Summerton, Mike Jones, Kirsty Stark. *Writer-Director:* Victoria Cocks. **Comment:** Enjoyable fantasy with a well written story and good overall production values. Once achieving their goal, the program could continue as stories set in mystical lands are endless and often fascinating to watch.

Episode List: *1.* Isaac and Rose. *2.* Arcayus and Rose.

555 *Water + Magic = Tail.* youtube.com. 2011 (Fantasy).

It appears to be a typical morning for a young girl (Bella) until she finds a pendant in her mailbox. Not knowing where it came from or who put it there, Bella decides to keep it. Later, when Bella comes in contact with water, a startling metamorphous occurs and she is transformed into a Mermaid. The program follows Bella as she struggles to lead the life of an ordinary girl while struggling to keep her Mermaid abilities secret. **Cast as Credited:** Kristen (Bella), Alexis (Rikki), Elle (Cleo), Olivia (Emma). **Comment:** Although episodes have been taken offline, photos depicting Bella as a Mermaid show her as very pretty but her Mermaid tail rather cheesy looking (just not what tails look like in other Mermaid-themed shows like *A Splashy Tail*). The episodes did span three seasons but just disappeared after the tenth episode played.

Episode List: Ten untitled episodes, labeled "Episode 1" through "Episode 10" have been produced.

556 *The Water Girls.* youtube.com. 2013 (Fantasy).

Three girls, Isabella, Sophia and Alonna each share the same secret (they are Mermaids) but are unaware of it at first. While studying together for a test, Isabella suggests they take a break and go outside to relax near the pool. Alonna becomes a little playful and begins splashing the water. As the water touches the girls, it activates a recessed gene that transforms each of them into a Mermaid (it is explained that "a water accident" each of the girls experienced earlier in life but at different times, set the stage for their current metamorphous). With their secrets revealed, the girls now must protect and help the other while pretending to be ordinary school girls. **Cast (as credited):** Jolie (Alonna), Bella (Sofia), Lilly (Isabella), Daisy (Athena), Chey (Serena), Katie (Mackenzie). **Comment:** The program has acceptable acting and pretty girls but suffers at times from poor sound.

Season 1 Episode List: *1.* Water Lies. *2.* The Argument. *3.* The Death of the Little One. *4.* Related Differently. *5.* The Fishy Secret. *6.* The Ring Dream. *7.* Finale.

Season 2 Episode List: *1.* The New Girl. *2.* The Wise One.

557 Water Lilly Mermaid. *youtube.com.* 2014 (Fantasy).

Sirens, evil creatures of the sea, are seeking a magical stone, protected by Water Lilly Mermaids that can grant them the power to rule the oceans of the world. Nixie is one such Water Lily Mermaid but her abilities have not yet manifested. One day, while home alone, a package arrives for Nixie that she finds contains a strange stone, a journal and a note: "I never wanted you to be in this position, but desperate times call for desperate measures. I am in danger and I trust you to keep it (the stone) safe. Don't tell anyone except the others (Water Lily Mermaids) and keep it (the stone) a secret. The reason will be explained in the journal." As Nixie looks at the stone, an orange light emerges and she is transformed into a Mermaid. She then learns, by reading the journal, about her mission to safeguard the stone. As Nixie begins her search for others like her, she meets Miranda, a Water Lily Mermaid who has agreed to help her. Two Sirens, however, have become aware of Nixie and the program charts Nixie and Miranda's efforts to avoid the Sirens and keep the stone from falling into evil hands. **Cast (as credited):** Elizabeth (Nixie), Catherine (Miranda), Tia and Taylor (Sirens), Farrah (Jade). **Comment:** Typical Mermaid program with acceptable acting and production values. **Episode List:** *1.* Pilot. *2.* The Capture. *3.* New Currents. *4.* Power Hour. *5.* Who Are You? *6.* The Return of the Sirens. *7.* First Full Moon.

558 Water Red. 2015 (Fantasy).

A young girl (Zuri) is by her bedroom's window when she notices a large red diamond that appears to have suddenly materialized. As she picks it up and examines it, she finds herself puzzled as to where it came from. Moments later, when she goes to wash her hands, the water transforms her into a Mermaid. Although she is able to cover up what happened, she fears trouble is just a stone's throw away as she has a twin sister (Zoey) who will reveal what happened if she finds out. The program follows Zuri as she struggles to adapt to what she has become while hoping to keep her secret from Zoey and the rest of the world. **Cast (as credited):** Aniyah (Zuri and Zoey). **Comment:** While the program, featuring a young African-American girl tries to be different (using the twin concept) it is rather slow moving (takes too long to establish a situation) and has rather badly framed scenes (essentials are cut off). The program has since been taken offline. **Season 1 Episode List:** *1.* Mermaid Girl. *2.* Mermaid Found. *3.* Twin Frozen. *4.* Sneaky Twin. *5.* Stop. *6.* The Curse Is Reversed. **Season 2 Episode List:** *1.* Zuri Is Better. *2.* Zuri Can Not Take It. *3.* Jungle of Mermaids. *4.* Zuri is Trapped. *5.* Finale.

Season 3 Episode List: *1.* Sirens and Lies. *2.* Sick and Trick.

559 The Water Secrets. *youtube.com.* 2014 (Fantasy).

In the Mariana Trench in the North Pacific Ocean there exists a race of beings known as Merfolk who fear exposure and an eventually end to their world by humans as they continue to explore the seven seas. To hopefully keep their world secret, the Oceanic Council has selected Rowena, a Princess chosen by the laws of the Ancient Mermaids, to join Adacora and Rikkia, Mermaids already blended into human society, to insure the safety of Merworld. Rowena's experiences are chronicled as she not only unites with her Mermaid sisters, but battles the evil Sirens who also pose a threat to their safety. **Cast (as credited):** Tara (Princess Rowena/Jackie), Eliya (Adacora), Joanna (Rikkia Norik), Brian (Chancellor), Kip (Rakah), Samantha (Solveig), Cali (Tiana), Natalie (Misty Rose/Megan), Kelton (Starena), Grace (Scarlet Moon). **Comment:** A number of episodes have been taken offline making it difficult to piece together information and figure out what is happening. The underwater sequence with Rowena being chosen for her mission is well done but the sound is very low and difficult to hear (even at full volume). There are also other sound problems (like wind blowing into the microphone) and very bad framing in some scenes (the girls' heads cut off). On the plus side, the leads perform their roles well in a good idea that, unfortunately, does not play well. **Season 1 Episode List:** *1.* A New Leader. *2.* The Sleepover. *3.* The Dream. *4.* The Return of Rikkia. *5.* Hidden Bracelets. *6.* Princesses. *7.* The Search. *8.* Battle Scars. *9.* Siren Curse. *10.* A Dark Christmas. **Season 2 Episode List:** *1.* Fairy Magic. *2.* Channel's Tale. *3.* Run Away. *4.* Adacora's Sister? *5.* Mermaid Hunters. *6.* Wishes? *7.* Intruder. *8.* The End … Or Is It? *9.* Clones Aren't Fun. *10.* A Dark Mermaid and Bionic Super Humans?!

560 Waterman. *youtube.com.* 2003–2009 (Cartoon).

Various, idiotic events that spark the lives of a young man (Waterman) and his friends: Ice Cream Girl, Pal and Roybot. See also *Puppets in the Park*, the spin off series. **Voice Cast:** Bryan Waterman, Chris Barnhill, Katie Yorra, Devin Farmer. **Credits:** *Producer-Writer-Director:* Bryan Waterman. **Comment:** A very early series that encompasses good animation and humor that, in some cases, is geared to a teenage or adult audience (as children simply will not get it). The official website has been taken offline and the only episodes available for viewing can be found on YouTube. **Episode List:** *1.* Pilot. *2.* The Tournament. *3.*

Meet Mr. Dillo. *4.* 16 Buttons of Justice. *5.* The Legend of Peg Leg Bill. *6.* Watergent. *7.* Bacones Addiction. *8.* Reel Big Fish—Awesome Music Video. *9.* The June Box Derby.

561 The Waters Call. 2012 (Fantasy).

While out for a walk, a young girl (Alice) spies a necklace on the ground and picks it up. After examining it, she tosses it away but it magically returns to her. Believing that maybe she was meant to have the necklace, she puts it on, feels a shock but nothing else. Later, when she returns home and comes in contact with water (taking a drink) she transforms into a Mermaid (with sea shells in her hair). As Alice struggles to cope with what has happened to her she also finds that, through a talking sea shell, that she has been chosen for a special mission: to battle the evil Black Mermaids, who are seeking to destroy the good Mermaids.

Cast (as credited): Alice, Cameron, Luna. **Comment:** There is a huge gap in episodes making it difficult to figure out what is happening. The five part first episode can be watched but the next (and last) episode that can be viewed is Episode 8, Part 3. The acting is good but the photography is simply quite bad (very jerky and truly annoying to watch). The program has since been taken offline.

Episode List: *1.* Part 1 (5 serial-like episodes), *2.* Part 2 (7 segments), *3.* Part 3 (4 segments), *4.* Part 4 (7 segments), *5.* Part 5 (6 segments), *6.* Part 6 (4 chapters), *7.* Part 7 (5 chapters), *8.* Part 8 (4 chapters).

562 Waters of Mysteries. *youtube.com.* 2014 (Fantasy).

Jenny and Violet are sisters who have just moved into a new house with their parents. When they discover that there is a hot tub in their backyard they decide to use it. Shortly after, the girls find a magical rock at the bottom of the hot tub and touch it. The water begins to bubble (although the water remains still, a bubbling effect is heard) and girls are transformed into Mermaids—something they accept but are not sure how it happened. Later that day, Lilli, their neighbor, stops by to welcome them and asks if she can use their hot tub (as the prior owners would not allow her). Sort of taking matters into her own hands, Lilli (who is wearing a swim suit under her clothes) enters the hot tub and, after hearing that bubbling effect, is also transformed into a Mermaid. The program follows their mishaps as they attempt to safeguard their secret while living lives as ordinary school girls.

Cast (as credited): Juniper S. (Violet), Caroline S. (Jenny), Aidan H. (Lilli), Fay (Miranda), Jane S. (Violet and Jenny's mother). **Comment:** It is hard to tell if Violet and Jenny are real life sisters or just acting as their scenes are quite convincing as sisters. Lilli comes off as a bit too pushy, sort of a girl who

gets what she wants, no matter what. Overall though, the production is good.

Episode List: *1.* Hot Tub Mysteries. *2.* Being a Mermaid Is a Mystery. *3.* Mentors, Movies and Other Magic.

563 The Wave Breaker (2014). *youtube. com.* 2014 (Fantasy).

Three hundred years ago two sisters, Alice and Ann, were anything but the ideal children to their parents. For reasons that are not stated, the sisters hated each other and constantly argued. One day, while Alice stood on the edge of a cliff overlooking the ocean, Ann pushed her, causing Alice to plunge into the ocean and drown. Although Ann did not mean to kill Alice, it has disgraced her family and made Ann rethink her ways. Years later on a stormy night in a lonely house near the ocean Ann, now married, gives birth to a baby boy. Ann is startled to see the ghost of Alice appear to her, looking as she did before she drowned. Alice speaks only once and curses the bloodline with shame for all eternity. As mysteriously as she appeared, Alice vanishes never to be seen again.

It is the present day when viewers are introduced to a very pretty but lonely teenage girl named Malice, a descendant of that boy born 300 years ago. Malice, however, is not a Mermaid, but a girl whose emotions can control storms. If, for example, Malice becomes angered, the ocean waters rage with waves; sadness causes rain; and jealousy produces floods. But Malice is not alone as her inner thoughts (heard as a female voice that calls her "Wave Breaker") appear to guide her and it is through that inner voice that Malice reacts to the situations that surround her and how she deals with all the misery that is a part of her life—a curse begun when an innocent girl named Alice lost her life to the ocean's waters centuries ago.

Cast: Shoshana Hetherington (Malice), Carrie (Voice). **Comment:** A captivating and very unusual program that while listed as a Mermaid series is actually not (although the second episode does encompass a Mermaid through shadow puppetry). The atmosphere, background music, acting and photography are outstanding and it is, without a doubt one of the best of its kind.

Episode List: *1.* From Start to Finish. *2.* Fear. *3.* Confusion.

564 Wave Breaker (2015). 2015 (Fantasy).

A young girl (Elle) is on a boat, about to embark on a fishing trip with a friend, when she spies a green and pink-like light streaking through the water. As she looks, she loses her balance, falls into the water and while swimming a Mermaid's tail is seen brushing against her. Seconds later, Elle transforms into a Mermaid. Elle must now keep secret what has happened as she struggles to control her developing powers and pretend to be an ordinary girl.

Cast (as credited): Elle as Herself. Comment: The opening sequence with Elle on the shore of a lake and a much older man approaching her and asking her if she would like to join him on a fishing trip is somewhat creepy. Although the man turns out to be a friend of the family, it is still a bit unacceptable. Overall it is a fairly nice production with capable acting and nice photography. The program has since been taken offline.

Episode List: 3 untitled episodes, labeled "Episode 1." "Episode 2" and "Episode 3" were produced.

565 *The Waves.* 2012 (Fantasy).

One day, while looking for something to do, a young girl (Britney) stumbles across an unknown gooey substance that she touches and transforms her into a Mermaid when she comes in contact with water. Britney's efforts to keep secret what happened as she adjusts to her Mermaid abilities are the focus of the program.

Cast (as credited): Ashton Rosenhagen (Britney), Zoey (Herself), Rocky (Himself). Comment: Typical Mermaid series with pretty girls and acceptable acting but poor sound. The program has since been taken offline.

Episode List: 3 untitled episodes, labeled "Episode 1" through "Episode 3" have been produced.

566 *We Are Mermaids (2011).* 2011 (Fantasy).

Delilah and Lily are young girls, enjoying themselves in a backyard pool when they are suddenly transformed into Mermaids. Nothing is explained as to what caused the metamorphoses and nothing is hinted at what might occur next; it can only be assumed they will have to adapt to what has happened to them and learn to keep it a secret while pretending to be ordinary girls.

Cast (as credited): Delilah and Lily as Themselves. Comment: All the action takes place in the swimming pool. The sound is very poor (muffled) and difficult to understand. Overall, it appears that after two episodes of just the girls in the pool, the project has been abandoned; it has since been taken offline.

Episode List: 2 untitled episodes, labeled "Episode 1" and "Episode 2" have been produced.

567 *We Are Mermaids (2013).* 2013 (Fantasy).

Three teenage girls (Lisa, Megan and Kaisa) are using what appears to be a homemade version of a Ouija Board when they invoke an unknown spirit (presumably that of a Mermaid). Other than frightening the girls, nothing happens until they each come in contact with water and it is assumed they will become Mermaids (the first and only episode that remains on line ends here without revealing anything else).

Cast (as credited): Alesya Alekseeva (Megan), Lisete Kumari (Lisa), Maria Smirnova (Kaisa). Comment: The program appears to have been abandoned. It is produced in Russia and both Russian and English are spoken. The girls are very pretty and the acting and photography are very good. The program has since been taken offline.

Episode List: 8 untitled episodes, labeled "Episode 1" through "Episode 8" have been produced. The final three episodes encompass only the Russian language.

568 *Whirl Girl. whirlgirl.com.* 1997–2001 (Cartoon).

It is the mid–21st century and Zone Werks, an evil media and technology corporation run by Ty Harden, has taken control of mankind. One woman, Morgan Cross, has become a symbol for freedom and become the head of a revolutionary group dedicated to destroying Ty. Morgan's fight ended in her death and her daughter, Kia, was captured and brainwashed to forget what had happened. But as time passed Kia's memory returned and, recalling her mother's actions, picks up where she left off and transforms herself into the super hero Whirl Girl (attired in blue bikini-like top, blue miniskirt and blue boots). With her weapon, the Whirl Blade and her fighting move, the Spin Kick, Kia begins her own battle against Ty to destroy him and return freedom to the world. Stekatta "Kat" Tressner and Sid X assist Kia; Victoria Thalios leads Free Vox, the rebel group opposed to Ty; Axxen Baines is Ty's top agent.

Voice Cast: Kim Campoli, David DiLeo, Betsy Hooper, Jennifer Richards, Kristen Johanssen, Jonathan Ellinghaus, Moe Fischer, Lani Ford, Angela Tweed, Sara Van Beckum. Credits: *Producer:* Buzz Potamkin, David B. Williams. *Writer:* Betsy Hooper, George Ostrin. *Director-Creator:* David B. Williams. Comment: A pioneering animated series that due to very limited high speed broadband in 1997 used comic strip-like panels to tell a story (using animation with dial-up connections would take several minutes to download). Flexible animation was encompassed the following year when Macromedia introduced Flash 2.0 Animation. Although the entire series cannot be watched the available episode is a good example of how early animation appeared on the Internet.

Episode List: 100 episodes were produced but only one episode and a trailer remains on line.

569 *Wings.* 2014 (Dolls).

The LPS (Littlest Pet Ship) dolls are encompassed to tell the story of a group of teenage girls who are just beginning their first year of high school.

Cast (as credited): Angel Davis, Charlie Reid, Queen Ava, Kimberly Davis, Dustin Smith, Princess

Samantha. Voices by Zoey. **Comment:** Good voices, photography and doll manipulation. The program has since been taken offline.

Episode List: 2 untitled episodes, labeled "Episode 1" and "Episode 2" have been produced.

570 *Wonder Woman and Super Girl Adventures. youtube.com.* 2011 (Fantasy).

The Wonder Woman and Super Girl dolls that are sold in stores each come with a pendant displaying a symbol of their being. The super heroes have a comic book life and, to continue their battle against evil, have been brought to "life" through their magically enhanced pendants. Serial-like (and very short) episodes relate their adventures as they battle injustice as a team.

Comment: A cast and credits are not given. It appears that a number of episodes (running about 20 seconds each) were produced but most have been deleted. While dolls are used, they are not hand held; instead a variation of stop motion photography is used (filming movement one frame at a time) here giving it a jerky movement. For unexplained reasons, the first episode has no sound.

Episode List: 3 untitled episodes, labeled "Episode 1," "Episode 2" and "Episode 3" remain on line.

571 *The Young Tails. youtube.com.* 2012 (Fantasy).

April and her friend Eskiane are swimming in what appears to be the ocean when they spot a cave. Curious, they venture into it and suddenly find themselves emerged in bubbling water. April and Eskiane are able to swim out of the cave and find their way back to safety but later, when they come in contact with water, they transform into Mermaids. The program, which appears to have been abandoned, just ends here with the assumption that they must now protect their secret while pretending to be ordinary girls.

Cast (as credited): Ashley (April), Autumn (Eskiana). **Comment:** Although there is only one episode, it is nicely photographed and has acceptable acting.

Episode List: *1.* Young Tails Pilot: Magical Swim.

572 *You're Invited to Mary Kate & Ashley's Coolest Parties. youtube.com.* 2008 (Comedy).

An Internet presentation of the 1995–2000 video series wherein Mary Kate and Ashley Olsen, the twins who became famous through the TV series *Full House* (as Michelle Tanner) simply prepare and host a different type of party in each episode. On occasion they are assisted by their younger sister, Elizabeth and older brother Trent.

Cast: Mary Kate Olsen, Ashley Olsen, Elizabeth Olsen, Trent Olsen as Themselves. **Credits:** *Director*: Alan Julian. *Writer*: Neil Steinberg. **Comment:** The program originally aired on the WB.com and was first presented on YouTube in 2008. Music and songs are combined with light comedy in a well produced and acted program. Although the video quality is very good, it does not compare to programs produced in HD.

Episode List: *1.* Sleepover Party. *2.* Hawaiian Beach Party. *3.* Christmas Party. *4.* Ballet Party. *5.* Costume Party. *6.* Mall Party. *7.* Camping Party. *8.* Fashion Party. *9.* School Dance Party. *10.* Birthday Party.

573 *The Ziggy and Gumboot Show. youtube.com.* 2013 (Puppets).

Ziggy, a guinea pig, and Gumboot, a rabbit (both puppets), share a cage and are apparently owned by a woman (who is never fully seen). They are punk rock enthusiasts and stories relate brief incidents as they pretend to be something they are not to escape their dreary lives.

Cast: Tiger Brown (Ziggy), Quentin Young (Gumboot), Kana Alf (Kawaii Sock), Kaylee Sunshine (Flowers), Marlon Dance-Hooi, Dean Allan (Various characters). **Credits:** *Producer-Writer-Director*: Dean Allan, Tiger Brown. **Comment:** Rather difficult to comprehend what is happening as just too much occurs at once and the viewer can easily become lost. The puppets are okay but they do use some foul language during song segments. A parental warning should be issued but is not.

Episode List: *1.* Hipster Sock. *2.* Conspiracy Sock. *3.* Hippy Sock. *4.* Tizzy Sock. *5.* Smart Sock. *6.* Kawaii Sock.

www.ingramcontent.com/pod-product-compliance
Lightning Source LLC
LaVergne TN
LVHW080116070326
832902LV00015B/2615